Go Programming - From Beginner to Professional

Learn everything you need to build modern software using Go

Samantha Coyle

Go Programming - From Beginner to Professional

Associate Group Product Manager: Kunal Sawant

Associate Publishing Product Manager: Akash Sharma

Associate Project Manager: Deeksha Thakkar

Senior Editor: Rounak Kulkarni

Technical Editor: Vidhisha Patidar and Jubit Pincy

Copy Editor: Safis Editing

Proofreader: Rounak Kulkarni

Indexer: Rekha Nair

Production Designer: Vijay Kamble

Senior Developer Relations Marketing Executive: Shrinidhi Monaharan

Business Development Executive: Debadrita Chatterjee

First published: December 2019

Second edition: March 2024

Production reference: 1220324

Published by Packt Publishing Ltd.

Grosvenor House

11 St Paul's Square

Birmingham

B3 1RB, UK.

ISBN 978-1-80324-305-4

www.packtpub.com

To my beloved mom, Susan Coyle, whose caring nature and dedication to lifting others instilled in me the drive to become a technical textbook author and to always bring others along on my journey through life. This book is dedicated to you, a tribute to your constant belief in me and my dreams, and your endless love that continues to inspire me every day. Your legacy lives on in every challenge I conquer and through each person I have a positive impact on. This endeavor is a testament to the incredible woman you were and the profound impact you had on my life. What Mom's life may have lacked in length, it made up for in light that continues to shine on.

Samantha Coyle

Contributors

About the author

Samantha Coyle, a Software Engineer at Diagrid, specializes in Go for cloud-native developer tooling, adept at abstracting application development challenges. Committed to Open Source, she actively contributes to projects like Dapr and Testcontainers. With a diverse background in retail computer vision solutions and successful stabilization of industrial edge use cases, particularly within biopharma data pipelines, Samantha brings invaluable expertise to her projects. Her expertise extends to being CKAD-certified and reviewing Go textbooks. She is passionate about empowering early-career, diverse professionals.

Samantha is part of a family of gophers, and enjoys GopherCon with her brother and identical twin sister. A seasoned speaker, she has presented at various conferences, including GopherCon.

About the reviewers

Stan Vangilder earned a Bachelor of Science in Electrical and Computer Engineering from the Georgia Institute of Technology, followed by a Master of Science in Management of Technology.

Throughout his career at a Fortune 150 company, he was an early adopter of technology and became a frequent speaker, trainer, coach, and consultant for diverse audiences within and beyond the organization.

Stan now channels his passion for learning and teaching by creating online courses tailored to simplify complex topics, facilitating swift and efficient integration into your projects and workflows.

Ivan Lemeshev is a seasoned software engineer with over 11 years of experience. He focuses on building large-scale cloud applications, microservices, and distributed systems using Go. He has used Go as his primary programming language for over seven years and likes its simplicity, performance, and ecosystem.

Table of Contents

2

Command and Control   53

3

Core Types   81

4

Complex Types   105

Part 2: Components

5

Functions – Reduce, Reuse, and Recycle   163

6

Don't Panic! Handle Your Errors   209

7

Interfaces   243

8

Generic Algorithm Superpowers 281

Part 3: Modules

9

Using Go Modules to Define a Project 297

10

Packages Keep Projects Manageable   313

11

Bug-Busting Debugging Skills   341

12

Part 4: Applications

13

14

15

Part 5: Building For The Web

16

Web Servers 475

17

Using the Go HTTP Client 511

Part 6: Professional

18

Concurrent Work   533

19

Testing   579

20

Using Go Tools   599

21

Go in the Cloud   617

Preface

Welcome to Go Programming - From Beginner to Professional! Here, you will learn everything you need to build modern software utilizing Go. Designed for beginners with no prior programming experience required, it offers a comprehensive approach to understanding and leveraging Go's power and idiomatic nature.

The best way to learn is by doing. You will do exactly that in this book. Go Programming – From Beginner to Professional will take you on an engaging step-by-step journey to understanding Go starting with the fundamentals. Each chapter includes exciting exercises and activities that you can do at your own pace or jump ahead to. As you continue reading, you will work your way to more advanced topics where you will discover how to harness Go's efficiency, simplicity, and concurrency to build robust and scalable software solutions. Learning at your own terms and pace, you will build up and reinforce key skills in a way that feels rewarding to you as you grow as a Go developer.

This book will highlight the latest features of Go 1.21 and onward, ensuring you're up-to-date with the cutting-edge capabilities of this versatile language as you grow your skills. You will build and iterate on your code like a Go Gopher does, learning along the way.

Join in on this exciting adventure as we unlock the full potential of Go and empower you to become a proficient Go developer. Whether you are building web applications, microservices, or tackling general software challenges and want to leverage Go, this book equips you with the knowledge and skills to succeed. Let us dive in and elevate your programming journey with Go.

Who this book is for

Designed for newcomers to Go, whether starting from scratch or transitioning from another language, this book empowers developers to build real-world projects and develop the necessary skills to launch their careers in Go. Offering a step-by-step approach, beginners can grasp the Go fundamentals even without prior programming experience. As readers progress, they uncover idiomatic Go best practices and explore the latest features of the language. Readers will gain expertise in building modern software in Go, equipping them to become professional developers through hands-on learning experiences.

What this book covers

Chapter 1, Variables and Operators, explains how variables hold data for you temporarily. It also shows how you can use operators to make changes or make comparisons to that data.

Chapter 2, Command and Control, teaches you how to make your code dynamic and responsive by creating rules that must be followed based on data in variables. Loops let you repeat logic over as you learn to take command of your control flow with Go.

Chapter 3, Core Types, introduces you to the building blocks of data. You'll learn what a type is and how the core types are defined.

Chapter 4, Complex Types, explains that complex types build on core types to allow you to model real-world data using data grouping and by composing new types from the core types. You'll also look at overcoming Go's type system when needed.

Chapter 5, Functions – Reduce, Reuse, and Recycle, teaches you the basics of constructing a function. Then, we will dive into more advanced features of using functions, such as passing a function as an argument, returning a function, assigning a function to a variable, and many more interesting things you can do with functions. You will learn the fundamentals of code reuse.

Chapter 6, Don't Panic! Handle Your Errors, teaches you how to work with errors, covering topics such as declaring your own error and handling errors the Go way. You will learn what a *panic* is and how to recover from one.

Chapter 7, Interfaces, starts by teaching the mechanics of interfaces and then demonstrates that interfaces in Go offer polymorphism, duck typing, the ability to have empty interfaces, and the implicit implementation of an interface.

Chapter 8, Generic Algorithm Superpowers, showcases the type parameter syntax Go offers to create a generic version of your code that is usable on more than one type. You will understand the when, why, and how to utilize generics to reduce code duplication.

Chapter 9, Using Go Modules to Define a Project, demonstrates how to leverage Go modules to structure and manage Go projects, covering essential Go dependency management files.

Chapter 10, Package Keep Projects Manageable, demonstrates how to leverage Go packages within our programs to keep code manageable and group code into useful subsystems of functionality.

Chapter 11, Bug-Busting Debugging Skills, teaches the fundamentals of finding bugs in our application. You will use various techniques of printing out markers in code, using values and types, and performing logging.

Chapter 12, About Time, gets you a head start in the concept of how Go manages time variables, and what features are provided for you to improve your applications, such as measuring execution time and navigating between time zones.

Chapter 13, Programming from the Command Line, teaches you how to create command line utilities with all that Go has to offer. You will practice flag parsing, handling large amounts of data, exit codes, terminal user interfaces, and learn best practices along the way.

Chapter 14, Files and Systems, shows how Go has great support for working with files and the underlying OS. You will be working with the filesystem, learning how to create, read, and modify files on the OS. You will also see how Go can read a CSV file, a common file format used by administrators.

Chapter 15, SQL and Databases, covers the most important aspects of connecting to databases and manipulating tables, which are very common tasks nowadays, and you'll learn how to work efficiently with databases using Go.

Chapter 16, Web Servers, teaches you how to use the Go standard packages to create an HTTP server, build websites, and create REST APIs You'll learn how to accept requests from a web form or from another program and respond in a human or machine readable format.

Chapter 17, Using the Go HTTP Client, instructs you how to use the Go standard packages to create an HTTP client and interact with REST APIs. You'll learn how to send GET requests to a server and process the response, as well as how to POST form data to a server and how to upload a file to a server.

Chapter 18, Concurrent Work, demonstrates how to make use of Go's concurrency features to enable your software to perform several tasks at the same time, splitting the work across independent Goroutines and reducing the processing time.

Chapter 19, Testing, helps understand the various types of testing that Go enables to include HTTP testing, fuzz testing, benchmark testing, using test suites, and generating test reports and code coverage of your code.

Chapter 20, Using Go Tools, familiarizes you with the tools that come with Go and explains how you can use them to improve your code. You'll learn how to automatically format your code with gofmt and goimports. You'll also learn how to do static analysis with go vet and how to detect race conditions using the Go race detector.

Chapter 21, Go in the Cloud, builds your understanding of preparing your Go code for deployment in the cloud. You will work through adding monitoring capabilities using tools such as Prometheus, OpenTelemetry, and how to containerize your Go application to work with orchestrators such as Kubernetes.

To get the most out of this book

Each great journey begins with a humble step. Our upcoming adventure with Go programming is no exception. Before we can do awesome things using Go, we need to be prepared with a productive environment. For this book to best serve you, you should install Git, Docker, and Go version 1.21 or higher. It is recommended that you have 4GB of RAM, and virtualization enabled in BIOS (usually enabled by default). The book is best suited for macOS or Linux, and will require minor tweaks for using Windows equivalent commands if needed. It is recommended to use a 1.6 GHz or faster desktop processor.

A helping hand on additional setup:

Install the Go Compiler

To turn your Go source code into something you can run, you'll need the Go compiler. For Windows and macOS, we recommend using the installer. Alternatively, to get more control you can download precompiled binaries. You can find both at https://packt.live/2PRUGjp. The install instructions for both methods on Windows, macOS, and Linux are at https://packt.live/375DQDA. The Go compiler is free to download and use.

Install Git

Go uses the version control tool Git to install extra tools and code. You can find the instructions for Windows, macOS, and Linux at https://packt.live/35ByRug. Git is free to install and use.

Install Visual Studio Code (Editor/IDE)

You need something to write your Go source code. This tool is called an editor or an **Integrated Development Environment** (IDE). If you already have an editor you like, you can use it with this course if you'd like to.

If you don't already have an editor, we recommend you use the free editor Visual Studio Code. You can download the installer from https://packt.live/35KD2Ek:

1. Once it's installed, open Visual Studio Code.
2. From the top menu bar, select **View**.
3. From the list of options, select **Extensions**.
4. A panel should appear on the left side. At the top is a search input box. Type Go.
5. The first option should be an extension called **Go by Microsoft**.
6. Click the **Install** button on that option.
7. Wait for a message that says it's successfully installed.

If you have Git installed, follow these steps:

1. Press *Ctrl/Cmd + Shift + P* all at the same time. A text input should appear at the top of the window.

2. Type `go tools`.

3. Select the option labelled something like **Go: Install/Update Tools**.

4. You'll see a list of options and checkboxes.

5. The very first checkbox next to the search input checks all the checkboxes. Select this checkbox, then select the **Go** button to the right of it.

6. A panel from the bottom should appear with some activity in it. Once this stops (and it may take a few minutes), you're all done.

Once done, select **View** from the top menu bar, then select **Explorer**.

Install Docker

Docker allows us to run things such as database servers without having to install them and containerize our applications. Docker is free to install and use.

For macOS users, follow the instructions at `https://packt.live/34VJLJD`.

For Windows users, follow the instructions at `https://packt.live/2EKGDG6`.

Linux users, you should be able to use your built-in package manager to install Docker. Instructions for common distributions are at `https://packt.live/2Mn8Cjc`.

You are safe to uninstall Docker, if you wish, once the book is complete.

Install PostgreSQL

PostgreSQL is used within the chapter covering database interactions. To install the PostgreSQL driver, follow the instructions at `https://www.postgresql.org/download/`.

If you are using the digital version of this book, we advise you to type the code yourself or access the code from the book's GitHub repository (a link is available in the next section). Doing so will help you avoid any potential errors related to the copying and pasting of code.

Download the example code files

You can download the example code files for this book from GitHub at `https://packt.link/sni2F`. If there's an update to the code, it will be updated in the GitHub repository.

We also have other code bundles from our rich catalog of books and videos available at `https://github.com/PacktPublishing/`. Check them out!

Conventions used

There are a number of text conventions used throughout this book.

`Code in text`: Indicates code words in text, database table names, folder names, filenames, file extensions, pathnames, dummy URLs, user input, and Twitter handles. Here is an example: "In the previous chapter, we learned how to use `if`, `if-else`, `else-if`, `switch`, `case`, `continue`, `break`, and `goto` in Go."

A block of code is set as follows:

```
package main
import "fmt"
func main() {
   fmt.Println(10 > 5)
   fmt.Println(10 == 5)
}
```

When we wish to draw your attention to a particular part of a code block, the relevant lines or items are set in bold:

```
go doc -all
```

Any command-line input or output is written as follows:

```
error, unexpected nil value
```

Bold: Indicates a new term, an important word, or words that you see onscreen. For instance, words in menus or dialog boxes appear in **bold**. Here is an example: " Once done, select **View** from the top menu bar, then select **Explorer**."

> **Tips or important notes**
> Appear like this.

Get in touch

Feedback from our readers is always welcome.

General feedback: If you have questions about any aspect of this book, email us at `customercare@packtpub.com` and mention the book title in the subject of your message.

Errata: Although we have taken every care to ensure the accuracy of our content, mistakes do happen. If you have found a mistake in this book, we would be grateful if you would report this to us. Please visit `www.packtpub.com/support/errata` and fill in the form.

Piracy: If you come across any illegal copies of our works in any form on the internet, we would be grateful if you would provide us with the location address or website name. Please contact us at `copyright@packt.com` with a link to the material.

If you are interested in becoming an author: If there is a topic that you have expertise in and you are interested in either writing or contributing to a book, please visit `authors.packtpub.com`.

Share Your Thoughts

Once you've read *Go Programming - From Beginner to Professional*, we'd love to hear your thoughts! Scan the QR code below to go straight to the Amazon review page for this book and share your feedback.

`https://packt.link/r/1803243058`

Your review is important to us and the tech community and will help us make sure we're delivering excellent quality content.

Download a free PDF copy of this book

Thanks for purchasing this book!

Do you like to read on the go but are unable to carry your print books everywhere?

Is your eBook purchase not compatible with the device of your choice?

Don't worry, now with every Packt book you get a DRM-free PDF version of that book at no cost.

Read anywhere, any place, on any device. Search, copy, and paste code from your favorite technical books directly into your application.

The perks don't stop there, you can get exclusive access to discounts, newsletters, and great free content in your inbox daily

Follow these simple steps to get the benefits:

1. Scan the QR code or visit the link below

https://packt.link/free-ebook/9781803243054

2. Submit your proof of purchase

3. That's it! We'll send your free PDF and other benefits to your email directly

Part 1: Scripts

Writing simple one-file software applications is often where most software development journeys begin. In this section, you'll delve into the world of scripting, empowering you to create cool and useful tools and helpers with ease.

This part has the following chapters:

- *Chapter 1, Variables and Operators*
- *Chapter 2, Command and Control*
- *Chapter 3, Core Types*
- *Chapter 4, Complex Types*

1

Variables and Operators

Overview

In this chapter, you will be introduced to various features of Go and gain a basic understanding of what Go code looks like. You will also be provided with a deep understanding of how variables work and will perform exercises and activities to get hands-on and get going.

By the end of this chapter, you will be able to use variables, packages, and functions in Go. You will also know how to change variable values in Go. Later in this chapter, you will use operators with numbers and design functions using pointers.

Technical requirements

For this chapter, you'll require Go version 1.21 or higher. The code for this chapter can be found at: `https://github.com/PacktPublishing/Go-Programming-From-Beginner-to-Professional-Second-Edition-/tree/main/Chapter01`.

Introduction to Go

Go (or Golang, as it's often called) is a programming language that's popular with developers because of how rewarding it is to use to develop software. It's also popular with companies because teams of all sizes can be productive with it. Go has also earned a reputation for consistently delivering software with exceptionally high performance.

Go has an impressive pedigree since it was created by a team from Google with a long history of building great programming languages and operating systems. They created a language that has the feel of a dynamic language such as JavaScript or PHP but with the performance and efficiency of strongly typed languages such as C++ and Java. They wanted a language that was engaging for the programmer but practical in projects with hundreds of developers.

Go is packed with interesting and unique features, such as being compliant with memory safety and channel-based concurrency. We'll explore these features in this chapter. By doing so, you'll see that their unique implementation within Go is what makes Go truly special.

Go is written in text files that are then compiled down to machine code and packaged into a single, standalone executable file. The executable is self-contained, with nothing needed to be installed first to allow it to run. Having a single file makes deploying and distributing Go software hassle-free. When compiling, you can pick one of several target operating systems, including – but not limited to – Windows, Linux, macOS, and Android. With Go, you write your code once and run it anywhere. Complied languages fell out of favor because programmers hated long waits for their code to compile. The Go team knew this and built a lightning-fast compiler that remains fast as projects grow.

Go has a statically typed and type-safe memory model with a garbage collector that automates memory management. This combination protects developers from creating many of the most common bugs and security flaws found in software while still providing excellent performance and efficiency. Dynamically typed languages such as Ruby and Python have become popular in part because programmers felt they could be more productive if they didn't have to worry about types and memory. The downside of these languages is that they give up performance and memory efficiency and can be more prone to type-mismatch bugs. Go has the same levels of productivity as dynamically typed languages while not giving up performance and efficiency.

A massive shift in computer performance has taken place. Going fast now means you need to be able to do as much work parallel or concurrently as possible. This change is due to the design of modern CPUs, which emphasize more cores over high clock speed. None of the currently popular programming languages have been designed to take advantage of this fact, which makes writing parallel and concurrent code in them error-prone. Go is designed to take advantage of multiple CPU cores, and it removes all the frustration and bug-filled code. Go is designed to allow any developer to easily and safely write parallel and concurrent code that enables them to take advantage of modern multicore CPUs and cloud computing – unlocking high-performance processing and massive scalability without the drama.

What does Go look like?

Let's take our first look at some Go code. This code randomly prints a message to the console from a pre-defined list of messages:

```
package main
// Import extra functionality from packages
import (
    "errors"
    "fmt"
    "log"
    "math/rand"
    "strconv"
    "time"
```

```
)// Taken from: https://en.wiktionary.org/wiki/Hello_
World#Translations
var helloList = []string{
  "Hello, world",
  "Καλημέρα κόσμε",
  "こんにちは世界",
  "السلام علیکم ای دنیا",
  "Привет, мир",
}
```

The `main()` function is defined as follows:

```
func main() {
  // Seed random number generator using the current time
  rand.NewSource(time.Now().UnixNano())
  // Generate a random number in the range of out list
  index := rand.Intn(len(helloList))
  // Call a function and receive multiple return values
  msg, err := hello(index)
  // Handle any errors
  if err != nil {
    log.Fatal(err)
  }
  // Print our message to the console
  fmt.Println(msg)
}
```

Let's consider the `hello()` function:

```
func hello(index int) (string, error) {
  if index < 0 || index > len(helloList)-1 {
    // Create an error, convert the int type to a string
    return "", errors.New("out of range: " + strconv.Itoa(index))
  }
  return helloList[index], nil
}
```

Now, let's step through this code piece by piece.

At the top of our script is the following:

```
package main
```

This code is our package declaration. All Go files must start with one of these. If you want to run the code directly, you'll need to name it `main`. If you don't name it `main`, then you can use it as a library and import it into other Go code. When creating an importable package, you can give it any name. All Go files in the same directory are considered part of the same package, which means all the files must have the same package name.

In the following code, we're importing code from packages:

```
// Import extra functionality from packages
import (
    "errors"
    "fmt"
    "log"
    "math/rand"
    "strconv"
    "time"
)
```

In this example, the packages are all from Go's standard library. Go's standard library is very high-quality and comprehensive. It's strongly recommended that you maximize your use of it. You can tell if a package isn't from the standard library because it'll look like a URL – for example, `github.com/fatih/color`.

Go has a module system that makes using external packages easy. To use a new module, add it to your import path. Go will automatically download it for you the next time you build code.

Imports only apply to the file they're declared in, which means you must declare the same imports over and over in the same package and project. But fear not – you don't need to do this by hand. There are many tools and Go editors that automatically add and remove the imports for you:

```
// Taken from: https://en.wiktionary.org/wiki/Hello_World#Translations
var helloList = []string{
    "Hello, world",
    "Καλημέρα κόσμε",
    "こんにちは世界",
    "سلام دنیای ",
    "Привет, мир",
}
```

Here, we're declaring a global variable, which is a list of strings, and initializing it with data. The text or strings in Go support multi-byte UFT-8 encoding, making them safe for any language. The type of list we're using here is called a slice. There are three types of lists in Go: slices, arrays, and maps. All three are collections of keys and values, where you use the key to get a value from the collection. Slice and array collections use a number as the key. The first key is always 0 in slices and arrays. Also, in slices and arrays, the numbers are contiguous, which means there is never a break in the sequence of numbers. With the map type, you get to choose the key type. You use this when you want to use some other data to look up the value in the map. For example, you could use a book's ISBN to look up its title and author:

```go
func main() {
...
}
```

Here, we're declaring a function. A function is some code that runs when called. You can pass data in the form of one or more variables to a function and optionally receive one or more variables back from it. The main() function in Go is special. The main() function is the entry point of your Go code. There may only be one main() function within the main package. When your code runs, Go automatically calls main to get things started:

```go
// Seed random number generator using the current time
rand.Seed(time.Now().UnixNano())
// Generate a random number in the range of out list
index := rand.Intn(len(helloList))
```

In the preceding code, we are generating a random number. The first thing we need to do is ensure it's a good random number; to do that, we must *seed* the random number generator. We seed it using the current time formatted to a Unix timestamp with nanoseconds. To get the time, we call the Now function in the time package. The Now function returns a struct type variable. Structs are a collection of properties and functions, a little like objects in other languages. In this case, we are calling the UnixNano function on that struct straight away. The UnixNano function returns a variable of the int64 type, which is a 64-bit integer or, more simply, a number. This number is passed into rand.Seed. The rand.Seed function accepts an int64 variable as its input. Note that the type of the variable from time.UnixNano and rand.Seed must be the same. With that, we've successfully seeded the random number generator.

What we want is a number we can use to get a random message. We'll use rand.Intn for this job. This function gives us a random number between 0 and 1, minus the number we pass in. This may sound a bit strange, but it works out perfectly for what we're trying to do. This is because our list is a slice where the keys start from 0 and increment by 1 for each value. This means the last index is 1 less than the length of the slice.

To show you what this means, here is some simple code:

```go
package main
import (
  "fmt"
)
func main() {
  helloList := []string{
```

```
        "Hello, world",
        "Καλημέρα κόσμε",
        "こんにちは世界",
        "سلام دنیای",
        "Привет, мир",
    }
    fmt.Println(len(helloList))
    fmt.Println(helloList[len(helloList)-1])
    fmt.Println(helloList[len(helloList)])
}
```

This code prints the length of the list and then uses that length to print the last element. To do that, we must subtract 1; otherwise, we'd get an error, which is what the last line causes:

```
5
Привет, мир
panic: runtime error: index out of range [5] with length 5

goroutine 1 [running]:
main.main()
        /Users/samcoyle/go/src/github.com/packt-book/Go-Programming---From-Beginner-to-Professional-Second-Edition-/Chapter01/Example01.01/main.go:17 +0x11c
exit status 2
```

Figure 1.1: Output displaying an error

Once we've generated our random number, we assign it to a variable. We do this with the short variable declaration seen with the : = notation, which is a very popular shortcut in Go within a function. It tells the compiler to go ahead and assign that value to the variable and select the appropriate type for that value implicitly. This shortcut is one of the many things that makes Go feel like a dynamically typed language:

```
// Call a function and receive multiple return values
msg, err := hello(index)
```

Then, we use that variable to call a function named hello. We'll look at hello in just a moment. The important thing to note is that we're receiving two values back from the function and we're able to assign them to two new variables, msg and err, using the : = notation and with err as the second value:

```
func hello(index int) (string, error) {
    ...
}
```

This code is the definition of the hello function; we're not showing the body for now. A function acts as a unit of logic that's called when and as often as is needed. When calling a function, the code that calls it stops running and waits for the function to finish running. Functions are a great tool for keeping your code organized and understandable. In the signature of hello, we've defined that it accepts a single int value and that it returns a string value and an error value. Having error as your last return value is a very common thing to have in Go. The code between { } is the body of the function. The following code is what's run when the function's called:

```
if index < 0 || index > len(helloList)-1 {
  // Create an error, convert the int type to a string
  return "", errors.New("out of range: " + strconv.Itoa(index))
}
return helloList[index], nil
```

Here, we are inside the function; the first line of the body is an `if` statement. An `if` statement runs the code inside its { } if its Boolean expression is true. The Boolean expression is the logic between `if` and `{`. In this case, we're testing to see if the passed `index` variable is less than 0 or greater than the largest possible slice index key.

If the Boolean expression were to be true, then our code would return an empty `string` and an `error` value. At this point, the function would stop running, and the code that called the function would continue to run. If the Boolean expression were not true, its code would be skipped over, and our function would return a value from `helloList` and `nil`. In Go, `nil` represents something with no value and no type:

```
// Handle any errors
if err != nil {
  log.Fatal(err)
}
```

After we've run `hello`, the first thing we need to do is check if it ran successfully. We can do this by checking the `error` value stored in `err`. If `err` is not equal to `nil`, then we know we have an error. You will see checks on whether `err` is not equal to `nil` as opposed to checks on whether `err` is equal to `nil`, as this simplifies the checks and logic for the code base. In the case of an error, we call `log.Fatal`, which writes out a logging message and kills our app. Once the app's been killed, no more code runs:

```
// Print our message to the console
fmt.Println(msg)
```

If there is no error, then we know that `hello` ran successfully and that the value of `msg` can be trusted to hold a valid value. The final thing we need to do is print the message to the screen via the Terminal.

Here's how that looks:

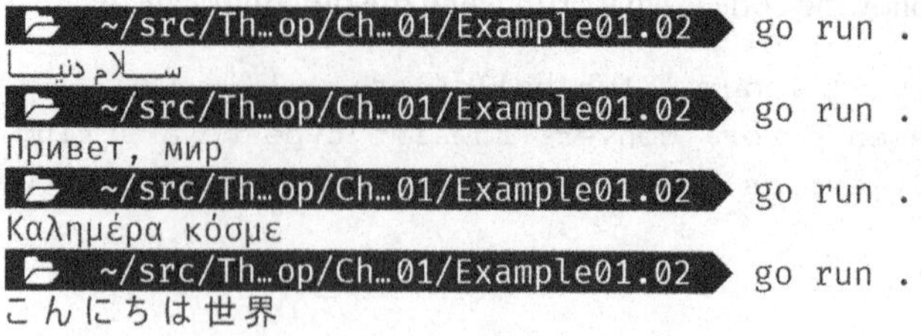

```
 ~/src/Th…op/Ch…01/Example01.02    go run .
سلام دنیا
 ~/src/Th…op/Ch…01/Example01.02    go run .
Привет, мир
 ~/src/Th…op/Ch…01/Example01.02    go run .
Καλημέρα κόσμε
 ~/src/Th…op/Ch…01/Example01.02    go run .
こんにちは世界
```

Figure 1.2: Output displaying valid values

In this simple Go program, we've been able to cover a lot of key concepts that we'll explore in full in the coming chapters.

Exercise 1.01 – using variables, packages, and functions to print stars

In this exercise, we'll use some of what we learned about in the preceding example to print a random number, between 1 and 5, of stars (*) to the console. This exercise will give you a feel of what working with Go is like and some practice with using the features of Go we'll need going forward. Let's get started:

1. Create a new folder and add a `main.go` file to it.

2. In `main.go`, add the `main` package name to the top of the file:

   ```
   package main
   ```

3. Now, add the imports we'll use in this file:

   ```
   import (
     "fmt"
     "math/rand"
     "strings"
     "time"
   )
   ```

4. Create a `main()` function:

   ```
   func main() {
   ```

5. Seed the random number generator:

   ```
   rand.Seed(time.Now().UnixNano())
   ```

6. Generate a random number between 0 and then add 1 to get a number between 1 and 5:

   ```
   r := rand.Intn(5) + 1
   ```

7. Use the string repeater to create a string with the number of stars we need:

```
stars := strings.Repeat("*", r)
```

8. Print the string with the stars to the console with a new line character at the end and close the main() function:

```
fmt.Println(stars)
}
```

9. Save the file. Then, in the new folder, run the following:

```
go run .
```

The following is the output:

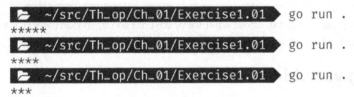

Figure 1.3: Output displaying stars

In this exercise, we created a runnable Go program by defining the main package with a main() function in it. We used the standard library by adding imports to packages. Those packages helped us generate a random number, repeat strings, and write to the console.

Activity 1.01 – defining and printing

In this activity, we are going to create a medical form for a doctor's office to capture a patient's name, age, and whether they have a peanut allergy:

1. Create a variable for the following:

    I. First name as a string.

    II. Family name as a string.

    III. Age as an int value.

    IV. Peanut allergy as a bool value.

2. Ensure they have an initial value.

3. Print the values to the console.

The following is the expected output:

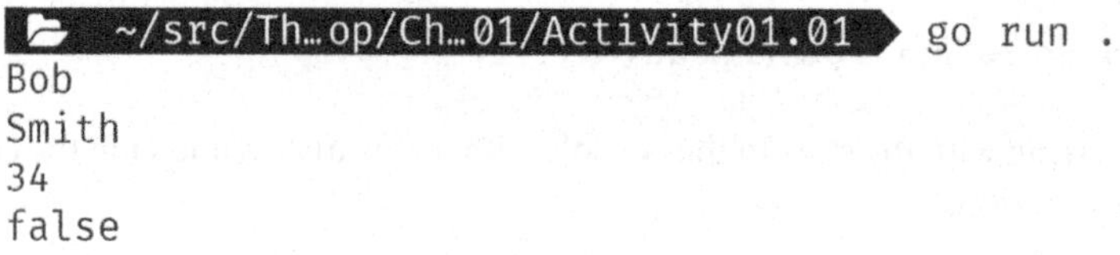

```
📂  ~/src/Th…op/Ch…01/Activity01.01    go run .
Bob
Smith
34
false
```

Figure 1.4: Expected output after assigning the variables

> **Note**
>
> The solution to all activities in this chapter can be found in the GitHub repository here: https://github.com/PacktPublishing/Go-Programming-From-Beginner-to-Professional-Second-Edition-/tree/main/Chapter01

Next, we'll start going into detail about what we've covered so far, so don't worry if you are confused or have any questions about what you've seen so far.

Declaring variables

Now that you've had a glimpse of Go and completed your first exercise, we're going to dive deep. Our first stop on our journey is variables.

A variable holds data for you temporarily so that you can work with it. When you declare a variable, it needs four things: a statement that you are declaring a variable, a name for the variable, the type of data it can hold, and an initial value for it. Fortunately, some of the parts are optional, but that also means there's more than one way of defining a variable.

Let's cover all the ways you can declare a variable.

Declaring a variable using var

Using var is the foundational way to declare a variable. Every other way we'll cover is a variation of this approach, typically by omitting parts of this definition. A full var definition with everything in place looks like this:

```
var foo string = "bar"
```

The key parts are var, foo, string, and = "bar":

- var is our declaration that we are defining a variable
- foo is the name of the variable
- string is the type of the variable
- = "bar" is its initial value

Exercise 1.02 – declaring a variable using var

In this exercise, we'll declare two variables using the full `var` notation. Then, we'll print them to the console. You'll see that you can use the `var` notation anywhere in your code, which isn't true for all variable declaration notations. Let's get started:

1. Create a new folder and add a `main.go` file to it.

2. In `main.go`, add the main package name to the top of the file:

    ```
    package main
    ```

3. Add the imports:

    ```
    import (
        "fmt"
    )
    ```

4. Declare a variable at the package-level scope. We'll cover what scopes are in detail later:

    ```
    var foo string = "bar"
    ```

5. Create the `main()` function:

    ```
    func main() {
    ```

6. Declare another variable using `var` in our function:

    ```
    var baz string = "qux"
    ```

7. Print both variables to the console:

    ```
    fmt.Println(foo, baz)
    ```

8. Close the `main()` function:

    ```
    }
    ```

9. Save the file. Then, in the new folder, run the following:

    ```
    go run .
    ```

The following is the output:

```
bar qux
```

In this example, `foo` is declared at the package level while `baz` is declared at the function level. Where a variable is declared is important because where you declare a variable also limits what notation you can use to declare it.

Next, we'll look at another way to use the `var` notation.

Declaring multiple variables at once with var

We can use a single `var` declaration to define more than one variable using a `var` block or statement. Using this method is common when declaring package-level variables. The variables don't need to be of the same type, and they can all have their own initial values. The notation looks like this:

```
var (
    <name1> <type1> = <value1>
    <name2> <type2> = <value2>
...
    <nameN> <typeN> = <valueN>
)
```

You can have multiple of these types of declarations. This is a nice way to group related variables, thereby making your code more readable. You can use this notation in functions, but it's rare to see it used there.

Exercise 1.03 – declaring multiple variables at once with var

In this exercise, we'll declare multiple variables using one `var` statement, each with a different type and initial value. Then, we'll print the value of each variable to the console. Let's get started:

1. Create a new folder and add a `main.go` file to it.

2. In `main.go`, add the `main` package name to the top of the file:

    ```
    package main
    ```

3. Add the imports:

    ```
    import (
      "fmt"
      "time"
    )
    ```

4. Start the `var` declaration:

    ```
    var (
    ```

5. Define three variables:

    ```
    Debug    bool   = false
    LogLevel  string = "info"
    startUpTime time.Time = time.Now()
    ```

6. Close the `var` declaration:

    ```
    )
    ```

7. In the `main()` function, print each variable to the console:

```
func main() {
   fmt.Println(Debug, LogLevel, startUpTime)
}
```

8. Save the file. Then, in the new folder, run the following:

```
go run .
```

The following is the output:

```
→  Exercise01.03 git:(main) ✗ go run .
false info 2024-03-15 20:53:10.866401 -0500 CDT m=+0.000094084
```

Figure 1.5: Output displaying three variable values

In this exercise, we declared three variables using a single `var` statement. Your output will look different for the `time.Time` variable, but that's correct. The format is the same, but the time itself is different.

Using the `var` notation like this is a good way to keep your code well organized and save you some typing.

Next, we'll start removing some of the optional parts of the `var` notation.

Skipping the type or value when declaring variables

In real-world code, it's not common to use the full `var` notation. There are a few cases where you need to define a package-level variable with an initial value and tightly control its type. In those cases, you need the full notation. It'll be obvious when this is needed as you'll have a type mismatch of some kind, so don't worry too much about this for now. The rest of the time, you'll remove an optional part or use the short variable declaration.

You don't need to include both the type and the initial value when declaring a variable. You can use just one or the other; Go works out the rest. If you have a type in the declaration but no initial value, Go uses the zero value for the type you picked. We'll talk about what a zero value is later in this book. On the other hand, if you have an initial value and no type, Go has a ruleset for how to infer the types that are needed from the literal value you use.

Exercise 1.04 – skipping the type or value when declaring variables

In this exercise, we'll update our previous exercise so that it skips the optional initial values or type declarations from our variable declaration. Then, we'll print the values to the console, as we did previously, to show that the result is the same. Let's get started:

1. Create a new folder and add a `main.go` file to it.

2. In `main.go`, add the `main` package name to the top of the file:

```
package main
```

3. Import the packages we'll need:

    ```
    import (
        "fmt"
        "time"
    )
    ```

4. Start the multi-variable declaration:

    ```
    var (
    ```

5. The `bool` value in the first exercise has an initial value of false. That's a `bool` value's zero value, so we'll drop the initial value from its declaration as it is set by default:

    ```
    Debug    bool
    ```

6. The next two variables both have a non-zero value for their type, so we'll drop their type declaration:

    ```
    LogLevel   = "info"
    startUpTime = time.Now()
    ```

7. Close the `var` declaration:

    ```
    )
    ```

8. In the `main()` function, print out each variable:

    ```
    func main() {
        fmt.Println(Debug, LogLevel, startUpTime)
    }
    ```

9. Save the file. Then, in the new folder, run the following:

    ```
    go run .
    ```

    The following is the output:

    ```
    → Exercise01.04 git:(main) ✗ go run .
    false info 2024-03-15 20:54:29.069746 -0500 CDT m=+0.000197001
    ```

Figure 1.6: Output displaying variable values despite not mentioning the type while declaring the variables

In this exercise, we were able to update the previous code so that it uses a much more compact variable declaration. Declaring variables is something you'll have to do a lot, and not having to use the notation makes for a better experience when writing code.

Next, we'll look at a situation where you can't skip any of the parts.

Type inference gone wrong

There are times when you'll need to use all the parts of the declaration – for example, when Go isn't able to guess the correct type you need. Let's take a look at an example of this:

```
package main
import "math/rand"
func main() {
   var seed = 1234456789
   rand.NewSource(seed)
}
```

The following is the output:

```
→  Example01.03 git:(main) ✗ go run .
# github.com/packt-book/Go-Programming---From-Beginner-to-Professional-Second-Edition-/Chapter01/Example01.03
./main.go:8:17: cannot use seed (variable of type int) as int64 value in argument to rand.NewSource
```

Figure 1.7: Output showing an error

The issue here is that `rand.NewSource` requires a variable of the `int64` type. Go's type inference rules interoperate a whole number, such as the one we used as an `int` value. We'll look at the difference between them in more detail later in this book. To resolve this, we will add `int64` type to the declaration. Here's how that looks:

```
package main
import "math/rand"
func main() {
   var seed int64 = 1234456789
   rand.NewSource(seed)
}
```

Next, we'll look at an even quicker way to declare variables.

Short variable declaration

When declaring variables in functions and functions only, we can use the `:=` shorthand. This shorthand allows us to make our declarations even shorter. It does this by allowing us to not have to use the `var` keyword and by always inferring the type from a required initial value.

Exercise 1.05 – implementing a short variable declaration

In this exercise, we'll update our previous exercise so that it uses a short variable declaration. Since you can only use a short variable declaration in a function, we'll move our variable out of the package scope. Where before `Debug` had a type but no initial value, we'll switch it back so that it has an initial value since that's required when using a short variable declaration. Finally, we'll print it to the console. Let's get started:

1. Create a new folder and add a `main.go` file to it.

2. In `main.go`, add the `main` package name to the top of the file:

    ```
    package main
    ```

3. Import the packages we'll need:

    ```
    import (
        "fmt"
        "time"
    )
    ```

4. Create the `main()` function:

    ```
    func main() {
    ```

5. Declare each variable using the short variable declaration notation:

    ```
    Debug := false
    LogLevel := "info"
    startUpTime := time.Now()
    ```

6. Print the variables to the console:

    ```
    fmt.Println(Debug, LogLevel, startUpTime)
    }
    ```

7. Save the file. Then, in the new folder, run the following:

    ```
    go run .
    ```

The following is the output:

```
→  Exercise01.05 git:(main) ✗ go run .
false info 2024-03-15 20:59:00.460143 -0500 CDT m=+0.000097209
```

Figure 1.8: Output displaying the variable values that were printed
after using short variable declaration notation

In this exercise, we updated our previous code to use a very compact way to declare variables when we have an initial value to use.

The : = shorthand is very popular with Go developers and the most common way in which variables get defined in real-world Go code. Developers like how it makes their code concise and compact while still being clear as to what's happening.

Another shortcut is declaring multiple variables on the same line.

Declaring multiple variables with a short variable declaration

It's possible to declare multiple variables at the same time using a short variable declaration. They must all be on the same line, and each variable must have a corresponding initial value. The notation looks like <var1>, <var2>, …, <varN> := <val1>, <val2>, …, <valN>. The variable names are on the left-hand side of : =, separated by , . The initial values are on the right-hand side of : = again, each separated by , . The leftmost variable name gets the leftmost value. There must be an equal number of names and values.

Here is an example that uses our previous exercise's code:

```
package main
import (
  "fmt"
  "time"
)
func main() {
  Debug, LogLevel, startUpTime := false, "info", time.Now()
  fmt.Println(Debug, LogLevel, startUpTime)
}
```

The following is the output:

```
→  Example01.04 git:(main) ✗ go run .
false info 2024-03-15 21:00:14.475672 -0500 CDT m=+0.000106459
```

Figure 1.9: Example output displaying the variable values for
the program with a variable declaring function

Sometimes, you do see real-world code like this. It's a little hard to read, so it's not common to see it in terms of literal values. This doesn't mean this isn't common, though – it's very common when calling functions that return multiple values. We'll cover this in detail when we look at functions later in this book.

Exercise 1.06 – declaring multiple variables from a function

In this exercise, we'll call a function that returns multiple values, and we'll assign each value to a new variable. Then, we'll print the values to the console. Let's get started:

1. Create a new folder and add a `main.go` file to it.

2. In `main.go`, add the `main` package name to the top of the file:

   ```
   package main
   ```

3. Import the packages we'll need:

   ```
   import (
       "fmt"
       "time"
   )
   ```

4. Create a function that returns three values:

   ```
   func getConfig() (bool, string, time.Time) {
   ```

5. In the function, return three literal values, each separated by `,`:

   ```
   return false, "info", time.Now()
   ```

6. Close the function:

   ```
   }
   ```

7. Create the `main()` function:

   ```
   func main() {
   ```

8. Using a short variable declaration, capture the values that were returned from the function's three new variables:

   ```
   Debug, LogLevel, startUpTime := getConfig()
   ```

9. Print the three variables to the console:

   ```
   fmt.Println(Debug, LogLevel, startUpTime)
   ```

10. Close the `main()` function:

    ```
    }
    ```

11. Save the file. Then, in the new folder, run the following:

    ```
    go run .
    ```

The following is the output:

```
→  Exercise01.06 git:(main) ✗ go run .
   false info 2024-03-15 21:01:09.87396 -0500 CDT m=+0.000322626
```

Figure 1.10: Output displaying the variable values for the program with the variable declaring function

In this exercise, we were able to call a function that returned multiple values and capture them using a short variable declaration in one line. If we used the `var` notation, it would look like this:

```
var (
  Debug bool
  LogLevel string
  startUpTime time.Time
)
Debug, LogLevel, startUpTime = getConfig()
```

Short variable notation is a big part of how Go has the feel of a dynamic language.

We're not quite done with `var` yet, though – it still has a useful trick up its sleeve.

Using var to declare multiple variables in one line

While it's more common to use a short variable declaration, you can use `var` to define multiple variables on a single line. One limitation of this is that, when declaring the type, all the values must have the same type. If you use an initial value, then each value infers its type from the literal value so that they can differ. Here's an example:

```
package main
import (
  "fmt"
  "time"
)
func getConfig() (bool, string, time.Time) {
  return false, "info", time.Now()
}
func main() {
  // Type only
  var start, middle, end float32
  fmt.Println(start, middle, end)
  // Initial value mixed type
  var name, left, right, top, bottom = "one", 1, 1.5, 2, 2.5
  fmt.Println(name, left, right, top, bottom)
  // works with functions also
  var Debug, LogLevel, startUpTime = getConfig()
```

```
    fmt.Println(Debug, LogLevel, startUpTime)
}
```

The following is the output:

```
→  Example01.05 git:(main) ✗ go run .
0 0 0
one 1 1.5 2 2.5
false info 2024-03-15 21:03:04.241447 -0500 CDT m=+0.000220501
```

Figure 1.11: Output displaying variable values

Most of these are more compact when using a short variable declaration. This fact means they don't come up in real-world code much. The exception is the same type-only example. This notation can be useful when you need many variables of the same type, and you need to control that type carefully.

Non-English variable names

Go is a UTF-8 compliant language, which means you can define variables' names using alphabets other than the Latin alphabet that, for example, English uses. There are some limitations regarding what the name of a variable can be. The first character of the name must be a letter or _. The rest can be a mixture of letters, numbers, and _. Let's have a look at what this looks like:

```
package main
import (
  "fmt"
  "time"
)
func main() {
  デバッグ := false
  日志级别 := "info"
  ළෑඝද := time.Now()
  _A1_Μείγμα := ""
"
  fmt.Println(デバッグ, 日志级别, ළෑඝද, _A1_Μείγμα)
}
```

The following is the output:

```
→  Example01.06 git:(main) ✗ go run .
false info 2024-03-15 21:03:11.338592 -0500 CDT m=+0.000107626 □
```

Figure 1.12: Output showing variable values

> **Note**
>
> **Languages and language**: Not all programming languages allow you to use UTF-8 characters as variables and function names. This feature could be one of the reasons why Go has become so popular in Asian countries, particularly in China.

Changing the value of a variable

Now that we've defined our variables, let's see what we can do with them. First, let's change the value from its initial value. To do that, we'll use a similar notation to when we set an initial value. This looks like `<variable>` = `<value>`.

Exercise 1.07 – changing the value of a variable

Follow these steps:

1. Create a new folder and add a `main.go` file to it.

2. In `main.go`, add the `main` package name to the top of the file:

   ```
   package main
   ```

3. Import the packages we'll need:

   ```
   import "fmt"
   ```

4. Create the `main()` function:

   ```
   func main() {
   ```

5. Declare a variable:

   ```
   offset := 5
   ```

6. Print the variable to the console:

   ```
   fmt.Println(offset)
   ```

7. Change the value of the variable:

   ```
   offset = 10
   ```

8. Print it to the console again and close the `main()` function:

   ```
   fmt.Println(offset)
   }
   ```

9.   Save the file. Then, in the new folder, run the following:

```
go run .
```

The following is the output before changing the variable's value:

```
5
10
```

In this example, we've changed the value of offset from its initial value of 5 to 10. Anywhere you use a raw value, such as 5 and 10 in our example, you can use a variable. Here's how that looks:

```
package main
import "fmt"
var defaultOffset = 10
func main() {
    offset := defaultOffset
    fmt.Println(offset)
    offset = offset + defaultOffset
    fmt.Println(offset)
}
```

The following is the output after changing the variable's value:

```
10
20
```

Next, we'll look at how we can change multiple variables in a one-line statement.

Changing multiple values at once

In the same way that you can declare multiple variables in one line, you can also change the value of more than one variable at a time. The syntax is similar, too; it looks like <var1>, <var2>, ..., <varN> = <val1>, <val2>, ..., <valN>.

Exercise 1.08 – changing multiple values at once

In this exercise, we'll define some variables and use a one-line statement to change their values. Then, we'll print their new values to the console. Let's get started:

1.   Create a new folder and add a main.go file to it.

2.   In main.go, add the main package name to the top of the file:

```
package main
```

3. Import the packages we'll need:

    ```
    import "fmt"
    ```

4. Create the main() function:

    ```
    func main() {
    ```

5. Declare our variables with an initial value:

    ```
    query, limit, offset := "bat", 10, 0
    ```

6. Change each variable's values using a one-line statement:

    ```
    query, limit, offset = "ball", offset, 20
    ```

7. Print the values to the console and close the main() function:

    ```
    fmt.Println(query, limit, offset)
    }
    ```

8. Save the file. Then, in the new folder, run the following:

    ```
    go run .
    ```

The following is the output showing the changed variable values using a single statement:

```
ball 0 20
```

In this exercise, we were able to change multiple variables in a single line. This approach would also work when calling functions, just as it does with a variable declaration. You need to be careful with a feature like this to ensure that, first and foremost, your code is easy to read and understand. If using a one-line statement like this makes it hard to know what the code is doing, then it's better to take up more lines to write the code.

Next, we'll look at what operators are and how they can be used to change your variables in interesting ways.

Operators

While variables hold the data for your application, they become truly useful when you start using them to build the logic of your software. Operators are the tools you use to work with your software's data. With operators, you can compare data to other data – for example, you can check whether a price is too low or too high in a trading application. You can also use operators to manipulate data. For example, you can use operators to add the costs of all the items in a shopping cart to get the total price.

The following list mentions groups of operators:

- **Arithmetic operators**: These are used for math-related tasks such as addition, subtraction, and multiplication.

- **Comparison operators**: These are used to compare two values; for example, whether they are equal, not equal, less than, or greater than each other.

- **Logical operators**: These are used with Boolean values to see whether they are both true, only one is true, or whether a `bool` value is false.

- **Address operators**: We'll cover these in detail soon when we look at pointers. These are used to work with them.

- **Receive operators**: These are used when working with Go channels. We'll cover this later in this book.

Exercise 1.09 – using operators with numbers

In this exercise, we are going to simulate a restaurant bill. To build our simulation, we'll need to use mathematic and comparison operators. We'll start by exploring all the major uses for operators.

In our simulation, we'll sum everything together and work out the tip based on a percentage. Then, we'll use a comparison operator to see whether the customer gets a reward. Let's get started:

> **Note**
>
> We have considered the US dollar as the currency for this exercise. You may consider any currency of your choice; the main focus here is the operations.

1. Create a new folder and add a `main.go` file to it.

2. In `main.go`, add the `main` package name to the top of the file:

    ```
    package main
    ```

3. Import the packages you'll need:

    ```
    import "fmt"
    ```

4. Create the `main()` function:

    ```
    func main() {
    ```

5. Create a variable to hold the total. For this item on the bill, the customer purchased two items that cost 13 USD. We must use `*` to do the multiplication. Then, we must print a subtotal:

    ```
    // Main course
    var total float64 = 2 * 13
    fmt.Println("Sub :", total)
    ```

6. Here, they purchased four items that cost 2.25 USD. We must use multiplication to get the total of these items, use + to add it to the previous total value, and then assign that back to the total:

```
// Drinks
total = total + (4 * 2.25)
fmt.Println("Sub :", total)
```

7. This customer is getting a discount of 5 USD. Here, we use – to subtract 5 USD from the total:

```
// Discount
total = total - 5
fmt.Println("Sub :", total)
```

8. Then, we use multiplication to calculate a 10% tip:

```
// 10% Tip
tip := total * 0.1
fmt.Println("Tip :", tip)
```

9. Finally, we add the tip to the total:

```
total = total + tip
fmt.Println("Total:", total)
```

10. The bill will be split between two people. Use / to divide the total into two parts:

```
// Split bill
split := total / 2
fmt.Println("Split:", split)
```

11. Here, we'll calculate whether the customer gets a reward. First, we'll set visitCount and then add 1 USD to this visit:

```
// Reward every 5th visit
visitCount := 24
visitCount = visitCount + 1
```

12. Then, we'll use % to give us any remainder after dividing visitCount by 5 USD:

```
remainder := visitCount % 5
```

13. The customer gets a reward on every fifth visit. If the remainder is 0, then this is one of those visits. Use the == operator to check whether the remainder is 0:

```
if remainder == 0 {
```

14. If it is, print a message stating that they get a reward:

```
fmt.Println("With this visit, you've earned a reward.")
```

```
        }
    }
```

15. Save the file. Then, in the new folder, run the following:

```
go run .
```

The following is the output:

```
📂  ~/src/Th…op/Ch…01/Exercise01.09   go run .
Sub  : 26
Sub  : 35
Sub  : 30
Tip  : 3
Total: 33
Split: 16.5
With this visit, you've earned a reward.
```

Figure 1.13: Output of operators used with numbers

In this exercise, we used the math and comparison operators with numbers. They allowed us to model a complex situation – calculating a restaurant bill. There are lots of operators and which ones you can use vary with the different types of values. For example, as well as there being an addition operator for numbers, you can use the + symbol to join strings together. Here's this in action:

```
package main
import "fmt"
func main() {
    givenName := "John"
    familyName := "Smith"
    fullName := givenName + " " + familyName
    fmt.Println("Hello,", fullName)
}
```

The following is the output:

```
Hello, John Smith
```

For some situations, there are some shortcuts we can make with operators. We'll go over this in the next section.

Bitwise operators

Go has all the familiar bitwise operators you'd find in programming languages. If you know what bitwise operators are, then there will be no surprises here for you. If you don't know what bitwise operators are, don't worry – they aren't common in real-world code.

Shorthand operators

There are a few shorthand assignment operators when you want to perform operations on an existing value with its own value:

- --: Reduce a number by 1
- ++: Increase a number by 1
- +=: Add and assign
- -=: Subtract and assign

Exercise 1.10 – implementing shorthand operators

In this exercise, we'll use some examples of operator shorthand to show how they can make your code more compact and easier to write. We'll create some variables and then use shorthand to change them, printing them out as we go. Let's get started:

1. Create a new folder and add a `main.go` file to it.

2. In `main.go`, add the `main` package name to the top of the file:

   ```
   package main
   ```

3. Import the packages we'll need:

   ```
   import "fmt"
   ```

4. Create the `main()` function:

   ```
   func main() {
   ```

5. Create a variable with an initial value:

   ```
   count := 5
   ```

6. We'll add to it and then assign the result back to itself. Then, we'll print it out:

   ```
   count += 5
   fmt.Println(count)
   ```

7. Increment the value by 1 and then print it out:

   ```
   count++
   fmt.Println(count)
   ```

8. Decrement it by 1 and then print it out:

   ```
   count--
   fmt.Println(count)
   ```

9. Subtract and assign the result back to itself. Print out the new value:

```
count -= 5
fmt.Println(count)
```

10. There is also a shorthand that works with strings. Define a string:

```
name := "John"
```

11. Next, we'll append another string to the end of it and then print it out:

```
name += " Smith"
fmt.Println("Hello,", name)
```

12. Close the main() function:

```
}
```

13. Save the file. Then, in the new folder, run the following:

```
go run .
```

The following is the output:

```
 ~/src/Th…op/Ch…01/Exercise01.10  go run .
10
11
10
5
Hello, John Smith
```

Figure 1.14: Output using shorthand operators

In this exercise, we used some shorthand operators. One set focused on modification and then assignment. This type of operation is common, and having these shortcuts makes coding more engaging. The other operators are increment and decrement. These are useful in loops when you need to step over data one at a time. These shortcuts make it clear what you're doing to anyone who reads your code.

Next, we'll look at comparing values to each other in detail.

Comparing values

Logic in applications is a matter of having your code make a decision. These decisions are made by comparing the values of variables to the rules you define. These rules come in the form of comparisons. We use another set of operators to make these comparisons. The result of these comparisons is always true or false. You'll also often need to make lots of these comparisons to make a single decision. To help with that, we have logical operators.

These operators, for the most part, work with two values and always result in a Boolean value. You can only use logical operators with Boolean values. Let's take a look at comparison operators and logical operators in more detail.

Comparison operators:

- ==: True if two values are the same
- !=: True if two values are not the same
- <: True if the left value is less than the right value
- <=: True if the left value is less or equal to the right value
- >: True if the left value is greater than the right value
- >=: True if the left value is greater than or equal to the right value

Logical operators:

- &&: True if the left and right values are both true
- ||: True if one or both the left and right values are true
- !: This operator only works with a single value and results in true if the value is false

Exercise 1.11 – comparing values

In this exercise, we'll use comparison and logical operators to see what Boolean results we get when testing different conditions. We are testing to see what level of membership a user has based on the number of visits they've had.

Our membership levels are as follows:

- **Silver**: Between 10 and 20 visits inclusively
- **Gold**: Between 21 and 30 visits inclusively
- **Platinum**: Over 30 visits

Let's get started:

1. Create a new folder and add a main.go file to it.
2. In main.go, add the main package name to the top of the file:

    ```
    package main
    ```

3. Import the packages we'll need:

    ```
    import "fmt"
    ```

4. Create the `main()` function:

```
func main() {
```

5. Define our `visits` variable and initialize it with a value:

```
visits := 15
```

6. Use the equals operator to see whether this is their first visit. Then, print the result to the console:

```
fmt.Println("First visit    :", visits == 1)
```

7. Use the not equal operator to see whether they are a returning visitor:

```
fmt.Println("Return visit   :", visits != 1)
```

8. Let's check whether they are a silver member using the following code:

```
fmt.Println("Silver member :", visits >= 10 && visits < 21)
```

9. Let's check whether they are a gold member using the following code:

```
fmt.Println("Gold member    :", visits > 20 && visits <= 30)
```

10. Let's check whether they are a platinum member using the following code:

```
fmt.Println("Platinum member :", visits > 30)
```

11. Close the `main()` function:

```
}
```

12. Save the file. Then, in the new folder, run the following:

```
go run .
```

The following is the output:

```
  ~/src/Th...op/Ch...01/Exercise01.11   go run .
First visit    : false
Return visit   : true
Silver member  : true
Gold member    : false
Platinum member : false
```

Figure 1.15: Output displaying the comparison result

In this exercise, we used comparison and logical operators to make decisions about data. You can combine these operators in an unlimited number of ways to express almost any type of logic your software needs to make.

Next, we'll look at what happens when you don't give a variable an initial value.

Zero values

The zero value of a variable is the empty or default value for that variable's type. Go has a set of rules stating that the zero values are for all the core types. Let's take a look:

Type	Zero Value
bool	false
Numbers (integers and floats)	0
String	"" (empty string)
pointers, functions, interfaces, slices, channels, and maps	nil (covered in detail in later chapters)

Figure 1.16: Variable types and their zero values

There are other types, but they are all derived from these core types, so the same rules still apply.

We'll look at the zero values of some types in the upcoming exercise.

Exercise 1.12 – zero values

In this example, we'll define some variables without an initial value. Then, we'll print out their values. We're using fmt.Printf to help us in this exercise as we can get more detail about a value's type. fmt.Printf uses a template language that allows us to transform passed values. The substitution we're using is %#v. This transformation is a useful tool for showing a variable's value and type. Some other common substitutions you can try are as follows:

Substitution	Formatting
%v	Any value. Use this if you don't care about the type you're printing.
%+v	Values with extra information, such as struct field names.
%#v	Go syntax, such as %+v with the addition of the name of the type of the variable.
%T	Print the variable's type.
%d	Decimal (base 10).
%s	String.

Figure 1.17: Table on substitutions

When using `fmt.Printf`, you need to add the new line symbol yourself. You can do this by adding `\n` to the end of the string. Let's get started:

1. Create a new folder and add a `main.go` file to it.

2. In `main.go`, add the `main` package name to the top of the file:

    ```
    package main
    ```

3. Import the packages we'll need:

    ```
    import (
        "fmt"
        "time"
    )
    ```

4. Create the `main()` function:

    ```
    func main() {
    ```

5. Declare and print an integer:

    ```
    var count int
    fmt.Printf("Count   : %#v \n", count)
    ```

6. Declare and print a `float` value:

    ```
    var discount float64
    fmt.Printf("Discount : %#v \n", discount)
    ```

7. Declare and print a `bool` value:

    ```
    var debug bool
    fmt.Printf("Debug   : %#v \n", debug)
    ```

8. Declare and print a `string` value:

    ```
    var message string
    fmt.Printf("Message : %#v \n", message)
    ```

9. Declare and print a collection of strings:

    ```
    var emails []string
    fmt.Printf("Emails : %#v \n", emails)
    ```

10. Declare and print a struct (a type composed of other types; we will cover this later in this book):

    ```
    var startTime time.Time
    fmt.Printf("Start   : %#v \n", startTime)
    ```

11. Close the `main()` function:

```
}
```

12. Save the file. Then, in the new folder, run the following:

```
go run .
```

The following is the output:

```
→  Exercise01.12 git:(main) ✗ go run .
Count    : 0
Discount : 0
Debug    : false
Message  : ""
Emails   : []string(nil)
Start    : time.Date(1, time.January, 1, 0, 0, 0, 0, time.UTC)
```

Figure 1.18: Output showing initial variable values

In this exercise, we defined a variety of variable types without an initial value. Then, we printed them out using `fmt.Printf` to expose more detail about the values. Knowing what the zero values are and how Go controls them allows you to avoid bugs and write concise code.

Next, we'll look at what pointers are and how they can enable you to write efficient software.

Value versus pointer

With values such as `int`, `bool`, and `string`, when you pass them to a function, Go makes a copy of the value, and it's the copy that's used in the function. This copying means that a change that's made to the value in the function doesn't affect the value that you used when calling the function.

Passing values by copying tends to result in code that has fewer bugs. With this method of passing values, Go can use its simple memory management system, called the stack. The downside is that copying uses up more and more memory as values get passed from function to function. In real-world code, functions tend to be small, and values get passed to lots of functions, so copying by value can sometimes end up using much more memory than is needed.

There is an alternative to copying that uses less memory. Instead of passing a value, we create something called a pointer and then pass that to functions. A pointer is not a value itself, and you can't do anything useful with a pointer other than getting a value using it. You can think of a pointer as the address of the value you want, and to get to the value, you must go to the address. If you use a pointer, Go won't make a copy of the value when passing a pointer to a function.

When creating a pointer to a value, Go can't manage the value's memory using the stack. This is because the stack relies on simple scope logic to know when it can reclaim the memory that's used by a value, and having a pointer to a variable means these rules don't work. Instead, Go puts the value on the heap. The heap allows the value to exist until no part of your software has a pointer to it anymore. Go reclaims these values in what it calls its garbage collection process. This process happens periodically in the background, and you don't need to worry about it.

Having a pointer to a value means that a value is put on the heap, but that's not the only reason that happens. Working out whether a value needs to be put on the heap is called escape analysis. There are times when a value with no pointers is put on the heap, and it's not always clear why.

You have no direct control over whether a value is put on the stack or the heap. Memory management is not part of Go's language specification. Memory management is considered an internal implementation detail. This means it could be changed at any time, and that what we've spoken about are only general guidelines and not fixed rules and could change at a later date.

While the benefits of using a pointer over a value that gets passed to lots of functions are clear for memory usage, it's not so clear for CPU usage. When a value gets copied, Go needs CPU cycles to get that memory and then release it later. Using a pointer avoids this CPU usage when passing it to a function. On the other hand, having a value on the heap means that it then needs to be managed by the complex garbage collection process. This process can become a CPU bottleneck in certain situations – for example, if there are lots of values on the heap. When this happens, the garbage collector has to do lots of checking, which uses up CPU cycles. There is no correct answer here, and the best approach is the classic performance optimization one. First, don't prematurely optimize. When you do have a performance problem, measure before you make a change, and then measure after you've made a change.

Beyond performance, you can use pointers to change your code's design. Sometimes, using pointers allows for a cleaner interface and simplifies your code. For example, if you need to know whether a value is present or not, a non-pointer value always has at least its zero value, which could be valid in your logic. You can use a pointer to allow for an `is not set` state as well as holding a value. This is because pointers, as well as holding the address to a value, can also be `nil`, which means there is no value. In Go, `nil` is a special type that represents something not having a value.

The ability for a pointer to be nil also means that it's possible to get the value of a pointer when it doesn't have a value associated with it, which means you'll get a runtime error. To prevent runtime errors, you can compare a pointer to `nil` before trying to get its value. This looks like `<pointer> != nil`. You can compare pointers with other pointers of the same type, but they only result in true if you are comparing a pointer to itself. No comparison of the associated values gets made.

Pointers are powerful tools in the language thanks to their efficiency, ability to pass by reference (instead of pass by value) to allow functions to modify the original values, and how they allow for dynamic memory allocation using the garbage collector. However, with any great tool comes great responsibility. Pointers can be dangerous if misused, such as in the event memory is freed (deallocated) and the pointer becomes a "dangling pointer," which could lead to undefined behavior if accessed. There is also the potential for memory leaks, unsafe operations due to direct memory access, and concurrency challenges if there are shared pointers that could introduce data races. Overall, Go's pointers are generally straightforward and less error-prone compared to other languages such as C.

Getting a pointer

To get a pointer, you have a few options. You can declare a variable as being a pointer type using a var statement. You can do this by adding * at the front of most types. This notation looks like var <name> *<type>. The initial value of a variable that uses this method is nil. You can use the built-in new function for this. This function is intended to be used to get some memory for a type and return a pointer to that address. The notation looks like <name> := new(<type>). The new function can be used with var too. You can also get a pointer from an existing variable using &, which you can read as "address of". This looks like <var1> := &<var2>.

Exercise 1.13 – getting a pointer

In this exercise, we'll use each of the methods we can use to get a pointer variable. Then, we'll print them to the console using fmt.Printf to see what their types and value are. Let's get started:

1. Create a new folder and add a main.go file to it.

2. In main.go, add the main package name to the top of the file:

   ```
   package main
   ```

3. Import the packages we'll need:

   ```
   import (
     "fmt"
     "time"
   )
   ```

4. Create the main() function:

   ```
   func main() {
   ```

5. Declare a pointer using a var statement:

   ```
   var count1 *int
   ```

6. Create a variable using new:

   ```
   count2 := new(int)
   ```

7. You can't take the address of a literal number. Create a temporary variable to hold a number:

   ```
   countTemp := 5
   ```

8. Using &, create a pointer from the existing variable:

   ```
   count3 := &countTemp
   ```

9.   It's possible to create a pointer from some types without a temporary variable. Here, we're using our trusty `time` struct:

```
t := &time.Time{}
```

10. Print each out using `fmt.Printf`:

```
fmt.Printf("count1: %#v\n", count1)
fmt.Printf("count2: %#v\n", count2)
fmt.Printf("count3: %#v\n", count3)
fmt.Printf("time : %#v\n", t)
```

11. Close the `main()` function:

```
}
```

12. Save the file. Then, in the new folder, run the following:

```
go run .
```

The following is the output:

```
→  Exercise01.13 git:(main) ✗ go run main.go
count1: (*int)(nil)
count2: (*int)(0x140000a4018)
count3: (*int)(0x140000a4020)
time : time.Date(1, time.January, 1, 0, 0, 0, 0, time.UTC)
```

Figure 1.19: Output showing pointers

In this exercise, we looked at three different ways of creating a pointer. Each one is useful, depending on what your code needs. With the `var` statement, the pointer has a value of `nil`, while the others already have a value address associated with them. For the `time` variable, we can see the value, but we can tell it's a pointer because its output starts with &.

Next, we'll see how we can get a value from a pointer.

Getting a value from a pointer

In the previous exercise, when we printed out the pointer variables for the `int` pointers to the console, we either got `nil` or saw a memory address. To get to the value a pointer is associated with, you must dereference the value using * in front of the variable name. This looks like `fmt.Println(*<val>)`.

Dereferencing a zero or `nil` pointer is a common bug in Go software as the compiler can't warn you about it, and it happens when the app is running. Therefore, it's always best practice to check that a pointer is not `nil` before dereferencing it unless you are certain it's not `nil`.

You don't always need to dereference – for example, when a property or function is on a struct. Don't worry too much about when you shouldn't be dereferencing as Go gives you clear errors regarding when you can and can't dereference a value.

Exercise 1.14 – getting a value from a pointer

In this exercise, we'll update our previous exercise to dereference the values from the pointers. We'll also add `nil` checks to prevent us from getting any errors. Let's get started:

1. Create a new folder and add a `main.go` file to it.

2. In `main.go`, add the `main` package name to the top of the file:

    ```
    package main
    ```

3. Import the packages we'll need:

    ```
    import (
      "fmt"
      "time"
    )
    ```

4. Create the `main()` function:

    ```
    func main() {
    ```

5. Our pointers are declared in the same way as they were previously:

    ```
    var count1 *int
    count2 := new(int)
    countTemp := 5
    count3 := &countTemp
    t := &time.Time{}
    ```

6. For counts 1, 2, and 3, we need to add a `nil` check and add `*` in front of the variable name:

    ```
    if count1 != nil {
       fmt.Printf("count1: %#v\n", *count1)
    }
    if count2 != nil {
       fmt.Printf("count2: %#v\n", *count2)
    }
    if count3 != nil {
       fmt.Printf("count3: %#v\n", *count3)
    }
    ```

7. We'll also add a `nil` check for our `time` variable:

    ```
    if t != nil {
    ```

8. We'll dereference the variable using `*`, just like we did with the `count` variables:

    ```
    fmt.Printf("time : %#v\n", *t)
    ```

9. Here, we're calling a function on our `time` variable. This time, we don't need to dereference it:

    ```
    fmt.Printf("time : %#v\n", t.String())
    ```

10. Close the `nil` check:

    ```
    }
    ```

11. Close the `main()` function:

    ```
    }
    ```

12. Save the file. Then, in the new folder, run the following:

    ```
    go run .
    ```

The following is the output:

```
→  Exercise01.14 git:(main) ✗ go run main.go
count2: 0
count3: 5
time  : time.Date(1, time.January, 1, 0, 0, 0, 0, time.UTC)
time  : "0001-01-01 00:00:00 +0000 UTC"
```

Figure 1.20: Output showing getting values from pointers

In this exercise, we used dereferencing to get the values from our pointers. We also used `nil` checks to prevent dereferencing errors. From the output of this exercise, we can see that `count1` was a `nil` value and that we'd have gotten an error if we tried to dereference. `count2` was created using `new`, and its value is a zero value for its type. `count3` also had a value that matched the value of the variable we got the pointer from. With our `time` variable, we were able to dereference the whole struct, which is why our output doesn't start with `&`.

Next, we'll look at how using a pointer allows us to change the design of our code.

Function design with pointers

We'll cover functions in more detail later in this book, but you know enough from what we've done so far to see how using a pointer can change how you use a function. A function must be coded to accept pointers, and it's not something that you can choose whether to do or not. If you have a pointer variable or have passed a pointer of a variable to a function, any changes that are made to the value of the variable in the function also affect the value of the variable outside of the function.

Exercise 1.15 – function design with pointers

In this exercise, we'll create two functions: one that accepts a number by value, adds 5 to it, and then prints the number to the console; and another function that accepts a number as a pointer, adds 5 to it, and then prints the number out. We'll also print the number out after calling each function to assess what effect it has on the variable that was passed to the function. Let's get started:

1. Create a new folder and add a `main.go` file to it.

2. In `main.go`, add the `main` package name to the top of the file:

    ```
    package main
    ```

3. Import the packages we'll need:

    ```
    import "fmt"
    ```

4. Create a function that takes an `int` pointer as an argument:

    ```
    func add5Value(count int) {
    ```

5. Add 5 to the passed number:

    ```
    count += 5
    ```

6. Print the updated number to the console:

    ```
    fmt.Println("add5Value    :", count)
    ```

7. Close the function:

    ```
    }
    ```

8. Create another function that takes an `int` pointer:

    ```
    func add5Point(count *int) {
    ```

9. Dereference the value and add 5 to it:

    ```
    *count += 5
    ```

10. Print out the updated value of `count` and dereference it:

    ```
    fmt.Println("add5Point    :", *count)
    ```

11. Close the function:

    ```
    }
    ```

12. Create the `main()` function:

```
func main() {
```

13. Declare an `int` variable:

```
var count int
```

14. Call the first function with the variable:

```
add5Value(count)
```

15. Print the current value of the variable:

```
fmt.Println("add5Value post:", count)
```

16. Call the second function. This time, you'll need to use & to pass a pointer to the variable:

```
add5Point(&count)
```

17. Print the current value of the variable:

```
fmt.Println("add5Point post:", count)
```

18. Close the `main()` function:

```
}
```

19. Save the file. Then, in the new folder, run the following:

```
go run .
```

The following is the output:

```
~/src/Th...op/Ch...01/Exercise01.15    go run .
add5Value       : 5
add5Value post: 0
add5Point       : 5
add5Point post: 5
```

Figure 1.21: Output displaying the current value of the variable

In this exercise, we showed you how passing values by a pointer can affect the value variables that are passed to them. We saw that, when passing by value, the changes you make to the value in a function do not affect the value of the variable that's passed to the function, while passing a pointer to a value does change the value of the variable passed to the function.

You can use this fact to overcome awkward design problems and sometimes simplify the design of your code. Passing values by a pointer has traditionally been shown to be more error-prone, so use this design sparingly. It's also common to use pointers in functions to create more efficient code, which Go's standard library does a lot.

Activity 1.02 – pointer value swap

In this activity, your job is to finish some code a co-worker started. Here, we have some unfinished code for you to complete. Your task is to fill in the missing code, where the comments are to swap the values of a and b. The swap function only accepts pointers and doesn't return anything:

```
package main
import "fmt"
func main() {
    a, b := 5, 10
    // call swap here
    fmt.Println(a == 10, b == 5)
}
func swap(a *int, b *int) {
    // swap the values here
}
```

Follow these steps:

1. Call the swap function, ensuring you are passing a pointer.

2. In the swap function, assign the values to the other pointer, ensuring you dereference the values.

The following is the expected output:

```
true true
```

Next, we'll look at how we can create variables with a fixed value.

Constants

Constants are like variables, but you can't change their initial values. These are useful for situations where the value of a constant doesn't need to or shouldn't change when your code is running. You could make the argument that you could hardcode those values into the code and it would have a similar effect. Experience has shown us that while these values don't need to change at runtime, they may need to change later. If that happens, it can be an arduous and error-prone task to track down and fix all the hardcoded values. Using a constant is a tiny amount of work now that can save you a great deal of effort later.

Constant declarations are similar to var statements. With a constant, the initial value is required. Types are optional and inferred if left out. The initial value can be a literal or a simple statement and can use the values of other constants. Like var, you can declare multiple constants in one statement. Here are the notations:

```
constant <name> <type> = <value>
constant (
    <name1> <type1> = <value1>
```

```
    <name2> <type2> = <value3>
...
    <nameN> <typeN> = <valueN>
)
```

Exercise 1.16 – constants

In this exercise, we have a performance problem: our database server is too slow. We are going to create a custom memory cache. We'll use Go's map collection type, which will act as the cache. There is a global limit on the number of items that can be in the cache. We'll use one map to help keep track of the number of items in the cache. We have two types of data we need to cache: books and CDs. Both use the ID, so we need a way to separate the two types of items in the shared cache. We need a way to set and get items from the cache.

We're going to set the maximum number of items in the cache. We'll also use constants to add a prefix to differentiate between books and CDs. Let's get started:

1. Create a new folder and add a main.go file to it.

2. In main.go, add the main package name to the top of the file:

    ```
    package main
    ```

3. Import the packages we'll need:

    ```
    import "fmt"
    ```

4. Create a constant that's our global limit size:

    ```
    const GlobalLimit = 100
    ```

5. Create a MaxCacheSize constant that is 10 times the global limit size:

    ```
    const MaxCacheSize int = 10 * GlobalLimit
    ```

6. Create our cache prefixes:

    ```
    const (
        CacheKeyBook = "book_"
        CacheKeyCD = "cd_"
    )
    ```

7. Declare a map value that has a string value for a key and a string value for its values as our cache:

    ```
    var cache map[string]string
    ```

8. Create a function to get items from the cache:

```
func cacheGet(key string) string {
  return cache[key]
}
```

9. Create a function that sets items in the cache:

```
func cacheSet(key, val string) {
```

10. In this function, check out the MaxCacheSize constant to stop the cache going over that size:

```
if len(cache)+1 >= MaxCacheSize {
  return
}
cache[key] = val
}
```

11. Create a function to get a book from the cache:

```
func GetBook(isbn string) string {
```

12. Use the book cache prefix to create a unique key:

```
  return cacheGet(CacheKeyBook + isbn)
}
```

13. Create a function to add a book to the cache:

```
func SetBook(isbn string, name string) {
```

14. Use the book cache prefix to create a unique key:

```
  cacheSet(CacheKeyBook+isbn, name)
}
```

15. Create a function to get CD data from the cache:

```
func GetCD(sku string) string {
```

16. Use the CD cache prefix to create a unique key:

```
  return cacheGet(CacheKeyCD + sku)
}
```

17. Create a function to add CDs to the shared cache:

```
func SetCD(sku string, title string) {
```

18. Use the CD cache prefix constant to build a unique key for the shared cache:

```
    cacheSet(CacheKeyCD+sku, title)
}
```

19. Create the `main()` function:

```
func main() {
```

20. Initialize our cache by creating a `map` value:

```
    cache = make(map[string]string)
```

21. Add a book to the cache:

```
    SetBook("1234-5678", "Get Ready To Go")
```

22. Add a CD cache prefix to the cache:

```
    SetCD("1234-5678", "Get Ready To Go Audio Book")
```

23. Get and print that Book from the cache:

```
    fmt.Println("Book :", GetBook("1234-5678"))
```

24. Get and print that CD from the cache:

```
    fmt.Println("CD :", GetCD("1234-5678"))
```

25. Close the `main()` function:

```
}
```

26. Save the file. Then, in the new folder, run the following:

```
go run .
```

The following is the output:

```
 ~/src/Th…op/Ch…01/Exercise01.16   go run .
Book : Get Ready To Go
CD   : Get Ready To Go Audio Book
```

Figure 1.22: Output displaying the Book and CD caches

In this exercise, we used constants to define values that don't need to change while the code is running. We declared then using a variety of notation options, some with the typeset and some without. We declared a single constant and multiple constants in a single statement.

Next, we'll look at a variation of constants for values that are more closely related.

Enums

Enums are a way of defining a fixed list of values that are all related. Go doesn't have a built-in type for enums, but it does provide tools such as iota to let you define your own using constants. We'll explore this now.

For example, in the following code, we have the days of the week defined as constants. This code is a good candidate for Go's iota feature:

```
...
const (
    Sunday    = 0
    Monday    = 1
    Tuesday   = 2
    Wednesday = 3
    Thursday  = 4
    Friday    = 5
    Saturday  = 6
)
...
```

With iota, Go helps us manage lists just like this. Using iota, the following code is equal to the preceding code:

```
...
const (
    Sunday = iota
    Monday
    Tuesday
    Wednesday
    Thursday
    Friday
    Saturday
)
...
```

Now, we have iota assigning the numbers for us. Using iota makes enums easier to create and maintain, especially if you need to add a new value to the middle of the code later. Order matters when using iota as it is an identifier that tells the Go compiler to start the first value at 0 and increment by 1 for each subsequent value in the case of this example. With iota, you can skip values using _, start with a different offset, and even use more complicated calculations.

Next, we'll take a detailed look at Go's variable scoping rules and how they affect how you write code.

Scope

All the variables in Go live in a scope. The top-level scope is the package scope. A scope can have child scopes within it. There are a few ways a child scope gets defined; the easiest way to think about this is that when you see {, you are starting a new child scope, and that child scope ends when you get to a matching }. The parent-child relationship is defined when the code compiles, not when the code runs. When accessing a variable, Go looks at the scope the code was defined in. If it can't find a variable with that name, it looks in the parent scope, then the grandparent scope, all the way until it gets to the package scope. It stops looking once it finds a variable with a matching name or raises an error if it can't find a match.

To put it another way, when your code uses a variable, Go needs to work out where that variable was defined. It starts its search in the scope of the code using the variable it's currently running in. If a variable definition using that name is in that scope, then it stops looking and uses the variable definition to complete its work. If it can't find a variable definition, then it starts walking up the stack of scopes, stopping as soon as it finds a variable with that name. This searching is all done based on a variable name. If a variable with that name is found but is of the wrong type, Go raises an error.

In this example, we have four different scopes, but we define the level variable once. This means that no matter where you use level, the same variable is used:

```go
package main
import "fmt"
var level = "pkg"
func main() {
  fmt.Println("Main start :", level)
  if true {
    fmt.Println("Block start :", level)
    funcA()
  }
}
func funcA() {
  fmt.Println("funcA start :", level)
}
```

The following is the output displaying variables when using level:

```
Main start : pkg
Block start : pkg
funcA start : pkg
```

In this example, we've shadowed the level variable. This new level variable is not related to the level variable in the package scope. When we print level in the block, the Go runtime stops looking for variables called `level` as soon as it finds the one defined in `main`. This logic results in a different value getting printed out once that new variable shadows the package variable. You can also see that it's a different variable because it's a different type, and a variable can't have its type changed in Go:

```
package main
import "fmt"
var level = "pkg"
func main() {
  fmt.Println("Main start :", level)
  // Create a shadow variable
  level := 42
  if true {
    fmt.Println("Block start :", level)
    funcA()
  }
  fmt.Println("Main end :", level)
}
func funcA() {
  fmt.Println("funcA start :", level)
}
```

The following is the output:

```
Main start : pkg
Block start : 42
funcA start : pkg
Main end : 42
```

Go's static scope resolution comes into play when we call `funcA`. That's why, when `funcA` runs, it still sees the package scope's `level` variable. The scope resolution doesn't pay attention to where `funcA` gets called.

You can't access variables defined in a child scope:

```
package main
import "fmt"
func main() {
  {
    level := "Nest 1"
    fmt.Println("Block end :", level)
  }
  // Error: undefined: level
  //fmt.Println("Main end   :", level)
}
```

The following is the output:

```
→  Example01.11 git:(main) ✗ go run .
# github.com/packt-book/Go-Programming---From-Beginner-to-Professional-Second-Edition-/Chapter01/Example01.11
./main.go:11:31: undefined: level
```

Figure 1.23: Output displaying an error

Activity 1.03 – message bug

The following code doesn't work. The person who wrote it can't fix it, and they've asked you to help them. Can you get it to work?

```
package main
import "fmt"
func main() {
  count := 5
  if count > 5 {
    message := "Greater than 5"
  } else {
    message := "Not greater than 5"
  }
  fmt.Println(message)
}
```

Follow these steps:

1. Run the code and see what the output is.

2. The problem is with message; make a change to the code.

3. Rerun the code and see what difference it makes.

4. Repeat this process until you see the expected output.

    The following is the expected output:

    ```
    Not greater than 5
    ```

In this activity, we saw that where you define your variables has a big impact on the code. Always think about the scope you need your variables to be in when defining them.

In the next activity, we are going to look at a similar problem that is a bit trickier.

Activity 1.04 – bad count bug

Your friend is back, and they have another bug in their code. This code should print `true`, but it's printing `false`. Can you help them fix the bug?

```
package main
import "fmt"
func main() {
    count := 0
    if count < 5 {
        count := 10
        count++
    }
    fmt.Println(count == 11)
}
```

Follow these steps:

1. Run the code and see what the output is.

2. The problem is with `count`; make a change to the code.

3. Rerun the code and see what difference it makes.

4. Repeat this process until you see the expected output.

The following is the expected output:

```
True
```

Summary

In this chapter, we got into the nitty-gritty of variables, including how variables are declared, and all the different notations you can use to declare them. This variety of notation gives you a nice compact notation to use for 90% of your work, while still giving you the power to be very specific when you need to the other 10% of the time. We looked at how to change and update the value of variables after you've declared them. Again, Go gives you some great shorthand to help in the most common use cases to make your life easier. All your data ends up in some form of variable. Data is what makes code dynamic and responsive. Without data, your code could only ever do exactly one thing; data unleashes the true power of software.

Now that your application has data, it needs to make choices based on that data. That's where variable comparison comes in. This helps us see whether something is true or false, bigger or smaller, and so on, and it also helps us make choices based on the results of those comparisons.

We explored how Go decided to implement its variable system by looking at zero values, pointers, and scope logic. At this point, we know that these are the details that can be the difference between delivering bug-free efficient software and not doing so.

We also took a look at how we can declare immutable variables by using constants and how `iota` can help manage lists or related constants to work, such as enums.

In the next chapter, we'll start to put our variables to work by defining logic and looping over collections of variables.

2

Command and Control

> **Overview**
>
> In this chapter, we'll use branching logic and loops to demonstrate how logic can be controlled and selectively run. With these tools, you'll have control of what you do and don't want to run based on the values of variables.
>
> By the end of this chapter, you will be able to implement branching logic using `if`, `else`, and `else if`; use `switch` statements to simplify complex branching logic; create looping logic using a `for` loop; loop over complex data collections using `range`; use `continue` and `break` to take control of the flow of loops; and use `goto` statements to jump to a labeled statement within a function.

Technical requirements

For this chapter, you'll require Go version 1.21 or higher. The code for this chapter can be found at: `https://github.com/PacktPublishing/Go-Programming-From-Beginner-to-Professional-Second-Edition-/tree/main/Chapter02`.

Introduction

In the previous chapter, we looked at variables and values and how we can temporarily store data in a variable and make changes to that data. We're now going to look at how we can use that data to run logic in code, or not, selectively. "Logic" refers to the sequence of instructions that control how your program operates or processes data. This logic allows you to control how data flows through your software. You can react to and perform different operations based on the values in your variables.

The logic could be for validating your user's inputs. If we were writing code to manage a bank account and the user asked to withdraw some money, we could check that they asked for a valid amount of money. We would check that they had enough money in their account. If the validation were successful, we would use logic to update their balance, transfer the money, and show a success message. If the validation failed, we'd show a message explaining what went wrong.

If your software is a virtual world, then logic is the physical law of that world. Like the physical laws of our world, those laws must be followed and can't be broken. If you create a law with a flaw in it, then your virtual world won't run smoothly and could even explode.

Another form of logic is a loop; using loops allows you to execute the same code multiple times. A common way to use loops is to iterate over a collection of data. For our imaginary banking software, we would use a loop to step through a user's transactions to display them to the user on request.

Loops and logic allow the software to have complex behavior that responds to changing and dynamic data.

if statements

An if statement is the most basic form of logic in Go. An if statement either will or will not run a block of code based on a Boolean expression. The notation looks like this: if <boolean expression> { <code block> }.

The Boolean expression can be simple code that results in a Boolean value. The code block can be any logic that you could also put in a function and are confined to the code block of that function. The code block runs when the Boolean expression is true. You can only use if statements within the scope of a function. In Go, the concept of "function scope" refers to the visibility and accessibility of variables and statements within a function. .

Exercise 2.01 – a simple if statement

In this exercise, we'll use an if statement to control whether certain code will or will not run. We'll define an int value that will be hardcoded, but in a real-world application, this could be user input. We'll then check whether the value is an odd or even number using the % operator, also known as a modulus expression, on the variable. The modulus gives you the amount remaining after division. We'll use the modulus to get the remainder after dividing by 2. If we get a remainder of 0, then we know the number is even. If the remainder is 1, then we know the number is odd. The modulus results in an int value, so we use == (comparison operator) to get a true or false Boolean value:

1. Create a new folder and add a main.go file.

2. In main.go, add the package and import:

    ```
    package main
    import "fmt"
    ```

3. Create a main function:

    ```
    func main() {
    ```

4. Define an `int` variable with an initial value. We are setting it to 5 here, which is an odd number, but we could also set it to 6, which is an even number:

```
input := 5
```

5. Create an `if` statement that uses a modulus expression, then check whether the result is equal to 0:

```
if input%2 == 0 {
```

6. When the Boolean expression results in `true`, that means the number is even. We then print that it's even to the console using the `fmt` package:

```
fmt.Println(input, "is even")
```

7. Close the code block:

```
}
```

8. Now do the same for odd numbers:

```
if input%2 == 1 {
    fmt.Println(input, "is odd")
}
```

9. Close `main`:

```
}
```

10. Save the file, and in the new folder, run the following code snippet:

```
go run main.go
```

The following is the expected output:

```
5 is odd
```

In this exercise, we used logic to run code selectively. Using logic to control which code runs lets you create flows through your code. This allows you to have code that reacts to its data. These flows allow you to be able to reason about what the code is doing with your data, making it easier to understand and maintain.

Try changing the value of the input to 6 to see how the even block gets executed instead of the odd block.

In the next topic, we'll explore how we can improve this code and make it more efficient.

if else statements

In the previous exercise, we did two evaluations. One evaluation was to check whether the number was even and the other was to see whether it was odd. As we know, a number can only ever be odd or even. With this knowledge, we can use deduction to know that if a number is not even, then it must be odd.

Using deductive logic such as this is common in programming in order to make programs more efficient by not having to do unnecessary work.

We can represent this kind of logic using an `if else` statement. The notation looks like this: `if <boolean expression> { <code block> } else { <code block> }`. The `if else` statement builds on the `if` statement and gives us a second block. The second block only runs if the first block doesn't run; both blocks can't run together.

Exercise 2.02 – using an if else statement

In this exercise, we'll update our previous exercise to use an `if else` statement:

1. Create a new folder and add a `main.go` file.

2. In `main.go`, add the package and import:

    ```
    package main
    import "fmt"
    ```

3. Create a `main` function:

    ```
    func main() {
    ```

4. Define an `int` variable with an initial value, and we'll give it a different value this time:

    ```
    input := 4
    ```

5. Create an `if` statement that uses a modulus expression, and then check whether the result is equal to 0:

    ```
    if input%2 == 0 {
      fmt.Println(input, "is even")
    ```

6. This time, we are not closing the code block but starting a new `else` code block:

    ```
    } else {
      fmt.Println(input, "is odd")
    }
    ```

7. Close `main`:

    ```
    }
    ```

8. Save the file, and in the new folder, run the following code snippet:

```
go run main.go
```

The following is the expected output:

```
4 is even
```

In this exercise, we were able to simplify our previous code by using an `if else` statement. As well as making the code more efficient, it also makes the code easier to understand and maintain.

In the next topic, we'll demonstrate how we can add as many code blocks as we want while still only letting one execute.

else if statements

`if else` solves the problem of running code for only one or two possible logical outcomes. With that covered, what if our preceding exercise's code was intended to only work for non-negative numbers? We'd need something that could evaluate more than one Boolean expression but only execute one of the code blocks; that is, the code block for negative numbers, even numbers, or odd numbers.

In that case, we can't use an `if else` statement on its own; however, we could cover it with another extension to `if` statements. In this extension, you can give the `else` statement its own Boolean expression. This is how the notation looks: `if <boolean expression> { <code block> } else if <boolean expression> { <code block> }`. You can also combine it with a final `else` statement at the end, which would look like this: `if <boolean expression> { <code block> } else if <boolean expression> { <code block> } else { <code block> }`. After the initial `if` statement, you can have as many `else if` statements as you need. Go evaluates Boolean expressions from the top of statements and works its way through each Boolean expression until one results in `true` or it finds an `else` instance. If there is no `else` instance and none of the Boolean expressions results in `true`, then no block is executed and Go moves on. When Go gets a Boolean `true` result, it executes the code block for that statement only, and it then stops evaluating any Boolean expressions of the `if` statement.

Exercise 2.03 – using an else if statement

In this exercise, we'll update our previous exercise. We're going to add a check for negative numbers. This check must run before the even and odd checks, as only one of the code blocks can run:

1. Create a new folder and add a `main.go` file.

2. In `main.go`, add the package and import:

```
package main
import "fmt"
```

3. Create a `main` function:

    ```
    func main() {
    ```

4. Define an `int` variable with an initial value, and we'll give it a negative value:

    ```
    input := -10
    ```

5. Our first Boolean expression is to check for negative numbers. If we find a negative number, we'll print a message saying that they are not allowed:

    ```
    if input < 0 {
        fmt.Println("input can't be a negative number")
    ```

6. We need to move our even check to an `else if` statement:

    ```
    } else if input%2 == 0 {
        fmt.Println(input, "is even")
    ```

7. The `else` statement stays the same, and we then close `main`:

    ```
    } else {
        fmt.Println(input, "is odd")
    }
    }
    ```

8. Save the file, and in the new folder, run the following code snippet:

    ```
    go run main.go
    ```

The following is the expected output:

```
input can't be a negative number
```

In this exercise, we added even more complex logic to our `if` statement. We added an `else if` statement to it, which allowed complex evaluation. This addition took what is usually a simple fork in the road that gives you many roads to go down but still with the restriction of only going down one of them.

In the next topic, we'll use a subtle but powerful feature of `if` statements that lets you keep your code nice and tidy.

initial if statements

It's common to need to call a function but not care too much about the returned value. Often, you'll want to check that it executed correctly and then discard the returned value; for example, sending an email, writing to a file, or inserting data into a database: most of the time, if these types of operations execute successfully, you don't need to worry about the variables they return. Unfortunately, the variables don't go anywhere as they are still in scope.

To stop these unwanted variables from hanging around, we can use what we know about scope rules to get rid of them. The best way to check for errors is to use `initial` statements on `if` statements. The notation looks like this: `if <initial statement>; <boolean expression> { <code block> }`. The initial statement is in the same section as the Boolean expression, with `;` to divide them.

Go only allows what it calls simple statements in the initial statement section, including the following:

- Assignment and short variable assignments:

```
i := 0
```

- Expressions such as math or logic expressions:

```
i = (j * 10) == 40
```

- Sending statements for working with channels, which we'll cover later in *Chapter 17* where we focus on concurrency

- Increment and decrement expressions:

```
i++
```

A common mistake is trying to define a variable using `var`. That's not allowed; you can use a short assignment in its place.

Exercise 2.04 – implementing initial if statements

In this exercise, we're going to continue to build on our previous exercises. We're going to add even more rules about which numbers can be checked as to whether they are odd or even. With so many rules, putting them all in a single Boolean expression is hard to understand. We'll move all the validation logic to a function that returns an error. This is a built-in Go type used for errors. If the value of the error is `nil`, then everything is okay. If not, you have an error, and you need to deal with it. We'll call the function in our initial statement and then check for errors:

1. Create a new folder and add a `main.go` file.

2. In `main.go`, add the package and imports:

```
package main
import (
  "errors"
  "fmt"
)
```

3. Create a function to do the validation. This function takes a single integer and returns an error:

```
func validate(input int) error {
```

4. We define some rules, and if any are `true`, we return a new error using the New function in the `errors` package:

```
if input < 0 {
    return errors.New("input can't be a negative number")
} else if input > 100 {
    return errors.New("input can't be over 100")
} else if input%7 == 0 {
    return errors.New("input can't be divisible by 7")
```

5. If the input passes all the checks, return `nil`:

```
} else {
    return nil
}
}
```

6. Create our `main` function:

```
func main() {
```

7. Define a variable with a value of `21`:

```
input := 21
```

8. Call the function using the initial statement; use the short variable assignment to capture the returned error. In the Boolean expression, check that the error is not equal to `nil` using `!=`:

```
if err := validate(input); err != nil {
    fmt.Println(err)
}
```

9. The rest is the same as before:

```
else if input%2 == 0 {
    fmt.Println(input, "is even")
} else {
    fmt.Println(input, "is odd")
}
}
```

10. Save the file, and in the new folder, run the following code snippet:

```
go run main.go
```

The following is the expected output, which displays an error statement:

```
input can't be divisible by 7
```

In this exercise, we used an initial statement to define and initialize a variable. That variable can be used in the Boolean expression and the related code block. Once the if statement completes, the variable goes out of scope and is reclaimed by Go's memory management system.

Expression switch statements

While it's possible to add as many else if statements to an if statement as you want, at some point, it'll get hard to read.

When this happens, you can use Go's logic alternative: switch. For situations where you would need a big if statement, switch can be a more compact alternative.

The notation for switch is shown in the following code snippet:

```
switch <initial statement>; <expression> {
case <expression>:
  <statements>
case <expression>, <expression>:
  <statements>
default:
  <statements>
}
```

The *initial* statement works the same in switch as it does in the preceding if statements. The expression is not the same because if is a Boolean expression. You can have more than just a Boolean in this expression. The cases are where you check to see whether the statements get executed. Statements are like code blocks in if statements, but with no need for the curly braces here.

Both the initial statement and expression are optional. To have just the expression, it would look like this: switch <expression> {.... To have only the initial statement, you would write switch <initial statment>; {.... You can leave them both off, and you'll end up with switch {.... When the expression is missing, it's as if you put the value of true there.

There are two main ways of using case expressions. They can be used just like if statements or Boolean expressions where you use logic to control whether the statements get executed. The alternative is to put a literal value there. In this case, the value is compared to the value in the switch expression. If they match, then the statements run. You can have as many case expressions as you want by separating them with , . The case expressions get checked from the top case and then from left to right if a case has multiple expressions.

When a case matches, only its statements are run, which is different from many other languages. To get the fall-through behavior found in those languages, a `fallthrough` statement must be added to the end of each case where you want that behavior. If you call `fallthrough` before the end of the case, it will fall through at that moment and move on to the next case.

An optional `default` case can be added anywhere in a `switch` statement, but it's best practice to add it to the end. The `default` case works just like using an `else` statement in an `if` statement.

This form of `switch` statement is called an *expression* `switch` statement. There is also another form of `switch` statement, called a *type* `switch` statement, which we'll look at in *Chapter 4*.

Exercise 2.05 – using a switch statement

In this exercise, we need to create a program that prints a particular message based on the day someone was born. We are using the `time` package for the set of days of the week constants. We'll use a `switch` statement to make a more compact logic structure:

1. Load the `main` package:

    ```
    package main
    ```

2. Import the `fmt` and `time` packages:

    ```
    import (
        "fmt"
        "time"
    )
    ```

3. Define a `main` function:

    ```
    func main() {
    ```

4. Define a variable that is the day of the week someone was born. Use the constants from the `time` package to do it. We'll set it to Monday, but it could be any day:

    ```
    dayBorn := time.Monday
    ```

5. Create a `switch` statement that uses the variable as its expression:

    ```
    switch dayBorn {
    ```

6. Each `case` expression will try to match its expression value against the `switch` expression value:

    ```
    case time.Monday:
    fmt.Println("Monday's child is fair of face")
    case time.Tuesday:
    fmt.Println("Tuesday's child is full of grace")
    case time.Wednesday:
    ```

```
fmt.Println("Wednesday's child is full of woe")
case time.Thursday:
fmt.Println("Thursday's child has far to go")
case time.Friday:
fmt.Println("Friday's child is loving and giving")
case time.Saturday:
fmt.Println("Saturday's child works hard for a living")
case time.Sunday:
fmt.Println("Sunday's child is bonny and blithe")
```

7. We'll use the `default` case here as a form of validation:

```
default:
fmt.Println("Error, day born not valid")
}
```

8. Close the `main` function:

```
}
```

9. Save the file, and in the new folder, run the following code snippet:

```
go run main.go
```

The following is the expected output:

```
Monday's child is fair of face
```

In this exercise, we used `switch` to create a compact logic structure that matches lots of different possible values to give a specific message to our users. It's quite common to see `switch` statements used with a constant as we did here, using the day-of-the-week constants from the `time` package.

Next, we'll use the `case` feature that lets us match multiple values.

Exercise 2.06 – switch statements and multiple case values

In this exercise, we're going to print out a message that tells us whether the day someone was born was a weekday or at the weekend. We only need two cases as each case can support checking multiple values:

1. Load the `main` package:

```
package main
```

2. Import the `fmt` and `time` packages:

```
import (
"fmt"
```

```
    "time"
)
```

3. Define a `main` function:

```
func main() {
```

4. Define our `dayBorn` variable using one of the `time` package's constants:

```
dayBorn := time.Sunday
```

5. `switch` starts the same by using the variable as the expression:

```
switch dayBorn {
```

6. This time, for `case`, we have weekday constants. Go checks each one against the `switch` expression, starting from the left, and sweeps through each one by one. Once Go gets a match, it stops evaluating and runs the statements for that case only:

```
case time.Monday, time.Tuesday, time.Wednesday, time.Thursday,
time.Friday:
    fmt.Println("Born on a weekday")
```

7. Then, it does the same for weekend days:

```
case time.Saturday, time.Sunday:
    fmt.Println("Born on the weekend")
```

8. We use `default` for validation again and close out the `switch` statement:

```
default:
    fmt.Println("Error, day born not valid")
}
```

9. Close the `main` function:

```
}
```

10. Save the file, and in the new folder, run the following code snippet:

```
go run main.go
```

The following is the expected output:

```
Born on the weekend
```

In this exercise, we used cases with multiple values. This allowed a very compact logic structure that could evaluate 7 days of the week with validation checking in a few lines of code. It makes the intention of the logic clear, which, in turn, makes it easier to change and maintain.

Next, we'll look at using more complex logic in `case` expressions.

Sometimes, you'll see code that doesn't evaluate anything in the `switch` statement but does checks in the `case` expression.

Exercise 2.07 – expressionless switch statements

It's not always possible to be able to match values using the value of the `switch` expression. Sometimes, you'll need to match on multiple variables. Other times, you'll need to match on something more complicated than an equality check. For example, you may need to check whether a number is in a specific range. In these cases, `switch` is still helpful in building compact logic statements, as `case` allows the same range of expressions that you have in `if` Boolean expressions.

In this exercise, let's build a simple `switch` expression that checks whether a day is at the weekend to show what can be done in `case`:

1. Load the `main` package:

    ```
    package main
    ```

2. Import the `fmt` and `time` packages:

    ```
    import (
        "fmt"
        "time"
    )
    ```

3. Define a `main` function:

    ```
    func main() {
    ```

4. Our `switch` expression is using the initial statement to define our variable. The expression is left empty as we won't be using it:

    ```
    switch dayBorn := time.Sunday; {
    ```

5. `case` is using some complex logic to check whether the day is at the weekend:

    ```
    case dayBorn == time.Sunday || dayBorn == time.Saturday:
      fmt.Println("Born on the weekend")
    ```

6. Add a `default` statement and close the `switch` expression:

    ```
    default:
      fmt.Println("Born some other day")
    }
    ```

7.   Close the `main` function:

```
}
```

8.   Save the file, and in the new folder, run the following code snippet:

```
go run main.go
```

The following is the expected output:

```
Born on the weekend
```

In this exercise, we learned that you can use complex logic in a case expression when a simple switch statement match is not enough. This still offers a more compact and easier way to manage a logic statement than if you have more than a couple of cases.

Next, we'll leave logic structures behind and start to look at ways in which we can run the same statements multiple times to make processing data easier.

Loops

In real-world applications, you're often going to need to run the same logic repeatedly. It's common to have to deal with multiple inputs and give multiple outputs. Loops are the simplest way of repeating your logic.

Go only has one looping statement, `for`, but it's a flexible one. There are two distinct forms: the first is used a lot for ordered collections such as arrays and slices, which we'll cover more later. The sort of loop used for ordered collections looks as follows:

```
for <initial statement>; <condition>; <post statement> {
    <statements>
}
```

The `initial` statement is just like the one found in `if` and `switch` statements. An `initial` statement runs before everything else and allows the same simple statements that we defined before. The condition is checked before each loop to see whether the statements should be run or whether the loop should stop. As with an `initial` statement, `condition` also allows simple statements. A `post` statement is run after the statements are run at the end of each loop and allows you to run simple statements. The `post` statement is mostly used for incrementing things such as loop counters, which get evaluated on the next loop by `condition`. The statements are any Go code you want to run as part of the loop.

`initial`, `condition`, and `post` statements are all optional, and it's possible to write a `for` loop like this:

```
for {
    <statements>
}
```

This form would result in a loop that would run forever, also known as an infinite loop, unless a `break` statement is used to stop the loop manually. In addition to `break`, there is also a `continue` statement that can be used to skip the remainder of an individual run of a loop but doesn't stop the whole loop.

Another form a `for` loop can take is when reading from a source of data that returns a Boolean when there is more data to read. Examples of this include when reading from databases, files, command-line inputs, and network sockets. This form looks like this:

```
for <condition> {
    <statements>
}
```

This form is just a simplified version of the form used to read from an ordered list but without the logic needed to control the loop yourself, as the source you're using is built to work easily in `for` loops.

The other form that a `for` loop takes is when looping over unordered data collections such as maps. We'll cover what maps are in more detail in a later chapter. When looping over these, you'll use a `range` statement in your loop. With maps, the form looks like this:

```
for <key>, <value> := range <map> {
    <statements>
}
```

Exercise 2.08 – using a for i loop

In this exercise, we'll use the three parts of a `for` loop to create a variable and use a variable in the loop. We'll be able to see how the variable changes after each iteration of the loop by printing out its value to the console:

1. Define a package as `main` and add the import:

    ```
    package main
    import "fmt"
    ```

2. Create a `main` function:

    ```
    func main() {
    ```

3. Define a `for` loop that defines an `i` variable with an initial value of `0` in the `initial` statement section. In the clause, check that `i` is less than 5. In the `post` statement, increment i by 1:

```
for i := 0; i < 5; i++ {
```

4. In the body of the loop, print out the value of `i`:

```
fmt.Println(i)
```

5. Close the loop:

```
}
```

6. Close `main`:

```
}
```

7. Save the file, and in the new folder, run the following code snippet:

```
go run main.go
```

The following is the expected output:

```
0
1
2
3
4
```

In this exercise, we used a variable that only exists in a `for` loop. We set up the variable, checked its value, modified it, and output it. Using a loop such as this is very common when working with ordered, numerically indexed collections such as arrays and slices. In this instance, we hardcoded the value for when to stop looping; however, when looking over arrays and slices, that value would be determined dynamically from the size of the collection.

Next, we'll use a `for i` loop to work with a slice.

Exercise 2.09 – looping over arrays and slices

In this exercise, we'll loop over a collection of strings. We'll be using a slice, but the loop logic will also be the same set of arrays. We'll define a collection; we'll then create a loop that uses the collection to control when to stop looping and a variable to keep track of where we are in the collection.

The way the index of arrays and slices works means that there are never any gaps in the number, and the first number is always 0. The built-in function, `len`, is used to get the length of any collection. We'll use it as part of the condition to check when we've reached the end of the collection:

1. Create a new folder and add a `main.go` file.

2. In `main.go`, add the package and import:

    ```
    package main
    import "fmt"
    ```

3. Create a `main` function:

    ```
    func main() {
    ```

4. Define a variable that is a slice of *strings* and initialize it with data:

    ```
    names := []string{"Jim", "Jane", "Joe", "June"}
    ```

    We will cover `collection` and `string` in more detail in the next chapter.

5. The `initial` and `post` statements for the loop are the same as before; the difference is in the `condition` statement, where we use `len` to check whether we are at the end of the collection:

    ```
    for i := 0; i < len(names); i++ {
    ```

6. The rest is the same as before:

    ```
    fmt.Println(names[i])
        }
    }
    ```

7. Save the file, and in the new folder, run the following code snippet:

    ```
    go run main.go
    ```

The following is the expected output:

```
Jim
Jane
Joe
June
```

In this exercise, we covered how to iterate over objects via indexing. Now, we will look at alternative ways of looping through objects using a `range` loop.

range loop

The `array` and `slice` types always have the number of an index, and that number always starts at 0. The `for i` loop we've seen so far is the most common choice you'll see in real-world code for these types.

The other collection type, map, doesn't give the same guarantee. That means you need to use range. You'll use range instead of the condition statement of a for loop, and, on each loop, range yields both a key and a value of an element in the collection, then moves on to the next element.

With a range loop, you don't need to define a condition to stop the loop as range takes care of that for us.

> **Callout map order**
>
> The order of items is randomized to stop developers from relying on the order of the elements in a map, which means you can use it as a form of pseudo-data randomization if needed.

Exercise 2.10 – looping over a map

In this exercise, we're going to create a map type that has a string for its key and a string for the values. We'll cover map types in more detail in a later chapter, so don't worry if you don't quite get what map types are yet. We'll then use range in the for loop to iterate over the map. We'll then write out the key and value data to the console:

1. Create a new folder and add a main.go file.

2. In main.go, add the package and import:

    ```
    package main
    import "fmt"
    ```

3. Create a main function:

    ```
    func main() {
    ```

4. Define a map type with a string key and a string value of the strings variable and initialize it with the data:

    ```
    config := map[string]string{
      "debug":    "1",
      "logLevel": "warn",
      "version": "1.2.1",
      }
    ```

5. Use range to get the key and value variables for an array element and assign them to variables:

    ```
    for key, value := range config {
    ```

6. Print out the key and value variables:

    ```
    fmt.Println(key, "=", value)
    ```

7. Close the loop and `main`:

```
    }
  }
```

8. Save the file, and in the new folder, run the following code snippet:

```
go run main.go
```

The following is the expected output, displaying a map that has a string for its key and a string for the values:

```
debug = 1
logLevel = warn
version = 1.2.1
```

In this exercise, we used `range` in a `for` loop to allow us to read out all the data from a map collection. map types don't give guarantees like arrays and slices do about starting at zero and having no gaps had we used an integer for the map keys. `range` also controls when to stop a loop.

If you don't need the `key` or the `value` variable, you can use _ as the variable name to tell the compiler you don't want it.

Activity 2.01 – looping over map data using range

Suppose you have been provided with the data in the following table. You have to find the word with the maximum count and print the word and its count using the following data:

Word	Count
Gonna	3
You	3
Give	2
Never	1
Up	4

Figure 2.1: Word and count data to perform the activity

> **Note**
>
> The preceding words are from the song *Never Gonna Give You Up*, sung by Rick Astley.

The steps to solve the activity are as follows:

1. Put the words into a map like this:

    ```
    words := map[string]int{
    "Gonna": 3,
    "You": 3,
    "Give": 2,
    "Never": 1,
    "Up":    4,
    }
    ```

2. Create a loop and use `range` to capture the word and the count.

3. Keep track of the word with the highest count using a variable for what the highest count is and its associated word.

4. Print the variables out.

The following is the expected output, displaying the most popular word with its count value:

```
Most popular word: Up
With a count of: 4
```

> **Note**
>
> The solution for this activity can be found in the GitHub repository folder for this chapter: `https://github.com/PacktPublishing/Go-Programming-From-Beginner-to-Professional-Second-Edition-/tree/main/Chapter02/Activity02.01`

Activity 2.02 – implementing FizzBuzz

When interviewing for a programming job, you'll be asked to do some coding exercises. These questions have you writing something from scratch and will have several rules to follow. To give you an idea of what that looks like, we'll run you through a classic one, *FizzBuzz*.

The rules are as follows:

*   Write a program that prints out the numbers from 1 to 100
*   If the number is a multiple of 3, print "Fizz"
*   If the number is a multiple of 5, print "Buzz"
*   If the number is a multiple of 3 and 5, print "FizzBuzz"

Here are some tips:

- You can convert a number to a string using `strconv.Itoa()`
- The first number to evaluate must be 1, and the last number to evaluate must be 100

These steps will help you to complete the activity:

1. Create a loop that does 100 iterations.
2. Have a variable that keeps count of the number of loops so far.
3. In the loop, use that count and check whether it's divisible by 3 or 5 using %.
4. Think carefully about how you'll deal with the "FizzBuzz" case.

The following screenshot shows the expected output:

> **Note**
>
> Considering that the output is too big to be displayed here, only a part of it will be visible in *Figure 2.2*.

```
 ~/src/Th…op/Ch…02/Activity02.01    go run .
1
2
Fizz
4
Buzz
Fizz
7
8
Fizz
Buzz
11
Fizz
13
14
FizzBuzz
16
17
Fizz
19
Buzz
Fizz
22
23
Fizz
Buzz
26
Fizz
28
29
FizzBuzz
31
```

Figure 2.2: The FizzBuzz output

> **Note**
>
> The solution for this activity can be found in the GitHub repository folder for this chapter: `https://github.com/PacktPublishing/Go-Programming-From-Beginner-to-Professional-Second-Edition-/tree/main/Chapter02/Activity02.02`

This activity can show you how `switch` statements can improve upon and tame `if else` statements that start to get too big.

Next, we'll look at how we can take manual control of a loop by skipping iterations or stopping the loop.

break and continue

There are going to be times when you need to skip a single loop or stop a loop from running altogether. It's possible to do this with variables and `if` statements, but there is an easier way.

The `continue` keyword stops the execution of the current loop and starts a new loop. The `post` loop logic runs, and the loop `condition` statement gets evaluated.

The `break` keyword also stops the execution of the current loop and stops any new loops from running.

Use `continue` when you want to skip a single item in a collection; for instance, perhaps it's okay if one of the items in a collection is invalid, but the rest may be okay to process. Use `break` when you need to stop processing when there are any errors in the data and there's no value in processing the rest of the collection.

Here, we have an example that generates a random number between 0 and 8. The loop skips on a number divisible by 3 and stops on a number divisible by 2. It also prints out the `i` variable for each loop to help us see that `continue` and `break` are stopping the execution of the rest of the loop.

Exercise 2.11 – using break and continue to control loops

In this exercise, we'll use `continue` and `break` in a loop to show you how you can take control of it. We're going to create a loop that keeps going forever. This means we have to stop it with `break` manually. We'll also randomly skip loops with `continue`. We'll do this skipping by generating a random number, and if that number is divisible by 3, we'll skip the rest of the loop:

1. Create a new folder and add a `main.go` file.

2. In `main.go`, add the package and imports:

    ```
    package main
    import (
      "fmt"
      "math/rand"
    )
    ```

3. Create a `main` function:

```
func main() {
```

4. Create an empty `for` loop. This will loop forever if you don't stop it:

```
    for {
```

5. Use `Intn` from the `rand` package to pick a random number between 0 and 8:

```
        r := rand.Intn(8)
```

6. If the random number is divisible by 3, print `"Skip"` and skip the rest of the loop using `continue`:

```
        if r%3 == 0 {
            fmt.Println("Skip")
            continue
```

7. If the random number is divisible by 2, then print `"Stop"` and stop the loop using `break`:

```
        } else if r%2 == 0 {
            fmt.Println("Stop")
            break
        }
```

8. If the number is neither of those things, then print the number:

```
        fmt.Println(r)
```

9. Close the loop and `main`:

```
    }
}
```

10. Save the file, and in the new folder, run the following code snippet:

```
go run main.go
```

The following is the expected output displaying random numbers, `Skip`, and `Stop`:

```
1
7
7
Skip
1
Skip
1
Stop
```

In this exercise, we created a `for` loop that would loop forever, and we then used `continue` and `break` to override normal loop behavior to take control of it ourselves. The ability to do this can allow us to reduce the number of nested `if` statements and variables needed to prevent logic from running when it shouldn't. Using `break` and `continue` helps to clean up your code and make it easier to work on.

If you use an empty `for` loop like this, the loop continues forever, and you must use `break` to prevent an infinite loop. An infinite loop is a loop in your code that never stops. Once you get an infinite loop, you'll need a way to kill your application; how you do that will depend on your operating system. If you are running your app in a terminal, closing the terminal normally does the trick. Don't panic – it happens to us all – your system may slow down, but it won't do it any harm.

Next, we'll work on some activities to test out all your new knowledge about logic and loops.

Activity 2.03 – bubble sort

In this activity, we'll sort a given slice of numbers by swapping the values. This sorting technique is known as the *bubble sort* technique. Go has built-in sorting algorithms in the `sort` package but we don't want you to use them; we want you to use the logic and loops you've just learned.

Here are the steps:

1. Define a slice with unsorted numbers in it.
2. Print this slice to the console.
3. Sort the values using swapping.
4. Once done, print the now sorted numbers to the console.

And here are some tips:

- You can do an in-place swap in Go like this:

```
nums[i], nums[i-1] = nums[i-1], nums[i]
```

- You can create a new slice with this code:

```
var nums2 []int
```

- You can add to the end of a slice like so:

```
nums2 = append(nums2, 1)
```

The following is the expected output:

```
Before: [5, 8, 2, 4, 0, 1, 3, 7, 9, 6]
After : [0, 1, 2, 3, 4, 5, 6, 7, 8, 9]
```

> **Note**
>
> The solution for this activity can be found in the GitHub repository folder for this chapter: https://github.com/PacktPublishing/Go-Programming-From-Beginner-to-Professional-Second-Edition-/tree/main/Chapter02/Activity02.03

goto statements

There may come a time when you want to skip certain logic within a function and go to a certain location within the function using the goto keyword. This may be accomplished using a label within the function and will result in a compilation error if attempting to use the goto label outside of the function scope.

goto statements are a way of adapting the Go control flow; however, they need to be used with caution as they can lead to difficulties in understanding function control flow and decrease code readability if used improperly. goto statements are used within the Go standard library in some cases, such as the math package, to make logic easier to read and reduce the need for unnecessary variables.

Exercise 2.12 – using goto statements

In this exercise, we'll use goto in a function to show you how you can take control of it. We're going to create a loop that keeps looping forever. This means we will have to stop it and exit manually under certain custom criteria. As with the previous exercise, we'll be generating a random number, and if that number is divisible by 2, we'll terminate the flow and go to our labeled statement:

1. Create a new folder and add a main.go file.

2. In main.go, add the package and imports:

    ```
    package main
    import (
        "fmt"
        "math/rand"
    )
    ```

3. Create a main function:

    ```
    func main() {
    ```

4. Create an empty for loop. This will loop forever if you don't stop it:

    ```
    for {
    ```

5. Use `Intn` from the `rand` package to pick a random number between 0 and 8:

    ```
    r := rand.Intn(8)
    ```

6. If the random number is divisible by 3, print `"Skip"` and skip the rest of the loop using `continue`:

    ```
    if r%3 == 0 {
        fmt.Println("Skip")
        continue
    ```

7. If the random number is divisible by 2, then print `"Stop"` and stop the loop using the `goto` keyword with the `STOP` custom-defined label to go to:

    ```
    } else if r%2 == 0 {
        fmt.Println("Stop")
        goto STOP
    }
    ```

8. If the number is neither of those things, then print the number:

    ```
    fmt.Println(r)
    ```

9. Close the loop:

    ```
    }
    ```

    Define a `goto` label named `STOP`, then print `"goto label reached"`:

    ```
    STOP:
        fmt.Println("Goto label reached")
        // Close main function
    }
    ```

10. Save the file, and in the new folder, run the following code snippet:

    ```
    go run main.go
    ```

The following is the expected output displaying random numbers, `Skip`, and `Stop`:

```
1
7
7
Skip
1
Skip
1
Stop
Goto label reached
```

In this exercise, we created a `for` loop that would loop forever, and we then used `goto` to override normal loop behavior to take control of it ourselves and terminate the forever loop under certain criteria. The ability to do this can allow us to adapt a control flow to suit our needs. Using `goto` in the case of this example is not difficult to understand the change in function logic to "go to" other areas of the function logic; however, in more complicated examples, `goto` can lead to challenges with code readability.

Next, we'll summarize what we have learned from this chapter.

Summary

In this chapter, we discussed logic and loops. These are the foundational building blocks to build complex software. They allow you to have data flow through your code. They let you deal with collections of data by letting you execute the same logic on every element of the data.

Being able to define the rules and laws of your code is the starting point of codifying the real world in software. If you are creating banking software and the bank has rules about what you can and can't do with money, then you can also define those rules in your code.

Logic and loops are essential tools that you'll use to build all your software.

In the next chapter, we'll look at Go's type system and the core types it has available.

3
Core Types

> **Overview**
>
> This chapter aims to show you how to use Go's basic core types to design your software's data. We'll work through each type to show what they are useful for and how to use them in your software. Understanding these core types provides you with the foundation required to learn how to create complex data designs.
>
> By the end of this chapter, you will be able to create variables of different types for Go programs and assign values to variables of different types. You will learn how to identify and pick a suitable type for any programming situation. You will also write a program to measure password complexity and implement empty value types.

Technical requirements

For this chapter, you'll require Go version 1.21 or higher. The code for this chapter can be found at: `https://github.com/PacktPublishing/Go-Programming-From-Beginner-to-Professional-Second-Edition-/tree/main/Chapter03`.

Introduction

In the previous chapter, we learned how to use `if`, `if-else`, `else-if`, `switch`, `case`, `continue`, `break`, and `goto` in Go.

Go is a strongly typed language, and all data is assigned a type. That type is fixed and can't be changed. What you can and can't do with your data is constrained by the types you assign. Understanding exactly what defines every one of Go's core types is critical to success with the Go language.

In later chapters, we'll talk about Go's more complex types, but those types are built on the core types defined in this chapter.

Go's core types are well-thought-out and easy to understand once you understand the details. Having to understand the details means Go's type system is not always intuitive. For example, Go's most common number type, `int`, may be either 32 bits or 64 bits in size depending on the computer used to compile the code.

Types are needed to make data easier for humans to work with. Computers only think about data in binary. Binary is hard for people to work with. By adding a layer of abstraction to binary data and labelling it as a number or some text, humans have an easier time reasoning about it. Reducing the cognitive load allows people to build more complex software because they're not overwhelmed by managing the details of the binary data.

Programming languages need to define what a number is or what a text is for. A programming language defines what you can call a number, and it defines what operations you can use on a number. For example, can a whole number such as 10 and a floating-point number such as 3.14 both be stored as the same type? While it seems obvious that you can multiply numbers, can you multiply text? As we progress through this chapter, we'll clearly define what the rules are for each type and what operations you can use with each of them.

The way data is stored is also a large part of what defines a type. To allow for the building of efficient software, Go places limits on how large some of its types can be. For example, the largest amount of storage for a number in Go's core types is 64 bits of memory. This allows for any number up to 18,446,744,073,709,551,615. Understanding these types of limitations is critical in building bug-free code.

The things that define a type are as follows:

- The kind of data that you can store in it
- What operations you can use with it
- What those operations do to it
- How much memory it can use

This chapter gives you the knowledge and confidence to use Go's type system correctly in your code.

True and false

True and false logic is represented using the Boolean type, `bool`. Use this type when you need an on/off switch in your code. The value of a `bool` instance can only ever be `true` or `false`. The zero value of a `bool` instance is `false`. A "zero value" refers to the default value that a variable takes when it's declared without an explicit initial value.

When using a comparison operator such as `==` or `>`, the result of that comparison is a `bool` value.

In this code example, we use comparison operators on two numbers. You'll see that the result is a `bool` value:

```
package main
import "fmt"
func main() {
  fmt.Println(10 > 5)
  fmt.Println(10 == 5)
}
```

Running the preceding code shows the following output:

```
true
false
```

Exercise 3.01 – Program to measure password complexity

An online portal creates user accounts for its users and accepts passwords that are only 8 to 15 characters long. In this exercise, we write a program for the portal to display whether the password entered meets the character requirements. The character requirements are as follows:

- Have a lowercase letter

- Have an uppercase letter

- Have a number

- Have a symbol

- Be 8 or more characters long

To do this exercise, we're going to use a few new features. Don't worry if you don't quite understand what they are doing; we'll cover them in detail in the next chapter. Consider this a sneak peek. We'll explain what everything is as we go, but your main focus should be on the Boolean logic:

1. Create a new folder and add a `main.go` file.

2. In `main.go`, add the main package name to the top of the file:

   ```
   package main
   ```

3. Now add the imports we'll use in this file:

   ```
   import (
     "fmt"
     "unicode"
   )
   ```

4. Create a function that takes a string argument and returns a `bool` value:

```
func passwordChecker(pw string) bool {
```

5. Convert the password string into a `rune` type, which is safe for multi-byte (UTF-8) characters:

```
pwR := []rune(pw)
```

We'll talk more about `rune` later in this chapter.

6. Count the number of multi-byte characters using `len`. This code results in a `bool` result that can be used in the `if` statement:

```
if len(pwR) < 8 {
  return false
}
```

7. Define some `bool` variables. We'll check these at the end:

```
hasUpper := false
hasLower := false
hasNumber := false
hasSymbol := false
```

8. Loop over the multi-byte characters one at a time:

```
for _, v := range pwR {
```

9. Using the `unicode` package, check whether this character is uppercase. This function returns a `bool` value that we can use directly in the `if` statement:

```
if unicode.IsUpper(v) {
```

10. If it is, we'll set the `hasUpper` bool variable to `true`:

```
hasUpper = true
}
```

11. Do the same thing for lowercase letters:

```
if unicode.IsLower(v) {
  hasLower = true
}
```

12. Also do it for numbers:

```
if unicode.IsNumber(v) {
   hasNumber = true
}
```

13. For symbols, we'll also accept punctuation. Use the or operator, which works with Booleans, to result in true if either of these functions returns true:

```
if unicode.IsPunct(v) || unicode.IsSymbol(v) {
   hasSymbol = true
   }
}
```

14. To pass all our checks, all our variables must be true. Here, we combine multiple and operators to create a one-line statement that checks all four variables:

```
return hasUpper && hasLower && hasNumber && hasSymbol
```

15. Close the function:

```
}
```

16. Create the main() function:

```
func main() {
```

17. Call the passwordChecker() function with an invalid password. As this returns a bool value, it can be used directly in an if statement:

```
if passwordChecker("") {
   fmt.Println("password good")
} else {
   fmt.Println("password bad")
}
```

18. Now, call the function with a valid password:

```
if passwordChecker("This!I5A") {
   fmt.Println("password good")
} else {
   fmt.Println("password bad")
}
```

19. Close the `main()` function:

    ```
    }
    ```

20. Save the file in the new folder and then run the following:

    ```
    go run main.go
    ```

Running the preceding code displays the following output:

```
password bad
password good
```

In this exercise, we highlighted a variety of ways that `bool` values manifest themselves in the code. `bool` values are critical to giving your code the ability to make a choice and be dynamic and responsive. Without `bool`, your code would have a hard time doing anything.

Next, we'll take a look at numbers and how Go categorizes them.

Numbers

Go has two distinct number types – integers, also known as whole numbers and floating-point numbers. The floating-point number type allows whole numbers and numbers that contain fractions of a whole number.

1, 54, and 5,436 are examples of whole numbers. 1.5, 52.25, 33.333, and 64,567.00001 are all examples of floating-point numbers.

> **Note**
> The default and empty value for all number types is 0.

Next, we'll start our number journey by looking at integers.

Integers

Integer types are classified in two ways, based on the following conditions:

- Whether or not they can store negative numbers
- The smallest and largest numbers they can store

Types that can store negative numbers are called signed integers. Types that can't store negative numbers are called unsigned integers. How big and small a number each type can store is determined by how many bytes of internal storage they have.

Here is an excerpt from the Go language specification with all the relevant integer types:

uint8	the set of all unsigned 8-bit integers (0 to 255)
uint16	the set of all unsigned 16-bit integers (0 to 65535)
uint32	the set of all unsigned 32-bit integers (0 to 4294967295)
uint64	the set of all unsigned 64-bit integers (0 to 18446744073709551615)
int8	the set of all signed 8-bit integers (-128 to 127)
int16	the set of all signed 16-bit integers (-32768 to 32767)
int32	the set of all signed 32-bit integers (-2147483648 to 2147483647)
int64	the set of all signed 64-bit integers (-9223372036854775808 to 9223372036854775807)
byte	alias for uint8
rune	alias for int32

Figure 3.1: Go language specification with relevant integer types

There are also the following special integer types:

uint	either 32 or 64 bits
int	same size as uint

Figure 3.2: Special integer types

uint and int are either 32 or 64 bits, depending on whether you compile your code for a 32-bit system or a 64-bit system. It's rare nowadays to run applications on a 32-bit system, as most systems nowadays are 64-bit.

An int type on a 64-bit system is not an int64 type. While these two types are identical, they are not the same integer type, and you can't use them together. If Go allowed this, there would be problems when the same code gets compiled for a 32-bit machine, so keeping them separate ensures that the code is reliable.

This incompatibility is not just an int type problem; you can't use any of the integer types together.

Picking the correct integer type to use when defining a variable is easy – use int. When writing code for an application, int does the job the majority of the time. Only think about using the other types when using an int type is causing a problem. The sorts of problems you see with int tend to be related to memory usage.

For example, let's say you have an app that's running out of memory. The app uses a massive number of integers, but these integers are never negative and won't go over 255. One possible fix is to switch from using `int` to using `uint8`. Doing this cuts its memory usage from 64 bits (8 bytes) per number to 8 bits (1 byte) per number.

We can show this by creating a collection of both types and then asking Go how much heap memory it is using. The output may vary on your computer, but the effect should be similar. This code creates a collection of `int` or `int8` numbers. It then adds 10 million values to the collection. Once that's done, it uses the runtime package to give us a reading of how much heap memory is being used. We can convert that reading to MB and then print it out:

```
package main
import (
  "fmt"
  "runtime"
)
func main() {
  var list []int
  //var list []int8
  for i := 0; i < 10000000; i++ {
    list = append(list, 100)
  }
  var m runtime.MemStats
  runtime.ReadMemStats(&m)
  fmt.Printf("TotalAlloc (Heap) = %v MiB\n", m.TotalAlloc/1024/1024)
}
```

Here's the output using `int`:

```
TotalAlloc (Heap) = 403 MiB
```

And here's the output using `int8`:

```
TotalAlloc (Heap) = 54 MiB
```

We saved a good amount of memory here, but we need 10 million values to make it worthwhile. Hopefully, now you are convinced that it's okay to start with `int` and only worry about performance when it's a problem.

Next, we'll look at floating-point numbers.

Floating-point numbers

Go has two floating-point number types, `float32` and `float64`. The bigger `float64` allows for more precision in numbers. `float32` has 32 bits of storage and `float64` has 64 bits of storage. Floats split their storage between whole numbers (everything to the left of the decimal point) and decimal numbers (everything to the right of the decimal point). How much space is used for the whole number or the decimal numbers varies according to the number being stored. For example, 9,999.9 would use more storage for the whole numbers, while 9.9999 would use more storage for the decimal numbers. With float64's bigger space for storage, it can store more whole numbers and/or more decimal numbers than float32 can.

Exercise 3.02 – Floating-point number accuracy

In this exercise, we're going to compare what happens when we do some divisions on numbers that don't divide equally. We'll be dividing 100 by 3. One way of representing the result is 33 ⅓. Computers, for the most part, can't compute fractions like this. Instead, they use a decimal representation, which is 33.3 recurring, where the 3 after the decimal point repeats forever. If we let the computer do that it uses up all the memory, which is not very helpful.

Luckily for us, we don't need to worry about this happening as the floating-point types have storage limits. The downside is that this leads to a number that doesn't reflect the true result; the result has a certain amount of inaccuracy. Your tolerance for inaccuracy needs and how much storage space you want to give to your floating-point numbers must be balanced out:

1. Create a new folder and add a main.go file.

2. In main.go, add the main package name to the top of the file:

    ```
    package main
    ```

3. Now add the imports we'll use in this file:

    ```
    import "fmt"
    ```

4. Create the main() function:

    ```
    func main() {
    ```

5. Declare an int variable and initialize it with a value of 100:

    ```
    var a int = 100
    ```

6. Declare a float32 variable and initialize it with a value of 100:

    ```
    var b float32 = 100
    ```

7. Declare a float64 variable and initialize it with a value of 100:

    ```
    var c float64 = 100
    ```

8. Divide each variable by 3 and print the result to the console:

    ```
    fmt.Println(a / 3)
    fmt.Println(b / 3)
    ```

```
    fmt.Println(c / 3)
  }
```

9. Save the file and in the new folder run the following:

```
go run main.go
```

Running the preceding code shows the following output displaying int-, float32-, and float64-typed equivalent starting values, divided by 3:

```
33
33.333332
33.333333333333336
```

In this exercise, we can see that the computer is not able to give perfect answers to this sort of division. You can also see that when doing this sort of math on integers, you don't get an error. Go ignores any fractional part of the number, which is usually not what you want. We can also see that float64 gives a much more precise answer than float32.

While this limit seems like it would lead to inaccuracy, for real-world business work, it gets the job done well enough the vast majority of the time. Use cases that involve highly precise counts, such as in finance and banking, require you to pay special attention to Go's numerical types to ensure mathematical accuracy.

Let's see what happens if we try to get our number back to 100 by multiplying it by 3:

```
package main
import "fmt"
func main() {
  var a int = 100
  var b float32 = 100
  var c float64 = 100
  fmt.Println((a / 3) * 3)
  fmt.Println((b / 3) * 3)
  fmt.Println((c / 3) * 3)
}
```

Running the preceding code shows the following output:

```
99
100
100
```

In this example, we saw that accuracy is not impacted as much as you'd expect. At first glance, floating-point math can seem simple, but it quickly gets complicated. When defining your floating-point variables, typically float64 should be your first choice, unless you need to be more memory efficient.

Next, we'll look at what happens when you go beyond the limits of a number type.

Overflow and wraparound

When you try to initialize a number with a value that's too big for the type you are using, you get an overflow error. The highest number you can have in an int8 type is 127. In the following code, we'll try to initialize it with 128 to see what happens:

```
package main
import "fmt"
func main() {
    var a int8 = 128
    fmt.Println(a)
}
```

Running the preceding code gives the following output:

```
📂  ~/src/Th…op/Ch…03/Example03.04   go run main.go
# command-line-arguments
./main.go:6:15: constant 128 overflows int8
```

Figure 3.3: Output after initializing with 128

This error is easy to fix and can't cause any hidden problems. The real problem is when the compiler can't catch it. When this happens, the number will "wraparound." Wraparound means the number goes from its highest possible value to its lowest possible value. Wraparound can be easy to miss when developing your code and can cause significant problems for your users.

Exercise 3.03 – Triggering number wraparound

In this exercise, we'll declare two small integer types – int8 and uint8. We'll initialize them near their highest possible value. Then we'll use a loop statement to increment them by 1 per loop, then print their value to the console. We'll be able to see exactly when they wraparound:

1. Create a new folder and add a main.go file.

2. In main.go, add the main package name to the top of the file:

    ```
    package main
    ```

3. Now add the imports we'll use in this file:

    ```
    import "fmt"
    ```

4. Create the main() function:

    ```
    func main() {
    ```

5. Declare an int8 variable with an initial value of 125:

    ```
    var a int8 = 125
    ```

6. Declare an uint8 variable with an initial value of 253:

    ```
    var b uint8 = 253
    ```

7. Create a for i loop that runs five times:

    ```
    for i := 0; i < 5; i++ {
    ```

8. Increment the two variables by 1:

    ```
    a++
    b++
    ```

9. Print the variables' values to the console:

    ```
    fmt.Println(i, ")", "int8 ", a, "uint8 ", b)
    ```

10. Close the loop:

    ```
    }
    ```

11. Close the main() function:

    ```
    }
    ```

12. Save the file, and, in the new folder, run the following:

    ```
    go run main.go
    ```

    Running the preceding code shows the following output:

    ```
    ~/src/Th…op/Ch…03/Exercise03.03    go run main.go
    0 ) int8 126 uint8 254
    1 ) int8 127 uint8 255
    2 ) int8 -128 uint8 0
    3 ) int8 -127 uint8 1
    4 ) int8 -126 uint8 2
    ```

    Figure 3.4: Output after wraparound

In this exercise, we saw that, for signed integers, you'd end up with a negative number while unsigned integers wrap around to 0. You must always consider the maximum possible value for your variable and be sure to have the appropriate type to support that number.

Next, we'll look at what you can do when you need a number that's bigger than the core types can give you.

Big numbers

If you need a number higher or lower than `int64` or `uint64` can store, you can use the `math/big` package. This package feels a little awkward to use compared to dealing with integer types, but you'll be able to do everything you can generally do with integers using its API.

Exercise 3.04 – Big numbers

In this exercise, we're going to create a number that's larger than Go's core number types can store. To demonstrate this, we'll use an addition operation. We'll also do the same to an `int` variable to show the difference. Then, we'll print the result to the console:

1. Create a new folder and add a `main.go` file.

2. In `main.go`, add the main package name to the top of the file:

    ```
    package main
    ```

3. Now add the imports we'll use in this file:

    ```
    import (
      "fmt"
      "math"
      "math/big"
    )
    ```

4. Create the `main()` function:

    ```
    func main() {
    ```

5. Declare an `int` variable and initialize it with `math.MaxInt64`, which is the highest possible value for an `int64` variable in Go and is defined as a constant:

    ```
    intA := math.MaxInt64
    ```

6. Add 1 to `int`:

    ```
    intA = intA + 1
    ```

7. Now we'll create a `big int` variable. This is a custom type and is not based on Go's `int` type. We'll also initialize it with Go's highest possible number value:

    ```
    bigA := big.NewInt(math.MaxInt64)
    ```

8. We'll add 1 to our `big int`. You can see that this feels clumsy:

    ```
    bigA.Add(bigA, big.NewInt(1))
    ```

9. Print out the max int size and the values for our Go int and our big int:

    ```
    fmt.Println("MaxInt64: ", math.MaxInt64)
    fmt.Println("Int    :", intA)
    fmt.Println("Big Int : ", bigA.String())
    ```

10. Close the main() function:

    ```
    }
    ```

11. Save the file, and in the new folder run the following:

    ```
    go run main.go
    ```

    Running the preceding code displays the following output:

    ```
     ~/src/Th…op/Ch…03/Exercise03.04    go run main.go
    MaxInt64:   9223372036854775807
    Int    : -9223372036854775808
    Big Int :   9223372036854775808
    ```

    Figure 3.5: Output displaying large numbers with Go's number types

In this exercise, we saw that while int has wrapped around, big.Int has added the number correctly.

If you have a situation where you have a number whose value is higher than Go can manage, then the big package from the standard library is what you need. Next, we'll look at a special Go number type used to represent raw data.

byte

The byte type in Go is just an alias for uint8, which is a number that has eight bits of storage. In reality, byte is a significant type, and you'll see it in lots of places. A bit is a single binary value – a single on/off switch. Grouping bits into groups of eight was a common standard in early computing and became a near-universal way to encode data. 8-bits have 256 possible combinations of "off" and "on," so uint8 has 256 possible integer values from 0 to 255. All combinations of on and off can are represented with this type.

You'll see byte used when reading and writing data to and from a network connection and when reading and writing data to files.

With this, we're all done with numbers. Now, let's look at how Go stores and manages text.

Text

Go uses a single `string` type to represent text.

When you write text to a `string` variable it's called a string literal. There are two kinds of string literals in Go:

- Raw – defined by wrapping text in a pair of `` ` ``
- Interpreted – defined by surrounding the text in a pair of "

With raw literals, what ends up in your variable is precisely the text that you see on the screen. With interpreted literals, Go scans what you've written and then applies transformations based on its own set of rules.

Here's what that looks like:

```
package main
import "fmt"
func main() {
   comment1 := `This is the BEST
thing ever!`
   comment2 := `This is the BEST\nthing ever!`
   comment3 := "This is the BEST\nthing ever!"
   fmt.Print(comment1, "\n\n")
   fmt.Print(comment2, "\n\n")
   fmt.Print(comment3, "\n")
}
```

Running the preceding code gives the following output:

```
 ~/src/Th…op/Ch…03/Example03.05   go run main.go
This is the BEST
thing ever!

This is the BEST\nthing ever!

This is the BEST
thing ever!
```

Figure 3.6: Output from printing text

In an interpreted string, \n represents a new line. In our raw string, \n doesn't do anything to our formatting and is printed out just as we typed it. To get a new line in the raw string, we must add an actual new line to our raw literal. The interpreted string must use \n to get a new line, as adding a real new line to an interpreted string is not allowed.

While there are a lot of things you can do with an interpreted string literal, in real-world code, the two you'll see most commonly are \n for a new line and, occasionally, \t for a tab.

Interpreted string literals are the most common kind in real-world code, but raw literals have their place. If you want to copy and paste text that contains a lot of new lines, or " or \ characters, it's easier to use raw literals.

In the following example, you can see how using raw literals makes the code more readable:

```go
package main
import "fmt"
func main() {
   comment1 := `In "Windows" the user directory is "C:\Users\"`
   comment2 := "In \"Windows\" the user directory is \"C:\\Users\\\""
   fmt.Println(comment1)
   fmt.Println(comment2)
}
```

Running the preceding code displays the following output:

```
📁  ~/src/Th…op/Ch…03/Example03.06   go run main.go
In "Windows" the user directory is "C:\Users\"
In "Windows" the user directory is "C:\Users\"
```

Figure 3.7: Output from more readable code

One thing you can't have in a raw literal is a ` character. If you need a literal with ` in it, you must use an interpreted string literal.

String literals are just ways of getting text into a string variable. Once you have the value in the variable, there are no differences.

Next, we'll look at how to work safely with multi-byte strings.

Rune

rune is a type with enough storage to store a single UTF-8 multi-byte character. String literals are encoded using UTF-8. UTF-8 is a massively popular and common multi-byte text encoding standard. The string type itself is not limited to UTF-8, as Go also needs to support other text encoding types. string not being limited to UTF-8 means there is often an extra step you need to take when working with your strings to prevent bugs.

The different encodings use a different number of bytes to encode text. Legacy standards use one byte to encode a single character. UTF-8 uses up to four bytes to encode a single character. When text is in the string type, to allow for this variability, Go stores all strings as a byte collection. To be able to safely perform operations with text of any kind of encoding, single- or multi-byte, it should be converted from a `byte` collection to a `rune` collection.

> **Note**
>
> If you don't know the encoding of the text, it's usually safe to convert it to UTF-8. Also, UTF-8 is backward-compatible with single-byte encoded text.

Go makes it easy to access the individual bytes of a string, as shown in the following example:

1. First, we define the package, import our needed libraries, and create the `main()` function:

```
package main
import "fmt"
func main() {
```

2. We'll create a string that contains a multi-byte character:

```
username := "Sir_King_Über"
```

3. We are going to use a `for i` loop to print out each byte of our string:

```
for i := 0; i < len(username); i++ {
   fmt.Print(username[i], " ")
}
```

4. Then we will close the `main()` function:

```
}
```

Running the preceding code gives the following output:

```
📂  ~/src/Th…op/Ch…03/Example03.07 ▶ go run main.go
83 105 114 95 75 105 110 103 95 195 156 98 101 114
```

Figure 3.8: Output displaying bytes according to input length

The numbers printed out are the byte values of the string. There are only 13 letters in our string. However, it contained a multi-byte character, so we printed out 14 byte values.

Let's convert our bytes back into strings. This conversion uses type conversion, which we'll cover in detail soon:

```
package main
import "fmt"
func main() {
  username := "Sir_King_Über"
```

```
    for i := 0; i < len(username); i++ {
      fmt.Print(string(username[i]), " ")
    }
  }
```

Running the preceding code gives the following output:

```
   ~/src/Th…op/Ch…03/Example03.08    go run main.go
  S i r _ K i n g _ Ã    b e r
```

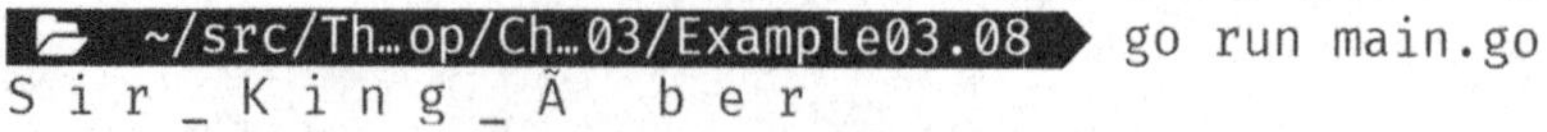

Figure 3.9: Output displaying bytes converted to strings

The output is as expected until we get to the Ü character. That's because Ü was encoded using more than one byte, and each byte on its own no longer makes sense.

To safely work with individual characters of a multi-byte string, you first must convert the string slice of byte types to a slice of rune types.

Consider the following example:

```
package main
import "fmt"
func main() {
  username := "Sir_King_Über"
  runes := []rune(username)
  for i := 0; i < len(runes); i++ {
    fmt.Print(string(runes[i]), " ")
  }
}
```

Running the preceding code gives the following output:

```
   ~/src/Th…op/Ch…03/Example03.09    go run main.go
  S i r _ K i n g _ Ü b e r
```

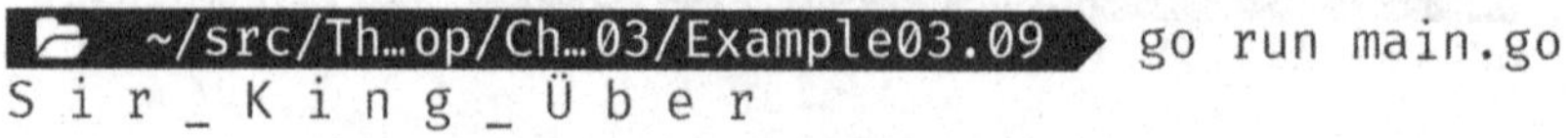

Figure 3.10: Output displaying strings

If we wish to work with each character in a loop like this, then using range would be a better choice. When using range, instead of moving one byte at a time, it moves along the string one rune at a time. The index is the byte offset, and the value is a rune value.

Exercise 3.05 – Safely looping over a string

In this exercise, we'll declare a string and initialize it with a multi-byte string value. We'll then loop over the string using range to give us each character, one at a time. We'll then print out the byte index and the character to the console:

1. Create a new folder and add a main.go file.

2. In main.go, add the main package name to the top of the file:

    ```
    package main
    ```

3. Now add the imports we'll use in this file:

    ```
    import "fmt"
    ```

4. Create the main() function:

    ```
    func main() {
    ```

5. Declare a string variable with a multi-byte string value:

    ```
    logLevel := "デバッグ"
    ```

6. Create a range loop that loops over the string, then capture index and rune in the variable:

    ```
    for index, runeVal := range logLevel {
    ```

7. Print index and rune to the console, casting the rune to a string:

    ```
    fmt.Println(index, string(runeVal))
    ```

8. Close the loop:

    ```
    }
    ```

9. Close the main() function:

    ```
    }
    ```

10. Save the file and in the new folder run the following:

    ```
    go run main.go
    ```

Running the preceding code gives the following output:

```
📂  ~/src/Th…op/Ch…03/Exercise03.05 ▶ go run main.go
0 デ
3 バ
6 ッ
9 グ
```

Figure 3.11: Output after safely looping over a string

In this exercise, we demonstrated that looping over a string in a safe, multi-byte way is baked right into the language. Using this method prevents you from getting invalid string data.

Another common way to find bugs is to check how many characters a string has by using len directly on it. Here is an example of how multi-byte strings can be mishandled:

```go
package main
import "fmt"
func main() {
  username := "Sir_King_Über"
  // Length of a string
  fmt.Println("Bytes:", len(username))
  fmt.Println("Runes:", len([]rune(username)))
  // Limit to 10 characters
  fmt.Println(string(username[:10]))
  fmt.Println(string([]rune(username)[:10]))
}
```

Running the preceding code gives the following output:

```
📂  ~/src/Th…op/Ch…03/Example03.10 ▶ go run main.go
Bytes: 14
Runes: 13
Sir_King_�
Sir_King_Ü
```

Figure 3.12: Output displaying bugs after using the len function

You can see that when using len directly on a string, you get the wrong answer. Checking the length of data input using len in this way would end up with invalid data. For example, if we needed the input to be exactly eight characters long and somebody entered a multi-byte character, using len directly on that input would allow them to enter less than eight characters.

When working with strings, be sure to check the strings package first. It's filled with useful tools that may already do what you need.

Next, let's take a close look at Go's special `nil` value.

The nil value

`nil` is not a type but a special value in Go. It represents an empty value of no type. When working with pointers, maps, and interfaces (we'll cover these in the next chapter), you need to be sure they are not `nil`. If you try to interact with a `nil` value, your code will crash.

If you can't be sure whether a value is `nil` or not, you can check it like this:

```go
package main
import "fmt"
func main() {
  var message [] string
  if message == nil {
    fmt.Println("error, unexpected nil value")
    return
  }
  fmt.Println(message)
}
```

Running the preceding code displays the following output:

```
error, unexpected nil value
```

In the preceding example, we declared the `message` variable as a slice of strings, but did not initialize it with any values. As such, the value of `message` is nil.

Activity 3.01 – Sales tax calculator

In this activity, we create a shopping cart application, where sales tax must be added to calculate the total:

1. Create a calculator that calculates the sales tax for a single item.

2. The calculator must take the item's cost and its sales tax rate.

3. Sum the sales tax and print the total amount of sales tax required for the following items:

Item	Cost	Sales Tax Rate
Cake	0.99	7.5%
Milk	2.75	1.5%
Butter	0.87	2%

Figure 3.13: List of items with their sales tax rates

Your output should look like this:

```
Sales Tax Total: 0.1329
```

> **Note**
>
> The solution for this activity can be found in the GitHub repository folder for this chapter: `https://github.com/PacktPublishing/Go-Programming-From-Beginner-to-Professional-Second-Edition-/tree/main/Chapter03/Activity03.01`.

Activity 3.02 – Loan calculator

In this activity, we must create a loan calculator for an online financial advisor platform. Our calculator should have the following rules:

1. A good credit score is a score of 450 or above.

2. For a good credit score, your interest rate is 15%.

3. If your score is less than good, your interest rate is 20%.

4. For a good credit score, your monthly payments can be no more than 20% of your monthly income.

5. If your credit score is not at least good, your monthly payment can be no more than 10% of your monthly income.

6. If a credit score, monthly income, loan amount, or loan term is less than 0, return an error.

7. If the term of the loan is not divisible by 12 months, return an error.

8. The interest payment will be a simple calculation of the loan amount * interest rate * loan term.

9. After doing these calculations, display the following details to the user:

    ```
    Applicant X
    -----------
    Credit Score : X
    Income : X
    Loan Amount : X
    Loan Term : X
    Monthly Payment : X
    Rate : X
    Total Cost : X
    Approved : X
    ```

This is the expected output:

```
📁  ~/src/Th…op/Ch…03/Activity03.02    go run main.go
Applicant 1
-----------
Credit Score    : 500
Income          : 1000
Loan Amount     : 1000
Loan Term       : 24
Monthly Payment : 47.916666666666664
Rate            : 15
Total Cost      : 150
Approved        : true

Applicant 2
-----------
Credit Score    : 350
Income          : 1000
Loan Amount     : 10000
Loan Term       : 12
Monthly Payment : 1000
Rate            : 20
Total Cost      : 2000
Approved        : false
```

Figure 3.14: Output of loan calculator

> **Note**
>
> The solution for this activity can be found in the `https://github.com/PacktPublishing/Go-Programming-From-Beginner-to-Professional-Second-Edition-/tree/main/Chapter03/Activity03.02`.

Summary

In this chapter, we took a big step in working with Go's type system. We took the time to define what types are and why they are needed. We then explored each of the core types in Go. We started with the simple `bool` type, and we were able to show how critical it is to everything we do in our code. We then moved on to the number types. Go has lots of types for numbers, reflecting the control that Go likes to give developers when it comes to memory usage and accuracy. After numbers, we looked at how strings work and how they are closely related to the rune type. With the advent of multi-byte characters, it's easy to make a mess of your text data. Go has provided powerful built-in features to help you get it right. Lastly, we looked at `nil` and how you use it within Go.

The concepts you've learned in this chapter have armed you with the knowledge needed to tackle Go's more complex types, such as collections and structs. We'll be looking at these complex types in the next chapter.

4
Complex Types

> **Overview**
>
> This chapter introduces Go's more complex types. This will build on what we learned in the previous chapter regarding Go's core types. These complex types are indispensable when you build more complex software as they allow you to logically group related data together. This ability to group data makes code easier to understand, maintain, and fix.
>
> By the end of this chapter, you will be able to use arrays, slices, and maps to group data together. You will learn to create custom types based on the core types. You will also learn to use structs to create structures composed of named fields of any other types and explain the importance of `interface{}`.

Technical requirements

For this chapter, you'll require Go version 1.21 or higher. The code for this chapter can be found at: `https://github.com/PacktPublishing/Go-Programming-From-Beginner-to-Professional-Second-Edition-/tree/main/Chapter04`.

Introduction

In the previous chapter, we covered Go's core types. These types are critical to everything you do in Go, but it can be challenging to model more complex data. In modern computer software, we want to be able to group data and logic where possible. We also want to be able to make our logic reflect the real-world solutions we're building.

If you were building software for cars, you would ideally want a custom type that embodies a car. This type should be named "car" and it should have properties that can store information about what kind of car it is. The logic that affects the car, such as starting and stopping, should be associated with the car type. If we had to manage more than one car, we would need to be able to group all the cars.

In this chapter, we'll learn about the features in Go that allow us to model the data part of this challenge. Then, in the next chapter, we'll solve the behavior part. By using custom types, you can extend Go's core types, and using structs allows you to compose a type made of other types and associate logic with them. Collections let you group data together and allow you to loop over and perform operations on them.

As the complexity of your tasks increases, Go's complex types help you keep your code easy to understand and maintain. Collections such as arrays, slices, and maps allow you to keep related data grouped together. Go's `struct` type allows you to create a single type that's made up of other strings, numbers, and Booleans, giving you the power to build models of complex real-world concepts. Structs also allow you to attach logic to them; this allows you to have the logic that controls your models closely tied together.

When things get complicated with types, we need to know how to use type conversions and assertions to manage type mismatches correctly. We'll also be looking at Go's `interface{}` type. This type is almost magical in that it allows you to overcome Go's struct typing system but in a way that's still type-safe.

Collection types

If you were dealing with a single email address, you would define a string variable to hold that value for you. Now, think about how you would structure your code if you needed to deal with between 0 and 100 email addresses. You could define a separate variable for each email address, but Go has something else we can use.

When dealing with lots of similar data, we put it in a collection. Go's collection types are arrays, slices, and maps. Go's collection types are strongly typed and easy to loop over, but they each have unique qualities that mean they are better suited to different use cases.

Arrays

Go's most basic collection type is an array. When you define an array, you must specify what type of data it may contain and how big the array is in the following form: `[<size>] <type>`. For example, `[10] int` is an array of size 10 that contains integers, while `[5] string` is an array of size 5 that contains strings. The key to making this an array is specifying the size. If your definition didn't have the size, it would seem like it works, but it would not be an array – it'd be a slice. A slice is a different, more flexible, type of collection that we'll look at after arrays. You can set the element values to be any type, including pointers and arrays.

You can initialize arrays with data using the following form:
`[<size>] <type>{<value1>,<value2>,...<valueN>}`. For example, `[5] string{1}` would initialize the array with the first value as 1, while `[5] string{9,9,9,9,9}` would fill the array with the value nine for each element. When initializing with data, you can have Go set the size of the array based on the number of elements you initialize it with. You can take advantage of this by replacing the length number with `....` For example, `[...] string{9,9,9,9,9}`

would create an array of length five because we initialized it with five elements. Just as with all arrays, the length is set at compile time and is not changeable at runtime.

Exercise 4.01 – Defining an array

In this exercise, we're going to define a simple array of size ten that takes integers. Then, we'll print out the contents. Let's get started:

1. Create a new folder and add a `main.go` file to it.

2. In `main.go`, add the package and imports:

    ```
    package main
    import "fmt"
    ```

3. Create a function that defines an array and then return it:

    ```
    func defineArray() [10]int {
      var arr [10]int
      return arr
    }
    ```

4. Define a `main` function, call the function, and print the result. We'll use `fmt.Printf` with `%#v` to get extra details about the value, including its type:

    ```
    func main() {
      fmt.Printf("%#v\n", defineArray())
    }
    ```

5. Save this. Then, from within the new folder, run the following:

    ```
    go run .
    ```

Running the preceding code provides us with the following output:

```
[10]int{0, 0, 0, 0, 0, 0, 0, 0, 0, 0}
```

In this exercise, we've defined an array but haven't filled it with any data. Since all arrays have a fixed size, when the array was printed out, it contained 10 values. These values are empty values for whatever type the array accepts.

Comparing arrays

The array's length is part of its type definition. If you have two arrays that accept the same type but they're different sizes, they are not compatible and aren't comparable with each other. To compare arrays, they must be of both the same length (size) and the same type.

Exercise 4.02 – Comparing arrays

In this exercise, we'll compare arrays. First, we'll define several arrays; some are comparable, while some are not. Then, we'll run the code and fix any problems that come up. Let's get started:

1. Create a new folder and add a `main.go` file to it.

2. In `main.go`, add the package and imports:

    ```
    package main
    import "fmt"
    ```

3. Create a function that defines four arrays:

    ```
    func compArrays() (bool, bool, bool) {
        var arr1 [5]int
        arr2 := [5]int{0}
        arr3 := [...]int{0, 0, 0, 0, 0}
        arr4 := [9]int{0, 0, 0, 0, 9}
    ```

4. Compare the arrays and return the result of the comparison. This closes off this function:

    ```
        return arr1 == arr2, arr1 == arr3, arr1 == arr4
    }
    ```

5. Define a `main` function so that it prints out the results:

    ```
    func main() {
        comp1, comp2, comp3 := compArrays()
        fmt.Println("[5]int == [5]int{0}           :", comp1)
        fmt.Println("[5]int == [...]int{0, 0, 0, 0, 0}:", comp2)
        fmt.Println("[5]int == [9]int{0, 0, 0, 0, 9} :", comp3)
    }
    ```

6. Save and run the code:

    ```
    go run .
    ```

Running the preceding code produces the following output:

```
→  Exercise04.02 git:(main) ✗ go run .
# github.com/packt-book/Go-Programming---From-Beginner-to-Professional-Second-Edition-/Chapter04/Exercise04.02
./main.go:10:45: invalid operation: arr1 == arr4 (mismatched types [5]int and [9]int)
```

Figure 4.1: Array type mismatch error

You should see an error. This error is telling you that `arr1`, which is a `[5] int` type, and `arr4`, which is a `[9] int` type, are not the same length arrays and therefore are not the same underlying type in Go, meaning they aren't comparable. Let's fix that.

1. Here, we have the following:

    ```
    arr4 := [9]int{0, 0, 0, 0, 9}
    ```

    We need to replace this with the following:

    ```
    arr4 := [5]int{0, 0, 0, 0, 9}
    ```

2. We also have the following code:

    ```
    fmt.Println("[5]int == [9]int{0, 0, 0, 0, 9} :", comp3)
    ```

    We need to replace this with the following:

    ```
    fmt.Println("[5]int == [5]int{0, 0, 0, 0, 9} :", comp3)
    ```

3. Save and run the code again using the following command:

    ```
    go run .
    ```

Running the preceding code produces the following output:

```
→  Exercise04.02 git:(main) ✗ go run .
[5]int == [5]int{0}                : true
[5]int == [...]int{0, 0, 0, 0, 0}: true
[5]int == [5]int{0, 0, 0, 0, 9}  : false
```

Figure 4.2: Output without error

In our exercise, we defined some arrays, and they were all defined in slightly different ways. At first, we had an error because we tried to compare arrays of different lengths, which, in Go, means they are different types. We fixed that and ran the code again. Then, we could see that even though the first three arrays were defined using different methods, they ended up being the same or equal to each other. The last array, now with its type fixed, had different data contained in it, so it's not the same or equal to the other arrays. The other collection types, that is, `slice` and `map`, are not comparable in this way. With maps and slices, you must loop over the contents of the two collections you're comparing and compare them manually. This ability gives arrays an advantage if comparing data in collections is a hot path, or frequent operation, in your code.

Initializing arrays using keys

So far, when we've initialized our arrays with data, we've let Go choose the keys for us. Keys refer to the indices or positions used to initialize specific values in an array. By setting values at specific indices using keys, you can initialize an array with desired values at specific positions while leaving other elements at their default values. Go allows you to pick the key you want for your data using `[<size>]<type>{<key1>:<value1>,…<keyN>:<valueN>}`. Go is flexible and lets you set keys with gaps and in any order. This ability to set values with a key is helpful if you've defined an array where the numeric keys have a specific meaning, and you want to set a value for a specific key but don't need to set any of the other values. Using keys when initializing arrays provides greater flexibility and control over the placement of values within an array.

Exercise 4.03 – Initializing an array using keys

In this exercise, we'll initialize a few arrays using some keys to set specific values. Then, we'll compare them to each other. After, we'll print out one of the arrays and look at its contents. Let's get started:

1. Create a new folder and add a `main.go` file to it.

2. In `main.go`, add the package and imports:

   ```
   package main
   import "fmt"
   ```

3. Create a function that defines three arrays:

   ```
   func compArrays() (bool, bool, [10]int) {
       var arr1 [10]int
       // set key 9 to value 0
       arr2 := [...]int{9: 0}
       // set key 0 to value 1, set key 9 to value 10,
       // and set key 4 to value 5
       arr3 := [10]int{1, 9: 10, 4: 5}
   ```

4. Compare the arrays and return the last one so that we can print it out later:

   ```
       return arr1 == arr2, arr1 == arr3, arr3
   }
   ```

5. Create a `main` function and call `compArrays`. Then, print out the results:

   ```
   func main() {
       comp1, comp2, arr3 := compArrays()
       fmt.Println("[10]int == [...]{9:0}           :", comp1)
       fmt.Println("[10]int == [10]int{1, 9: 10, 4: 5}}:", comp2)
       fmt.Println("arr3                     :", arr3)
   }
   ```

6. Save the file. Then, in the new folder, run the following:

   ```
   go run .
   ```

Running the preceding code produces the following output:

```
 ~/src/Th…op/Ch…04/Exercise04.03    go run .
[10]int == [...]{9:0}              : true
[10]int == [10]int{1, 9: 10, 4: 5}}: false
arr3                               : [1 0 0 0 5 0 0 0 0 10]
```

Figure 4.3: Array initialized using keys

In this exercise, we used keys when initializing the data for an array. For `arr2`, we combined the `. . .` shortcut with setting a key to make the array length directly relate to the key we set. With `arr3`, we mixed it using keys and without using keys to initialize the array, and we also used the keys out of order when setting key 0 to value 1, key 9 to value 10, and key 4 to value 5. Go's flexibility when using keys is strong and makes using arrays in this way pleasant.

Now that we've looked at initializing arrays, let's take a further look at reading their values.

Reading from an array

So far, we've defined an array and initialized it with some data. Now, let's read that data out. It's possible to access a single element of the array using `<array>[<index>]`. For example, this accesses the first element of an array, `arr[0]`. I know 0 is the first element of the array because arrays always use a zero-indexed integer key. The zero index means the first index for an array is always 0 and the last index is always the array's length minus 1.

The order of items in an array is guaranteed to be stable. Order stability means that an item placed at index 0 is always the first item in the array.

Being able to access specific parts of an array can be helpful in a few ways. It's often necessary to validate the data in an array by checking either the first and/or last elements. Sometimes, the position of the data in an array is important so that you know you can get, for example, a product's name from the third index. This positional significance is common when reading **comma-separated value** (**CSV**) files or other similar delimiter-separated value files. CSV is still in common use as it is a popular choice for exporting data from spreadsheet documents.

Exercise 4.04 – Reading a single item from an array

In this exercise, we'll define an array and initialize it with some words. Then, we'll read the words out in the form of a message and print it. Let's get started:

1. Create a new folder and add a file named `main.go` to it.

2. In `main.go`, add the package and imports:

    ```
    package main
    import "fmt"
    ```

3. Create a function that defines an array with words. The order of the words is important:

```
func message() string {
  arr := [...]string{
    "ready",
    "Get",
    "Go",
    "to",
  }
```

4. Now, create a message by joining the words in a specific order and returning it. We're using the `fmt.Sprintln` function here since it allows us to capture the formatted text before it's printed:

```
  return fmt.Sprintln(arr[1], arr[0], arr[3], arr[2])
}
```

5. Create our `main()` function, call the `message` function, and print it to the console:

```
func main() {
  fmt.Print(message())
}
```

6. Save and run the code:

```
go run .
```

Running the preceding code produces the following output:

```
Get ready to Go
```

We now understand how to access specific elements in an array using indices. Next, we will explore writing to an array.

Writing to an array

Once an array is defined, you're able to make changes to individual elements using its index using `<array>[<index>]` = `<value>`. This assignment works the same as it does for other types of variables.

In real-world code, you often need to modify the data in your collections after it has been defined based on inputs or logic.

Exercise 4.05 – Writing to an array

In this exercise, we'll define an array and initialize it with some words. Then, we'll make some changes to the words. Finally, we'll read the words out to form a message and print it. Let's get started:

1. Create a new folder and add a file named `main.go` to it.

2. In `main.go`, add the package and imports:

    ```
    package main
    import "fmt"
    ```

3. Create a function that defines an array with words. The order of the words is important:

    ```
    func message() string {
        arr := [4]string{"ready", "Get", "Go", "to"}
    ```

4. We'll change some of the words in the array by assigning new values using an array index. The order this is done in doesn't matter:

    ```
    arr[1] = "It's"
    arr[0] = "time"
    ```

5. Now, create a message by joining the words in a specific order and return it:

    ```
        return fmt.Sprintln(arr[1], arr[0], arr[3], arr[2])
    }
    ```

6. Create our `main()` function, call the `message` function, and print it to the console:

    ```
    func main() {
        fmt.Print(message())
    }
    ```

7. Save and run the code:

    ```
    go run .
    ```

Running the preceding code produces the following output:

```
It's time to Go
```

You now know the basics when it comes to initializing, reading, and writing to an array using an index. Knowing that arrays contain multiple values, let's peek at how to loop over an array.

Looping over an array

The most common way you'll work with arrays is by using them in loops. Due to the way an array's indexes work, they are easy to loop over. The index always starts at 0, there are no gaps, and the last element is the array's length, minus 1.

Because of this, it's also common to use a loop where we create a variable to represent the index and increment it manually. This type of loop is often called a `for i` loop since i is the name that's given to the index variable.

> **Note**
>
> You can use a different letter than i; however, i is very representative of the word index in the case of looping an array and thereby represents idiomatic Go stylistically.

As you'll remember from the previous chapter, a `for` loop has three possible parts: the logic that can run before the loop, the logic that runs on each loop interaction to check whether the loop should continue, and the logic that runs at the end of each loop iteration. A `for i` loop looks like this: `i := 0; i < len(arr); i++ {`. What happens is that we define i to be zero, which also means i only exists in the scope of the loop. Then, i is checked on the loop's iteration to ensure it's less than the length of the array. We check that it's less than the length of the array since the length is always 1 more than the last index key. Lastly, we increment i by 1 on each loop to let us step over each element in the array, one by one, until we've reached the length of the array.

When it comes to the length of an array, it can be tempting to hardcode the value of the last index instead of using `len` since you know the length of your array is always the same. Hardcoding length is a bad idea. Hardcoding would make your code harder to maintain. It's common for your data to change and evolve. If you ever need to come back and change the size of an array, having hardcoded array lengths introduces hard-to-find bugs and even runtime panics. In Go, a runtime panic is essentially an event that occurs when the program encounters an exceptional situation it cannot or should not recover from. When a panic is triggered, the program will terminate immediately.

Using loops with arrays allows you to repeat the same logic for every element – that is, validating the data, modifying the data, or outputting the data – without having to duplicate the same code for multiple variables.

Exercise 4.06 – Looping over an array using a "for i" loop

In this exercise, we'll define an array and initialize it with some numbers. We'll loop over the numbers and do an operation on each one, putting the result in a message. Then, we'll return the message and print it. Let's get started:

1. Create a new folder and add a file named `main.go` to it.

2. In `main.go`, add the package and imports:

    ```
    package main
    import "fmt"
    ```

3. Create a function. We'll define an array with data and an m variable before the loop:

    ```
    func message() string {
        m := ""
        arr := [4]int{1,2,3,4}
    ```

4. Define the start of the loop. This manages the index and the loop:

    ```
    for i := 0; i < len(arr); i++ {
    ```

5. Then, write the body of the loop, which does an operation on each element of the array and adds it to the message:

    ```
    arr[i] = arr[i] * arr[i]
    m += fmt.Sprintf("%v: %v\n", i, arr[i])
    ```

6. Now, close the loop, return the message, and close the function:

    ```
        }
        return m
    }
    ```

7. Create our `main` function, call the `message` function, and print it to the console:

    ```
    func main() {
        fmt.Print(message())
    }
    ```

8. Save this code. Then, from the new folder, run the code:

    ```
    go run .
    ```

Running the preceding code produces the following output after looping over the array using the `for i` loop and multiplying the values times themselves:

```
0: 1
1: 4
2: 9
3: 16
```

A `for i` loop is very common, so pay close attention to the `for` loop, and be sure to understand what each of the three parts is doing.

> **Note**
>
> **Using len in a loop**: In other languages, it's not efficient to count the number of elements on each iteration of a loop. In Go, it's okay. The Go runtime tracks the length of the array internally, so it doesn't count the items when you call `len`. This feature is also true for the other collection types; that is, slice and map.

Modifying the contents of an array in a loop

In addition to reading from an array in a loop, you can also change the contents of the array in a loop. Working with the data in each element works like working with variables. You use the same `for i` loops too.

Just as with reading data from arrays, being able to change data in collections reduces the amount of code you need to write if each element were a standalone variable.

Exercise 4.07 – Modifying the contents of an array in a loop

In this exercise, we're going to define an empty array, fill it with data, and then modify that data. Finally, we'll print the filled and modified array to the console. Let's get started:

1. Create a new folder and add a file named `main.go` to it.

2. In `main.go`, add the package and imports:

   ```
   package main
   import "fmt"
   ```

3. Create a function that fills an array with numbers from 1 to 10:

   ```
   func fillArray(arr [10]int) [10]int {
       for i := 0; i < len(arr); i++ {
        arr[i] = i + 1
       }
       return arr
   }
   ```

4. Create a function that multiples the number from an array by itself and then sets the result back to the array:

   ```
   func opArray(arr [10]int) [10]int {
       for i := 0; i < len(arr); i++ {
          arr[i] = arr[i] * arr[i]
       }
       return arr
   }
   ```

5. In our `main()` function, we need to define our empty array, fill it, modify it, and then print its contents to the console:

```
func main() {
    var arr [10]int
    arr = fillArray(arr)
    arr = opArray(arr)
    fmt.Println(arr)
}
```

6. Save this code. Then, from the new folder, run the code:

```
go run .
```

Running the preceding code produces the following output:

```
[1 4 9 16 25 36 49 64 81 100]
```

Working with data in arrays is simple once you've understood how to use them in a `for i` loop. One nice thing about working with arrays over other collections is their fixed length. With arrays, it's not possible to accidentally change the size of the array and end up in an infinite loop, which is a loop that can't end and results in software that runs forever while using lots of resources.

Activity 4.01 – Filling an array

In this activity, we're going to define an array and fill it using a `for i` loop. The following are the steps for this activity:

1. Create a new Go program.

2. Define an array with 10 elements.

3. Use a `for i` loop to fill that array with the numbers 1 through 10.

4. Use `fmt.Println` to print the array to the console.

The expected output is as follows:

```
[1 2 3 4 5 6 7 8 9 10]
```

> **Note**
>
> The solution for this activity can be found in the GitHub repository folder for this chapter: `https://github.com/PacktPublishing/Go-Programming-From-Beginner-to-Professional-Second-Edition-/tree/main/Chapter04/Activity04.01`.

Slices

Arrays are great, but their rigidity around size can cause issues. If you wanted to create a function that accepted an array and sorted the data in it, it could only work for one size of an array. That requires you to create a function for each size of an array. This strictness around size makes working with arrays feel like a hassle and unengaging. The flip side of arrays is that they are an efficient way of managing sorted collections of data. Wouldn't it be great if there were a way to get the efficiency of arrays but with more flexibility? Go gives you this in the form of slices.

A slice is a thin layer around arrays that lets you have a sorted numeric indexed collection without having to worry about the size. Underneath the thin layer is still a Go array, but Go manages all the details, such as how big an array to use. You use a slice just like you would an array; it only holds values of one type, you can read and write to each element using [and], and they are easy to loop over using for i loops.

The other thing a slice can do is be easily expanded using the built-in append function. This function accepts your slice and the values you'd like to add and returns a new slice with everything merged. It's common to start with an empty slice and expand it as needed.

Since a slice is a thin layer around an array, this means it's not a true type like an array. You need to understand how Go uses the hidden array behind a slice. If you don't, it'll lead to subtle and difficult-to-debug errors.

In real-world code, you should be using slices as your go-to for all sorted collections. You'll be more productive because you won't need to write as much code as you would with an array. Most code you'll see in real-world projects uses lots of slices and rarely uses arrays. Arrays are only used when the size needs to be exactly a certain length, and even then, slices get used most of the time as they can be passed around the code more easily.

Exercise 4.08 – Working with slices

In this exercise, we'll show you how flexible slices are by reading some data from a slice, passing a slice to a function, looping over a slice, reading values from a slice, and appending values to the end of a slice. Let's get started:

1. Create a new folder and add a file named main.go to it.

2. In main.go, add the package and imports:

```
package main
import (
    "fmt"
    "os"
)
```

3. Create a function that takes an `int` argument and returns a `string` slice:

```
func getPassedArgs(minArgs int) []string {
```

4. In the function's body, check if we have the correct number of arguments being passed in through the command line. If not, we exit the program with an error. When we run our program from the command line, Go automatically places all arguments into `os.Args`, which is a slice of strings:

```
if len(os.Args) < minArgs {
  fmt.Printf("At least %v arguments are needed\n", minArgs)
  os.Exit(1)
}
```

5. The first element of the `os.Args` slice, `os.Args[0]`, is how the code is called and not an argument, so we'll skip that and start our `for i` loop at index 1:

```
var args []string
for i := 1; i < len(os.Args); i++ {
  args = append(args, os.Args[i])
}
```

6. Then, we'll return the arguments:

```
  return args
}
```

7. Now, create a function that loops over a slice and finds the longest string. When two words are of the same length, the first word is returned:

```
func findLongest(args []string) string {
  var longest string
  for i := 0; i < len(args); i++ {
    if len(args[i]) > len(longest) {
      longest = args[i]
    }
  }
  return longest
}
```

8. In the `main()` function, we call the functions and check for errors. If there is an error, we tell the user then terminate the program with `os.Exit(1)`, which also returns error code 1 to the operating system:

```
func main() {
  if longest := findLongest(getPassedArgs(3)); len(longest) > 0 {
    fmt.Println("The longest word passed was:", longest)
  } else {
```

```
        fmt.Println("There was an error")
        os.Exit(1)
    }
}
```

9. Save the file. Then, in the folder it's saved in, run the code using the following command:

```
go run . Get ready to Go
```

Running the preceding code produces the following output:

```
The longest word passed was: ready
```

In this exercise, we were able to see how flexible slices are and, at the same time, how they work just like arrays. This way of working with slices is another reason why Go has the feel of a dynamic language.

Appending multiple items to a slice

The built-in append function can add more than one value to a slice. You can add as many parameters to append as you need since the last parameter is variadic. Since it's variadic, this means that you can also use the . . . notation to use a slice as the variadic parameter, allowing you to pass an arbitrary number of arguments to append.

Being able to pass more than one argument to append comes up all the time in real-world code, and having it keeps Go code compact by not requiring multiple calls or loops to add multiple values.

Exercise 4.09 – Appending multiple items to a slice

In this exercise, we'll use the variadic parameter of append to add multiple values in the form of predefined data to a slice. Then, we'll add a dynamic amount of data based on user input to the same slice. Let's get started:

1. Create a new folder and add a file named main.go to it.

2. In main.go, add the package and imports:

```
package main
import (
    "fmt"
    "os"
)
```

3. Create a function to safely grab user input:

```
func getPassedArgs() []string {
    var args []string
    for i := 1; i < len(os.Args); i++ {
```

```
        args = append(args, os.Args[i])
    }
    return args
}
```

4. Create a function that accepts a slice of strings as a parameter and returns a slice of strings. Then, define a slice of `strings` variable:

```
func getLocales(extraLocales []string) []string {
    var locales []string
```

5. Add multiple strings to the slice using `append`:

```
locales = append(locales, "en_US", "fr_FR")
```

6. Add more data from the parameter:

```
locales = append(locales, extraLocales...)
```

7. Return the variable and close the function definition:

```
    return locales
}
```

8. In the `main()` function, get the user input, pass it to our function, and then print the result:

```
func main() {
    locales := getLocales(getPassedArgs())
    fmt.Println("Locales to use:", locales)
}
```

9. Save the file. Then, in the folder you created in *step 1*, run the code using the following command:

```
go run . fr_CN en_AU
```

Running the preceding code produces the following output:

```
Locales to use: [en_US fr_FR fr_CN en_AU]
```

In this exercise, we used two methods of adding multiple values to a slice. You would also use this technique if you needed to join two slices together.

While appending a slice like this to add it to another slice may seem inefficient, the Go runtime can spot when you're doing an explode in an append and optimizes the call in the background to ensure no resources get wasted.

Creating slices from slices and arrays

By using a similar notation to accessing a single element in an array or a slice, you can create new slices derived from the contents of arrays and slices. The most common notation is [<low>:<high>]. This notation tells Go to create a new slice with the same value type as the source slice or array and to populate the new slice with values by starting at the low index and then going up to, but not including, the high index. Low and high are optional. If you omitted low, then Go defaults to the first element in the source. If you omit high, then it goes all the way to the last value. It's possible to skip both, and if you do, then the new slice has all the values from the source.

When you create new slices this way, Go doesn't copy the values. If the source is an array, then that source array is the hidden array for the new slice. If the source is a slice, then the hidden array for the new slice is the same hidden array the source slice uses.

This is an important concept because modifying *ANY* slice also changes the underlying array, not a copy of it. Think of a slice as a "view" of the underlying array.

Exercise 4.10 – Creating slices from a slice

In this exercise, we'll use the slice range notation to create slices with a variety of initial values. Commonly, in real-world code, you need to work with only a small part of a slice or an array. The range notation is a quick and straightforward way of getting only the data you need. Let's get started:

1. Create a new folder and add a file named main.go to it.

2. In main.go, add the package and imports:

    ```
    package main
    import "fmt"
    ```

3. Create a function and define a slice with nine int values:

    ```
    func message() string {
        s := []int{1, 2, 3, 4, 5, 6, 7, 8, 9}
    ```

4. We'll extract the first value, first directly as an int value, then as a slice using both low and high, and finally using just high and skipping low. We'll write the values to a message string:

    ```
    m := fmt.Sprintln("First :", s[0], s[0:1], s[:1])
    ```

5. Now, we'll get the last element. To get the int value, we'll use the length and subtract 1 from the index. We use that same logic when setting the low for the range notation. For high, we can use the length of the slice. Finally, we can see we can skip high and get the same result:

    ```
    m += fmt.Sprintln("Last    :", s[len(s)-1], s[len(s)-1:len(s)],
    s[len(s)-1:])
    ```

6. Now, let's get the first five values and add them to the message:

```
m += fmt.Println("First 5 :", s[:5])
```

7. Next, we'll get the last four values and add them to the message as well:

```
m += fmt.Println("Last 4 :", s[5:])
```

8. Finally, we'll extract five values from the middle of the slice and get them in the message too:

```
m += fmt.Println("Middle 5:", s[2:7])
```

9. Then, we'll return the message and close the function:

```
    return m
}
```

10. In main, we'll print the message out:

```
func main() {
    fmt.Print(message())
}
```

11. Save the file. Then, in the folder you created in *step 1*, run the code using the following command:

```
go run .
```

Running the preceding code produces the following output:

```
→  Exercise04.10 git:(main) x go run .
First   : 1 [1] [1]
Last    : 9 [9] [9]
First 5 : [1 2 3 4 5]
Last 4  : [6 7 8 9]
Middle 5: [3 4 5 6 7]
```

Figure 4.5: Output after creating slices from a slice

In this exercise, we tried out a few ways to create slices from another slice. You can also use these same techniques on an array as the source. We saw that both start and stop indexes are optional. If you don't have a start index, it'll start at the beginning of the source slice or array. If you don't have a stop index, then it'll stop at the end of the array. If you skip both start and stop indexes, it'll make a copy of the slice or array. This trick is useful for turning an array into a slice but not helpful for copying slices because the two slices share the same hidden array.

Understanding slice internals

Slices are great and should be your go-to when you need an ordered list, but if you don't know how they work under the hood, they cause hard-to-spot bugs.

An array is a value type that's like a `string` or an `int` type. Value types can be copied and compared to themselves. These value types, once copied, are not connected to their source values. Slices don't work like value types; they work more like pointers, but they are also not pointers.

The key to staying safe with a slice is to understand that there is a hidden array that stores the values and that making changes to the slice changes the underlying array. These changes may or may not require that the hidden array be replaced with a bigger one. The fact that the management of the hidden array happens in the background is what makes it hard to reason well about what's going on with your slices.

Slices have three hidden properties: length, a pointer to the hidden array, and wherein the hidden array its starting point is. When you append to a slice, one or all of these properties get updated. Which properties get updated depends on whether the hidden array is full or not.

The size of the hidden array and the size of the slice are not always the same. The size of the slice is its length, which we can find out by using the `len` built-in function. The size of the hidden array is the capacity of the slice. There is also a built-in function that tells you the capacity of a slice; that is, `cap`. When you add a new value to a slice using `append`, one of two things happens: if the slice has extra capacity – that is, the hidden array is not full yet – it adds the value to the hidden array and then updates the slice's length property. If the hidden array is full, Go creates a new, larger, array. Go then copies all the values from the old array into the new array and adds the new value too. Then, Go updates the slice from pointing to the old array to the new array and updates the length of the slice and, possibly, its starting point.

The starting point only comes into play if the slice is a subset of values from an array or a slice not starting at the first element, as in our example, where we got the last five elements of a slice. The rest of the time, it'll be the first element in the hidden array.

It's possible to control the size of the hidden array when you define a slice. Go's built-in `make` function allows you to set the length and capacity of a slice when creating it. The syntax looks like this: `make(<sliceType>, <length>, <capacity>)`. When creating a slice using `make`, the capacity is optional, but the length is required.

Exercise 4.11 – Using make to control the capacity of a slice

In this exercise, using the `make` function, we'll create several slices and display their length and capacity. Let's get started:

1. Create a new folder and add a file named `main.go` to it.

2. In `main.go`, add the package and imports:

    ```
    package main
    import "fmt"
    ```

3.   Create a function that returns three int slices:

```
func genSlices() ([]int, []int, []int) {
```

4.   Define a slice using the var notation:

```
var s1 []int
```

5.   Define a slice using make and set only the length:

```
s2 := make([]int, 10)
```

6.   Define a slice that uses both the length and capacity of the slices:

```
s3 := make([]int, 10, 50)
```

7.   Return the three slices and close the function definition:

```
return s1, s2, s3
}
```

8.   In the main() function, call the function we created and capture the returned values. For each slice, print its length and capacity to the console:

```
func main() {
    s1, s2, s3 := genSlices()
    fmt.Printf("s1: len = %v cap = %v\n", len(s1), cap(s1))
    fmt.Printf("s2: len = %v cap = %v\n", len(s2), cap(s2))
    fmt.Printf("s3: len = %v cap = %v\n", len(s3), cap(s3))
}
```

9.   Save the file. Then, in the folder you created in *step 1*, run the code using the following command:

```
go run .
```

Running the preceding code produces the following output:

```
→  Exercise04.11 git:(main) ✗ go run .
s1: len = 0 cap = 0
s2: len = 10 cap = 10
s3: len = 10 cap = 50
```

Figure 4.6: Output displaying slices

In this exercise, we used make, len, and cap to control and display the length and capacity of a slice when defining one.

If you already know the maximum size your slice will need, setting the capacity upfront can improve performance because Go won't have to spend extra resources resizing the underlying array.

Background behavior of slices

Due to the complexity of what a slice is and how it works, you can't directly compare slices to one another. If you try, Go gives you an error. You can compare a slice to nil, but that's it.

A slice is not a value, and it's not a pointer, so what is it? A slice is a special construct in Go. A slice doesn't store its own values directly. In the background, it's using an array that you can't access directly. What a slice does store is a pointer to that hidden array, its own starting point in that array, how long the slice is, and what the capacity of the slice is. These values provide slices with a window for the hidden array. The window can be the whole hidden array or just a smaller portion of it. The pointer to the hidden array can be shared by more than one slice. This pointer sharing can result in multiple slices that can share the same hidden array, even though not all the slides contain the same data. This means that one of the slices can have more data than the other slices.

When a slice needs to grow beyond its hidden array, it creates a new bigger array, copies the contents from the old array to the new one, and points the slice at the new array. This array swap is why our preceding slices became disconnected. At first, they were pointing to the same hidden array, but when we grow the first slice, the array it's pointing to changes. This change means that changes to the grown slice no longer affect the other slices since they are still pointing to the old, smaller, array.

If you need to make a copy of a slice and need to be sure they are not connected, you have a few choices. You can use append to copy the contents of the source slice into another array or use the built-in copy function. When using copy, Go won't change the size of the destination slice, so be sure it has enough room for all the elements you want to copy.

Exercise 4.12 – Controlling internal slice behavior

In this exercise, we're going to explore five different ways to copy data from slice to slice and how that has an impact on a slice's internal behavior. Let's get started:

1. Create a new folder and add a file named main.go to it.

2. In main.go, add the package and imports:

    ```
    package main
    import "fmt"
    ```

3. Create a function that returns three int values:

    ```
    func linked() (int, int, int) {
    ```

4. Define an `int` slice, initialized with some data:

```
s1 := []int{1, 2, 3, 4, 5}
```

5. Then, we'll make a simple variable copy of that slice:

```
s2 := s1
```

6. Create a new slice by copying all the values from the first slice as part of a slice range operation:

```
s3 := s1[:]
```

7. Change some data in the first slice. Later, we'll see how this affects the second and third slices:

```
s1[3] = 99
```

8. Return the same index for each slice and close the function definition:

```
    return s1[3], s2[3], s3[3]
}
```

9. Create a function that will return two `int` values:

```
func noLink() (int, int) {
```

10. Define a slice with some data and do a simple copy again:

```
s1 := []int{1, 2, 3, 4, 5}
s2 := s1
```

11. This time, we'll append to the first slice before we do anything else. This operation changes the length and capacity of the slice:

```
s1 = append(s1, 6)
```

12. Then, we'll change the first slice, return the same indexes from the two slices, and close the function:

```
s1[3] = 99
return s1[3], s2[3]
}
```

13. In our next function, we'll be returning two `int` values:

```
func capLinked() (int, int) {
```

14. We'll define our first slice using `make` this time. When doing this, we'll be setting a capacity that's larger than its length:

```
s1 := make([]int, 5, 10)
```

15. Let's fill the first array with the same data as before:

```
s1[0], s1[1], s1[2], s1[3], s1[4] = 1, 2, 3, 4, 5
```

16. Now, we'll create a new slice by copying the first slice, like we did previously:

```
s2 := s1
```

17. We'll append a new value to the first slice, which changes its length but not its capacity:

```
s1 = append(s1, 6)
```

18. Then, we'll change the first slice, return the same indexes from the two slices, and close the function:

```
s1[3] = 99
return s1[3], s2[3]
}
```

19. In this function, we'll use make again to set a capacity, but we'll use append to add elements that will go beyond that capacity:

```
func capNoLink() (int, int) {
    s1 := make([]int, 5, 10)
    s1[0], s1[1], s1[2], s1[3], s1[4] = 1, 2, 3, 4, 5
    s2 := s1
    s1 = append(s1, []int{10: 11}...)
    s1[3] = 99
    return s1[3], s2[3]
}
```

20. In the next function, we'll use copy to copy the elements from the first slice to the second slice. copy returns how many elements were copied from one slice to another, so we'll return that too:

```
func copyNoLink() (int, int, int) {
    s1 := []int{1, 2, 3, 4, 5}
    s2 := make([]int, len(s1))
    copied := copy(s2, s1)
    s1[3] = 99
    return s1[3], s2[3], copied
}
```

21. In the final function, we'll use append to copy the value into the second slice. Using append in this way results in the values being copied into a new hidden array:

```
func appendNoLink() (int, int) {
    s1 := []int{1, 2, 3, 4, 5}
    s2 := append([]int{}, s1...)
```

```
        s1[3] = 99
        return s1[3], s2[3]
    }
```

22. In main, we'll print out all the data we returned and print it to the console:

```
func main() {
    l1, l2, l3 := linked()
    fmt.Println("Linked    :", l1, l2, l3)
    nl1, nl2 := noLink()
    fmt.Println("No Link    :", nl1, nl2)
    cl1, cl2 := capLinked()
    fmt.Println("Cap Link  :", cl1, cl2)
    cnl1, cnl2 := capNoLink()
    fmt.Println("Cap No Link :", cnl1, cnl2)
    copy1, copy2, copied := copyNoLink()
    fmt.Print("Copy No Link: ", copy1, copy2)
    fmt.Printf(" (Number of elements copied %v)\n", copied)
    a1, a2 := appendNoLink()
    fmt.Println("Append No Link:", a1, a2)
}
```

23. Save the file. Then, in the folder you created in *step 1*, run the code using the following command:

```
go run .
```

Running the preceding code produces the following output:

```
→ Exercise04.12 git:(main) ✗ go run .
Linked        : 99 99 99
No Link       : 99 4
Cap Link      : 99 99
Cap No Link   : 99 4
Copy No Link  : 99 4 (Number of elements copied 5)
Append No Link: 99 4
```

Figure 4.7: Output displaying data

In this exercise, we stepped through five different scenarios where we made copies of slice data. In the Linked scenario, we made a simple copy of the first slice and then a range copy of it. While the slices themselves are distinct and are no longer the same slices, in reality, it doesn't make a difference to the data they hold. Each of the slices pointed to the same hidden array, so when we made a change to the first slice, it affected all of the slices.

In the `No Link` scenario, the setup was the same for the first and second slices, but before we made a change to the first slice, we appended a value to it. When we appended this value to it, in the background, Go needed to create a new array to hold the now large number of values. Since we were appending to the first slice, its pointer was to look at the new, bigger slice. The second slice didn't get its pointer updates. That's why, when the first slice had its value change, the second slice wasn't affected. The second slice isn't pointing to the same hidden array anymore, meaning they are not linked.

For the `Cap Link` scenario, the first slice was defined using `make` and with an oversized capacity. This extra capacity meant that when the first slice had a value appended to it, there was already extra room in the hidden array. This extra capacity means there was no need to replace the hidden array. The effect was that when we updated the value on the first slice, it and the second slice were still pointing to the same hidden array, meaning the change affected both.

In the `Cap No Link` scenario, the setup was the same as the previous scenario, but when we appended values, we appended more values than there was available capacity. Even though there was extra capacity, there was not enough, and the hidden array in the first slice got replaced. The result was that the link between the two slices broke.

In `Copy No Link`, we used the built-in `copy` function to copy the value for us. While this does copy the values into a new hidden array, `copy` won't change the length of the slice. This fact means that the destination slice must be the correct length before you do the copy. You don't see copy much in real-world code; this could be because it's easy to misuse it.

Lastly, with `Append No Link`, we used append to do something similar to `copy` but without having to worry about the length. This method is most commonly seen in real-world code when you need to ensure you get a copy of the values that are not linked to the source. This is easy to understand since append gets used a lot, and it's a one-line solution. There is one slightly more efficient solution that avoids the extra memory allocation of the empty slice in the first argument of append. You can reuse the first slice by creating a 0-capacity range copy of it. This alternative looks like this:

```
s1 := []int{1, 2, 3, 4, 5}
s2 := append(s1[:0:0], s1...)
```

Can you see something new here? This uses the seldom-used slice range notation of `<slice>[<low>:<high>:<capacity>]`. With the current Go compiler, this is the most memory-efficient way to copy a slice.

Map fundamentals

While arrays and slices are similar and can sometimes be interchangeable, Go's other collection type, `map`, is quite different and is not interchangeable with `array` and `slice`. Go's map type serves a different purpose.

Go's map is a hashmap in computer science terms. The main difference between a map and the other collection types relates to its key. In an array or slice, the key is a placeholder (the index number), and it has no meaning of its own. It's only there to act as a counter and has no direct relationship with the value.

With a map, the key is data – data that has a real relationship with the value. For example, you could have a collection of user account records in a map. The key would be the users' employee IDs. An employee ID is real data and not just an arbitrary placeholder. If someone were to give you their employee ID, you'd be able to look up their account records without needing to loop over the data to find it. With a map, you can set, get, and delete data quickly.

You can access individual elements of a map in the same way as you do with a slice or an array: using [and]. Maps can have any type that is directly comparable as a key, such as an int or a string type. You can't compare slices, so they can't be keys. A map's value can be of any type, including pointers, slices, and maps.

You shouldn't use a map as an ordered list. Even if you were to use an int type for a map's keys, maps are not guaranteed to always start at index 0, and they are not guaranteed to not have any gaps in the keys. This feature could be an advantage, even if you did want int keys. If you had sparsely populated data – that is, values with gaps between keys– in a slice or an array, it would contain lots of zero data. In a map, it would only contain the data you set.

To define a map, you use the following notation: map [<key_type>] <value_type>

You can use make to create maps, but the arguments for make are different when using make to create a map. Go can't create keys for a map, so it's not possible to create a map of an arbitrary length like you can with a slice. You can suggest a capacity for the compiler to use for your map. Suggesting the capacity for a map is optional, and map can't be used with cap to check what its capacity is.

Maps are like slices in that they are not a value and not a pointer. A map is a special construct in Go. You'll need to take the same care when copying the variable or the values. Since you can't control or check the capacity of a map, they are even more challenging when you want to know what's going to happen when you add elements.

Since Go does not help you manage your keys with maps, this means you must specify keys when initializing a map with data. It's the same notation as the other collection types; that is, map [<key_type>] <value_type>{<key1>: <value>, … <keyN>:, <valueN>}.

Once defined, you can set values without needing to worry about the length of the map like you do with arrays and slices. Setting a value is just like the other collections; that is, <map> [<key>] = <value>. Something that you do need to do before setting the value of a map is to make sure you've initialized it first. If you try to set a value of an uninitialized map, it causes a runtime panic. To avoid this, it's good practice to avoid defining a map using var. If you initialize the map with data or use make to create your maps, you won't have this problem.

Exercise 4.13 – Creating, reading, and writing a map

In this exercise, we're going to define a map with some data and then add a new element to it. Finally, we'll print the map to the console. Let's get started:

1. Create a new folder and add a file named `main.go` to it.

2. In `main.go`, add the package and imports:

    ```
    package main
    import "fmt"
    ```

3. Create a function that returns a `map` type with `string` keys and `string` values:

    ```
    func getUsers() map[string]string {
    ```

4. Define a `map` type with `string` keys and `string` values and then initialize it with some elements:

    ```
    users := map[string]string{
        "305": "Sue",
        "204": "Bob",
        "631": "Jake",
    }
    ```

5. Next, we'll add a new element to the map type:

    ```
    users["073"] = "Tracy"
    ```

6. Return the map type and close the function:

    ```
    return users
    }
    ```

7. In the `main` function, print the map type to the console:

    ```
    func main() {
        fmt.Println("Users:", getUsers())
    }
    ```

8. Save the file. Then, in the folder you created in *step 1*, run the code using the following command:

    ```
    go run .
    ```

Running the preceding code produces the following output:

```
Users: map[073:Tracy 204:Bob 305:Sue 631:Jake]
```

In this exercise, we created a map, initialized it with data, and then added a new element. This exercise shows that working with maps is similar to working with arrays and slices. When you should use a map comes down to the kinds of data you'll store in it and if your access pattern needs access to individual items rather than a list of items.

Reading from maps

You won't always know whether a key exists in a map before needing to use it to get a value. When you're getting a value for a key that doesn't exist in a map, Go returns the zero value for the map's value type. Having logic that works with zero values is a valid way to program in Go, but that's not always possible. If you can't use zero-value logic, maps can return an extra return value when you need it. The notation looks like this: `<value>, <exists_value> := <map>[<key>]`. Here, `exists_value` is a Boolean value that is `true` if a key exists in the map; otherwise, it's `false`. This is typically represented with a Boolean value called `ok`. When looping over a map, you should use the `range` keyword and never rely on the order of the items in it. Go doesn't guarantee the order of items in a map. To ensure no one replies on the order of the elements, Go purposely randomizes the order of them when you range over a map. If you did need to loop over the elements of your map in a specific order, you'd need to use an array or a slice to assist you with that.

Exercise 4.14 – Reading from a map

In this exercise, we're going to read from a map using direct access and a loop. We'll also check to see if a key exists in the map. Let's get started:

1. Create a new folder and add a file named `main.go` to it.

2. In `main.go`, add the package and imports:

```
package main
import (
  "fmt"
  "os"
)
```

3. Create a function that returns a map type with a string key and a string value:

```
func getUsers() map[string]string {
```

4. Define a map type and initialize it with data. Then, return the map type and close the function:

```
return map[string]string{
  "305": "Sue",
  "204": "Bob",
  "631": "Jake",
  "073": "Tracy",
  }
}
```

5.   In this function, we'll accept a string as input. The function will also return a string and a Boolean:

```go
func getUser(id string) (string, bool) {
```

6.   Get a copy of the `users` map from our earlier function:

```go
users := getUsers()
```

7.   Get a value from the `users` maps using the passed-in ID as the key. Capture both the value and the `exists` value:

```go
user, exists := users[id]
```

8.   Return both values and close the function:

```go
return user, exists
}
```

9.   Create a `main` function:

```go
func main() {
```

10. Check that at least one argument gets passed in. If not, exit:

```go
if len(os.Args) < 2 {
    fmt.Println("User ID not passed")
    os.Exit(1)
}
```

11. Capture the passed argument and call the `getUser` function:

```go
userID := os.Args[1]
name, exists := getUser(userID)
```

12. If the key is not found, print a message, and then print all the users using a `range` loop. After that, exit:

```go
if !exists {
    fmt.Printf("Passed user ID (%v) not found.\nUsers:\n",
userID)
    for key, value := range getUsers() {
        fmt.Println("  ID:", key, "Name:", value)
    }
    os.Exit(1)
}
```

13. If everything is okay, print the name we found:

```go
fmt.Println("Name:", name)
}
```

14. Save the file. Then, in the folder you created in *step 1*, run the code using the following command:

```
go run . 123
```

15. Then, run the following command:

```
go run . 305
```

Running the preceding code produces the following output:

```
→ Exercise04.14 git:(main) ✗ go run . 123
Passed user ID (123) not found.
Users:
    ID: 073 Name: Tracy
    ID: 305 Name: Sue
    ID: 204 Name: Bob
    ID: 631 Name: Jake
exit status 1
→ Exercise04.14 git:(main) ✗ go run . 305
Name: Sue
```

Figure 4.8: Output displaying all the users and the name that was found

In this exercise, we learned how we can check to see if a key exists in a map. It may look a little strange coming from other languages that require you to check for the existence of a key before getting the value, not after. This way of doing things does mean there is much less chance of runtime errors. If a zero value is not possible in your domain logic, then you can use that fact to check if a key exists.

We used a `range` loop to print all the users in our map nicely. Your output is probably in a different order to the output shown in the preceding screenshot, which is due to Go randomizing the order of the elements in a map when you use `range`.

Activity 4.02 – Printing a user's name based on user input

It's now your turn to work with maps. We're going to define a map and create logic to print the data in the map based on the key that's passed to your app. The following are the steps for this activity:

1. Create a new Go program.

2. Define a map type with the following key-value pairs:

   Key: 305, *Value*: Sue

   Key: 204, *Value*: Bob

   Key: 631, *Value*: Jake

   Key: 073, *Value*: Tracy

3. Using os.Args, read a key that's been passed in and print the corresponding name; for instance, go run . 073.

4. Correctly handle when no argument gets passed or if the passed argument doesn't match a value in the map type.

5. Print a message to the user with the name in the value.

The expected output is as follows:

```
Hi, Tracy
```

> **Note**
>
> The solution for this activity can be found in the GitHub repository folder for this chapter: https://github.com/PacktPublishing/Go-Programming-From-Beginner-to-Professional-Second-Edition-/tree/main/Chapter04/Activity04.02.

Activity 4.03 – Slicing the week

In this activity, we're going to create a slice and initialize it with some data. Then, we're going to modify that slice using what we've learned about sub-slices. The following are the steps for this activity:

1. Create a new Go program.

2. Create a slice and initialize it with all the days of the week, starting on Monday and ending on Sunday.

3. Change the slice using slice ranges and append it so that the week now starts on Sunday and ends on Saturday.

4. Print the slice to the console.

The expected output is as follows:

```
[Sunday Monday Tuesday Wednesday Thursday Friday Saturday]
```

> **Note**
>
> The solution for this activity can be found in the GitHub repository folder for this chapter: https://github.com/PacktPublishing/Go-Programming-From-Beginner-to-Professional-Second-Edition-/tree/main/Chapter04/Activity04.03.

Deleting elements from a map

If you need to remove an element from a map, you'll need to do something different than you would with an array or a slice. In an array, you can't remove elements since the length's fixed; the best you can do is zero out the value. With a slice, you can zero out, but it's also possible to use a combination of a slice `range` and `append` to cut out one or more elements. With a map, you could zero the value out, but the element still exists, so it causes problems if you're checking whether a key exists in your logic. You can't use slice ranges on a map to cut elements out either.

To remove an element, we need to use the built-in `delete` function. The function signature for `delete`, when used with maps, is `delete(<map>, <key>)`. The `delete` function doesn't return anything, and if a key doesn't exist, nothing happens.

Exercise 4.15 – Deleting an element from a map

In this exercise, we'll define a map and then delete an element from it using user input. Then, we'll print the now possibly smaller map to the console. Let's get started:

1. Create a new folder and add a file named `main.go` to it.

2. In `main.go`, add the package and imports:

```go
package main
import (
    "fmt"
    "os"
)
```

3. We're going to define our `users` map in the package scope:

```go
var users = map[string]string{
    "305": "Sue",
    "204": "Bob",
    "631": "Jake",
    "073": "Tracy",
}
```

4. Create a function that deletes from the `users` map using a passed-in string as the key:

```go
func deleteUser(id string){
    delete(users, id)
}
```

5. In `main`, we'll grab the passed-in `userID` value and print the `users` map to the console:

```go
func main() {
    if len(os.Args) < 2 {
```

```
        fmt.Println("User ID not passed")
        os.Exit(1)
    }
    userID := os.Args[1]
    deleteUser(userID)
    fmt.Println("Users:", users)
}
```

6.   Save the file. Then, in the folder you created in *step 1*, run the code using the following command:

```
go run . 305
```

Running the preceding code produces the following output:

```
Users: map[073:Tracy 204:Bob 631:Jake]
```

In this exercise, we used the built-in `delete` function to totally remove an element from a map. This requirement is unique for maps; you can't use `delete` on arrays or slices.

Activity 4.04 – Removing an element from a slice

Go doesn't have anything built in to remove elements from a slice, but it's possible with the techniques you've learned. In this activity, we're going to set up a slice with some data and one element to remove. Then, you need to work out how to do this. There are many ways to get this done, but can you work out the most compact way?

Here are the steps for this activity:

1.   Create a new Go program.

2.   Create a slice with the following elements in the following order:

```
Good
Good
Bad
Good
Good
```

3.   Write the code to remove the `Bad` element from the slice.

4.   Print the result to the console.

The following is the expected output:

```
[Good Good Good Good]
```

> **Note**
>
> The solution for this activity can be found in the GitHub repository folder for this chapter: `https://github.com/PacktPublishing/Go-Programming-From-Beginner-to-Professional-Second-Edition-/tree/main/Chapter04/Activity04.04`.

Simple custom types

You can create custom types using Go's simple types as a starting point. The notation is `type <name> <type>`. If we were to create an ID type based on a string, this would look like `type id string`. The custom type acts the same as the type you based it on, including getting the same zero value and having the same abilities to compare with other values of the same type. A custom type is not compatible with its base type, but you can convert your custom type back into the type it's based on to allow for interaction.

Exercise 4.16 – Creating a simple custom type

In this exercise, we'll define a map and then delete an element from it using user input and a simple custom type. Then, we'll print the now possibly smaller map to the console. Let's get started:

1. Create a new folder and add a file named `main.go` to it.

2. In `main.go`, add the package and imports:

    ```
    package main
    import "fmt"
    ```

3. Define a custom type called `id` based on the `string` type:

    ```
    type id string
    ```

4. Create a function that returns three `id` instances:

    ```
    func getIDs() (id, id, id) {
    ```

5. For `id1`, we'll initialize it and leave it at its zero value:

    ```
    var id1 id
    ```

6. For `id2`, we'll initialize it using a string literal:

    ```
    var id2 id = "1234-5678"
    ```

7. Finally, for `id3`, we'll initialize it to zero and then set a value separately:

    ```
    var id3 id
    id3 = "1234-5678"
    ```

8. Now, return the `id` instances and close the function:

```
    return id1, id2, id3
}
```

9. In `main`, call our function and do some comparisons:

```
func main() {
    id1, id2, id3 := getIDs()
    fmt.Println("id1 == id2    :", id1 == id2)
    fmt.Println("id2 == id3    :", id2 == id3)
```

10. For this preceding comparison, we'll convert the `id` type back into a string:

```
    fmt.Println("id2 == \"1234-5678\":", string(id2) == "1234-5678")
}
```

11. Save the file. Then, in the folder you created in *step 1*, run the code using the following command:

```
go run .
```

Running the preceding code produces the following output:

```
→  Exercise04.16 git:(main) ✗ go run .
id1 == id2       : false
id2 == id3       : true
id2 == "1234-5678": true
```

Figure 4.9: Output after comparison

In this exercise, we created a custom type called `id`, set data on it, and then compared it with values of the same type and with its base type of `string`.

Simple custom types are a foundational part of modeling the data problems you'll see in the real world. Having types designed to reflect the data you need to work with closely helps keep your code easy to understand and maintain.

Structs

Collections are perfect for grouping values of the same type and purpose together. There is another way of grouping data together in Go for a different purpose. Often, a simple string, number, or Boolean doesn't fully capture the essence of the data you'll have.

For example, for our user map, a user was represented by their unique ID and their first name. That is rarely going to be enough detail to be able to work with user records. The data you could capture about a person is almost infinite, such as their given, middle, and family names. Their preferred prefix and suffix, their date of birth, their height, weight, or where they work can also be captured. It would be possible to store this data in multiple maps, all with the same key, but that is hard to work with and maintain.

The ideal thing to do is to collect all these different bits of data into a single data structure that you can design and control. That's what Go's `struct` type is: it's a custom type that you can name and then specify the field properties and their types.

The notation for structs looks like this:

```
type <name> struct {
  <fieldName1> <type>
  <fieldName2> <type>
  ...
  <fieldNameN> <type>
}
```

Field names must be unique within a struct. You can use any type for a field, including pointers, collections, and other structs.

You can access a field on a struct using the following notation: `<structValue>.<fieldName>`. To set a value, you use this notation: `<structValue>.<fieldName> = <value>`. To read a value, you use the following notation: `value = <structValue>.<fieldName>`.

Structs are the closest thing that Go has to what are called classes in other languages, but structs have purposely been kept stripped down by Go's designers. A key difference is that structs don't have any form of inheritance. The designers of Go feel that inheritance causes more problems than it solves in real-world code.

Once you've defined your custom `struct` type, you can use it to create a value. You have several ways to create values from `struct` types. Let's take a look at them now.

Exercise 4.17 – Creating struct types and values

In this exercise, we're going to define a user struct. We'll define some fields of different types. Then, we'll create some struct values using a few different methods. Let's get started:

1. Create a new folder and add a file named `main.go` to it.

2. In `main.go`, add the package and imports:

```
package main
import "fmt"
```

3. The first thing we'll do is define our `struct` type. You generally do this in the package scope (outside of any function body). We need to give it a name that's unique at the package-level scope:

```
type user struct {
```

4. We'll add some fields of different types and then close the struct definition:

```
name    string
age     int
balance float64
member bool
}
```

5. We'll create a function that returns a slice of our newly defined `struct` type:

```
func getUsers() []user {
```

6. Our first user is initialized using this key-value notation. This notation is the most common form to use when initializing structs:

```
u1 := user{
  name:    "Tracy",
  age:     51,
  balance: 98.43,
  member: true,
}
```

7. When using the key-value notation, the order of the fields doesn't matter, and any you leave out will get a zero value for their type:

```
u2 := user{
  age: 19,
  name: "Nick",
}
```

8. It's possible to initialize a struct with values only. If you do this, all the fields must be present, and their order must match how you defined them in the struct:

```
u3 := user{
  "Bob",
  25,
  0,
  false,
}
```

9. This `var` notation will create a struct where all the fields have zero values:

```
var u4 user
```

10. Now, we can set values on the fields using . and the field name:

```
u4.name = "Sue"
u4.age = 31
u4.member = true
u4.balance = 17.09
```

11. Now, we will return the values wrapped in a slice and close the function:

```
    return []user{u1, u2, u3, u4}
}
```

12. In main, we'll get the slice of users, loop over it, and print it to the console:

```
func main() {
  users := getUsers()
  for i := 0; i < len(users); i++ {
    fmt.Printf("%v: %#v\n", i, users[i])
  }
}
```

13. Save the file. Then, in the folder you created in *step 1*, run the code using the following command:

```
go run .
```

Running the preceding code produces the following output:

```
→ Exercise04.17 git:(main) ✗ go run .
0: main.user{name:"Tracy", age:51, balance:98.43, member:true}
1: main.user{name:"Nick", age:19, balance:0, member:false}
2: main.user{name:"Bob", age:25, balance:0, member:false}
3: main.user{name:"Sue", age:31, balance:17.09, member:true}
```

Figure 4.10: Output as per the new struct

In this exercise, you defined a custom struct type that contained multiple fields, each of a different type. Then, we created values from that struct using a few different methods. Each of these methods is valid and useful in different contexts.

We defined the struct at the package scope, and while it's not typical, you can define struct types in the function scope too. If you do define a struct type in a function, it'll only be valid for use in that function. When defining a type at the package level, it's available for use throughout the package.

It's also possible to define and initialize a struct at the same time. If you do this, you can't reuse the type, but it's still a useful technique. The notation looks like this:

```
type <name> struct {
  <fieldName1> <type>
  <fieldName2> <type>
```

```
   ...
   <fieldNameN> <type>
}{
   <value1>,
   <value2>,
   ...
   <valueN>,
}
```

You can also initialize using the key-value notation, but initializing with only the values is the most common when this is done.

Comparing structs to each other

If all a struct's fields are comparable types, then the struct is also comparable. So, if your struct is made up of `string` and `int` types, then you can compare whole structs to one another. If your struct has a slice in it, then you can't. Go is strongly typed, so you can only compare values of the same type, but with structs, there is a little bit of flexibility. If the struct was defined anonymously and has the same structure as a named struct, then Go allows the comparison.

Exercise 4.18 – Comparing structs to each other

In this exercise, we'll define a comparable struct and create a value with it. We'll also define and create values with anonymous structs that have the same structure as our named struct. Finally, we'll compare them and print the results to the console. Let's get started:

1. Create a new folder and add a file named `main.go` to it:

2. In `main.go`, add the package and imports:

    ```
    package main
    import "fmt"
    ```

3. Let's define a simple, comparable struct:

    ```
    type point struct {
        x int
        y int
    }
    ```

4. Now, we'll create a function that returns two Booleans:

    ```
    func compare() (bool, bool) {
    ```

5. We'll now create our first anonymous struct:

```
point1 := struct {
   x int
   y int
}{
   10,
   10,
}
```

> **Note**
>
> The struct is considered anonymous because the struct type does not have a name. point1 is a variable that contains an instance of the anonymous struct.

6. With the second anonymous struct, we're initializing it to zero and then changing the value after initialization:

```
point2 := struct {
   x int
   y int
}{}
point2.x = 10
point2.y = 5
```

7. The final struct to create uses the named struct type we created previously:

```
point3 := point{10, 10}
```

8. Compare them. Then, return and close the function:

```
   return point1 == point2, point1 == point3
}
```

9. In main, we'll call our function and print the results:

```
func main() {
   a, b := compare()
   fmt.Println("point1 == point2:", a)
   fmt.Println("point1 == point3:", b)
}
```

10. Save the file. Then, in the folder you created in *step 1*, run the code using the following command:

```
go run .
```

Running the preceding code produces the following output:

```
→   Exercise04.18 git:(main) ✗ go run .
point1 == point2: false
point1 == point3: true
```

Figure 4.11: Output comparing structs

In this exercise, we saw that we can work with anonymous struct values in the same way as named `struct` types, including comparing them. With named types, you can only compare structs of the same type. When you compare types in Go, Go compares all the fields to check for a match. Go allows a comparison of these anonymous structs to be made because the field names and types match. Go is a little flexible with comparing structs like this.

Struct composition using embedding

While inheritance is not possible with Go structs, the designers of Go did include an exciting alternative. The alternative is to embed types in `struct` types. Using embedding, you can add fields to a struct from other structs. This composition feature has the effect of letting you add to a struct using other structs as components. Embedding is different than having a field that is a `struct` type. When you embed, the fields from the embedded struct get promoted. Once promoted, a field acts as if it's defined on the target struct.

To embed a struct, you add it like you would a field, but you don't specify a name. To do this, you add a `struct` type name to another struct without giving it a field name, which looks like this:

```
type <name> struct {
  <Type>
}
```

Though not common, you can embed any other type into structs. There is nothing to promote, so to access the embedded type, you access it using the type's name; for example, `<structValue>.<type>`. This way of accessing embedded types by their type name is also true for structs. This means there are two valid ways to work with an embedded struct's fields: `<structValue>.<fieldName>` or `<structValue>.<type>.<fieldName>`. This ability to access a type by its name also means that the type's names must be unique between the embedded types and the root field names. When embedding pointer types, the type's name is the type without the pointer notation, so the name `*<type>` becomes `<type>`. The field is still a pointer, and only the name is different.

When it comes to promotion, if you were to have any overlap with your struct's field names, Go allows you to embed, but the promotion of the overlapping field doesn't happen. You can still access the field by going through the type name path.

You can't use promotion when initializing structs with embedded types. To initialize the data, you must use the embedded type's name.

Exercise 4.19 – Struct embedding and initialization

In this exercise, we'll define some structs and custom types. We'll embed those types into a struct. Let's get started:

1. Create a new folder and add a file named `main.go` to it.

2. In `main.go`, add the package and imports:

   ```
   package main
   import "fmt"
   ```

3. Create a custom `string` type called `name`:

   ```
   type name string
   ```

4. Create a struct called `location` with two `int` fields; that is, x and y:

   ```
   type location struct {
       x int
       y int
   }
   ```

5. Create a `size` struct with two `int` fields; that is, `width` and `height`:

   ```
   type size struct {
       width int
       height int
   }
   ```

6. Create a struct named `dot`. This embeds each of the preceding structs in it:

   ```
   type dot struct {
       name
       location
       size
   }
   ```

7. Create a function that returns a slice of dots:

   ```
   func getDots() []dot {
   ```

8. Our first `dot` instance uses the `var` notation. This will result in all the fields having a zero value:

   ```
   var dot1 dot
   ```

9. With `dot2`, we're also initializing with zero values:

   ```
   dot2 := dot{}
   ```

10. To set the name, we use the type's name as if it were a field:

```
dot2.name = "A"
```

11. For `size` and `location`, we'll use the promoted fields to set their value:

```
dot2.x = 5
dot2.y = 6
dot2.width = 10
dot2.height = 20
```

12. When initializing embedded types, you can't use promotion. For `name`, the result is the same, but for `location` and `size`, you need to put more work into this:

```
dot3 := dot{
  name: "B",
  location: location{
    x: 13,
    y: 27,
  },
  size: size{
    width: 5,
    height: 7,
  },
}
```

13. For `dot4`, we'll use the type names to set data:

```
dot4 := dot{}
dot4.name = "C"
dot4.location.x = 101
dot4.location.y = 209
dot4.size.width = 87
dot4.size.height = 43
```

14. Return all the dots in a slice and then close the function:

```
    return []dot{dot1, dot2, dot3, dot4}
}
```

15. In `main`, call the function. Then, loop over the slice and print it to the console:

```
func main() {
    dots := getDots()
    for i := 0; i < len(dots); i++ {
```

```
        fmt.Printf("dot%v: %#v\n", i+1, dots[i])
    }
}
```

16. Save the file. Then, in the folder you created in *step 1*, run the code using the following command:

```
go run .
```

Running the preceding code produces the following output:

```
→  Exercise04.19 git:(main) ✗ go run .
dot1: main.dot{name:"", location:main.location{x:0, y:0}, size:main.size{width:0, height:0}}
dot2: main.dot{name:"A", location:main.location{x:5, y:6}, size:main.size{width:10, height:20}}
dot3: main.dot{name:"B", location:main.location{x:13, y:27}, size:main.size{width:5, height:7}}
dot4: main.dot{name:"C", location:main.location{x:101, y:209}, size:main.size{width:87, height:43}}
```

Figure 4.12: Output after struct embedding and initialization

In this exercise, we were able to define a complex struct by embedding other types into it. Embedding allows you to reuse common structures by reducing the duplicated code but still giving your struct a flat API.

We may not see much embedding in real-world Go code. It does come up, but the complexity and exception mean that Go developers prefer to have the other structs as named fields.

Activity 4.05 – Creating a locale checker

In this activity, we're going to create a locale validator. A locale is an internationalization and localization concept that is a combination of both a language and a country or region. We'll create a struct that represents a locale. After, we're going to define a list of locales our code supports. Then, we'll read in some locale code from the command line and print out whether our code accepts that locale or not.

Here are the steps for this activity:

1. Create a new Go program.

2. Define a struct with a field for language and a separate field for country or region.

3. Create a collection to hold the local definitions for at least five locales; for instance, en_US, en_CN, fr_CN, fr_FR, and ru_RU.

4. Read in the locale from the command line; for example, using os.Args. Be sure to have error checking and validation working.

5. Load the passed locale string into a new locale struct.

6. Use that struct to check whether the passed struct is supported.

7. Print a message to the console stating whether the locale is supported or not.

The expected output is as follows:

```
→  Activity04.05 git:(main) x go run . en_CN
Locale passed is supported
→  Activity04.05 git:(main) x go run . en_ZH
Locale not supported: en_ZH
exit status 1
```

Figure 4.13: Expected output

> **Note**
>
> The solution for this activity can be found in the GitHub repository folder for this chapter:
> `https://github.com/PacktPublishing/Go-Programming-From-Beginner-to-Professional-Second-Edition-/tree/main/Chapter04/Activity04.05`.

Type conversions

There are times when your types won't match up, and with Go's strict type system, if types are not the same, they can't interact with one another. In these cases, you have two options. If the two types are compatible, you can do type conversion – that is, you can create a new value by changing one type to another. The notation to do this is `<value>.(<type>)`. When working with strings, we used this notation to cast a string to a slice of runes or bytes and back again. This works because a string is a special type that stores the string's data as a slice of bytes.

It's important to note that not all type conversions preserve the original value. When working with numeric type conversion, the numbers can change from their original value. If you convert from a large `int` type (for example, `int64`) into a smaller `int` type (for example, `int8`), it causes the number to overflow. If you were to convert from an unsigned `int` type (for example, `uint64`) into a signed `int` type (for example, `int64`), this overflow happens because unsigned `int` types can store a higher number than a signed `int` type. This overflowing is the same when converting an `int` type into a `float` type since the `float` type splits its storage space between whole numbers and decimals. When converting from a `float` type to an `int` type, the decimal part is truncated.

It's still perfectly reasonable to do these types of lossy conversions, and they happen all the time in real-world code. If you know that the data you're dealing with doesn't cross these thresholds, then there's no need to worry.

Go does its best to guess at the types that need conversion. This is called implicit type conversion. For example, `math.MaxInt8` is an `int` type, and if you try to assign it to a number other than an `int` type, Go does an implicit type conversion for you.

Exercise 4.20 – Numeric type conversions

In this exercise, we'll do some numeric type conversions and intentionally cause some data issues. Let's get started:

1. Create a new folder and add a file named `main.go` to it.

2. In `main.go`, add the package and imports:

    ```
    package main
    import (
      "fmt"
      "math"
    )
    ```

3. Create a function that returns a string:

    ```
    func convert() string{
    ```

4. Define some variables to do our work. Go is doing an implicit conversion of the `math.MaxInt8` int into an `int8` type:

    ```
    var i8 int8 = math.MaxInt8
    i := 128
    f64 := 3.14
    ```

5. Here, we'll convert from a smaller `int` type into a larger `int` type. This is always a safe operation:

    ```
    m := fmt.Sprintf("int8  = %v > int64  = %v\n", i8, int64(i8))
    ```

6. Now, we'll convert from an `int` type that's 1 above `int8`'s maximum size. This will cause an overflow to `int8`'s minimum size:

    ```
    m += fmt.Sprintf("int  = %v > int8  = %v\n", i, int8(i))
    ```

7. Next, we'll convert our `int8` type into a `float64` type. This doesn't cause an overflow and the data is unchanged:

    ```
    m += fmt.Sprintf("int8  = %v > float32 = %v\n", i8,
    float64(i8))
    ```

8. Here, we'll convert a `float` type into an `int` type. All the decimal data is lost but the whole number is kept as is:

    ```
    m += fmt.Sprintf("float64 = %v > int  = %v\n", f64, int(f64))
    ```

9. Return the message and then close the function:

```
      return m
}
```

10. In the main() function, call the function and print it to the console:

```
func main() {
   fmt.Print(convert())
}
```

11. Save the file. Then, in the folder you created in *step 1*, run the code using the following command:

```
go run .
```

Running the preceding code produces the following output:

```
→ Exercise04.20 git:(main) x go run .
int8    = 127  > int64   = 127
int     = 128  > int8    = -128
int8    = 127  > float32 = 127
float64 = 3.14 > int     = 3
```

Figure 4.14: Output after conversion

Type assertions and interface{}

We've used fmt.Print and its siblings a great deal for writing our code, but how does a function such as fmt.Print take any type of value when Go is a strongly typed language? Let's take a look at the actual Go standard library code for fmt.Print:

```
// Print formats using the default formats for its operands and writes
to standard output.
// Spaces are added between operands when neither is a string.
// It returns the number of bytes written and any write error
encountered.
func Print(a ...interface{}) (n int, err error) {
   return Fprint(os.Stdout, a...)
}
```

I hope you can see that looking at Go's source code is not scary – it's a great way to see how you should do things, and I recommend looking at it whenever you are curious about how they do something properly using idiomatic Go.

By looking at this code, we can see that fmt.Print has a variadic of the interface{} type. We'll cover interfaces in more detail later, but for now, what you need to know is that an interface in

Go describes which functions a type must have to conform to that interface. Interfaces in Go don't describe fields and don't describe a type's core value, such as being a string or a number. In Go, any type can have functions, including strings and numbers. What `interface{}` is describing is a type with no functions. What use is a value with no function, no fields, and no core value? None, but it's still a value, and it can still be passed around. This interface is not setting the type of the value but controlling which values it will allow for a variable with that interface. Which types in Go conform to `interface{}`? All of them! Any of Go's types or any custom type you create conform to `interface{}`, and this is how `fmt.Print` can accept any type. You can also use `interface{}` in your code to achieve the same result.

The Go 1.18 release included an alias of the `interface{}` type called any. Since they are equivalent in usage, any is interchangeable with `interface{}` in the earlier code example that we saw at the beginning of this section.

Once you have your variable that conforms to `interface{}`, what can you do with it? Even if the underlying value of your `interface{}` variable has functions, fields, or a core value, you can't use them because Go is enforcing the interface's contract, which is why this is still all type-safe.

To unlock the capabilities of the value masked by `interface{}` or any, we need to use type assertion. The notation for type assertion is `<value>.(<type>)`. Type assertion results in a value of the type that was requested and, optionally, a Boolean value regarding whether it was successful or not. This looks like `<value> := <value>.(<type>)` or `<value>, <ok> := <value>.(type)`. If you leave the Boolean value out and the type assertion fails, Go raises a panic.

Go doesn't remove anything from a value when you place it in an `interface{}` type or any variable. What happens is the Go compiler prevents you from using it because it's not able to perform its type-safety checks at compile time. Using type assertion is your instruction to Go that you want to unlock the value. When you do type assertion, Go performs the type-safety checks it would have done at compile time and at runtime, and those checks may fail. It's then your responsibility to deal with the type-safety checks failing. Type assertions are a feature that causes runtime errors and panics, which means you must be extra careful around them.

Exercise 4.21 – Type assertions

In this exercise, we will perform some type assertions and ensure that all the safety checks are in place when we do so. Let's get started:

1. Create a new folder and add a file named `main.go` to it.

2. In `main.go`, add the package and imports:

```
package main
import (
    "errors"
```

```
    "fmt"
)
```

3. Create a function that accepts an `interface{}` type and returns a string and an error:

```
func doubler(v interface{}) (string, error) {
```

4. First, we'll check to see if our argument is an `int` type, and if it is, we'll multiply it by 2 and return it:

```
if i, ok := v.(int); ok {
    return fmt.Sprint(i * 2), nil
}
```

5. Here, we'll check if it's a string, and if it is, we'll concatenate it to itself and return it:

```
if s, ok := v.(string); ok {
    return s + s, nil
}
```

6. If we don't get any matches, return an error. Then, close the function:

```
    return "", errors.New("unsupported type passed")
}
```

7. In `main`, call `doubler` with a variety of data and print the results to the console:

```
func main() {
    res, _ := doubler(5)
    fmt.Println("5 :", res)
    res, _ = doubler("yum")
    fmt.Println("yum :", res)
    _, err := doubler(true)
    fmt.Println("true:", err)
}
```

8. Save the file. Then, in the folder you created in *step 1*, run the code using the following command:

```
go run .
```

Running the preceding code produces the following output:

```
→  Exercise04.21 git:(main) ✗ go run .
5  : 10
yum : yumyum
true: unsupported type passed
```

Figure 4.15: Output showing matches

The combination of interface{}, any, and type assertions allows you to overcome Go's strict type controls, in turn allowing you to create functions that can work with any type of variable. The challenge is that you lose the protection that Go gives you at compile time for type safety. It's still possible to be safe, but the responsibility is yours now – do it wrong, and you'll get a nasty runtime error.

Type switch

If we wanted to expand our `doubler` function to include all `int` types, we'd end up with a lot of duplicated logic. Go has an excellent way of dealing with more complex type assertion situations, known as a type switch. Here's what it looks like:

```
switch <value> := <value>.(type) {
case <type>:
  <statement>
case <type>, <type>:
  <statement>
default:
  <statement>
}
```

The type switch only runs your logic if it matches the type you're looking for, and it sets the value to that type. You can match on more than one type in a case but Go can't change the type of the value for you, so you'll still need to do type assertion. One of the things that makes this a type switch and not an expression switch is the `<value>.(type)` notation. You can only use that as part of a type switch. Something else that's unique to type switches is that you can't use a `fallthrough` statement.

Exercise 4.22 – Type switch

In this exercise, we'll update our `doubler` function to use a type switch and expand its abilities to deal with more types. Let's get started:

1. Create a new folder and add a file named `main.go` to it.

2. In `main.go`, add the package and imports:

    ```
    package main
    import (
      "errors"
      "fmt"
    )
    ```

3. Create our function, which takes a single `interface{}` argument and returns a string and an error:

    ```
    func doubler(v interface{}) (string, error) {
    ```

4. Create a type switch using our argument:

```
switch t := v.(type) {
```

5. For `string` and `bool`, since we're only matching on one type, we don't need to do any extra safety checks and can work with the value directly:

```
case string:
 return t + t, nil
case bool:
 if t {
   return "truetrue", nil
 }
 return "falsefalse", nil
```

6. For the floats, we're matching on more than one type. This means we need to do type assertion to be able to work with the value:

```
case float32, float64:
 if f, ok := t.(float64); ok {
   return fmt.Sprint(f * 2), nil
 }
```

7. If this type assertion were to fail, we'd panic, but we can rely on the logic that only `float32` can work directly with the result of type assertion:

```
return fmt.Sprint(t.(float32) * 2), nil
```

8. Match all the `int` and `uint` types. We've been able to remove lots of code here by not needing to do the type-safety checks ourselves:

```
case int:
 return fmt.Sprint(t * 2), nil
case int8:
 return fmt.Sprint(t * 2), nil
case int16:
 return fmt.Sprint(t * 2), nil
case int32:
 return fmt.Sprint(t * 2), nil
case int64:
 return fmt.Sprint(t * 2), nil
case uint:
 return fmt.Sprint(t * 2), nil
case uint8:
 return fmt.Sprint(t * 2), nil
case uint16:
```

```
    return fmt.Sprint(t * 2), nil
  case uint32:
    return fmt.Sprint(t * 2), nil
  case uint64:
    return fmt.Sprint(t * 2), nil
```

9. We'll use `default` to return an error. Then, we'll close the `switch` statement and function:

```
  default:
    return "", errors.New("unsupported type passed")
  }
}
```

10. In the `main()` function, call our function with even more data and print the results to the console:

```
func main() {
  res, _ := doubler(-5)
  fmt.Println("-5 :", res)
  res, _ = doubler(5)
  fmt.Println("5 :", res)
  res, _ = doubler("yum")
  fmt.Println("yum :", res)
  res, _ = doubler(true)
  fmt.Println("true:", res)
  res, _ = doubler(float32(3.14))
  fmt.Println("3.14:", res)
}
```

11. Save the file. Then, in the folder you created in *step 1*, run the code using the following command:

```
go run .
```

Running the preceding code produces the following output:

```
→  Exercise04.22 git:(main) ✗ go run .
-5  : -10
5   : 10
yum : yumyum
true: truetrue
3.14: 6.28
```

Figure 4.16: Output after calling functions

In this exercise, we used a type switch to build a complex type-assertion scenario. Using the type switch still gives us full control of the type assertions but also lets us simplify the type-safety logic when we don't need that level of control.

Activity 4.06 – Type checker

In this activity, you're going to write some logic that has a slice or different types of data. These data types are as follows:

- `int`
- `float`
- `string`
- `bool`
- `struct`

Create a function that accepts a value of any type. The function returns a string with the name of the type:

- For `int`, `int32`, and `int64`, it returns `int`
- For all floats, it returns `float`
- For a string, it returns `string`
- For a Boolean, it returns `bool`
- For anything else, it returns `unknown`
- Loop all the data by passing each one to your function.
- Then, print the data and its type name to the console.

The expected output is as follows:

```
 ~/src/Th…op/Ch…04/Activity04.06    go run .
1 is int
3.14 is float
hello is string
true is bool
{} is unknown
```

Figure 4.17: Expected output

> **Note**
>
> The solution for this activity can be found in the GitHub repository folder for this chapter: `https://github.com/PacktPublishing/Go-Programming-From-Beginner-to-Professional-Second-Edition-/tree/main/Chapter04/Activity04.06`. Think about the different ways you could implement this solution depending on which Go version you are using; for example, solving this with Go 1.18's any or `interface{}` type alias.

Summary

In this chapter, we got into advanced uses of variables and types in Go. Real-world code gets complicated quickly because the real world is complicated. Being able to model the data accurately and keep that data logically organized in your code helps reduce the complexity of your code to a minimum.

You now know how to group similar data, either in a fixed-length ordered list using an array, in a dynamic-length ordered list using a slice, or in a key-value hash using a map.

We learned to go beyond Go's core types and start to create custom types based either directly on the core types or by creating a struct, which is a collection of other types held in a single type and value.

There are times when you'll have type mismatches, so Go gives us the ability to convert compatible types so that they can interact in a type-safe way.

Go also lets us break free of its type-safety rules and gives us full control. By using type assertions, we can accept any type using the magic of `interface{}` and `any`, and then get those types back.

In the next chapter, we'll explore how to group our logic into reusable components and attach them to our custom types to make our code more straightforward and easier to maintain and build with.

Part 2: Components

As scripts evolve, they can become unwieldy and difficult to manage. To maintain control over your codebase, it's essential to break it down into smaller, more manageable components. This not only enhances code organization but also facilitates code reuse.

This section delves into the realm of componentization, empowering you to create modular and reusable code structures.

This part has the following chapters:

- *Chapter 5, Functions – Reduce, Reuse, and Recycle*
- *Chapter 6, Don't Panic! Handle Your Errors*
- *Chapter 7, Interfaces*
- *Chapter 8, Generic Algorithm Superpowers*

5

Functions – Reduce, Reuse, and Recycle

Overview

This chapter will describe the various ways in which you can reduce, reuse, and recycle code. It will include a large overview of functions so that you can include parts of a function, such as defining the function, function identifiers, parameter lists, return types, and the function body. We will also look at best practices when designing code so that you can make it reusable and flexible and make your functional logic small and purposeful.

By the end of this chapter, you will be able to see how easy Go makes it to reduce, reuse, and recycle code. This will include how to describe a function and the different parts that make up a function and evaluate the scope of variables with functions. You will know how to create and call a function, as well as how to utilize variadic and anonymous functions and create closures for various constructs. You will also know how to use functions as parameters and return values and how to use `defer` statements with functions. Finally, you will know how to separate similar functionality into logical sections by using multiple files and directories in your projects.

Technical requirements

For this chapter, you will need to install the Go programming language. This chapter's code can be found in this book's GitHub repository: `https://github.com/PacktPublishing/Go-Programming-From-Beginner-to-Professional-Second-Edition-/tree/main/Chapter05`.

Introduction

The ability to write code in a way that is easy to maintain and iterate on is a vital skill for an engineer. This means crafting it so that it may be reused, easily expanded upon, and understood by others. Go makes it easy to keep code clean and readable, and separate logical chunks together. The first major way of writing code that is easy to reduce, reuse, and recycle is through the use of functions.

Functions are a core part of many languages and Go is no exception. A function is a section of code that has been declared to perform a task. Go functions can have zero or more inputs and outputs. One feature that sets Go apart from other programming languages is the multiple return values; most programming languages are limited to one return value. This leads into Go's flexibility and the ability for developers to continuously write adaptable code.

In the following section, we will see some features of Go functions that differ from other languages, such as returning multiple types. We will also see that Go has support for first-class functions. This means that Go can assign a variable to a function, pass a function as an argument, and have a function as a return type for a function. We will show how functions can be used to break up complex parts into smaller parts.

Functions in Go are considered first-class citizens and higher-order functions. First-class citizens are the functions that are assigned to a variable. Higher-order functions are functions that can take a function as an argument. The rich features of Go functions empower them to be used in various segments in the following ways:

- To pass a function as an argument to another function

- To return a function as a value from a function

- To use functions as a type

- To use functions as closures

- To use anonymous functions

- To assign functions to a variable

We will be looking at each of these features since they are all supported in Go.

Functions

Functions are a critical part of Go and we should understand their place. Let's examine some of the reasons for using functions:

- **Breaking up a complex task**: Functions are used to perform a task, but if that task is complicated, it should be broken down into smaller tasks. Functions can be used for small tasks to solve a bigger problem. Smaller tasks are more manageable, and using a function to solve specific tasks will make the entire code base easier to maintain.

- **Reducing code**: A good indication that you should use a function is when you see similar code repeating throughout your program. When you have duplicate code, it increases the difficulty of maintenance. If you have one change to make, you will have multiple instances where your code needs to change.

- **Reusability**: Once you have defined your function, you can use it repeatedly. It can also be used by other programmers. This sharing of functions will reduce lines of code and save time by allowing you to not have to reinvent the wheel. There are a couple of guidelines we should follow when we design functions:

  - **Single responsibility**: A function should perform one task. For example, a single function should not calculate the distance between two points and estimate the time to travel between those two points. There should be a function for each of those tasks. This allows for better testing of that function and easier maintenance. It is difficult to narrow a function to perform a single task, so do not get discouraged if you do not get it right the first time. Even seasoned programmers struggle with assigning a single responsibility to a function, and responsibilities can shift over time.

  - **Small in size**: Functions should not span over hundreds of lines of code. This is an indication that the code needs some refactoring. When we have large functions, it's more likely that the single responsibility principle will be violated. A good rule of thumb is trying to limit the function size to approximately 25 lines of code; however, that's not a hard-and-fast rule. The benefit of keeping the code concise is that it reduces the complexity of debugging a large function. It also makes writing unit tests with better code coverage easier.

Parts of a function

Let's look at the different components that are involved in defining a function. The following is the typical layout of a function:

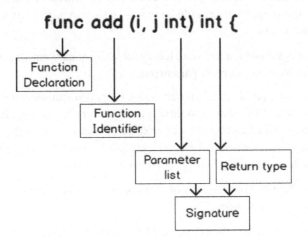

Figure 5.1: Different parts of a function

The different parts of a function are described here:

- `func`: In Go, the function declaration starts with the `func` keyword.

- **Identifier**: This is also referred to as the function name. It is idiomatic in Go to use camelCase for the function name. camelCase is the practice of having the first letter of the function name in lowercase and the first letter of each word following in uppercase. Examples of function names that follow this convention include `calculateTax`, `totalSum`, and `fetchId`.

  The identifier should be something descriptive that makes the code easy to read and makes the purpose of the function easy to understand. The identifier is not required. You can have a function with no name; this is known as an anonymous function. Anonymous functions will be discussed in detail later in this chapter.

> **Note**
>
> When the first letter of the function name is in lowercase, then the function can't be exported outside of a package. This means it's private and cannot be called from outside the package. It can only be called within the package.
>
> Keep this in mind when you use the camelCase naming convention. If you want your function to be exportable, the first letter of the function name must be capitalized. This will mean other packages can consume and use your function if it is exported and starts with a capital letter.

- **Parameter list**: Parameters are input values to a function. A parameter is data that is required by the function to help solve the task of the function. Parameters are defined as follows: name, type. An example parameter list could be (`name string`, `age int`). Parameters are local variables of the function.

  Parameters are optional for a function. It is possible to not have any parameters for a function. A function can have zero or more parameters.

  When two or more parameters have the same type, you can use what is called shorthand parameter notation. This removes specifying the same type for each parameter. For instance, if your parameters are (`firstName string`, `lastName string`), they can be shortened to (`firstName, lastName string`). This reduces the verbosity of the parameter inputs and increases the readability of the function parameter list.

- **Return types**: Return types are a list of data types, such as Boolean, string, map, or another function that can be returned.

  In the context of declaring a function, we refer to these types as return types. However, in the context of calling a function, they are called return values.

  Return types are the output of the function. Often, they are the result of the arguments provided to the function. They are optional. Most programming languages return a single type; in Go, you can return multiple types.

- **Function body**: The function body is the coding statements between curly braces, { }.

  The statements in the function are what determine what the function does. The function code is the code that is being used to perform the task that the function was created to accomplish.

  If return types were defined, then a `return` statement is required in the function body. The `return` statement causes the function to immediately stop and return the value types listed after the `return` statement. The types in the return type list and the `return` statement must match.

  In the function body, there can be multiple `return` statements. You often see this in the case of errors, where you might return different values than, say if the function processed logic successfully.

- **Function signature**: Though not listed in the preceding code snippet, a function signature is a term that references the input parameters combined with the return types. Both of those units make up a function signature.

  Often, when you define the function signature when it is being used by others, you want to strive to not make changes to it as this can adversely impact your code and the code of others.

We will be diving deep into each of the parts of a function as we progress through this chapter. These parts of a function will become easier to understand through the following discussion and will become clearer as we go through this chapter.

The checkNumbers function

Now that we have looked at the different parts of the function, let's see how these parts work with various examples. Let's start with a simple approach with a `checkNumbers` function. The `checkNumbers` function prints out various messages based on some math results of whether a number is even or odd. The rules perform one of the actions based on the number given:

- If the number is even, print Even
- If the number is odd, print Odd

The following is the code snippet to achieve this output:

```
func checkNumbers() {
    for i := 1; i <= 30; i++ {
        if i%2 == 0 {
            fmt.Println("Even")
        } else {
            fmt.Println("Odd")
        }
    }
}
```

Let's look at the code in sections:

```
func checkNumbers() {
```

- `func`, as you may recall, is the keyword to declare a function. This informs Go that the following piece of code is going to be a function.
- `checkNumbers` is the name of our function. It is idiomatic (standard practice) in Go to use a camelCase name.
- `()`, the parenthesis following the name of our function, is empty: our current implementation of the `checkNumbers` game does not require any input parameters. If it *did* require input parameters, they would be contained within parentheses.
- The space between the parameter list, `()`, and the opening brace would be the return type. Our current implementation does not require a return type.
- Regarding `{`, unlike other programming languages that you may know, Go requires that the opening curly brace is on the same line as the function declaration. If the opening brace is not on the same line as the function signature when you attempt to run the program, you will get an error:

```
for i := 1; i <= 30; i++ {
```

The preceding line is a `for` loop that increments the `i` variable from 1 to 30:

```
if i%2 == 0 {
```

> **Note**
>
> `%` is a modulus operator; it gives the remainder of the two integers being divided. Using our function, if `i` is evenly divisible by 2, then it will print out the word `"Even"`; otherwise, it will print "Odd".
>
> As we become more familiar with Go concepts and language syntax, the explanation of the code will exclude items that we would otherwise be going over multiple times.

We have now defined our function. It has a specific task we want it to perform, but it doesn't do any good if we do not execute the function. So, how do we execute a function? We must call our function. When we call a function, we are telling our program to execute the function. We will be calling our function inside the `main()` function.

Functions can call other functions. When this occurs, control is given to the function that was called. After the called function has returned data or reached the ending curly brace, `}`, control is given back to the caller. Let's look at an example to understand this better:

```
func main() {
    fmt.Println("Main is in control")
```

```
    checkNumbers()
    fmt.Println("Back to main")
}
```

- fmt.Println("Main is in control"): This print statement is for demonstration purposes. It shows that we are in the main() function.

- checkNumbers(): We are now calling the function inside the main() function. Even though there are no parameters for our function, the parentheses are still required, and control of the program is given to the checkNumbers() function. After the checkNumbers() function completes, control is then given back to the main() function.

- fmt.Println("Back to main"): The print statement is for demonstration purposes to show that control has been given back to the main() function.

The output will be as follows:

```
Main is in control
Even
Odd
Even
Odd
Even
Odd
Even
Odd
Even
Odd
Even
Odd
Even
Odd
Even
Odd
Even
Odd
Even
Odd
Even
Odd
Even
Odd
Even
Odd
Even
Odd
Even
Odd
Even
Back to main
```

Figure 5.2: Output for checkNumbers

> **Note**
>
> The parentheses following the checkNumbers function are still required, even though there are no input parameters. If they are omitted, the Go compiler will generate an error that states checkNumbers was evaluated but not used. This is a common error.

Exercise 5.01 – creating a function to print salesperson expectation ratings from the number of items sold

In this exercise, we will be creating a function that will not have any parameters or return types. The function will iterate over a map and print the name and number of items sold on the map. It will also print a statement based on how the salesperson performed based on their sales. The following steps will help you with the solution:

1. Use the IDE of your choice.

2. Create a new file and save it as main.go.

3. Enter the following code in main.go. The first function that main will call is itemsSold(); it does not have any parameters and has no return values:

```
package main
import (
    "fmt"
)
func main() {
    itemsSold()
}
```

4. Next, we'll define our function for logic regarding items sold:

```
func itemsSold() {
```

5. In the itemsSold() function, initialize a map that will have a key-value pair of string, int. The map will hold a name(string) and the number of items(int) sold by the individual. The name is the key for the map. We assign various names to number of items sold:

```
items := make(map[string]int)
items["John"] = 41
items["Celina"] = 109
items["Micah"] = 24
```

6. We iterate over the items map and assign k to key(name) and v to value(items):

```
for k, v := range items{
```

7. We print out `Name` and the number of sold `items`:

```
fmt.Printf("%s sold %d items and ", k, v)
```

8. Depending on the value of `v`(`items`), we will determine the statement we print:

```
if v < 40 {
  fmt.Println("is below expectations.")
} else if v > 40 && v <= 100 {
  fmt.Println("meets expectations.")
} else if v > 100 {
  fmt.Println("exceeded expectations.")
  }
 }
}
```

9. Open your terminal and navigate to the code's directory.

10. Run `go build` and then run the executable.

The expected output is as follows:

```
John sold 41 items and meets expectations.
Celina sold 109 items and exceeded expectations.
Micah sold 24 items and is below expectations.
```

In this exercise, we saw some of the fundamental parts of a function. We demonstrated how to declare a function using the `func` keyword, followed by how to give our function an identifier or name, such as `itemsSold()`. Then, we added code to the function body. In the next few sections, we will expand on these core parts of the function and learn how to pass data into a function using parameters.

> **Note**
>
> It is best to type the code into an IDE. The benefit is that if you type something incorrectly, you will see the error message and can perform some debugging to solve the problem.

Parameters

Parameters define what arguments can be passed to our function. Functions can have zero or more parameters. Even though Go allows us to define multiple parameters, we should take care not to have a huge parameter list; that would make the code harder to read. It may also be an indication that the function is doing more than one specific task. If that is the case, we should refactor the function. Take, for example, the following code snippet:

```
func calculateSalary(lastName string, firstName string, age int, state
string, country string, hoursWorked int, hourlyRate, isEmployee bool)
```

```
{
// code
}
```

The preceding code is an example of a function whose parameter list is bloated. The parameter list should pertain only to the single responsibility of the function. We should only define the parameters that are needed to solve the specific problem that the function is built for.

Parameters are the input types that our function will use to perform its task. Function parameters are local to the function, meaning they are only available to that function. They are not available outside of the context of the function. Also, the order of the parameters must match the parameter types in the correct sequence.

Correct:

```
func main() {
    greeting("Cayden", 45)
}
func greeting(name string, age int) {
    fmt.Printf("%s is %d", name, age)
}
```

The output when the correct parameter matches would be as follows:

```
Cayden is 45
```

Incorrect:

```
func main() {
    greeting(45,"Cayden")
}
func greeting(name string, age int) {
    fmt.Printf("%s is %d",name, age)
}
```

The output looks as follows:

```
prog.go:5:11: cannot use 45 (type int) as type string in argument to greeting
prog.go:5:14: cannot use "Cayden" (type string) as type int in argument to greeting

Go build failed.
```

Figure 5.3: Output for incorrect parameter matching

In the incorrect version of the code, we are calling the greeting() function with the age argument, which is of the integer type, when the parameter is of the string type. The sequence of your arguments must match the sequence of the parameter input list.

Additionally, users would want to have more control over the data the code iterates over. Going back to the checkNumbers example, the current implementation only does 1 to 30. Users may need to work on different number ranges, so we need a way to decide the ending range of the loop. We can change our checkNumbers function so that it accepts an input parameter. This would meet the needs of our user:

```
func main() {
  checkNumbers(10)
}
func checkNumbers(end int) {
  for i := 1; i <= end; i++ {
    if i%2 == 0 {
      fmt.Println("Even")
    } else {
      fmt.Println("Odd")
    }
  }
}
```

The preceding code snippet can be explained as follows:

- For checkNumbers(10) in the main() function, we pass 10 as an argument to our checkNumbers function
- For checkNumbers(end int), end is the name of our parameter and it is of the int type
- Now, our function will only iterate up to the value of our end parameter; in this example, it will iterate to 10

The difference between an argument and a parameter

This is a good time to discuss the difference between an argument and a parameter. When you are defining your function, using our example, checkNumbers(end int) is called a parameter. When you call a function, such as checkNumbers(10), 10 is called the argument. Also, the argument and parameter names do not need to match.

Functions in Go can also have more than one parameter defined. We need to add another parameter to our checkNumbers function to accommodate this enhancement:

```
func main() {
  start:= 10
  end:= 20
  checkNumbers(start, end)
}
func checkNumbers(start int, end int) {
```

```
    for i := start; i <= end; i++ {
        // code omitted for brevity
    }
}
```

The preceding code snippet can be explained as follows:

- Regarding checkNumbers(start, end), we are now passing two arguments to the checkNumbers function. When there are multiple arguments, they must be separated by a comma.

- Regarding func checkNumbers(start int, end int), when multiple parameters are defined in a function, they are separated by commas, following the convention of name type, name type, name type, and so on.

Our checkNumbers parameters are more verbose than what is necessary. When we have multiple input parameters of the same type, we can separate the input name by a comma followed by the type. This is referred to as shorthand parameter notation. See the following example of using shorthand parameter notation:

```
func main() {
    start, end := 10,20
    checkNumbers(start, end)
}
func checkNumbers(start, end int) {
    // code...
}
```

The preceding code snippet can be explained as follows:

- There is no change to the caller when using shorthand parameter notation.

- Regarding checkNumbers(start, end int), start and end are of the int type. Nothing needs to change in the body of the function to accommodate the shorthand parameter notation.

Exercise 5.02 – mapping index values to column headers

The function that we are going to create will be taking a slice of column headers from a CSV file. It will print out a map of an index value of the headers we are interested in:

1. Open the IDE of your choice.

2. Create a new file and save it as main.go.

3. Enter the following code in `main.go`:

```go
package main
import (
  "fmt"
  "strings"
)
func main() {
   hdr :=[]string{"empid", "employee", "address", "hours worked",
"hourly rate", "manager"}
   csvHdrCol(hdr)
   hdr2 :=[]string{"employee", "empid", "hours worked",
"address", "manager", "hourly rate"}
   csvHdrCol(hdr2)
}
func csvHdrCol(header []string) {
        csvHeadersToColumnIndex:= make(map[int]string)
```

First, we assign a variable to a key-value pair of `int` and `string`. `key(int)` will be the index of our `header(string)` column. The index will map to a column header.

4. We range over `header` to process each string that is in the slice. In the following `for` loop, `i` will store the index, and `v` will be assigned to each value in the header:

```go
for i, v := range header {
```

5. For each string, remove any trailing spaces in front of and after the string. In general, we should always assume that our data may have some erroneous characters:

```go
v = strings.TrimSpace(v)
```

6. In our `switch` statement, we lower all the casing for exact matches. As you may recall, Go is a case-sensitive language. We need to ensure that the casing is the same for matching purposes. When our code finds the header, it sets the index value for the header in the map:

```go
switch strings.ToLower(v) {
case "employee":
        csvHeadersToColumnIndex[i] = v
case "hours worked":
        csvHeadersToColumnIndex[i] = v
case "hourly rate":
        csvHeadersToColumnIndex[i] = v

}
}
```

7. Typically, we would not print out the results. We should return csvHeadersToColumnIndex, but since we have not gone over how to return a value, we will print it for now:

```
fmt.Println(csvHeadersToColumnIndex)
}
```

8. Open your terminal and navigate to the code's directory.

9. Run go build and run the executable.

The expected output is as follows:

```
Map[1:employee 3:hours worked 4: hourly rate]
Map[0:employee 2:hours worked 5: hourly rate]
```

In this exercise, we saw how to accept data into a function: by defining a parameter for our function. The callers of our function were able to pass arguments to the function. We will continue to discover various abilities that functions in Go can provide. So far, we have seen how to get data into our function. In the next section, we will see how to get data out of our function.

Function variable scope

When designing functions, we need to consider the variable scope. The scope of a variable determines where the variable is accessible or visible to the different parts of the application. Variables declared inside the function are considered local variables. This means that they are only accessible to the code within the body of the function. You cannot access variables from outside of the function. The calling function does not have access to variables inside the called function. The input parameter's scope is the same as the local variable's scope to the function.

Variables declared in the calling function are scoped to that function. This means that the variables are local to the function and those variables are not accessible outside of the function. Our function cannot reach into the calling function's variables. To gain access to those variables, they must be passed into our function as input parameters:

```
func main() {
   m:= "Uncle Bob"
   greeting()
}
func greeting() {
   fmt.Printf("Greeting %s", m)
}
```

Here's the output:

```
prog.go:10:28: undefined: m

Go build failed.
```

Figure 5.4: Error output for the m variable being undefined

The previous code snippet will result in an error in func greeting() that states that m is undefined. That is because the m variable is declared inside main(). The greeting() function does not have access to the m variable. For it to have access, the m variable must be passed to the greeting() function as an input parameter:

```
func main() {
    m:= "Uncle Bob"
    greeting(m)
    fmt.Printf("Hi from main: %s", s)
}
func greeting(name string) {
    fmt.Printf("Greeting %s", name)
    s := "Slacker"
    fmt.Printf("Greeting %s", s)
}
```

Here's the output:

```
prog.go:7:33: undefined: s

Go build failed.
```

Figure 5.5: Error output for the s variable being undefined

The previous code snippet will result in an error in func main(). The error will state that s is undefined. This is because the s variable is declared in the greeting() function. The main() function does not have access to the s variable. The s variable is only visible to code inside the function body of greeting().

These are just some considerations that we need to keep in mind when we are declaring and accessing variables. It is important to understand the scope of the variables inside a function concerning the variables declared outside of a function. It can cause some confusion when you are trying to access variables but you are not scoped to the context that you are trying to access. The examples in this chapter should help you in understanding the scope of variables.

Return values

So far, the functions that we have created do not have any return values. Functions typically accept inputs, perform some action on those inputs, and then return the results of those actions. Functions in some programming languages return only one value. Go allows you to return multiple values from a function. This is one of the features of Go functions that distinguishes it from other programming languages.

Exercise 5.03 – creating a checkNumbers function with return values

In this exercise, we are going to make some enhancements to our checkNumbers function. We are going to change it so that it accepts only an integer. We will leave the onus on the caller to perform the looping if they desire to do so. Also, we are going to have two returns. The first will be the number provided and the corresponding text indicating if the number is Even or Odd. The following steps will help you with the solution:

1. Open the IDE of your choice.

2. Create a new file in a different directory and save it as main.go.

3. In the main() function, assign variables to the return values of our function. The n, and s variables correspond to the values being returned from our function, which are int and string, respectively:

    ```
    func main() {
        for i := 0; i <= 15; i++ {
        num, result := checkNumbers(i)
        fmt.Printf("Results:   %d %s\n", num, result)
        }
    }
    ```

4. The checkNumbers function now returns two values; the first being an int value, followed by a string value:

    ```
    func checkNumbers(i int) (int, string) {
        switch {
    ```

5. Simplify the if{}else{} statements by replacing them with switch statements. As you are writing code, you should look for ways to simplify things and make the code more readable. case i%2 ==0 is equivalent to our previous if i%2 == 0 statements. Instead of our previous fmt.Println() statements, replace them with return. The return statement will immediately stop the execution of the function and return the results to the caller:

    ```
    case i%2 == 0:
      return i, "Even"
    default:
    ```

```
            return i, "Odd"
        }
    }
```

The expected output is as follows:

```
        Results:  0 Even
        Results:  1 Odd
        Results:  2 Even
        Results:  3 Odd
        Results:  4 Even
        Results:  5 Odd
        Results:  6 Even
        Results:  7 Odd
        Results:  8 Even
        Results:  9 Odd
        Results: 10 Even
        Results: 11 Odd
        Results: 12 Even
        Results: 13 Odd
        Results: 14 Even
        Results: 15 Odd
```

Figure 5.6: Output for the checkNumbers function with return values

In this exercise, we saw how we can return multiple values from a function. We were able to assign variables to the multiple return values from the function. We also noticed that the variables that were assigned to the function matched the order of the return values. In the following section, we will learn that in the body of the function, we can perform naked returns, where we do not need to specify the variable being returned in our return statement.

We also saw a switch statement that was used to clean up the if{}else{} logic. We had a case for even numbers and a default "catch-all" case where odd numbers would fall. The default case is just as it sounds and will be the default case if a case is not before it.

Activity 5.01 – calculating the working hours of employees

In this activity, we'll be creating a function that will calculate the working hours of employees for a week. Then, we'll use this to calculate the payable salary amount. The developer struct has a field called Individual that is of the Employee type. The developer struct keeps track of the HourlyRate value that they charge and how many hours they work each day. The following steps will help you to reach the solution:

1. Create an Employee type that has the following fields: Id as int, FirstName as string, and LastName as string.

2. Create a developer type that has the following fields: Individual as Employee, HourlyRate as int, and WorkWeek as [7]int.

3. Create an enum type (enums are types that contain only a limited number of fixed values) for the seven days of the week. This will be of the `Weekday int` type with a constant declaration for each day of the week.

4. Create a pointer receiver method called `LogHours` for `Developer` that will take the `WeekDay` type and `int` type as input. Assign the hours worked that day to the `Developer` workweek slice.

5. Create a method that is a pointer receiver called `HoursWorked()`. This method will return the total hours that have been worked.

6. In the `main()` function, initialize and create a variable of the `Developer` type.

7. In the `LogHours` method, call the method for two days (such as Monday and Tuesday).

8. Print the hours for the two days of the previous step.

9. Next, print the results of the `HoursWorked` method.

The following is the expected output:

```
Hours worked on Monday:    8
Hours worked on Tuesday:   10

Hours worked this week:    18
```

> **Note**
>
> The solution for this activity can be found in the GitHub repository folder for this chapter: `https://github.com/PacktPublishing/Go-Programming-From-Beginner-to-Professional-Second-Edition-/tree/main/Chapter05/Activity05.01`

This activity aims to demonstrate the ability to break problems down into manageable tasks to be implemented by functions, such that each of our functions has a single responsibility. `LogHours` is responsible for assigning the hours worked for each day. `HoursWorked` uses the values that were assigned in `LogHours` to display the hours worked each day. We used return types from our functions to display the data. This exercise demonstrates utilizing functions correctly to provide a solution to a problem.

Naked returns

> **Note**
>
> Functions that have return values must have a return statement as the last statement in the function. If you omit the return statement, the Go compiler will give you an error stating "missing return at the end of the function."
>
> Typically, when a function returns two types, the second type is an `error`. We have not gone over errors yet, so we won't be demonstrating them in these examples. It is good to know that, in Go, it is idiomatic for the second return type to be of the `error` type.

Go also allows you to ignore a variable being returned. For example, say we are not interested in the `int` value that is being returned from our `checkNumbers` function. In Go, we can use what is called a blank identifier, which allows us to ignore values in an assignment:

```
_, err := file.Read(bytes)
```

For example, when reading a file, we might not be concerned about the number of bytes read. So, in that case, we can ignore the value being returned by using the blank identifier, `_`. When extra data is being returned from a function that does not provide any information that is needed by our program, such as the reading of a file, it is a good candidate for ignoring the return:

> **Note**
>
> As you will discover later, many functions return an error as the second return value. You should not ignore return values from functions that are errors. Ignoring an error returned by a function could result in unexpected behavior. Error return values should be handled appropriately.

```
func main() {
  for i := 0; i <= 15; i++ {
    _, result := checkNumbers(i)
    fmt.Printf("Results: %s\n", result)
  }
}
```

In the preceding example, we used the blank identifier, `_`, to ignore the `int` value being returned:

```
    _, result := checkNumbers(i)
```

You must always have a placeholder for the values being returned when assigning values from a function. When performing an assignment, the placeholders must match the number of return values from the function. `_` and `result` are the placeholders for the return values of `int` and `string`.

Go also has a feature that allows you to name your returns. If you use this feature, it can make your code more readable, as well as self-documenting. If you name your return variables, they are under the same constraints as the local variables, as discussed in the previous section. By naming your returns, you are creating local variables in the function. You can then assign values to those return variables, just as you do with input parameters:

```
func greeting() (name string, age int) {
    name = "John"
    age = 21
    return name, age
}
```

In the preceding code, (name string, age int) are named returns. They are now local variables to the function.

Since name and age are local variables that were declared in the return list of the function, you can now assign values to them. They can be treated as local variables. In the return statement, specify the return values. If you do not specify the variable name in the return, it is called a *naked return*:

```
func greeting() (name string, age int) {
    name = "John"
    age = 21
    return
}
```

Consider the preceding code block. This code is the same as before with the exception that the return value does not name the variables to return. The return statement will return the variables that are named in the return list.

One of the disadvantages of naked returns is that it can cause confusion when reading code. To avoid confusion and the possibility of other issues, it is recommended that you avoid using the naked returns feature as it can make it difficult to follow the variable that is to be returned. There can also be issues with shadowing when using naked returns:

```
func message() (message string, err error) {
    message = "hi"
    if message == "hi"{
        err := fmt.Errorf("say bye\n")
        return
    }
    return
}
```

The preceding code will result in the following error:

```
prog.go:15:7: err is shadowed during return
```

Figure 5.7: Output of shadowing with naked returns

This is because the `err` variable is named in `return` and is initialized in an `if` statement. Recall that variables that are initialized within curly braces, such as `for` loops, `if` statements, and `switch` statements, are scoped to that context, meaning that they are only visible and accessible within those curly braces.

Exercise 5.04 – mapping a CSV index to a column header with return values

In *Exercise 5.02 – mapping index values to column headers*, we only printed the results of the index to the column header. In this exercise, we are going to return the map as the result. The map that's being returned is the index-to-column header mapping. The following steps will help you with the solution:

1. Open the IDE of your choice.

2. Open the file from the previous column header exercise called `main.go`.

3. Enter the following code in `main.go`:

```
package main
import (
    "fmt"
    "strings"
)
```

4. Next, in the `main()` function, define the headers for the columns. First, we will assign a variable to a key-value pair of `int` and `string`. `key(int)` will be the index of our `header(string)` column. The index will map to a column header:

```
func main() {
    hdr := []string{"empid", "employee", "address", "hours
worked", "hourly rate", "manager"}
    result := csvHdrCol(hdr)
    fmt.Println("Result: ")
    fmt.Println(result)
    fmt.Println()
    hdr2 := []string{"employee", "empid", "hours worked",
"address", "manager", "hourly rate"}
    result2 := csvHdrCol(hdr2)
    fmt.Println("Result2: ")
    fmt.Println(result2)
```

```
        fmt.Println()
    }
    func csvHdrCol(hdr []string) map[int]string {
        csvIdxToCol := make(map[int]string)
```

5. We use `range` over `header` to process each string that is in the slice:

```
    for i, v := range hdr {
```

6. For each string, we remove any trailing spaces in front of and after the string. In general, we should always assume that our data may have some erroneous characters:

```
    v = strings.TrimSpace(v)
```

7. In our `switch` statement, we lower all the casing for exact matches. As you may recall, Go is a case-sensitive language. We need to ensure the casing is the same for matching purposes. When our code finds the header, it sets the index value for the header in the map:

```
    switch strings.ToLower(v) {
        case "employee":
          csvIdxToCol[i] = v
        case "hours worked":
          csvIdxToCol[i] = v
        case "hourly rate":
          csvIdxToCol[i] = v
        }
    }
    return csvIdxToCol
    }
```

8. Open a terminal and navigate to the code's directory.

9. Run `go build` and run the executable.

The expected output for return values is as follows:

```
Result1:
Map[1:employee 3:hours worked 4: hourly rate]
Result2:
Map[0:employee 2:hours worked 5: hourly rate]
```

In this exercise, we saw a real-world example of mapping a CSV index to column headers. We used a function to solve this complex problem. We were able to have the function have a single return value of the map type. In the next section, we are going to see how functions can accept a variable number of argument values within a single argument.

Variadic functions

A variadic function is a function that accepts a variable number of argument values. It is good to use a variadic function when the number of arguments of a specified type is unknown:

```
func f(parameterName ...Type)
```

The preceding function is an example of what a variadic function looks like. The three dots (...) in front of the type are called a *pack operator*. The pack operator is what makes it a variadic function. It tells Go to store all the arguments of Type in parameterName. The variadic variable can accept zero or more variables as the argument:

```
func main() {
    nums(99, 100)
    nums(200)
    nums()
}
func nums(i ...int) {
    fmt.Println(i)
}
```

The nums function is a variadic function that accepts an int type. As stated previously, you can pass zero or more arguments of the type. If there is more than one value, you separate them with a comma, as in nums(99, 100). If there is only one argument to pass, you only pass that argument, as in nums(200). If there isn't an argument to pass, you can leave it empty, as in nums().

Variadic functions can have other parameters. However, if your function requires multiple parameters, the variadic parameter must be the last in the function. Also, there can only be one variadic variable per function. The following function is incorrect and will result in an error at compile time as the variadic variable is not the last parameter of the function.

Incorrect function:

```
package main
import "fmt"
func main() {
    nums(99, 100, "James")
}
func nums(i ...int, str person) {
    fmt.Println(str)
    fmt.Println(i)
}
```

The expected output is as follows:

```
./prog.go:8:11: syntax error: cannot use ... with non-final parameter i
```

Figure 5.8: Variadic syntax error output

Correct function:

```
package main
import "fmt"
func main() {
  nums("James", 99, 100)
}
func nums(str string, i ...int) {
  fmt.Println(str)
  fmt.Println(i)
}
```

The output will look as follows:

```
James
[99 100]
```

You may have guessed by now that the actual type of Type inside the function is a slice. The function takes the arguments being passed in and converts them into the new slice being specified. For example, if the variadic type is int, then once you are inside the function, Go converts that variadic int type into a slice of integers:

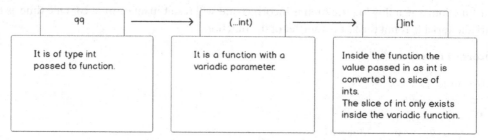

Figure 5.9: Converting a variadic int into a slice of integers

Let's make some tweaks to this example by having the variadic function take in integer values:

```
package main
import "fmt"
func main() {
  nums(99, 100)
```

```
}
func nums(i ...int) {
  fmt.Println(i)
  fmt.Printf("%T\n", i)
  fmt.Printf("Len: %d\n", len(i))
  fmt.Printf("Cap: %d\n", cap(i))
}
```

The variadic function's output is as follows:

```
[99 100]
[] int
Len: 2
Cap: 2
```

The nums() function shows that the variadic type of i is a slice of integers. Once in the function, i will be a slice of integers. The variadic type has a length and capacity, which is to be expected for a slice. In the following code snippet, we will try to pass a slice of integers to a variadic function, nums():

```
package main
import "fmt"
func main() {
  i := []int{ 5, 10, 15}
  nums(i)
}
func nums(i ...int) {
  fmt.Println(i)
}
```

The expected output is as follows:

```
./prog.go:7:6: cannot use i (type []int) as type int in argument to nums
```

Figure 5.10: Variadic function error

Why didn't this code snippet work? We just proved that the variadic variable inside the function is of the slice type. The reason is that the function expects a list of arguments of the int type to be converted into a slice. Variadic functions work by converting the arguments that are passed into a slice of the type being specified. However, Go has a mechanism for passing a slice to a variadic function. For this, we need to use the unpack operator; it is three dots (...). When you call a variadic function and you want to pass a slice as an argument to a variadic parameter, you need to place the three dots before the variable:

```
func main() {
  i := []int{ 5, 10, 15}
```

```
    nums(i...)
}
func nums(i ...int) {
    fmt.Println(i)
}
```

The difference between this version of the function and the previous is the calling code to the function, nums. The three dots that are put after the i variable are a slice of integers. This allows a slice to be passed to the variadic function.

Exercise 5.05 – summing numbers

In this exercise, we are going to sum up a variable number of arguments. We will pass the arguments as a list of arguments and as a slice. The return value will be an int type – that is, the sum of the values we passed to the function. The following steps will help you with the solution:

1.　Open the IDE of your choice.

2.　Create a new file in a new directory and save it as main.go.

3.　Enter the following code in main.go:

```
package main
import (
    "fmt"
)
func main() {
    i := []int{ 5, 10, 15}
    fmt.Println(sum(5, 4))
    fmt.Println(sum(i...))
}
```

4.　The sum function accepts a variadic argument of the int type. Since it gets converted into a slice, we can range over the values and return the sum of all the values that get passed:

```
func sum(nums ...int) int {
    total := 0
    for _, num := range nums {
        total += num
    }
    return total
}
```

5.　Open a terminal and navigate to the code's directory.

6.　Run go build and run the executable.

The expected output for summing numbers is as follows:

```
9
30
```

In this exercise, we saw that by using a variadic parameter, we can accept an unknown number of arguments. Our function allows us to sum up any number of integers. We can see that variadic parameters can be utilized to solve specific problems where the number of values of the same type being passed as an argument is unknown. In the next section, we are going to look at how to create a function without a name and assign a function to a variable.

Anonymous functions

So far, we have been using named functions. As you may recall, named functions are functions that have an identifier or a function name. Anonymous functions, also referred to as function literals, are functions that do not have a function name, hence the name "anonymous functions." An anonymous function is declared in a similar way to how a named function is declared. The only difference with the declaration is that the name for the function is omitted. Anonymous functions can do whatever a normal function in Go does, including accepting arguments and returning values. Anonymous functions can also be declared within another function.

In this section, we will be introducing the fundamentals of anonymous functions and some of their basic uses. Later, you will see how anonymous functions can be fully utilized. Anonymous functions are used for (and in conjunction with) the following:

- Closure implementations
- `defer` statements
- Defining a code block to be used with a goroutine
- Defining a function for one-time use
- Passing a function to another function

    The following is a basic declaration for an anonymous function:

    ```
    func main() {
      func() {
        fmt.Println("Greeting")
      }()
    }
    ```

Let's take a closer look:

- Notice that we are declaring a function inside another function. As with named functions, you must start with the `func` keyword to declare a function.

- Following the `func` keyword would normally be the name of the function, but with anonymous functions, there is no function name. Instead, there are empty parentheses.

- The empty parentheses following the func keyword are where the function's parameters would be defined for the function.

- Next is the open curly brace, {, which starts the function body.

- The function body is only a one-liner; it will print "Greeting".

- The closing curly brace, }, denotes the end of the function.

- The last set of parentheses is called the execution parentheses. These parentheses invoke the anonymous function. The function will execute immediately. Later, we will see how to execute an anonymous function at a later location within the function.

You can also pass arguments to an anonymous function. To be able to pass arguments to an anonymous function, they must be supplied in the execution parentheses:

```
func main() {
    message := "Greeting"
    func(str string) {
        fmt.Println(str)
    }(message)
}
```

Here, we have the following:

- func (str string): The anonymous function being declared has an input parameter of the string type.

- } (message): The argument message that's being passed to the execution parentheses.

We have been executing anonymous functions as they are declared, but there are other ways to execute anonymous functions. You can also save the anonymous function to a variable. This leads to a different set of opportunities that we will look at in this chapter:

```
func main() {
    f := func() {
        fmt.Println("Executing an anonymous function using a variable")
    }
    fmt.Println("Line after anonymous function declaration")
    f()
}
```

Let's take a closer look:

- We are assigning the f variable to our anonymous function.

- f is now of the func() type.

- f can now be used to invoke the anonymous function, in a fashion similar to that for a named function. You must include () after the f variable to execute the function.

Exercise 5.06 – creating an anonymous function to calculate the square root of a number

Anonymous functions are great for small snippets of code that you want to execute within a function. Here, we are going to create an anonymous function that is going to have an argument passed to it. It will then calculate the square root. The following steps will help you with the solution:

1.   Use the IDE of your choice.

2.   Create a new file and save it as main.go.

3.   Enter the following code in main.go. We are assigning our x variable to our anonymous function. Our anonymous function takes a parameter, (i int). It also returns a value of int:

```go
package main
import (
  "fmt"
)
func main() {
   j := 9
   x := func(i int) int {
     return i * i
   }
```

4.   Notice that the last curly brace does not have () to execute the function. We call our anonymous function using x(j):

```go
   fmt.Printf("The square of %d is %d\n", j, x(j))
 }
```

5.   Open a terminal and navigate to the code's directory.

6.   Run go build and run the executable.

The expected output is as follows:

```
The square of 9 is 81
```

In this exercise, we saw how to assign a variable to a function and later call that function by using the variable that was assigned to it. We saw that when we need a small function that might not be reusable in our program, we can create an anonymous function and assign it to a variable. In the next section, we are going to expand the use of anonymous functions to closures.

Closures

So far, we have introduced anonymous function syntax using some basic examples. Now that we have a fundamental understanding of how anonymous functions work, we will look at how we can use this powerful concept.

Closures are a form of anonymous functions. Regular functions cannot reference variables outside of themselves; however, an anonymous function can reference variables external to their definition. A closure can use variables declared at the same level as the anonymous function's declaration. These variables do not need to be passed as parameters. The anonymous function has access to these variables when it is called:

```
func main() {
  i := 0
  incrementor := func() int {
    i +=1
    return i
  }
  fmt.Println(incrementor())
  fmt.Println(incrementor())
  i +=10
  fmt.Println(incrementor())
}
```

Code synopsis:

1. We initialize a variable in the `main()` function called `i` and set it to `0`.

2. We assign `incrementor` to our anonymous function.

3. The anonymous function increments `i` and returns it. Notice that our function does not have any input parameters.

4. Then, we print the results of `incrementor` twice and get 1 and 2.

5. Notice that, outside our function, we increment `i` by `10`. This is a problem. We want `i` to be isolated and for it not to change as this is not the desired behavior. When we print the results of `incrementor` again, it will be 12. We want it to be 3. We will correct this in our next example.

One problem with the previous example that we noticed is that any code in the main function has access to `i`. As we saw in the example, `i` can be accessed and changed outside of our function. This is not the desired behavior; we want the incrementor to be the only one to change that value. In other words, we want `i` to be protected from other functions changing it. The only function that should be changing is our anonymous function when we call it:

```
func main() {
  increment := incrementor()
```

```
  fmt.Println(increment())
  fmt.Println(increment())
}
func incrementor() func() int {
  i := 0
  return func() int {
    i += 1
    return i
  }
}
```

Code synopsis:

1. We declared a function called `incrementor()`. This function has a return type of `func()` `int`.

2. Using `i := 0`, we initialize our variable at the level of the `incrementor()` function; this is similar to what we did in the previous example, except it was at the `main()` function level and anyone at that level had access to `i`. Only the `incrementor()` function has access to the `i` variable with this implementation.

3. We are returning our anonymous function, `func()` `int`, which increments the `i` variable.

4. In the `main()` function, `increment := incrementor()` assigns a variable to `func()` `int` that gets returned. It is important to note that `incrementor()` only gets executed once here. In our `main()` function, it is no longer being referenced or executed.

5. `increment()` is of the `func()` `int` type. Each call to `increment()` runs the anonymous function code. It is referencing the `i` variable, even after `incrementor()` has been executed.

The preceding example demonstrated how we can protect our variable by wrapping it with an anonymous function, thereby restricting access to updating the variable only through invoking the anonymous function itself. This is shown through the expected output, where we've incremented `i` twice, as follows:

```
1
2
```

Exercise 5.07 – creating a closure function to decrement a counter

In this exercise, we are going to create a closure that decrements from a given starting value. We will combine what we have learned about passing an argument to an anonymous function and use that knowledge with a closure. The following steps will help you with the solution:

1. Open the IDE of your choice.

2. Create a new file in a new directory and save it as `main.go`.

3. Enter the following code in main.go:

```
func main() {import "fmt"
    counter := 4
```

4. We will look at the decrement function first. It takes an argument of the int type and has a return value of func() int. In previous examples, the variable was declared inside the function but before the anonymous function. In this exercise, we have it as an input parameter:

```
x:= decrement(counter)
    fmt.Println(x())
    fmt.Println(x())
    fmt.Println(x())
    fmt.Println(x())
}
```

5. We decrement i by one inside the anonymous function:

```
func decrement(i int) func() int {
```

6. In the main() function, we initialize a variable counter to be used as our starting integer to be decremented:

```
return func() int {
```

7. Here, we have x:= decrement(counter); x is assigned to func() int. Each call to x() runs the anonymous function:

```
I--
        return i
    }
}
```

8. Open a terminal and navigate to the code's directory.

9. Run go build and run the executable.

The expected output for the decrement counter is as follows:

```
3
2
1
0
```

In this exercise, we saw that closures have access to variables that are external to them. This allowed our anonymous function to make changes to the variable that a normal function would not be able to make. In the next section, we are going to look at how functions can be passed as arguments to another function.

Function types

As we have seen so far, Go has rich feature support for functions. In Go, functions are types too, just like `int`, `string`, and `bool` are types. This means we can pass functions as arguments to other functions, functions can be returned from a function, and functions can be assigned to variables. We can even define our own function types. A function's type signature defines the types of its input parameters and return values. For a function to be of the type of another function, it must have the exact signature of the type 'unction that is declared. Let's examine a few function types:

```
type message func()
```

The preceding code snippet creates a new function type called `message`. It has no input parameters and does not have any return types.

Let's examine another one:

```
type calc func(int, int) string
```

The preceding code snippet creates a new function type called `calc`. It accepts two arguments of the `int` type and its return value is of the `string` type.

Now that we have a fundamental understanding of function types, we can write some code to demonstrate their uses:

```
package main
import (
   "fmt"
)
type calc func(int, int) string
func main() {
   calculator(add, 5, 6)
}
func add(i, j int) string {
   result := i + j
   return fmt.Sprintf("Added %d + %d = %d", i, j, result)
}
func calculator(f calc, i, j int) {
   fmt.Println(f(i, j))
}
```

Let's look at the code by the line:

```
type calc func(int, int) string
```

`type calc` declares `calc` to be of the `func` type, determining that it takes two integers as arguments and returns a string:

```
func add(i, j int) string {
    result := i + j
    return fmt.Sprintf("Added %d + %d = %d", i, j, result)
}
```

`func add(i,j int) string` has the same signature as the `calc` type. It takes two integers as arguments and returns a string stating "Adding i + j = result." Functions can be passed to other functions, just like any other type in Go:

```
func calculator(f calc, i, j int) {
    fmt.Println(f(i, j))
}
```

`func calculator(f calc, i, j int)` accepts `calc` as input. The `calc` type, as you may remember, is a function type that has input parameters of `int` and a return type of `string`. Anything that matches that signature can be passed to the function. The `func calculator` function returns the result of the function of the `calc` type.

In the `main` function, we call `calculator(add, 5, 6)`. We are passing it the `add` function. `add` satisfies the signature of the `calc func` type.

Figure 5.11 summarizes each of the preceding functions and how they relate to each other. This figure shows how `func add` is of the `func calc` type, which then allows it to be passed as an argument to `func calculator`:

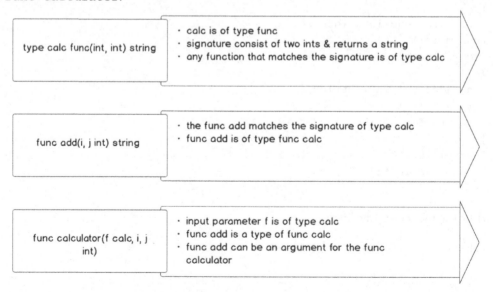

Figure 5.11: Function types and uses

We have just seen how to create a function type and pass it as an argument to a function. It is not that far of a stretch to pass a function as a parameter to another function. We will change our previous example slightly to reflect passing a function as a parameter:

```go
func main() {
    calculator(add, 5, 6)
    calculator(subtract, 10, 5)
}
func calculator(f func(int, int) int, i, j int) {
    fmt.Println(f(i, j))
}
func add(i, j int) int {
    return i + j
}
func subtract(i, j int) int {
    return i - j
}
```

Let's take a closer look:

- We modified the add function signature so that it returns an int type instead of a string type.

- We added a second function called subtract. Note that its function signature is the same as that of the add function. The subtract function simply returns the result of subtracting two numbers:

  ```go
  func calculator(f func(int, int) int, i, j int) {
      fmt.Println(f(i, j))
  }
  ```

- Here, we have calculator(f func(int, int) int, i, j int). The calculator function now has an input parameter of the func type. The input parameter, f, is a function that accepts two integers and returns an int type. Any function that satisfies the signature can be passed to the function.

- In the main() function, calculator is called twice: once with the add function and some integer values being passed and once with the subtract function being passed as an argument with some integer values.

The expected output is as follows:

```
11
5
```

The ability to pass functions as a type is a powerful feature where you can pass functions to other functions if their signatures match the passed-to function's input parameter. An integer type for a function can be any value if it is an integer. The same goes for passing functions: a function can be any value if it is the correct type.

A function can also be returned from another function. We saw this when using anonymous functions combined with closures. Here, we will take a brief look since we saw this syntax previously:

```
package main
import "fmt"
func main() {
   v:= square(9)
   fmt.Println(v())
   fmt.Printf("Type of v: %T",v)
}
func square(x int) func() int {
   f := func() int {
      return x * x
   }
   return f
}
```

Returning a function looks as follows:

```
81
Type of v: func() int
```

- Here, we have `square(x int) func() int`. The `square` function accepts an `int` type as an argument and returns a function type that returns an `int` type:

  ```
  func square(x int) func() int {
     f := func() int {
        return x * x
     }
     return f
  }
  ```

- In the `square` body, we assign a variable, `f`, to an anonymous function that returns the square value of the input parameter, `x`.

- The `return` statement for the `square` function returns an anonymous function that is of the `func() int` type.

- v is assigned to the return of the `square` function. As you may recall, the return value is of the `func() int` type.

- v has been assigned the `func () int` type; however, it has not been invoked. We will invoke it inside the `print` statement.

- Finally, we have `fmt.Printf("Type of v: %T",v)`. This statement just prints out the type for v, which is `func() int`.

Exercise 5.08 – creating various functions to calculate salary

In this exercise, we are going to be creating several functions. We need the ability to calculate the salary of a developer and a manager. We want this solution to be extensible for the future possibilities of other salaries to be calculated. We will be creating functions to calculate the developer's and manager's salary. Then, we will create another function that will take the previously mentioned function as an input parameter. The following steps will help you with the solution:

1. Use the IDE of your choice.

2. Create a new file in a new directory and save it as `main.go`.

3. Enter the following code in `main.go`:

```go
package main
import "fmt"
func main() {
    devSalary := salary(50, 2080, developerSalary)
    bossSalary := salary(150000, 25000, managerSalary)
    fmt.Printf("Boss salary: %d\n", bossSalary)
    fmt.Printf("Developer salary: %d\n", devSalary)
}
```

4. The `salary` function accepts a function that accepts two integers as arguments and returns an int `type`. So, any function that matches that signature can be passed as an argument to the `salary` function:

```go
func salary(x, y int, f func(int, int) int) int{
```

5. In the body of the `salary()` function, pay, is assigned the value that gets returned from the f function. It passes x and y as parameters to the f parameter:

```go
    pay := f(x, y)
    return pay
}
```

6. Notice that the `managerSalary` and `developerSalary` signatures are identical and that they match the `f` function for `salary`. This means that both `managerSalary` and `developerSalary` can be passed as `func(int, int) int`:

```
func managerSalary(baseSalary, bonus int) int {
   return baseSalary + bonus
}
```

7. `devSalary` and `bossSalary` get assigned to the results of the `salary` function. Since `developerSalary` and `managerSalary` satisfy the signature of `func(int, int) int`, they can both be passed in as arguments:

```
func developerSalary(hourlyRate, hoursWorked int) int {
   return hourlyRate * hoursWorked
}
```

8. Open a terminal and navigate to the code's directory.

9. Run `go build` and run the executable.

The expected output is as follows:

```
Boss salary: 175000
Developer salary: 104000
```

In this exercise, we saw how a function type can be a parameter for another function. This allows a function to be an argument to another function. This exercise showed how our code can be simplified by having one `salary` function. If, in the future, we need to calculate the salary for a tester position, we would only need to create a function that matches the function type for `salary` and pass it as an argument. The flexibility that this gives is that we do not have to change our `salary` function's implementation. In the next section, we are going to see how we can change the execution flow of a function, specifically after the function returns.

defer

The `defer` statement defers the execution of a function until the surrounding function returns. Let's try to explain this a bit better. Inside a function, you have a `defer` statement in front of a function that you are calling. Essentially, that function will execute right before the function you are currently inside completes. Still confused? Perhaps an example will make this concept a little clearer:

```
package main
import "fmt"
func main() {
   defer done()
   fmt.Println("Main: Start")
```

```
    fmt.Println("Main: End")
}
func done() {
    fmt.Println("Now I am done")
}
```

The output for the `defer` example is as follows:

```
Main: Start
Main: End
Now I am done
```

Inside the `main()` function, we have a deferred function, `defer done()`. Notice that the `done()` function has no new or special syntax. It just does a simple print to the console.

Next, we have two `print` statements. The results are interesting. The two `print` statements in the `main()` function print first. Even though the deferred function was first in `main()`, it printed last. Isn't that interesting? Its ordering in the `main()` function did not dictate its order of execution.

These deferred functions are commonly used for performing "cleanup" activities. This includes releasing resources, closing files, closing database connections, and removing `configuration\ temp` files created by a program. `defer` functions are also used to recover from a panic; this will be discussed later in this book.

Using the `defer` statement is not limited to just named functions – you can also utilize the `defer` statement with anonymous functions. Taking our previous code snippet, let's turn it into a deferred call with an anonymous function:

```
package main
import "fmt"
func main() {
    defer func() {
        fmt.Println("Now I am done")
    }()
    fmt.Println("Main: Start")
    fmt.Println("Main: End")
}
```

Let's take a closer look:

- There's not much that has changed from the previous code. We took the code that was in the `done` function and created a deferred anonymous function.

- The `defer` statement is placed before the `func()` keyword. Our function has no function name. As you may recall, a function without a name is an anonymous function.

- The results are the same as those from the previous example. Its readability, to a certain extent, is easier than having the deferred function declared as a named function, as in the previous example.

It is also possible and common to have multiple `defer` statements in a function. However, they may not execute in the order that you expect. When using `defer` statements in front of functions, the execution follows the order of **First In, Last Out (FILO)**. Think of it as how you would stack plates. The first plate to start the stack will have a second plate placed on it, the second plate will have a third plate placed on it, and so on. The first plate to get taken off the stack is the last plate that was placed on the stack. The first plate that was placed to start the stack will be the last plate to come off the stack. Let's look at an example that declares multiple anonymous functions with the `defer` statement placed in front of them:

```go
package main
import "fmt"
func main() {
  defer func() {
    fmt.Println("I was declared first.")
  }()
  defer func() {
    fmt.Println("I was declared second.")
  }()
  defer func() {
    fmt.Println("I was declared third.")
  }()
  f1 := func() {
    fmt.Println("Main: Start")
  }
  f2 := func() {
    fmt.Println("Main: End")
  }
  f1()
  f2()
}
```

The multiple `defer` output looks as follows:

```
Main: Start
Main: End
I was declared third.
I was declared second.
I was declared first.
```

Let's take a closer look:

- The first three anonymous functions have their execution deferred.

- We declare f1 and f2 to be of the func() type. These two functions are anonymous.

- As you can see, f1() and f2() executed as expected, but the order of the multiple defer statements executed in the reverse order of how they were declared in the code. The first defer statement was the last to execute and the last defer statement was the first to execute.

Careful consideration must be given when using defer statements. A situation that you should consider is when you use defer statements in conjunction with variables. When a variable is passed to a deferred function, the variable's value at that time is what will be used in the deferred function. If that variable is changed after the deferred function, it will not be reflected when the deferred function runs:

```go
func main() {
   age := 25
   name := "John"
   defer personAge(name, age)
   age *= 2
   fmt.Printf("Age double %d.\n", age)
}
func personAge(name string, i int) {
    fmt.Printf("%s is %d.\n", name, i)
}
```

The output would be as follows:

```
Age double 50.
John is 25.
```

Let's take a closer look:

- age := 25: We initialize the age variable to 25 before the defer function.

- name := "John": We initialize the name variable to "John" before the defer function.

- defer personAge(name, age): We state that the function is going to be deferred.

- age *= 2: We double the age after the deferred function. Then, we print the current value of age doubled.

- personAge(name string, i int): This is the function that is deferred; it only prints out the person and age.

- The results show the value of age (25) after it has been doubled in the main function.

- When the execution of the program reaches the line that has `defer personAge(name, age)`, the value of age is 25. Before the `main()` function completes, the deferred function runs and the value of age is still 25. Variables used in the deferred function are the values before it was deferred, regardless of what happens after it.

Activity 5.02 – calculating the payable amount for employees based on working hours

This activity is based on the previous activity. We will keep the same functionality, but we will be adding three additional features. In this version of the application, we would like to give the employee the ability to track their hours throughout the day without having logged them yet. This will allow the employees to keep better track of their hours before they log them at the end of the day. We will also enhance the application so that it calculates the employee's pay. The application will calculate their pay for any overtime they've worked. The application will also print out details of how many hours were worked each day:

1. Create a function called `nonLoggedHours() func(int) int`. Each time this function is called, it will calculate the hours of the employee that have not been logged. You will be using a closure inside the function.

2. Create a method called `PayDay() (int,bool)`. This method will calculate the weekly pay. It needs to consider overtime pay. The method will pay twice the hourly rate for hours greater than 40. The function will return `int` as the weekly pay and `bool` if the pay is overtime pay. The Boolean value will be true if the employee worked more than 40 hours and false if they worked less than 40 hours.

3. Create a method called `PayDetails()`. This method will print each day and the hours worked that day by the employee. It will print the total hours for the week, the pay for the week, and if the pay contains overtime pay.

4. Inside the main function, initialize a variable of the `Developer` type. Assign a variable to `nonLoggedHours`. Print the variable that was assigned to `nonLoggedHours` with values of 2, 3, and 5.

5. Also, in the `main()` function, log the hours for the following days: Monday 8, Tuesday 10, Wednesday 10, Thursday 10, Friday 6, and Saturday 8.

6. Finally, run the `PayDetails()` method.

The following is the expected output:

```
Tracking hours worked thus far today:  2
Tracking hours worked thus far today:  5
Tracking hours worked thus far today:  10

Sunday hours:  0
Monday hours:  8
Tuesday hours:  10
Wednesday hours:  10
Thursday hours:  10
Friday hours:  6
Saturday hours:  8

Hours worked this week:  52
Pay for the week: $ 544
Is this overtime pay:  true
```

Figure 5.12: Output for the payable amount activity

> **Note**
>
> The solution for this activity can be found in the GitHub repository folder for this chapter: `https://github.com/PacktPublishing/Go-Programming-From-Beginner-to-Professional-Second-Edition-/tree/main/Chapter05/Activity05.02`.

This activity aims to go a step further than *Activity 5.01 – calculating the working hours of employees*, by using some more advanced programming with Go's functions. In this activity, we continued to use functions, as we did previously; however, we returned multiple values and returned a function from a function. We also demonstrated the use of closures for calculating hours not logged by an employee.

Separating similar code

So far, we have covered a lot regarding functions since they are a vital aspect of what makes Go successful and flexible as a language. To continue with the idea of making flexible code for others to understand, iterate on, and work with, we will discuss how to expand this mentality.

In the world of software development, organizing code effectively is crucial for creating maintainable and scalable applications. In Go programming, one approach to achieving code organization is by separating related functions into different directories and utilizing multiple packages.

Thus far, we have been working with just one file to understand the fundamentals of Go. However, there is life beyond just a `main.go` file. We will briefly discuss ways Go developers keep in mind the reusability and cleanliness of their code, beyond the scope of functions. However, we will keep things at a high level at this point as we dive into the details of this when we cover Go modules.

A well-structured directory layout enhances code readability and maintainability. It allows developers to locate and work with specific functionality quickly. In Go, it is common to group related functions into separate directories based on their purpose, context, or domain. By organizing code into feature-based or domain-specific directories, developers can easily identify and modify code pertaining to a particular functionality. This separation fosters modularity and makes it easier to understand the application's architecture.

As projects grow in size and complexity, splitting code into functions and purposeful directories becomes essential for managing dependencies and reducing cognitive load. Large applications often benefit from a directory structure that aligns with the project's modules or components. There are many benefits as to why you, as a developer, should care about separating your Go code into logical chunks:

- Enhanced code reusability
- Improved readability and maintainability
- Testability and isolation

A concrete example of this can be seen in the following example:

1. Use the IDE of your choice.
2. Create a new file in a new directory and save it as main.go.
3. Enter the following code in main.go:

```
package main
import "fmt"
func main() {
calculateSalary()
playGame()
    getWeather()
}
func calculateSalary() {
    // do stuff
}
func playGame() {
    // do stuff
}
func getWeather() {
    // do stuff
}
```

The `calculateSalary`, `playGame`, and `getWeather` functions are independent of each other, each can contain complex logic, and they may rely on different, unrelated dependencies.

Placing the unrelated functions, and even withholding their actual logic, makes the code file bloated; it can become messy and unmanageable as you continue to iterate on the code and add logic. It could make sense to separate the three functions into their own files, such as `salary.go`, `game.go`, and `weather.go`. Eventually, you could separate them into different directories, and so forth, as you go.

It is important to start small, and then think about how you can separate similar code to continue writing manageable Go code that others can easily understand and iterate on. Again, this idea of code separation will be discussed in more detail when we cover Go modules since that is a vital way Go enables simple and reusable code.

Summary

In this chapter, we studied why and how functions are an essential part of the Go programming language. We also discussed various features of functions in Go that make Go stand apart from other programming languages. Go has features that allow us to solve a lot of real-world problems and do so in a small, iterable, and manageable way. Functions in Go serve many purposes, including enhancing the usage and readability of code.

Next, we learned how to create and call functions. We studied the various types of functions that are used in Go and discussed scenarios where each of the function types can be used. We also expounded on the concept of closures. Closures are essentially a type of anonymous function that can use variables declared at the same level as that at which the anonymous function was declared. Then, we discussed various parameters and return types and studied `defer`. We also discussed how to keep your code clean and separated such that similar logic can be packaged up nicely together. This mentality of thinking about how to reduce, reuse, and recycle your code will enable you to become a better developer.

In the next chapter, we'll explore errors and error types and learn how to build custom errors, thus building a recovery mechanism to handle errors in Go.

6

Don't Panic! Handle Your Errors

Overview

In this chapter, we will be looking at various code snippets from the Go standard packages to get an understanding of Go's idiomatic way of performing error handling. We will also look at how to create custom error types in Go and see more examples in the standard library.

By the end of this chapter, you will be able to distinguish between the different types of errors and compare error handling and exception handling. You will also be able to create error values, `panic()`, and properly recover after a panic and handle your errors. Lastly, we will briefly discuss adding context to our errors through error wrapping.

Technical requirements

For this chapter, you'll require Go version 1.21 or higher. The code for this chapter can be found at: `https://github.com/PacktPublishing/Go-Programming-From-Beginner-to-Professional-Second-Edition-/tree/main/Chapter06`.

Introduction

In the previous chapter, we learned how to reduce, reuse, and recycle good code practices with Go through the help of functions, separating logical components, and more! We also discovered more regarding functions, such as the fact that functions can be passed as parameters and returned from a function. In this chapter, we will work with errors and learn how to return those from functions.

Developers are not perfect and, by extension, neither is the code that they produce. All software at some point in time has had errors. Handling errors is critical when you are developing software. These errors can have a negative impact of varying degrees on its users. The impact on the users of your software can be more far-reaching than you realize.

For instance, let's consider the Northeast Blackout of 2003. On August 14, there was a blackout for about 50 million people in the United States and Canada that lasted for 14 days. This was due to a race condition bug in the alarm system in a control room. Technically, a race condition bug is when two separate threads try to access the same memory location for a write operation. This race condition can cause a program to crash. In this instance, it resulted in over 250 power plants going offline. One way to handle a race condition is to ensure proper synchronization between the various threads, or small units of execution within a process, and allow memory locations to be accessed for write operations by only one thread at a time. We will discuss concurrency in more detail later in this book; however, this example illustrates how it is important that we, as developers, ensure we handle errors properly so that we can try our best to avoid issues such as this. If we do not handle errors properly, this can harm the users of our application and their way of life, as seen by the power outage incident described here. Yes, this is an event from years ago; however, we should take the opportunity to learn from the past and work toward handling errors properly to avoid this in the future. Further information on the Northeast Blackout can be found online: `https://en.wikipedia.org/wiki/Northeast_blackout_of_2003`.

In this chapter, we will be looking at what an error is, what an error looks like in Go, and, more specifically, how to handle errors the Go way. Let's get started!

What are errors?

An error is something that causes your program to produce unintended results. Those unintended results could range from the application crashing, an incorrect data calculation (such as a bank transaction not being processed correctly), or not providing any results. These unintended results are referred to as software bugs. Any software will contain errors during its lifetime due to numerous scenarios that programmers do not anticipate. The following are possible outcomes when errors occur:

- The erroneous code could cause the program to crash without warning
- The output of the program was not the intended result
- An error message is displayed

There are three types of errors that you might encounter:

- Syntax errors
- Runtime errors
- Semantic errors

Let's explore each one in more detail.

Syntax errors

Syntax errors result from improper use of the programming language. This often occurs due to mistyping the code. Most modern IDEs will have some visual way of bringing syntax errors to the attention of the programmer. In most modern IDEs, syntax errors can be caught at an early stage. They may occur more frequently when you are learning a new programming language. A few occurrences of syntax errors could be due to the following:

- Incorrect use of syntax for a loop

- Misplacing or omitting curly braces, parentheses, or brackets

- Misspelled function names or package names

- Passing the wrong type of argument to a function

Here is an example of a syntax error:

```
package main
import (
    "fmt"
)
func main() {
    fmt.println("Enter your city:")
}
```

The output appears as follows:

```
fmt.println("Enter your city:")
cannot refer to unexported name fmt.println
undefined: fmt.println
```

Go is case-sensitive, so `println` should be `Println`.

Syntax errors are errors that you receive quick feedback on from `golint` that runs within your IDE thanks to the `gopls` language server. `gopls` is the official Go language server developed by the Google Go team and provides various language features, including code completion and diagnostics on syntax warnings and errors, as well as formatting issues. Working with Go code within an IDE that supports the **Language Server Protocol** (**LSP**) communicates with `gopls` to enable these features. `golint` itself is a separate command-line tool that can provide code analysis and can integrate with `gopls`. It is recommended to run your code through a linter before committing. This process is often automated when you're opening up code for team members to review in a **continuous integration** (**CI**) environment so that team-based and/or larger projects all have good code quality standards.

Runtime errors

These errors occur when the code is asked to perform a task that it cannot do. Unlike syntax errors, these are typically only found during the execution of the code.

The following are common examples of runtime errors:

- Opening a connection to a database that does not exist
- Performing a loop that is bigger than the number of elements in the slice or array you are iterating over
- Opening a file that does not exist
- Performing a mathematical operation, such as dividing a number by zero

Exercise 6.01 – runtime errors while adding numbers

In this exercise, we are going to write a simple program that sums up a slice of numbers. This program will demonstrate an example of a runtime error and will crash when it is executed:

1. Create a directory called `Exercise06.01` inside the `Chapter06` directory.

2. Create a file called `main.go` inside the directory you created in *step 1*.

3. This program will be in `package main`. Import the `fmt` package:

    ```
    package main
    import "fmt"
    ```

4. Inside the `main` function, we will have a slice of integers that will have four elements:

    ```
    func main() {
        nums := []int{2, 4, 6, 8}
    ```

5. We will have a variable, `total`, to be used to sum all the integer variables in the slice. Use a `for` loop to sum the variables:

    ```
    total := 0
    for i := 0; i <= 10; i++ {
        total += nums[i]
    }
    ```

6. Next, we print the results of the total:

    ```
    fmt.Println("Total: ", total)
    }
    ```

With that, we have introduced an example of a runtime error to the program; so, we will not get the following output:

```
Total: 20
```

7. At the command line, navigate to the directory you created in *step 1*.

8. At the command line, type the following:

```
go build main.go
```

The go build command will compile your program and create an executable named after the directory you created in *step 1*.

9. Type the name of the file you created in *step 8* and hit *Enter* to run the executable (Add the ./main command). The expected output will be as follows:

```
panic: runtime error: index out of range [4] with length 4

goroutine 1 [running]:
main.main()
        /tmp/sandbox265689164/prog.go:9 +0x120
```

Figure 6.1: Output after executing

As you can see, the program crashed. The index out of range panic is a common error to new Go developers and veterans alike.

In this example, the error – a panic (we will discuss what a panic is later in this chapter) in this program – is the result of iterating in the for loop by a greater number – in our case, 10 – than the actual number of elements in the slice – in our case, 4. One possible solution would be to use a for loop with a range:

```
package main
import "fmt"
func main() {
  nums := []int{2, 4, 6, 8}
  total := 0
  for i := range nums {
    total += nums[i]
  }
  fmt.Println("Total: ", total)
}
```

In this exercise, we saw how we can avoid runtime errors by paying attention to minute details.

To capture issues more easily before they become runtime errors, it is best to do the following:

-   Properly test your code
-   Avoid nil pointer dereferences

- Use proper input validation as necessary
- Perform boundary checks to check bounds on data before accessing
- Use proper synchronization mechanisms
- Avoid global state
- Use panic and recover sparingly
- Conductor thorough code reviews on teammates
- Use code linters and analyzers
- Conduct version management for dependencies

While several of these include trying to be mindful of proper coding practices, many of them will also be discussed in subsequent chapters of this book.

Semantic errors

Syntax errors are the easiest to debug, followed by runtime errors, while logic errors are the hardest. Semantic errors are sometimes very hard to spot as they are a result of logical errors that can lead to unexpected behavior.

For example, in 1998, when the Mars Climate Orbiter was launched, its purpose was to study the climate of Mars, but due to a logic error in the system, the Mars Climate Orbiter, valued at $235 million, was destroyed. After some analysis, it was discovered that the calculations of units on the ground controller system were done in imperial units and the software on the Orbiter was done in metric units. This was a logic error that caused the navigation system to incorrectly calculate its maneuvers in space. As indicated by this historical tale of a semantic error, these are defects in the way code processes elements of a program. These types of errors are often caught at runtime. This is another illustration of the significant consequences erroneous code can cause since the Mars Climate Orbiter was very expensive and included many hours of engineering efforts.

Here are some reasons for semantic errors to occur:

- Logical errors such as incorrect computations
- Accessing incorrect resources (files, databases, servers, and variables)
- Incorrect setting of variables for negation (not equal versus equal)
- Type errors on variables
- Incorrect use of functions, data structures, pointers, and concurrency

Exercise 6.02 – a semantic error with walking distance

We are writing an application that will determine whether we should walk to our destination or take a car. If our destination is greater than or equal to 2 km, we are going to take a car. If it is less than 2 km, then we will walk to our destination. We are going to demonstrate a semantic error with this program.

The expected output of this exercise is as follows:

```
Take the car
```

Follow these steps:

1. Create a directory called Exercise6.02 inside the Chapter06 directory.

2. Save a file called main.go inside the directory you created in the previous step. This program will be inside package main.

3. Import the fmt package:

    ```
    package main
    import "fmt"
    ```

4. Inside the main function, display a message to take the car when km is greater than 2, and when km is less than 2, to send a message for walking:

    ```
    func main() {
       km := 2
       if km > 2 {
          fmt.Println("Take the car")
       } else {
          fmt.Println("Going to walk today")
       }
    }
    ```

5. At the command line, navigate to the directory you created.

6. At the command line, type the following:

    ```
    go build main.go
    ```

    The go build command will compile your program and create an executable named after the directory you created.

7. Type the name of the file you created in *Step 6* and hit *Enter* to run the executable (Add the ./main command). The expected output will be as follows:

You will get the following output:

```
Going to walk today
```

The program will run with no errors, but the message that's displayed won't be what we expected.

As mentioned previously, the program runs with no errors, but the results are not what we expected. This is because we have a logic error. Our `if` statement does not account for km equal to 2. It only checks that the distance is greater than 2. Fortunately, this is a simple fix: replace > with >=. Now, the program will give the results that we expect:

```
func main() {
  km := 2
  if km >= 2 {
    fmt.Println("Take the car")
  } else {
    fmt.Println("Going to walk today")
  }
}
```

This simple program made it easy to debug the logic error, but these types of errors in a larger program may not be as easy to spot.

Semantic errors involve understanding the intended logic of the code. It is best to be thorough in testing. This includes various types of tests, such as unit, integration, end-to-end, and others. Each type of test serves a specific purpose in capturing different aspects of errors and preventing unintended consequences. Later in this book, we will discuss the various types of testing in further detail. Additionally, adopting best practices for Go and a continuous learning mindset can help!

The remainder of this chapter will focus on the runtime errors we've covered. However, it is good to understand the various types of errors that you, as a programmer, could encounter.

Error handling using other programming languages

Programmers who are new to Go and who have a background in other programming languages may initially find Go's methodology for dealing with errors a bit odd. Go does not handle errors in the same fashion as other languages, such as Java, Python, C#, and Ruby. Those languages perform exception handling.

The following code snippets are some examples of how other languages handle errors by performing exception handling:

```
//java
try {
  // code
}catch (exception e){
  // block of code to handle the error
}
//python
try:
```

```
   //code
except:
   //code
else:
   try:
   // code
   except:
   // code
finally:
   //code
```

Typically, exceptions, if not handled, will crash your application. In most cases, exception handling tends to be implicit checking versus Go's explicit checking for errors returned by its functions. In the exception-handling paradigm, anything can fail, and you must account for that. Each function can throw an exception, but you do not know what that exception could be.

In the error handling paradigm that Go uses, it is obvious when the programmer does not handle the error because the function returns the error code, and you can see that they did not check for the error. We will be looking at the specifics of checking for error code later in this chapter.

Most programming languages follow a similar pattern to the one shown in the previous code snippet. It is usually some sort of `try..catch..finally` block. One point of contention with the `try.. catch..finally` block is that the control flow of the program's execution gets interrupted and can follow a different path. This can lead to several logic errors and difficulty in the readability of the code. Here is a quick peek at how Go handles errors:

```
val, err := someFunc() err
if err != nil{
   return err
}
return nil
```

The preceding code snippet is a very simple syntax for handling the error. We will look at this in greater detail in the following sections.

Error interface type

What is an error in Go? An error in Go is a value. Here's a quote from Rob Pike, one of the pivotal pioneers of Go:

"Values can be programmed, and since errors are values, errors can be programmed. Errors are not like exceptions. There's nothing special about them, whereas an unhandled exception can crash your program."

Since errors are values, they can be passed into a function, returned from a function, and evaluated just like any other value in Go.

An error in Go is anything that implements the error interface. Interfaces will be explained in detail in the following chapter, so we will keep the details light in this chapter concerning interface references. We need to look at some fundamental aspects that make up the error type in Go. To be an error type in Go, it must first satisfy type error interface:

```
//https://golang.org/pkg/builtin/#error
type error interface {
   Error() string
}
```

The wonderful thing about Go is its simplistic design regarding language features. This can easily be seen with the error interface that Go's standard library uses. To satisfy the error interface, only two things are required:

- The method name, Error()

- The Error() method to return a string

It is important to understand that an error type is an interface type. Any value that is an error can be described as a string. When performing error handling in Go, the functions will return error values. The Go language uses this throughout the standard library.

Look at the following code snippet for a starting discussion point on errors:

```
package main
import (
   "fmt"
   "strconv"
)
func main() {
   v := "10"
   if s, err := strconv.Atoi(v); err == nil {
     fmt.Printf("%T, %v\n", s, s)
   }else{
     fmt.Println(err)
   }
   v = "s2"
   s, err := strconv.Atoi(v)
   if err != nil{
     fmt.Println(s, err)
   }
}
```

We will not go into every detail of the function and instead focus on the error portion of the code. In *Chapter 5, Reduce, Reuse, and Recycle*, we learned that functions can return multiple values. This is a powerful feature that most languages do not have. This is powerful, especially when dealing with error values. The `strconv.Atoi()` function returns an `int` type and an error, as seen in the example stated previously. It is a function that is in the Go standard library. For functions that return error values, the error value should be the last return value.

It is Go-idiomatic to evaluate the error value for functions or methods that return an error. It is generally bad practice to not handle an error that is returned from a function. When returned and ignored, an error can lead to lots of wasted debugging efforts. It can also cause unforeseen consequences in your program. If the value is not `nil`, then we have an error and must decide how we want to handle it. Depending on the scenario, we might want to do one of the following things:

- Return the error to the caller
- Log the error and continue execution
- Stop the execution of the program
- Ignore it (this is highly not recommended)
- Panic (only in very rare conditions; we will discuss this in more detail later)

If the value of error is `nil`, this means there is no error. No further steps are necessary.

Let's take a closer look at the standard package regarding the error type. We will start by looking at each piece of code in the `https://packt.live/2rk6r8Z` file:

```
type errorString struct {
    s string
}
```

The `errorString` struct is in the `errors` package. This struct is used to store the string version of the error. `errorString` has a single field of `s` that is of the `string` type. `errorString` and the field are unexportable. This means that we can't access the `errorString` type or its field, `s`, directly. The following code shows an example of trying to access an unexported `errorString` type and its field, `s`:

```
package main
import (
  "errors"
  "fmt"
)
func main() {
  es := errors.errorString{}
  es.s = "slacker"
  fmt.Println(es)
}
```

Here's the output:

```
./prog.go:9:8: cannot refer to unexported name errors.errorString
./prog.go:10:4: es.s undefined (cannot refer to unexported field or method s)
```

Figure 6.2: Expected output for the unexported field

On the surface, it appears that `errorString` is neither accessible nor useful, but we should keep digging into the standard library:

```
func (e *errorString) Error() string {
    return e.s
}
```

The `errorString` type has a method that implements the error interface. It satisfies the requirements, provides a method called `Error()`, and returns a string. The error interface has been satisfied. We now have access to the `errorString` field, `s`, through the `Error()` method. This is how an error gets returned within the standard library.

You should now have a basic understanding of what an error is in Go. Next, we'll learn how to create error types in Go.

Creating error values

In the standard library, the `errors` package has a method that we can use to create errors:

```
// https://golang.org/src/errors/errors.go
// New returns an error that formats as the given text.
func New(text string) error {
    return &errorString{text}
}
```

It is important to understand that the `New` function takes a string as an argument, converts it into `*errors.errorString`, and returns an error value. The underlying value of the error type that gets returned is of the `*errors.errorString` type.

We can prove this by running the following code:

```
package main
import (
    "errors"
    "fmt"
)
```

```
func main() {
    ErrBadData := errors.New("Some bad data")
    fmt.Printf("ErrBadData type: %T", ErrBadData)
}
```

Here is an example from Go's standard library, `http`, that uses the `errors` package to create package-level variables:

```
var (
    ErrBodyNotAllowed = errors.New("http: request method or response
status code does not allow body")
    ErrHijacked = errors.New("http: connection has been hijacked")
    ErrContentLength = errors.New("http: wrote more than the declared
Content- Length")
    ErrWriteAfterFlush = errors.New("unused")
)
```

When creating errors in Go, it is idiomatic to start with the `Err` variable.

Exercise 6.03 – creating an application to calculate pay for the week

In this exercise, we are going to create a function that calculates pay for the week. This function will accept two arguments – the hours worked during the week and the hourly rate. The function is going to check whether the two parameters meet the criteria for being valid. The function will need to calculate regular pay, which is hours less than or equal to 40, and overtime pay, which is hours greater than 40 for the week.

We will create two error values using `errors.New()`. The one error value will be used when there is an invalid hourly rate. An invalid hourly rate in our app is an hourly rate that is less than 10 or greater than 75. The second error value will be when hours per week are not between 0 and 80.

Use the IDE of your choice. One option would be Visual Studio Code. Follow these steps:

1. Create a directory called `Exercise6.03` inside the `Chapter06` directory.

2. Save a file called `main.go` inside the directory you created in the previous step The `main.go` file will be in `package main`.

3. Import the two Go standard libraries, `errors` and `fmt`:

    ```
    package main
    import (
        "errors"
        "fmt"
    )
    ```

4. With that, we have declared our error variables using `errors.New()`. Now, we can use idiomatic Go for the variable name, starting it with `Err` and camel casing. Our error string is in lowercase with no punctuation:

```go
var (
        ErrHourlyRate = errors.New("invalid hourly rate")
        ErrHoursWorked = errors.New("invalid hours worked per
week")
)
```

5. Inside the `main` function, we will be calling our `payday()` function three times. We will declare our error variables using `errors.New()` and check `err` after the function:

```go
func main() {
    pay, err := payDay(81, 50)
    if err != nil {
        fmt.Println(err)
    }
}
```

6. Create the `payDay` function and make it accept two arguments (`hoursWorked` and `hourlyRate`). The function will return an `int` type and an error. We will discuss this step by step afterward:

```go
func payDay(hoursWorked, hourlyRate int) (int, error) {
        if hourlyRate < 10 || hourlyRate > 75 {
            return 0, ErrHourlyRate
        }
    if hoursWorked < 0 || hoursWorked > 80 {
        return 0, ErrHoursWorked
    }
    if hoursWorked > 40 {
        hoursOver := hoursWorked - 40
        overTime := hoursOver * 2
        regularPay := hoursWorked * hourlyRate
        return regularPay + overTime, nil
    }
    return hoursWorked * hourlyRate, nil
}
```

7. We will use an `if` statement to check whether the hourly rate is less than 10 or greater than 75. If `hourlyRate` meets those conditions, we will return 0 and our custom error, `ErrHourlyRate`. If `hourlyRate` does not meet those conditions, then the returned value will be `return hoursWorked * hourlyRate, nil`. We return `nil` for the error because there was no error:

```
func payDay(hoursWorked, hourlyRate int) (int, error) {
    if hourlyRate < 10 || hourlyRate > 75 {
        return 0, ErrHourlyRate
    }
    return hoursWorked * hourlyRate, nil
}
```

8. In *step 7*, we validated `hourlyRate`. Now, we will need to validate `hoursWorked`. We will add another `if` statement to the `payDay()` function that will check whether `hoursWorked` is less than 0 or greater than 80. If `hoursWorked` matches that condition, we will return 0 and the error, `ErrHoursWorked`:

```
func payDay(hoursWorked, hourlyRate int) (int, error) {
    if hourlyRate < 10 || hourlyRate > 75 {
        return 0, ErrHourlyRate
    }
    if hoursWorked < 0 || hoursWorked > 80 {
        return 0, ErrHoursWorked
    }
    return hoursWorked * hourlyRate, nil
}
```

9. In the previous two steps, we added `if` statements to validate the arguments being passed to the function. In this step, we will add another `if` statement to calculate overtime pay. Overtime pay is hours greater than 40. The hours over 40 are double `hourlyRate`. The hours less than or equal to 40 are at `hourlyRate`:

```
func payDay(hoursWorked, hourlyRate int) (int, error) {
    if hourlyRate < 10 || hourlyRate > 75 {
        return 0, ErrHourlyRate
    }
    if hoursWorked < 0 || hoursWorked > 80 {
        return 0, ErrHoursWorked
    }
    if hoursWorked > 40 {
        hoursOver := hoursWorked - 40
        overTime := hoursOver * 2
        regularPay := hoursWorked * hourlyRate
        return regularPay + overTime, nil
```

```
    }
        return hoursWorked * hourlyRate, nil
    }
```

10. In the `main()` function, we will call the `payDay()` function three times with various arguments. We will check the error after each call and print the error message if applicable. If there is no error, then we print the pay for the week:

```
func main() {
    pay, err := payDay(81, 50)
    if err != nil {
        fmt.Println(err)
    }
    pay, err = payDay(80, 5)
    if err != nil {
        fmt.Println(err)
    }
    pay, err = payDay(80, 50)
    if err != nil {
        fmt.Println(err)
    }
    fmt.Println(pay)
}
```

11. In the command line, navigate to the directory you created previously.

12. In the command line, type the following:

```
go build main.go
```

The `go build` command will compile your program and create an executable named after the directory you created.

13. Type the name of the file you created and hit *Enter* to run the executable:

```
./main
```

The expected output is as follows:

```
Invalid hours worked per week
Invalid hourly rate
4080
```

In this exercise, we saw how to create custom error messages that can be used to easily determine why the data was considered invalid. We also showed how to return multiple values from a function and to check for errors from the function. In the next section, we will look at how to use panic in our applications.

Panic

Several languages use exceptions for handling errors. However, Go does not use exceptions – it uses something called a panic. This is a built-in function that causes a program to crash. It stops the normal execution of the current goroutine where the panic happened and all other ongoing goroutines and shows a stack trace of what occurred.

In Go, a panic is not the norm, unlike other languages where an exception is the norm. A panic signal indicates something abnormal that is occurring within your code. Usually, when a panic is initiated by runtime or the developer, it is to protect the integrity of the program.

Errors and panics differ in their purposes and how they are handled by the Go runtime. An error in Go indicates that something unexpected occurred, but it will not adversely impact the integrity of the program. Go expects that the developer will handle the error properly. The function or other programs will not typically crash if you do not handle the error. However, panics differ in this regard. When a panic occurs, it will ultimately crash the system unless there are handlers to handle the panic. If there are no handlers for the panic, it will go all the way up the stack and crash the program.

One example that we will look at later in this chapter is where a panic occurs due to an index being out of range. This is typical when trying to access the index of a collection that doesn't exist. If Go did not panic in this case, it could harm the integrity of the program, such as other parts of the program trying to store or retrieve data that is not there in the collection.

> **Note**
> Review the topic of goroutines to understand what occurs in Go when you panic. At a high level, the `main()` function is a Goroutine. When a panic occurs, you will see references to "Goroutine running" in the error message.

Panics can be initiated by the developer and can be caused during the execution of a program by runtime errors. A `panic()` function accepts an empty interface. For now, suffice to say, this means it can accept anything as an argument. However, in most cases, you should pass an error type to the `panic()` function. It is more intuitive to the user of our function to have some details on what caused the panic. Passing an error to the panic function is also idiomatic in Go. We will also see how recovering from a panic that has an error type passed to it gives us some different options when dealing with panic. When a panic occurs, it will generally follow these steps:

I.   The execution is stopped.

II.   Any deferred functions in the panicking function will be called.

III. Any deferred functions in the stack of the panicking function will be called.

IV.   It will continue up the stack until it reaches `main()`.

V.   Statements after the panicking function will not execute.

VI.   The program then crashes.

Here's how a panic works:

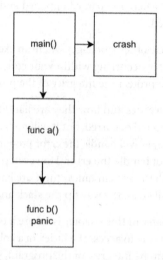

Figure 6.3: The working of a panic

The preceding diagram illustrates code in the main function that calls the a () function. This function then calls the b () function. Inside b (), a panic occurs. The panic () function is not handled by any of the code upstream (a () or the main () function), so the program will crash the main () function.

Here's an example of a panic that occurs in Go. Try to determine why this program panics:

```
package main
import (
    "fmt"
)
func main() {
    nums := []int{1, 2, 3}
    for i := 0; i <= 10; i++ {
        fmt.Println(nums[i])
    }
}
```

The output of this panic is shown here:

```
1
2
3
panic: runtime error: index out of range [3] with length 3

goroutine 1 [running]:
main.main()
        /tmp/sandbox076956134/prog.go:10 +0x100
```

Figure 6.4: Panic example

The panic runtime error is a common one that you will encounter while developing. It is an index out of range error. Go generated this panic because we are trying to iterate over a slice more times than there are elements. Go felt that this is a reason to panic because it puts the program in an abnormal condition.

Here's a snippet of code that demonstrates the basics of using a panic:

```
package main
import (
    "errors"
    "fmt"
)
func main() {
    msg := "good-bye"
    message(msg)
    fmt.Println("This line will not get printed")
}
func message(msg string) {
    if msg == "good-bye" {
        panic(errors.New("something went wrong"))
    }
}
```

Code synopsis:

- The function panics because the argument to the function message is `"good-bye"`.

- The `panic()` function prints the error message. Having a good error message helps with the debugging process.

- Inside the panic, we are using `errors.New()`, which we used in the previous section to create an error type.

- As you can see, `fmt.Println()` does not get executed in the `main()` function. Since there are no `defer` statements, execution stops immediately.

The expected output for this code snippet is as follows:

```
panic: something went wrong

goroutine 1 [running]:
main.message(...)
        /tmp/sandbox741915746/prog.go:16
main.main()
        /tmp/sandbox741915746/prog.go:10 +0x140
```

Figure 6.5: Panic example output

The following code snippet shows how `panic` and a `defer` statement function together:

main.go

```go
func test() {
    n := func() {
    fmt.Println("Defer in test")
    }
    defer n()
    msg := "good-bye"
    message(msg)
}
func message(msg string) {
    f := func() {
    fmt.Println("Defer in message func")
    }
    defer f()
    if msg == "good-bye" {
    panic(errors.New("something went wrong"))
```

The output of this panic example is as follows:

```
Defer in message func
Defer in test
panic: something went wrong

goroutine 1 [running]:
main.message(0x116057, 0x8)
        /tmp/sandbox806116420/prog.go:24 +0x140
main.test()
        /tmp/sandbox806116420/prog.go:16 +0x60
main.main()
        /tmp/sandbox806116420/prog.go:7 +0x20
```

Figure 6.6: Panic example output

Let's understand the code in parts:

I.   We start by examining the code in the message() function since that is where the panic starts. When the panic occurs, it runs the defer statement within the panicking function, message().

II.   The deferred function, func f(), runs in the message() function.

III.   Going up the call stack, the next function is the test() function, and its deferred function, n(), will execute.

IV.   Finally, we get to the main() function, where the execution is stopped by the panicking function. The print statement in main() does not get executed.

Note

You may have seen os.Exit() used to stop the execution of a program. os.Exit() stops execution immediately and returns a status code. No deferred statements are run when os.Exit() is performed. Panic is preferred over os.Exit() in certain cases as a panic will run deferred functions.

Exercise 6.04 – Crashing the program on errors using a panic

In this exercise, we will be modifying *Exercise 6.03 – creating an application to calculate pay for the week*. Consider the following scenario, where the requirements have changed.

We no longer need to return error values from our payDay() function. It has been decided that we cannot trust the user of the program to respond properly to the errors. There have been complaints of incorrect paychecks. We believe this is due to the caller of our function ignoring the errors being returned.

The payDay() function will now only return the pay amount and no errors. When the arguments provided to the function are invalid, instead of returning an error, the function will panic. This will cause the program to stop immediately and, therefore, not process a paycheck.

Use the IDE of your choice. One option could be Visual Studio Code. Now, follow these steps:

1.   Create a directory called Exercise6.04 inside the Chapter06 directory.

2.   Save a file called main.go inside the directory you created in the previous step. This program will be inside package main.

3.   Enter the following code in main.go:

```
package main
import (
    "fmt"
    "errors"
)
```

```
var (
    ErrHourlyRate = errors.New("invalid hourly rate")
    ErrHoursWorked = errors.New("invalid hours worked per week")
)
```

4. Inside the `main` function, call the `payDay()` function, assign it to only one variable, `pay`, and then print it:

```
func main() {
    pay := payDay(81, 50)
    fmt.Println(pay)
}
```

5. Change the return type of the `payDay()` function so that it only returns `int`:

```
func payDay(hoursWorked, hourlyRate int) int {
```

6. Inside the `payDay()` function, assign a variable, `report`, to an anonymous function. This anonymous function provides details of the arguments provided to the `payDay()` function. Even though we are not returning errors, this will provide some insight as to why the function panics. Since it is a deferred function, it will always execute before the function exits:

```
func payDay(hoursWorked, hourlyRate int) int {
    report := func() {
        fmt.Printf("HoursWorked: %d\nHourldyRate: %d\n",
    hoursWorked, hourlyRate)
    }
    defer report()
}
```

The business rule for valid `hourlyRate` and `hoursWorked` stays the same as in the previous exercise. Instead of returning an error, we will be using the `panic` function. When the data is invalid, we panic and pass the argument of `ErrHourlyRate` or `ErrHoursWorked`.

The arguments that are passed to the `panic()` function assist the user of our function in understanding the cause of the panic.

7. When a panic occurs in the `payDay()` function, the `defer` function, `report()`, will give the caller some insight into why the panic occurred. The panic will bubble up the stack to the `main()` function and execution will stop immediately. The following code must be added after the `defer` function in the `payDay()` function:

```
if hourlyRate < 10 || hourlyRate > 75 {
    panic(ErrHourlyRate)
}
if hoursWorked < 0 || hoursWorked > 80 {
    panic(ErrHoursWorked )
```

```
        }
        if hoursWorked > 40 {
            hoursOver := hoursWorked - 40
            overTime := hoursOver * 2
            regularPay := hoursWorked * hourlyRate
            return regularPay + overTime
        }
        return hoursWorked * hourlyRate
    }
```

8. At the command line, navigate to the directory you created.

9. At the command line, type the following:

```
go build main.go
```

10. The go build command will compile your program and create an executable named after the directory you created.

11. Type in the name of the file you created and hit *Enter* to run the executable.

The expected output should be as follows:

```
HoursWorked: 81
HourldyRate: 50
panic: invalid hours worked per week

goroutine 1 [running]:
main.payDay(0x51, 0x32, 0x0, 0x28e8)
        /tmp/sandbox697228173/prog.go:28 +0x1e0
main.main()
        /tmp/sandbox697228173/prog.go:14 +0x40
```

Figure 6.7: Panic exercise output

In this exercise, we learned how to perform a panic and pass an error to the panic() function. This aids the user of the function in gaining a good understanding of the cause of the panic. In the next section, we will learn how to regain control of the program after a panic occurs using recover(). We will also discuss guidelines on panic() and recover() in Go thereafter.

Recover

Go provides us with the ability to regain control after a panic has occurred. recover() is a function that is used to regain control of a panicking goroutine.

The signature of the recover() function is as follows:

```
func recover() interface{}
```

The `recover()` function accepts no arguments and returns an empty `interface{}`. For now, an empty `interface{}` indicates that any type can be returned. The `recover()` function will return the value sent to the `panic()` function.

The `recover()` function is only useful inside a deferred function. As you may recall, a deferred function gets executed before the encompassing function terminates. Executing a call to the `recover()` function inside a deferred function stops the panicking by restoring normal execution. If the `recover()` function is called outside a deferred function, it will not stop the panicking.

The following diagram shows the steps a program would take when using `panic()`, `recover()`, and a `defer()` function:

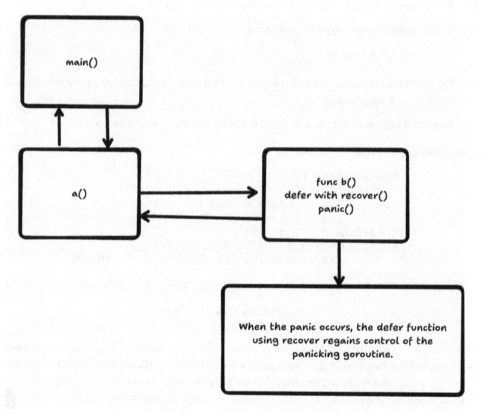

Figure 6.8: The recover() function's flow

The steps that are taken in the preceding diagram can be explained as follows:

I.   The `main()` function calls `func a()`.

II.   `func a()` calls `func b()`.

III. Inside func b(), there is a panic.

IV. The panic() function gets handled by a deferred function that uses the recover() function.

V. The deferred function is the last function to execute inside func b().

VI. The deferred function calls the recover() function.

VII. The call to recover() causes normal flow back to the caller, func a().

VIII. Normal flow continues, and control is finally given back with the main() function.

The following code snippet mimics the behavior of the preceding diagram:

main.go

```
func main() {
    a()
    fmt.Println("This line will now get printed from main() function")
}
func a() {
    b("good-bye")
    fmt.Println("Back in function a()")
}
func b(msg string) {
    defer func() {
        if r := recover(); r!= nil{
            fmt.Println("error in func b()", r)
        }
    }()
```

The full code is available at https://github.com/PacktPublishing/Go-Programming-From-Beginner-to-Professional-Second-Edition-/blob/main/Chapter06/Examples/Example06.02/main.go.

Code synopsis:

- The main() function calls the a() function. This calls the b() function.

- b() accepts a string type and assigns it to the msg variable. If msg evaluates to true in the if statement, a panic will occur.

- The argument for the panic is a new error created by the errors.New() function:

```
if msg == "good-bye" {
    panic(errors.New("something went wrong"))
}
```

Once the panic occurs, the next call will be to the deferred function.

The deferred function uses the `recover()` function. The value of the panic is returned from `recover()`; in this case, the value of `r` is an error type. Then, the function prints out some details:

```
defer func() {
    if r := recover(); r!= nil {
        fmt.Println("error in func b()", r)
    }
}()
```

- The control flow goes back to `a()`. Then, the `a()` function prints out some details.

- Next, control goes back to the `main()` function, where it prints out some details and terminates:

```
error in func b() something went wrong
Back in function a()
This line will now get printed from main() function
```

Figure 6.9: recover() example output

Exercise 6.05 – recovering from a panic

In this exercise, we will enhance our `payDay()` function so that it can recover from a panic. When our `payDay()` function panics, we will inspect the error from that panic. Then, depending on the error, we will print an informative message to the user. Let's get started:

1. Create a directory called `Exercise6.05` inside the `Chapter06` directory.

2. Save a file called `main.go` inside the directory you created in the previous step. This program will be inside `package main`.

3. Enter the following code in `main.go`:

```
package main
import (
    "errors"
    "fmt"
)
var (
    ErrHourlyRate = errors.New("invalid hourly rate")
    ErrHoursWorked = errors.New("invalid hours worked per week")
)
```

4. Call the payDay() function with various arguments and then print the return value of the function:

```
func main() {
    pay := payDay(100, 25)
    fmt.Println(pay)
    pay = payDay(100, 200)
    fmt.Println(pay)
    pay = payDay(60, 25)
    fmt.Println(pay)
}
```

5. Then, add a defer function to your payDay() function:

```
func payDay(hoursWorked, hourlyRate int) int {
    defer func() {
```

6. We can check for the return value from the recover() function, as follows:

```
        if r := recover(); r != nil {
            if r == ErrHourlyRate {
```

If r is not nil, this means a panic occurs and we should perform an action.

7. We can evaluate r and see whether it equals one of our error values – ErrHourlyRate or ErrHoursWorked:

```
                fmt.Printf("hourly rate: %d\nerr: %v\n\n",
    hourlyRate, r)
            }
            if r == ErrHoursWorked {
                fmt.Printf("hours worked: %d\nerr: %v\n\n",
    hoursWorked, r)
            }
        }
```

8. If our if statements evaluate to true, we print some details about the data and the error values from the recover() function. Then, we print how our pay was calculated:

```
            fmt.Printf("Pay was calculated based on:\nhours worked:
    %d\nhourly Rate: %d\n", hoursWorked, hourlyRate)
        }()
```

9. The rest of the code in the payDay() function remains unchanged. To see a description of it, please refer to *Exercise 6.04 – crashing the program on errors using a panic*:

```
if hourlyRate < 10 || hourlyRate > 75 {
    panic(ErrHourlyRate)
}
if hoursWorked < 0 || hoursWorked > 80 {
    panic(ErrHoursWorked)
}
if hoursWorked > 40 {
    hoursOver := hoursWorked - 40
    overTime := hoursOver * 2
    regularPay := hoursWorked * hourlyRate
    return regularPay + overTime
}
return hoursWorked * hourlyRate
}
```

10. At the command line, navigate to the directory you created.

11. At the command line, type the following:

```
go build main.go
```

The go build command will compile your program and create an executable named after the directory you created.

12. Type the name of the file you created and hit *Enter* to run the executable:

```
./main
```

The expected output is as follows:

```
hours worked: 100
err: invalid hours worked per week

Pay was calculated based on:
hours worked: 100
hourly Rate: 25
0
hourly rate: 200
err: invalid hourly rate

Pay was calculated based on:
hours worked: 100
hourly Rate: 200
0
Pay was calculated based on:
hours worked: 60
hourly Rate: 25
1540
```

Figure 6.10: Recovering from a panic exercise output

In the preceding exercises, we have seen the progression of creating a custom error and returning that error. From this, we have been able to crash programs when needed using panic(). In the previous exercise, we demonstrated the ability to recover from panics and display error messages based on the error type that was passed to the panic() function. In the following section, we will discuss some basic guidelines when performing error handling in Go.

Guidelines when working with errors and panics

Guidelines are just for guidance. They are not set in stone. This means that the majority of the time, you should follow the guidelines; however, there could be exceptions. Some of these guidelines have been mentioned previously, but we have consolidated them here for quick reference:

- When declaring an error type, the variable needs to start with Err. It should also follow the camel case naming convention:

  ```
  var ErrExampleNotAllowd= errors.New("error example text")
  ```

- The error string should start in lowercase and not end with punctuation. One of the reasons for this guideline is that the error can be returned and concatenated with other information relevant to the error.

- If a function or method returns an error, it should be evaluated. Errors that are not evaluated can cause the program to not function as expected.

- When using panic(), pass an error type as the argument, instead of an empty value.

- Do not evaluate the string value of an error to extract information directly from the string representation of an error. Instead, use type assertions or the error interface methods to retrieve specific details about the error.

- Use the panic() function sparingly.

Errors should be used for expected situations, such as when you come across a recoverable issue in your code. When a function cannot return its intended result due to specific conditions, returning an error allows the caller to handle the situation gracefully. panic() should never be your first line of defense. panic() is meant for exceptional or unexpected situations and using it for regular error handling can lead to hard-to-debug issues, making your code less maintainable. Additionally, logging your errors in DEBUG mode, which is a state where a program provides more detailed information for debugging purposes, can be useful when debugging why an error occurred.

Following these suggestions will help improve the reliability and maintainability of your Go code and help you handle errors gracefully.

Error wrapping

When propagating errors up the call stack, there are ways to improve the context around why an error occurred. This is extremely useful in complex systems to aid in understanding an error case. Error wrapping helps preserve the original error information while adding additional context to the error. This can be seen with the use of `fmt.Errorf` or the `errors.Wrap` function from `github.com/pkg/errors`. Error wrapping provides more detailed information about where an error occurred or what caused it, making it easier to understand and handle errors in your code.

A simple example of error wrapping can be seen in the following function:

```
func readConfig() error {
    _, err := readFile("file.txt")
    if err != nil {
        return errors.Wrap(err, "failed to read config file")
    }
    return nil
}
```

Alternatively, the wrapped error return can be represented by the following code:

```
return fmt.Errorf("failed to read config file: %w", err)
```

The preceding code shows how you can easily chain errors using error wrapping. `%w` in the format string on the error provided previously allows errors to be chained, which provides additional context on why the error occurred. This approach is supported in the standard library, so it should be considered the preferred and most simplistic method.

However, there is another third-party Go package that can be used to handle multiple errors together using `github.com/hashicorp/go-multierror`. These options give you the flexibility to understand additional error context or aggregate multiple errors into a single error, which can be convenient in certain scenarios.

The Go standard library introduced error wrapping in Go 1.13, and you can see this type of functionality in use today by professional teams and in more complex applications. Providing additional context around an error can be useful in debugging scenarios. To illustrate this, consider a situation where an error occurs in code you are unfamiliar with, and the error provides no context. It will be very challenging to pinpoint the origin of the error. Debugging becomes very difficult when you lack information about the specific part of the code where the error occurred. However, you must be mindful of not propagating too much context up the call stack so that you're not compromising the security of your code base.

Activity 6.01 – creating a custom error message for a banking application

A bank wants to add some custom errors when checking for last names and valid routing numbers. They have found that the direct deposit procedure allows invalid names and routing numbers to be used. The bank wants a descriptive error message for when these incidents occur. Our job is to create two descriptive custom error messages. Remember to use an idiomatic naming convention for the error variable and a proper structure for the error message.

You need to do the following:

1. First, you must create two error values for `ErrInvalidLastName` and `ErrInvalidRoutingNumber`.

2. Then, you must print the custom message in the `main()` function to show the bank the error message they will receive when those errors are encountered.

The expected output is as follows:

```
invalid last name
invalid routing number
```

By the end of this activity, you will be familiar with the steps that are needed to create a custom error message.

> **Note**
> The solution to this activity can be found `https://github.com/PacktPublishing/Go-Programming-From-Beginner-to-Professional-Second-Edition-/tree/main/Chapter06/Activity06.01`.

Activity 6.02 – validating a bank customer's direct deposit submission

The bank was pleased with the custom error messages that you created in *Activity 6.01 – creating a custom error message for a banking application*. They are so pleased that they now want you to implement two methods. These two methods are for validating the last name and the routing number:

1. You will need to create a struct called `directDeposit`.

2. The `directDeposit` struct will have three string fields: `lastName`, `firstName`, and `bankName`. It will also have two `int` fields called `routingNumber` and `accountNumber`.

3. The `directDeposit` struct will have a `validateRoutingNumber` method. The method will return `ErrInvalidRoutingNum` when the routing number is less than 100.

4. The `directDeposit` struct will have a `validateLastName` method. It will return `ErrInvalidLastName` when `lastName` is an empty string.

5. The `directDeposit` struct will have a method report. It will print out each of the fields' values.

6. In the `main()` function, assign values to the `directDeposit` struct's fields and call each of the `directDeposit` struct's methods.

The expected output is as follows:

```
invalid routing number
invalid last name
*********************************************************************************
Last Name:
First Name:    Abe
Bank Name:    XYZ Inc
Routing Number:    17
Account Number:    1809
```

Figure 6.11: Validating a bank customer's direct deposit submission

By the end of this activity, you will have learned how to return errors from functions and how to check for errors returned from a function. You will also be able to check for a condition and, based on that condition, return a custom error.

> **Note**
>
> The solution to this activity can be found `https://github.com/PacktPublishing/ Go-Programming-From-Beginner-to-Professional-Second-Edition-/ tree/main/Chapter06/Activity06.02`.

Activity 6.03 – panic on invalid data submission

The bank has now decided that it would rather crash the program when an invalid routing number is submitted. The bank feels that the erroneous data should cause the program to stop processing the direct deposit data. You need to raise panic on an invalid data submission instance. Build this on top of *Activity 6.02 – validating a bank customer's direct deposit submission*.

For this activity, you only need to do one thing – change the `validateRoutingNumber` method so that it doesn't return `ErrInvalidRoutingNum`, but instead performs a panic:

The expected output is as follows:

```
panic: invalid routing number

goroutine 1 [running]:
main.(*directDeposit).validateRoutingNumber(...)
          /tmp/sandbox561135516/prog.go:44
main.main()
          /tmp/sandbox561135516/prog.go:30 +0x160
```

Figure 6.12: Panic on an invalid routing number

By the end of this activity, you will be able to cause a panic to occur and see how that impacts the flow of the program.

> **Note**
>
> The solution to this activity can be found https://github.com/PacktPublishing/
> Go-Programming-From-Beginner-to-Professional-Second-Edition-/
> tree/main/Chapter06/Activity06.03.

Activity 6.04 – preventing a panic from crashing the app

After some initial alpha testing, the bank no longer wants the app to crash, Instead, in this activity, we need to recover from the panic that we added in *Activity 6.03 – panic on invalid data submission*, and print the error that caused the panic:

1. Add a defer function inside the validateRoutingNumber method.

2. Add an if statement that checks the error that's returned from the recover() function. If there is an error, then print it:

The expected output is as follows:

```
→  Activity06.04 git:(main) ✗ go run .
invalid routing number
invalid last name
*******************************************************************************
Last Name:
First Name:  Abe
Bank Name:  WilkesBooth Inc
Routing Number:  17
Account Number:  1809
```

Figure 6.13: Recovering from a panic on an invalid routing number

By the end of this activity, you will have caused a panic, but you will be able to prevent it from crashing the application. You will get an understanding of how the recover() function, used in conjunction with the defer statement, can be used to prevent the application from crashing.

> **Note**
>
> The solution for this activity can be found https://github.com/PacktPublishing/
> Go-Programming-From-Beginner-to-Professional-Second-Edition-/
> tree/main/Chapter06/Activity06.04.

Summary

In this chapter, we looked at the different types of errors that you will encounter while programming, such as syntax, runtime, and semantic errors. We focused more on runtime errors since they are challenging to debug.

Then, we examined the difference between various language philosophies when it comes to dealing with errors. We saw how Go's syntax for errors is simpler to understand compared to the exception handling that various languages utilize.

An error in Go is a value. Values can be passed around to functions. Any error can be a value, so long as it implements the error interface type. We learned how easily we can create errors. We also learned that we should name our error values so that they start with `Err`, followed by a descriptive camel case name.

Next, we discussed panics and the similarities between a panic and an exception. We also discovered that panics are pretty similar to exceptions; however, if panics aren't handled, they will cause the program to crash. However, Go has a mechanism that will return control of the program to normal: the `recover()` function. The requirement for recovering from a panic is the usage of the `recover()` function in a deferred function. Then, we learned about the general guidelines for using errors, `panic()`, and `recover()` before exploring how to add additional context to errors using error wrapping.

In the next chapter, we will look at interfaces and their uses, as well as how they differ from how other programming languages implement interfaces. We will see how they can be used to solve various problems that you will face as a programmer.

7

Interfaces

Overview

This chapter aims to demonstrate the implementation of interfaces in Go. It is quite simple compared to other languages because it is done implicitly in Go, whereas other languages require interfaces to be implemented explicitly.

In the beginning, you will be able to define and declare an interface for an application and implement an interface in your applications. This chapter introduces you to using duck typing and polymorphism, accepting interfaces, and returning structs.

By the end of this chapter, you will have learned how to use type assertion to access your interface's underlying concrete value and use the type switch statement.

Technical requirements

For this chapter, you'll require Go version 1.21 or higher. The code for this chapter can be found at: `https://github.com/PacktPublishing/Go-Programming-From-Beginner-to-Professional-Second-Edition-/tree/main/Chapter07`.

Introduction

In the previous chapter, we discussed error handling in Go. We looked at what an error is in Go; it is anything that implements the error interface. At the time, we did not investigate what an interface was. In this chapter, we are going to look at what an interface is.

For example, your manager requests that you create an API that can accept JSON data. The data contains information about various employees, such as their address and the hours they worked on a project. The data will need to be parsed into an `employee` struct, a relatively simple task. You then create a function called `loadEmployee(s string)`. The function will accept a string that is formatted as JSON, and then parse that string to load the `employee` struct.

Your manager is happy with the work; however, they have another requirement. The clients need the ability to accept a file with the employee data in JSON format. The functionality to be performed is the same underlying task as before. You create another function called `loadEmployeeFromFile(f *os.File)` that reads the data from the file, parses the data, and loads the `employee` struct.

Your manager has yet another requirement that the employee data should now also come from an HTTP endpoint. You will need to be able to read the data from the HTTP request, so you create another function called `loadEmployeeFromHTTP(r *Request)`.

All three functions that were written have a common behavior that they are performing. They all need to be able to read the data. The underlying type could be different (such as `string`, `os.File`, or `http.Request`) but the behavior, or reading the data, is the same in all cases.

The `func loadEmployee(s string)`, `func loadEmployeeFromFile(f *os.File)`, and `func loadEmployeeFromHTTP(r *Request)` functions can all be replaced using an interface, `func loadEmployee (r io.Reader)`. `io.Reader` is an interface, and we will discuss it in more depth later in the chapter, but for now, it is enough to say it can be used to solve the given problem.

In this chapter, we will see how interfaces can solve such a problem; by defining the behavior that is being performed as an interface type, we can accept any underlying concrete type. Don't worry if that does not make sense right now; it will start to become clearer as we progress in this chapter. We will discuss how interfaces give us the ability to perform duck typing and polymorphism. We will see how accepting interfaces and returning structs will decrease coupling and increase the use of functions in more areas of our programs. We will also examine the empty interface and discuss use cases to fully utilize it, along with type assertion and type switch statements.

Interface

An interface is a set of methods that describe the behavior of the data type. Interfaces define the behavior(s) of the type that must be satisfied to implement that interface. A behavior describes what that type can do. Almost everything exhibits certain behavior. For example, a cat can meow, walk, jump, and purr. All of those are behaviors of a cat. A car can start, stop, turn, and speed up. All of those are behaviors of a car. Similarly, behaviors for types are called methods.

> **Note**
>
> The definition that the official documentation provides is *Interfaces in Go provide a way to specify the behavior of an object.* (`https://go.dev/doc/effective_go#interfaces_and_types`)

There are several ways to describe an interface:

- A collection of method signatures is methods with only the name of the method, its arguments, types, and a return type. This is an example of a collection of method signatures for the `Speaker{}` interface:

```
type Speaker interface {
    Speak(message string) string
    Greet() string
}
```

- Blueprints of the type's methods are needed to satisfy the interface. Using the `Speaker{}` interface, the blueprint (interface) states that to satisfy the `Speaker{}` interface, the type must have a `Speak()` method that accepts a string and returns a string. It also must have a `Greet()` method that returns a string.

- Behaviors are what the interface type must exhibit. For example, the `Reader{}` interface has a Read method. Its behavior is the reading of data. The following code is from the Go standard library's `Reader{}` interface:

```
type Reader interface {
    Read(b []byte) (n int, err error)
}
```

- Interfaces can be described as having no implementation details. When defining an interface, such as the `Reader{}` interface, it only contains the method signatures without the actual code implementation. The responsibility for supplying the code or implementation details lies with the type that implements the interface, not the interfaces themselves.

Behaviors of a type are collectively called method sets, which are collections of methods associated with that type. A method set encompasses the names of methods defined by an interface, along with any input parameters and return types. For example, a type may exhibit behaviors such as `Read()`, `Write()`, and `Save()`. These behaviors collectively form the method sets of the type, providing a clear definition of what actions or functionalities the type can perform.

It is important to note that the reasoning behind the selection of these behaviors and the type's characteristics should be clearly documented. Understanding why a type has specific behaviors adds context to the design decisions and enhances overall code comprehension.

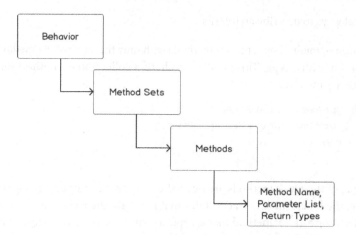

Figure 7.1: Graphical representation of interface elements

When talking about behaviors, note that we did not discuss the implementation details. Implementation details are omitted when you define an interface. It is important to understand that no implementation is specified or enforced in the declaration of an interface. Each type that we create that implements an interface can have its own implementation details. An interface that has a method called Greeting() can be implemented in different ways by various types. A struct type of person can implement Greeting() in a different way than a struct type of animal.

Interfaces focus on the behaviors that the type must exhibit. It is not the job of the interface to provide method implementations. That is the job of the type that is implementing the interface. The types, usually a struct, contain the implementation details of the method sets. Now that we have a basic understanding of an interface, in the next topic, we will be looking at how to define an interface.

Defining an interface

Defining an interface involves the following steps:

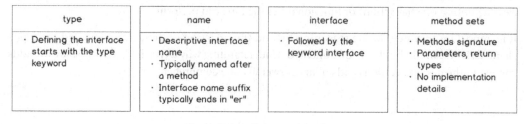

Figure 7.2: Defining an interface

Here is an example of declaring an interface:

```
type Speaker interface {
    Speak() string
}
```

Let's look at each part of this declaration:

- Start with the `type` keyword, followed by the name, and then the `interface` keyword.
- We are defining an interface type called `Speaker{}`. It is idiomatic in Go to name the interface with an `er` suffix. If it is a one-method interface, it is typical to name the interface after that one method.
- Next, you define the method set. Defining an interface type specifies the method(s) that belong to it. In this interface, we are declaring an interface type that has one method called `Speak()` and it returns a string.
- The method set of the `Speaker{}` interface is `Speak()`.

Here is an interface that is used frequently in Go:

```
// https://golang.org/pkg/io/#Reader
type Reader interface {
    Read(p []byte) (n int, err error)
}
```

Let's look at the parts of this code:

- The interface name is `Reader{}`
- The method set is `Read()`
- The signature of the `Read()` method is `(p []byte)(n int, err error)`

Interfaces can have more than one method as its method set. Let's look at an interface used in the Go package:

```
// https://golang.org/pkg/os/#FileInfo
type FileInfo interface {
    Name() string // base name of the file
    Size() int64 // length in bytes for regular files; system-
dependent for others
    Mode() FileMode // file mode bits
    ModTime() time.Time // modification time
    IsDir() bool // abbreviation for Mode().IsDir()
    Sys() interface{} // underlying data source (can return nil)
}
```

As you can see, `FileInfo{}` has multiple methods.

In summary, interfaces are types that declare method sets. Similar to other languages that utilize interfaces, they do not implement the method sets. Implementation details are not part of defining an interface. In the next topic, we will be looking at what Go requires for you to be able to implement the interface.

Implementing an interface

Interfaces in other programming languages implement an interface explicitly. Explicit implementation means that the programming language directly and clearly states that this object is using this interface. For example, this is in Java:

```
class Dog implements Pet
```

The code segment explicitly states that the `Dog` class will implement the `Pet` interface.

In Go, interfaces are implemented implicitly. This means that a type will implement the interface by having all the methods and the signature of the interface. Here is an example:

```go
package main
import (
    "fmt"
)
type Speaker interface {
    Speak() string
}
type cat struct {
}
func main() {
    c := cat{}
    fmt.Println(c.Speak())
    c.Greeting()
}
func (c cat) Speak() string {
    return "Purr Meow"
}
func (c cat) Greeting() {
    fmt.Println("Meow,Meow!!!!mmmeeeeooooowwww")
}
```

Let's break this code down into parts:

```
type Speaker interface {
  Speak() string
}
```

We are defining a `Speaker{}` interface. It has one method that describes the `Speak()` behavior. The method returns a string. For a type to implement the `Speaker{}` interface, it must have the method listed in the interface declaration. Then, we create an empty struct type called `cat`:

```
type cat struct {
}
func (c cat) Speak() string {
  return "Purr Meow"
}
```

The `cat` type has a `Speak()` method that returns the string. This satisfies the `Speaker{}` interface. It is now the responsibility of the implementer of `cat` to provide the implementation details for the `cat` type's `Speak()` method.

Notice that there was no explicit statement that declares `cat` implements the `Speaker{}` interface; it does so by just having met the requirements of the interface.

It is also important to notice that the `cat` type has a method called `Greeting()`. The type can have methods that are not needed to satisfy the `Speaker{}` interface. However, the `cat` must have at least the required method sets to be able to satisfy the interface.

The output will be as follows:

```
Purr Meow
Meow,Meow!!!!mmmeeeeeooooowwww
```

Advantages of implementing interfaces implicitly

There are some advantages to implementing interfaces implicitly. We have seen that when you create an interface, you have to go to each type and explicitly state that the type implements the interface. In Go, the type that satisfies the interface is said to implement it. There is no `implements` keyword like in other languages; you do not need to say that a type implements the interface. In Go, if it has the method sets and signatures of the interface, it implicitly implements the interface.

When you change the method sets of an interface, in other languages you would have to go to all those types that did not satisfy the interface and remove the explicit declaration for the type. This is not the case in Go, since it is an implicit declaration.

Another advantage is you can use interfaces for types that are in another package. This decouples the definition of an interface from its implementation. We will discuss packages and their scope in *Chapter 10, Packages Keep Projects Manageable*.

Let's look at an example of using an interface from a different package in our main package. The `Stringer` interface is an interface that is in the Go language. It is used by several packages through the Go language. One example is the `fmt` package, which is used for formatting when printing values:

```go
type Stringer interface {
    String() string
}
```

`Stringer` is an interface that is a type that can describe itself as a string. Interface names typically follow the method name but with the addition of the `er` suffix:

```go
package main
import (
    "fmt"
)
type Speaker interface {
    Speak() string
}
type cat struct {
    name string
    age int
}
func main() {
    c := cat{name: "Oreo", age:9}
    fmt.Println(c.Speak())
    fmt.Println(c)
}
func (c cat) Speak() string {
    return "Purr Meow"
}
func (c cat) String() string {
    return fmt.Sprintf("%v (%v years old)", c.name, c.age)
}
```

Let's break down this code into parts:

- We have added a `String()` method to our `cat` type. It returns the field data for name and age.

- When we call the `fmt.Println()` method in `main()` with the argument of cat, `fmt.Println()` calls the `String()` method on the `cat` type.

- Our cat type now implements two interfaces: the Speaker{} interface and the Stringer{} interface. It has the methods required to satisfy both of those interfaces:

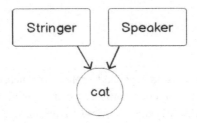

Figure 7.3: Types can implement multiple interfaces

Exercise 7.01 – implementing an interface

In this exercise, we are going to create a simple program that demonstrates how to implement interfaces implicitly. We will have a person struct that will implicitly implement the Speaker{} interface. The person struct will contain name, age, and isMarried as its fields. The program will call the Speak() method of our person struct and display a message displaying the person struct's name. The person struct will also satisfy the requirements for the Stringer{} interface by having a String() method. You may recall previously, in the *Advantages of implementing interfaces implicitly* section, that the Stringer{} interface is an interface that is in the Go language. It can be used for formatting when printing values. That is how we are going to use it in this exercise to format the printing of the fields of the person struct:

1. Create a new file and save it as main.go.

2. We will have package main and will be using the fmt package in this program:

```
package main
import (
   "fmt"
)
```

3. Create a Speaker{} interface with a method called Speak() that returns a string:

```
type Speaker interface {
   Speak() string
}
```

We have created a Speaker{} interface. Any type that wants to implement our Speaker{} interface must have a Speak() method that returns a string.

4. Create our person struct with name, age, and isMarried as its fields:

```
type person struct {
  name string
  age int
  isMarried bool
}
```

Our person type contains name, age, and isMarried fields. We will later print the contents of these fields in our main function using a Speak() method that returns a string. Having a Speak() method will satisfy the Speaker{} interface.

5. In the main() function, we will initialize a person type, print the Speak() method, and print the person field values:

```
func main() {
  p := person{name: "Cailyn", age: 44, isMarried: false}
  fmt.Println(p.Speak())
  fmt.Println(p)
}
```

6. Create a String() method for person and return a string value. This will satisfy the Stringer{} interface, which will now allow it to be called by the fmt.Println() method:

```
func (p person) String() string {
  return fmt.Sprintf("%v (%v years old).\nMarried status: %v ",
p.name, p.age, p.isMarried)
}
```

7. Create a Speak() method for person that returns a string. The person type has a Speak() method that has the same signature as the Speak() method of the Speaker{} interface. The person type satisfies the Speaker{} interface by having a Speak() method that returns the string. To satisfy interfaces, you must have the same methods and method signatures of the interface:

```
func (p person) Speak() string {
  return "Hi my name is: " + p.name
}
```

8. Open the terminal and navigate to the code's directory.

9. Run go build main.go.

10. Correct any errors that are returned and ensure your code matches the code snippet here.

11. Run the executable by typing the executable name in the command line with the ./main command.

You should get the following output:

```
Hi my name is Cailyn
Cailyn (44 years old).
Married status: false
```

In this exercise, we saw how simple it is to implement interfaces implicitly. In the next topic, we will build on this by having different data types, such as structs, implement the same interface, which can be passed to any function that has the argument of that type of interface. We will go into greater detail about how that is possible in the next topic and see why it is a benefit for a type to appear in various forms.

Duck typing

We have been basically doing what is called duck typing. Duck typing is a test in computer programming: *If it looks like a duck, swims like a duck, and quacks like a duck, then it must be a duck.* If a type matches an interface, then you can use that type wherever that interface is used. Duck typing is matching a type based upon methods, rather than the expected type:

```
type Speaker interface {
    Speak() string
}
```

Anything that matches the Speak() method can be a Speaker{} interface. When implementing an interface, we are essentially conforming to that interface by having the required method sets:

```
package main
import (
    "fmt"
)
type Speaker interface {
    Speak() string
}
type cat struct {
}
func main() {
    c := cat{}
    fmt.Println(c.Speak())
}
func (c cat) Speak() string {
    return "Purr Meow"
}
```

cat matches the `Speak()` method of the `Speaker{}` interface, so a cat is a `Speaker{}`:

```
package main
import (
    "fmt"
)
type Speaker interface {
    Speak() string
}
type cat struct {
}
func main() {
    c := cat{}
    chatter(c)
}
func (c cat) Speak() string {
    return "Purr Meow"
}
func chatter(s Speaker) {
    fmt.Println(s.Speak())
}
```

Let's examine this code in parts:

- In the preceding code, we declare a `cat` type and create a method for the `cat` type called `Speak()`. This fulfills the required method sets for the `Speaker{}` interface.

- We create a method called `chatter` that takes the `Speaker{}` interface as an argument.

- In the `main()` function, we are able to pass a `cat` type into the `chatter` function, which can evaluate to the `Speaker{}` interface. This satisfies the required method sets for the interface.

Polymorphism

Polymorphism is the ability to appear in various forms. For example, a shape can appear as a square, circle, rectangle, or any other shape:

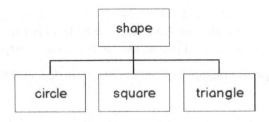

Figure 7.4: Polymorphism example for shape

Go does not do subclassing like other object-oriented languages because Go does not have classes. Subclassing in object-oriented programming is inheriting from one class to another. By doing subclassing, you are inheriting the fields and methods of another class. Go provides a similar behavior through embedding structs and by using polymorphism through interfaces.

One of the advantages of using polymorphism is that it allows the reuse of methods that have been written once and tested. Code is reused by having an **Application Programming Interface (API)** that accepts an interface; if our type satisfies that interface, it can be passed to that API. There is no need to write additional code for each type; we just need to ensure we meet the interface method's set requirements. Obtaining polymorphism through the use of interfaces will increase the reusability of the code. If your API only accepts concrete types such as int, float, and bool, only that concrete type can be passed. However, if your API accepts an interface, then the caller can add the required method sets to satisfy that interface regardless of the underlying type. This reusability is accomplished by allowing your APIs to accept interfaces. Any type that satisfies the interface can be passed to the API. We have seen this type of behavior in a previous example. This is a good time to take a closer look at the Speaker{} interface.

As we have seen in previous examples, each concrete type can implement one or more interfaces. Recall that our Speaker{} interface can be implemented by a dog, cat, or person type:

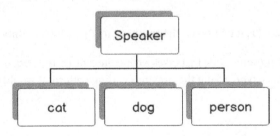

Figure 7.5: The Speaker interface implemented by multiple types

When a function accepts an interface as an input parameter, any concrete type that implements that interface can be passed as an argument. Now, you have achieved polymorphism by being able to pass various concrete types to a method or function that has an interface type as an input parameter.

Let's look at some progressive examples that will enable us to demonstrate how polymorphism is achieved in Go:

```go
package main
import (
  "fmt"
)
type Speaker interface {
  Speak() string
}
type cat struct {
}
func main() {
  c := cat{}
  catSpeak(c)
}
func (c cat) Speak() string {
  return "Purr Meow"
}
func catSpeak(c cat) {
  fmt.Println(c.Speak())
}
```

Let's examine the code in parts:

- cat satisfies the Speaker{} interface. The main() function calls catSpeak() and takes a type of cat.

- Inside catSpeak(), it prints out the results of its Speak() method.

We are going to implement some code that takes a concrete type (cat, dog, or person) and satisfies the Speaker{} interface type. Using the previous coding pattern, it would look like the following code snippet:

```go
package main
import (
  "fmt"
)
type Speaker interface {
  Speak() string
}
```

```
type cat struct {
}
type dog struct {
}
type person struct {
  name string
}
func main() {
  c := cat{}
  d := dog{}
  p := person{name:"Heather"}
  catSpeak(c)
  dogSpeak(d)
  personSpeak(p)
}
func (c cat) Speak() string {
  return "Purr Meow"
}
func (d dog) Speak() string {
  return "Woof Woof"
}
func (p person) Speak() string {
  return "Hi my name is " + p.name +"."
}
func catSpeak(c cat) {
  fmt.Println(c.Speak())
}
func dogSpeak(d dog) {
  fmt.Println(d.Speak())
}
func personSpeak(p person) {
  fmt.Println(p.Speak())
}
```

Let's look at this code in parts:

```
type cat struct {
}
type dog struct {
}
type person struct {
  name string
}
```

We have three concrete types (cat, dog, and person). The cat and dog types are empty structs, while the person struct has a name field:

```go
func (c cat) Speak() string {
    return "Purr Meow"
}
func (d dog) Speak() string {
    return "Woof Woof"
}
func (p person) Speak() string {
    return "Hi my name is " + p.name +"."
}
```

Each of our types implicitly implements the Speaker{} interface. Each of the concrete types implements it differently from the others:

```go
func main() {
    c := cat{}
    d := dog{}
    p := person{name:"Heather"}
    catSpeak(c)
    dogSpeak(d)
    personSpeak(p)
}
```

In the main() function, we call catSpeak(), dogSpeak(), and personSpeak() to invoke their respective Speak() methods. The preceding code has a lot of redundant functions that perform similar actions. We can refactor this code to be simpler and easier to read. We will use some of the features you get with implementing interfaces to provide a more concise implementation:

```go
package main
import (
    "fmt"
)
type Speaker interface {
    Speak() string
}
func saySomething(say ...Speaker) {
    for _, s := range say {
        fmt.Println(s.Speak())
    }
}
type cat struct {}
func (c cat) Speak() string {
```

```
    return "Purr Meow"
}
type dog struct {}
func (d dog) Speak() string {
    return "Woof Woof"
}
type person struct {
    name string
}
func (p person) Speak() string {
    return "Hi my name is " + p.name + "."
}
func main() {
    c := cat{}
    d := dog{}
    p := person{name: "Heather"}
    saySomething(c,d,p)
}
```

Let's look at the code in parts:

```
func saySomething(say ...Speaker)
```

Our `saySomething()` function is using a variadic parameter. If you recall, a variadic parameter can accept zero or more arguments for that type. For more information on variadic functions, review *Chapter 5, Reduce, Reuse, and Recycle*. The parameter type is `Speaker`. An interface can be used as an input parameter:

```
func saySomething(say ...Speaker) {
    for _, s := range say {
        fmt.Println(s.Speak())
    }
}
```

We range over the slice of `Speaker`. For each `Speaker` type, we call the `Speak()` method. In our code, we passed the `cat` and `dog` struct types to the `person` function. The function accepts an argument as an interface of `Speaker{}`. Any of the methods that make up that interface can be invoked. For each of those concrete types, the `Speak()` method is called.

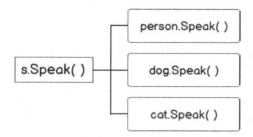

Figure 7.6: Multiple types implementing the Speaker interface

In the main() function, we will see polymorphism being demonstrated through the use of interfaces:

```
func main() {
    c := cat{}
    d := dog{}
    p := person{name: "Heather"}
    saySomething(c,d,p)
}
```

We implement each of the concrete types, cat, dog, and person. The cat, dog, and person types all satisfy the Speaker{} interface. Since they match an interface, you can use that type wherever that interface is used. As you can see, this also includes being able to pass the cat, dog, and person types into a method.

Through the use of interfaces and polymorphism, this code is more concise than the previous code snippets. The example at the beginning of the chapter showed a single concrete type that satisfied the Speaker{} interface that invoked the Speak() method. We then added a few more concrete types to our running example (cat, dog, and person), each of these separately invoking their own Speak() method. We noticed redundant code in that example and started looking for a better way to implement the solution. We discovered that interface types can be parameter input types. Through duck typing and polymorphism, our third and final code snippet was able to have a single function that would call the Speak() method on each type that satisfied the Speaker() interface.

Exercise 7.02 – calculating the area of different shapes using polymorphism

We will be implementing a program that will calculate the area of a triangle, rectangle, and square. The program will use a single function that accepts a Shape interface. Any type that satisfies the Shape interface can be passed as an argument to the function. This function should then print the area and the name of the shape:

1.   Use the IDE of your choice.

2.   Create a new file and save it as main.go.

3. We will have a package called `main`, and we will be using the `fmt` package in this program:

    ```
    package main
    import (
        "fmt"
    )
    ```

4. Create the `Shape{}` interface, which has two method sets called `Area() float64` and `Name() string`:

    ```
    type Shape interface {
        Area() float64
        Name() string
    }
    ```

5. Next, we will create `triangle`, `rectangle`, and `square` struct types. These types will each satisfy the `Shape{}` interface. `triangle`, `rectangle`, and `square` have appropriate fields that are needed to calculate the area of the shape:

    ```
    type triangle struct {
        base float64
        height float64
    }
    type rectangle struct {
        length float64
        width float64
    }
    type square struct {
        side float64
    }
    ```

6. We create the `Area()` and `Name()` methods for the `triangle` struct type. The area of a triangle is *base * height/2*. The `Name()` method returns the name of the shape:

    ```
    func (t triangle) Area() float64 {
        return (t.base * t.height) / 2
    }
    func (t triangle) Name() string {
        return "triangle"
    }
    ```

7. We create the `Area()` and `Name()` methods for the `rectangle` struct type. The area of a rectangle is `length * width`. The `Name()` method returns the name of the shape:

    ```
    func (r rectangle) Area() float64 {
        return r.length * r.width
    }
    ```

```
func (r rectangle) Name() string {
  return "rectangle"
}
```

8. We create the Area() and Name() methods for the square struct type. The area of a square is side * side. The Name() method returns the name of the shape:

```
func (s square) Area() float64 {
  return s.side * s.side
}
func (s square) Name() string {
  return "square"
}
```

Now, each of our shapes (triangle, rectangle, and square) satisfies the Shape interface because they each have an Area() and Name() method with the appropriate signatures:

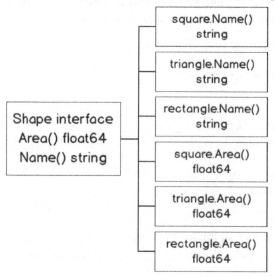

Figure 7.7: square, triangle, and rectangle areas of the Shape type

9. We will now create a function that accepts the Shape interface as a variadic parameter. The function will iterate over the Shape type and execute each of its Name() and Area() methods:

```
func printShapeDetails(shapes ...Shape) {
  for _, item := range shapes {
    fmt.Printf("The area of %s is: %.2f\n", item.Name(), item.
Area())
  }
}
```

10. Inside the `main()` function, set the fields for `triangle`, `rectangle`, and `square`. Pass all three to the `printShapeDetail()` function. All three can be passed because they each satisfy the `Shape` interface:

```
func main() {
    t := triangle{base: 15.5, height: 20.1}
    r := rectangle{length: 20, width: 10}
    s := square{side: 10}
    printShapeDetails(t, r, s)
}
```

11. Build the program by running `go build` at the command line:

```
go build main.go
```

12. Correct any errors that are returned and ensure your code matches the code snippet here.

13. Run the executable by typing the name of the executable and hit *Enter* to run it:

```
./main
```

You should see the following output:

```
The area of triangle is: 155.78
The area of rectangle is: 200.00
The area of square is: 100.00
```

In this exercise, we saw the flexibility and the reusable code that interfaces provide to our programs. Further, we will discuss how accepting interfaces and returning structs for our functions and methods increase code reusability and low coupling by not being dependent on the concrete types. When we use interfaces as input arguments to an API, we are stating that a type needs to satisfy the interface. When using concrete types, we require that the argument for the API must be of that type. For instance, if a function signature is `func greeting(msg string)`, we know that the argument being passed must be a string. Concrete types can be thought of as types that are not abstract (`float64`, `int`, `string`, and so on); however, interfaces could be considered an abstract type because you are satisfying the method sets of the interface type. The underlying interface type is a concrete type, but the underlying type is not what needs to be passed into the API. The type must meet the requirements of having the method sets that the interface type defines.

In the future, if we require another type to be passed, this will mean the code upstream to our API will need to change, or if the caller of our API needs to change its data type, it might request we change our API to accommodate it. If we use interfaces, this is not an issue; the caller of our code needs to satisfy the interface's method sets. The caller can then change the underlying type if it complies with the interface requirements.

Accepting interfaces and returning structs

There is a Go proverb that states, *Accept interfaces, return structs*. It can be restated as accept interfaces and return concrete types. This proverb is talking about accepting interfaces for your APIs (functions, methods, and so on) and the return to be structs or concrete types. This proverb follows Postel's Law, which states, *Be conservative with what you do, be liberal with what you accept*. We are focusing on the *be liberal with what you accept* part. By accepting interfaces, you are increasing the flexibility of the API for your functi0on or method. By doing this, you are allowing for the user of the API to meet the requirements of the interface, but not forcing the user to use a concrete type. If our functions or methods only accept concrete types, then we are limiting the users of our functions to a specific implementation. In this chapter, we are going to explore the previously mentioned Go proverb and learn why it is a good design pattern to follow. We will see that as we go over the code example:

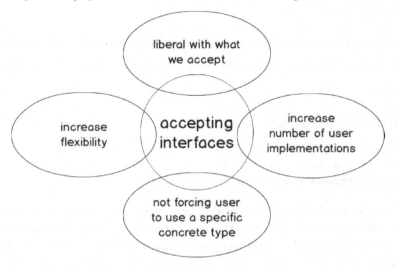

Figure 7.8: Benefits of accepting interfaces

The following example will illustrate the benefits of accepting interfaces versus using concrete types. We will have two functions that perform the same task of decoding JSON, but each has different inputs. One of these functions is superior to the other, and we will go over the reasons why that is the case.

Look at the following example:

main.go

```
package main
import (
    "encoding/json"
    "fmt"
    "io"
```

```
        "strings"
)
type Person struct {
    Name string `json:"name"`
    Age int `json:"age"`
}
```

The full code is available at `https://github.com/PacktPublishing/Go-Programming-From-Beginner-to-Professional-Second-Edition-/blob/main/Chapter07/Example01/main.go`.

The expected output is as follows:

```
{Joe 18}
{Jane 21}
```

Let's examine each part of this code. We will discuss some parts of the code in the upcoming chapters. This code decodes some data into a struct. There are two functions being used for that purpose, `loadPerson2()` and `loadPerson()`:

```
func loadPerson2(s string) (Person, error) {
    var p Person
    err := json.NewDecoder(strings.NewReader(s)).Decode(&p)
    return p, err
}
```

The `loadPerson2()` function accepts an argument that is a concrete string and returns a struct. The returning of the struct meets half of *Accept interfaces, return structs*. However, it is very limited and not liberal in what it accepts. This limits the user of the function to a narrow implementation. The only thing that can ever be passed is a string. Granted, in some cases that might be acceptable, but in other situations, it could be a problem. For example, if your function or method should only accept a specific data type, then you may not want to accept interfaces:

```
func loadPerson(r io.Reader) (Person, error) {
    var p Person
    err := json.NewDecoder(r).Decode(&p)        return p, err
}
```

In this function, we are accepting the `io.Reader{}` interface. The `io.Reader{}` (`https://pkg.go.dev/io#Reader`) and `io.Writer{}` (`https://pkg.go.dev/io#Writer`) interfaces are among the most utilized interfaces in Go packages. `json.NewDecoder` accepts anything that satisfies the `io.Reader{}` interface. The caller code just needs to make sure whatever they pass satisfies the `io.Reader{}` interface:

```
p, err := loadPerson(strings.NewReader(s))
```

strings.NewReader returns a Reader type that has a Read(b []byte) (n int, err error) method that satisfies the io.Reader{} interface. It can be passed to our loadPerson() function. You may be thinking that each function still does what it was intended for. You would be correct, but let's say the caller is no longer going to pass a string, or another caller will be passing a file that contains the JSON data:

```
f, err := os.Open("data.json")
if err != nil {
  fmt.Println(err)
}
```

Our loadPerson2() function would not work; however, our loadPerson() data would work because the return type from os.Open() satisfies the io.Reader{} interface.

Say, for instance, the data will be coming through an HTTP endpoint. We will be getting the data from *http.Request. Again, the loadPerson2() function would not be a good choice. We would get the data from request.Body, which just so happens to implement the io.Reader{} interface.

You may be wondering whether interfaces are good for input arguments. If so, why would we not return them too? If you return an interface, it adds unnecessary difficulty for the user. The user will have to look up the interface to then find the method set and the method set's signature:

```
func someFunc() Speaker{} {
  // code
}
```

You would need to look at the definition of the Speaker{} interface and then spend time looking at the implementation code, all of which is unnecessary for the user of the function. If an interface is needed from the return type of the function, the user of the function can create the interface for that concrete type and use it in their code.

As you start to follow this Go proverb, check to see whether there is an interface in the Go standard packages. This will increase the number of different implementations that your function can provide. Our users of the function can have various implementations using strings.newReader, http.Request.Body, and os.File, just like in our code example, by using the io.Reader{} interface from the Go standard packages.

Empty interface

An empty interface is an interface that has no method sets and no behaviors. An empty interface specifies no methods:

```
interface{}
```

This is a straightforward yet complex concept to wrap your head around. As you may recall, interfaces are implemented implicitly; there is no `implements` keyword. Since an empty interface specifies no methods, that means that every type in Go implements an empty interface automatically. All types satisfy the empty interface.

In the following code snippet, we will demonstrate how to use the empty interface. We will also see how a function that accepts an empty interface allows any type to be passed to that function:

main.go

```go
package main
import "fmt"
type Speaker interface {
    Speak() string
}
type cat struct {
    name string
}
```

The full code is available at `https://github.com/PacktPublishing/Go-Programming-From-Beginner-to-Professional-Second-Edition-/blob/01d1c9d340172a55335add4ad7adc285b7a51fe4/Chapter07/Example02/main.go`.

The expected output is as follows:

```
({oreo}, main.cat)
({oreo}, main.cat)
(99, int)
(false, bool)
(test, string)
```

Let's evaluate the code in sections:

```go
func emptyDetails(s interface{}) {
   fmt.Printf("(%v, %T)\n", i, i)
}
```

The function accepts an empty `interface{}`. Any type can be passed to the function since all types implement the empty `interface{}`. It prints the value and the concrete type. The `%v` verb prints the value and the `%T` verb prints the concrete type:

```go
func main() {
   c := cat{name: "oreo"}
   i := 99
```

```
    b := false
    str := "test"
    catDetails(c)
    emptyDetails(c)
    emptyDetails(i)
    emptyDetails(b)
    emptyDetails(str)
}
```

We pass a cat type, integer, bool, and string. The emptyDetails() function will print each of them:

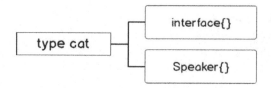

Figure 7.9: The cat type implements an empty interface{} and the Speaker interface

The cat type implements the empty interface{} and the Speaker{} interface implicitly.

Now that we have a basic understanding of empty interfaces, we will be looking at various use cases for them in the upcoming topics, including the following:

- Type switching

- Type assertion

- Examples of Go packages

Type assertion and switches

Type assertion provides access to an interface's concrete type. Remember that interface{} can be any value:

```
package main
import (
  "fmt"
)
func main() {
    var str interface{} = "some string"
    var i interface{} = 42
    var b interface{} = true
    fmt.Println(str)
    fmt.Println(i)
```

```
    fmt.Println(b)
}
```

The type assertion output would look as follows:

```
some string
42
true
```

In each instance of the variable declaration, each variable is declared as an empty interface, but the concrete value for `str` is a string, for `i` is an integer, and for `b` is a Boolean.

When there is an empty `interface{}` type, sometimes, it is beneficial to know the underlying concrete type. For instance, you may need to perform data manipulation based on that type. If that type is a string, you would perform data modification and validation differently from how you would if it was an integer value. This also comes into play when you are consuming JSON data of an unknown schema. The values in that JSON might be known during the ingesting process. We would need to convert that data to `map[string]interface{}` and perform various data massaging, or transformation of the data based on its underlying type or structure. We have an activity later in this chapter that will show us how to perform such an action. We could perform a type conversion with the `strconv` package:

```
package main
import (
  "fmt"
  "strconv"
)
func main() {
  var str interface{} = "some string"
  var i interface{} = 42
  fmt.Println(strconv.Atoi(i))
}
```

```
prog.go:15:26: cannot use i (type interface {}) as type string in argument to strconv.Atoi: need type assertion
```

Figure 7.10: Error when type assertion is needed

So, it appears we cannot use type conversion because the types are not compatible with type conversion. We will need to use type assertion:

```
v := s.(T)
```

The preceding statement says that it asserts that the interface value s is of type T and assigns the underlying value of v:

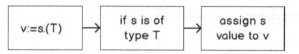

Figure 7.11: Type assertion flow

Consider the following code snippet:

```
package main
import (
    "fmt"
    "strings"
)
func main() {
    var str interface{} = "some string"
    v := str.(string)
    fmt.Println(strings.Title(v))
}
```

Let's examine the preceding code:

- The preceding code asserts that str is of the string type and assigns it to the variable v
- Since v is a string, it will print it with title casing

The result is as follows:

```
Some String
```

It is good when the assertion matches the expected type. So, what will happen if s is not of type T? Let's take a look:

```
package main
import (
    "fmt"
    "strings"
)
func main() {
    var str interface{} = 49
    v := str.(string)
    fmt.Println(strings.Title(v))
}
```

Let's examine the preceding code:

- `str{}` is an empty interface and the concrete type is `int`

- The type assertion is checking whether `str` is of the string type, but in this scenario, it is not, so the code will panic

- The result is as follows:

```
panic: interface conversion: interface {} is int, not string

goroutine 1 [running]:
main.main()
          /tmp/sandbox011356825/main.go:11 +0x40
```

Figure 7.12: Failed type assertion

Having a panic being thrown is not desirable. However, Go has a way to check whether `str` is a string:

```
package main
import (
  "fmt"
)
func main() {
  var str interface{} = "the book club"
  v, isValid := str.(int)
  fmt.Println(v, isValid)
}
```

Let's examine the preceding code:

- A type assertion returns two values, the underlying value and a Boolean value.

- `isValid` is assigned to a return type of `bool`. If it returns `true`, that indicates that `str` is of the `int` type. It means that the assertion is true. We can use the Boolean that was returned to determine what action we can take on `str`.

- When the assertion fails, it will return `false`. The return value will be the zero value that you are trying to assert to. It also will not panic.

There will be times when you do not know the empty interface concrete type. This is when you will use a type switch. A type switch can perform several types of assertions; it is similar to a regular switch statement. It has a case and default clauses. The difference is that type switch statements evaluate for a type rather than a value.

Here is a basic syntax structure:

```
switch v := i.(type) {
case S:
  // code to act upon the type S
}
```

Let's examine the preceding code:

```
i.(type)
```

The syntax is like that of the type assertion, `i.(int)`, except the specified type, `int` in our example, is replaced with the `type` keyword. The type being asserted of type `i` is assigned to `v`; then, it is compared to each of the `case` statements:

```
case S:
```

In the `switch` type, the statements evaluate for types. In regular switching, they evaluate for values. Here, it is evaluated for a type of S.

Now that we have a fundamental understanding of the type switch statement, let's look at an example that uses the syntax we have just evaluated:

main.go

```
func typeExample(i []interface{}) {
    for _, x := range i {
    switch v := x.(type) {
        case int:
            fmt.Printf("%v is int\n", v)
        case string:
            fmt.Printf("%v is a string\n", v)
        case bool:
            fmt.Printf("a bool %v\n", v)
        default:
            fmt.Printf("Unknown type %T\n", v)
        }
    }
}
```

The full code is available at https://github.com/PacktPublishing/Go-Programming-From-Beginner-to-Professional-Second-Edition-/blob/main/Chapter07/Example03/main.go.

Let's now explore the code in pieces:

```
func main() {
  c := cat{name: "oreo"}
  i := []interface{}{42, "The book club", true, c}
  typeExample(i)
}
```

In the `main()` function, we are initializing a variable, `i`, to a slice of interfaces. In the slice, we have the `int`, `string`, `bool`, and `cat` types:

```
func typeExample(i []interface{})
```

The function accepts a slice of interfaces:

```
for _, x := range i {
  switch v := x.(type) {
    case int:
      fmt.Printf("%v is int\n", v)
    case string:
      fmt.Printf("%v is a string\n", v)
    case bool:
      fmt.Printf("a bool %v\n", v)
    default:
      fmt.Printf("Unknown type %T\n", v)
  }
}
```

The `for` loop ranges over the slice of interfaces. The first value in the slice is 42. The `switch` case asserts that the slice value of 42 is an `int` type. The `case int` statement will evaluate to `true` and print that 42 is `int`. When the `for` loop iterates over the last value of the `cat` type, the `switch` statement will not find that type in its case evaluations. Since there is no `cat` type being checked for in the `case` statements, the default will execute its `print` statement. Here are the results of the code being executed:

```
42 is int
The book club is string
a bool true
Unknown type main.cat
```

Exercise 7.03 – analyzing empty interface{} data

In this exercise, we are given a map. The map's key is a string and its value is an empty `interface{}`. The map's value contains different types of data stored in the value portion of the map. Our job is to determine each key's value type. We are going to write a program that will analyze the data of map[string] interface{}. Understand that the values of the data can be of any type. We need to write logic to catch types we are not looking for. We are going to store that information in a slice of structs that will hold the key name, data, and the type of data:

1. Create a new file called main.go.

2. Inside the file, we will have a main package and will need to import the fmt package:

    ```
    package main
    import (
        "fmt"
    )
    ```

3. We will create a struct called record that will store the key, type of value, and data from map[string] interface{}. This struct is used to store the analysis that we are performing on the map. The key field is the name of the map key. The valueType field stores the type of data stored as a value in the map. The data field stores the data we are analyzing. It is an empty interface{}, since there can be various types of data in the map:

    ```
    type record struct {
        key string
        valueType string
        data interface{}
    }
    ```

4. We will create a person struct that will be added to our map[string] interface{}:

    ```
    type person struct {
        lastName string
        age int
        isMarried bool
    }
    ```

5. We will create an animal struct that will be added to our map[string] interface{}:

    ```
    type animal struct {
        name string
        category string
    }
    ```

6. Create a newRecord() function. The key parameter will be our map's key. The function also takes interface{} as an input parameter. i will be our map's value for the key that is passed to the function. It will return a record type:

    ```
    func newRecord(key string, i interface{}) record {
    ```

7. Inside the `newRecord()` function, we initialize `record{}` and assign it to the `r` variable. We then assign `r.key` to the key input parameter.

8. The `switch` statement assigns the type of `i` to the `v` variable. The `v` variable type gets evaluated against a series of `case` statements. If a type evaluates to `true` for one of the `case` statements, then the `valueType` record gets assigned to that type, along with the value of `v` to `r.data`, and then returns the `record` type:

```
r := record{}
r.key = key
switch v := i.(type) {
case int:
   r.valueType = "int"
   r.data = v   case bool:
   r.valueType = "bool"
   r.data = v   case string:
   r.valueType = "string"
   r.data = v   case person:
   r.valueType = "person"
```

9. The `r.data = vA default` statement is needed for the `switch` statement. If the type of `v` does not get evaluated to `true` in the `case` statements, then `default` will be executed. `record.valueType` will be marked as unknown:

```
default:
   r.valueType = "unknown"
   r.data = v   }
   return r

}
```

10. Inside the `main()` function, we will initialize our map. The map is initialized to a string for the key and an empty interface for the value. We then assign `a` to an `animal` struct literal and `p` to a `person` struct literal. Then, we start adding various key-value pairs to the map:

```
func main() {
  m := make(map[string]interface{})
  a := animal{name: "oreo", category: "cat"}
  p := person{lastName: "Doe", isMarried: false, age: 19}
  m["person"] = p
  m["animal"] = a
  m["age"] = 54
  m["isMarried"] = true
  m["lastName"] = "Smith"
```

11. Next, we initialize a slice of `record`. We iterate over the map and add records to `rs`:

```
rs := []record{}
for k, v := range m {
    r := newRecord(k, v)
    rs = append(rs, r)
}
```

12. Now, print out the record field values. We range over the slice of records and print each record value:

```
for _, v := range rs {
    fmt.Println("Key: ", v.key)
    fmt.Println("Data: ", v.data)
    fmt.Println("Type: ", v.valueType)
    fmt.Println()
}
}
```

Iterating over maps may produce output in different orders. An example of the expected output is as follows:

```
Key:    lastName
Data:   Smith
Type:   string

Key:    person
Data:   {Doe 19 false}
Type:   person

Key:    animal
Data:   {oreo cat}
Type:   unknown

Key:    age
Data:   54
Type:   int

Key:    isMarried
Data:   true
Type:   bool
```

Figure 7.13: Output for the exercise

The exercise has demonstrated Go's ability to identify the underlying type of an empty interface. As you can see from the results, our type switch was able to identify each type except for the value of the key of `animal`. It has its type marked as `unknown`. Also, it was even able to identify the `person` struct type, and the data has the field values of the struct.

Activity 7.01 – calculating pay and performance review

In this activity, we are going to calculate the annual pay for a manager and a developer. We will print out the developer's and manager's names and their pay for the year. The developer pay will be based on an hourly rate. The developer type will also keep track of the number of hours they have worked in a year. The developer type will also include their review. The review will need to be a collection of keys of strings. These strings are the categories that the developer is being reviewed on, for example, work quality, teamwork, and communication.

The aim of this activity is to use an interface to demonstrate polymorphism by calling a single function called payDetails() that accepts an interface. This payDetails() function will print the salary information for a developer type and a manager type.

The following steps should help you with the solution:

1. Create an Employee type that has Id, FirstName, and LastName fields.

2. Create a Developer type that has the following fields: Individual of the Employee type and HourlyRate, HoursWorkedInYear, and Review of the map[string] interface{} type.

3. Create a Manager type with the following fields: Individual of the Employee type, Salary, and CommissionRate.

4. Create a Payer interface that has a Pay() method that returns a string and float64.

5. The Developer type should implement the Payer{} interface by returning the Developer name and returning the developer year pay based on the calculation of Developer. HourlyRate * Developer.HoursWorkInYear.

6. The Manager type should implement the Payer{} interface by returning the Manager name and returning the Manager year pay based on the calculation of Manager.Salary + (Manager.Salary * Manager.CommissionRate).

7. Add a function called payDetails(p Payer) that accepts a Payer interface and prints fullName and the pay that is returned from the Pay() method.

8. We now need to calculate the review rating for a developer. Review is obtained by map[string] interface{}. The key of the map is a string; it is what the developer is being rated on, such as work quality, teamwork, and skills.

9. The empty interface{} of the map is needed because some managers give the rating as a string and others as a number. Here is the mapping of the string to the integer:

```
"Excellent" - 5
"Good" - 4
"Fair" - 3
"Poor" - 2
"Unsatisfactory" - 1
```

10. We need to calculate the performance review value as a `float` type. It is the sum of the map `interface{}` divided by the length of the map. Take into consideration that the rating can be a string or an integer, so you will need to be able to accept both and convert it into a float.

The expected output is as follows:

```
Eric Davis got a review rating of 2.80
Eric Davis got paid 84000.00 for the year
Mr. Boss got paid 160500.00 for the year
```

> **Note**
>
> The solution for this activity can be found in the GitHub repository folder for this chapter: `https://github.com/PacktPublishing/Go-Programming-From-Beginner-to-Professional-Second-Edition-/tree/main/Chapter07/Activity7.01`.

In this activity, we saw the benefits of using an empty interface that allows us to accept any type of data. We then used type assertion and type switch statements to perform certain tasks based on the underlying concrete type of the empty interface.

any

The any keyword as of **Go 1.18** is basically an alias to `interface{}`. With the any type definition, Go has replaced all references to the empty interface. However, it is important to note that they are interchangeable, being type aliases.

Summary

This chapter presented some fundamental and advanced topics when using interfaces. We learned that Go's implementation of interfaces has some similarities with other languages; for example, an interface does not contain the implementation details of the behaviors it is representing, and an interface is the blueprint of the methods. The different types that implement the interface can differ in their implementation details. However, Go differs in how you implement an interface compared to other languages. We learned that the implementation is done implicitly and not explicitly like in other languages.

This concludes that Go does not do subclassing; so, for it to implement polymorphism, it uses interfaces. It allows an interface type to appear in different forms, such as a `Shape` interface appearing as a rectangle, square, or circle.

We also discussed a design pattern of accepting interfaces and returning structs. We demonstrated that this pattern allows for broader uses by other callers. We examined the empty interface and saw how it can be used when you do not know the type being passed or when there could be multiple different types being passed to your API. Even though we did not know the type at runtime, we showed you how to use type assertion and type switching to determine the type. We also saw updates regarding the any keyword being a type alias to the empty interface. The knowledge and practice of these various tools will help you build robust and fluid programs.

In the following chapter, we will look at more Go 1.18 updates regarding generics, and how that allows developers to use code for more than one type of variable!

8

Generic Algorithm Superpowers

Overview

This chapter will discuss the versatility and expressive strength that Go's type parameter syntax brings developers. As we explore this chapter, we'll uncover the means to create algorithms that transcend the limitations of single variable types. By harnessing the power of type parameters, developers gain the ability to craft generic versions of their code, enabling it to seamlessly operate on multiple types. This chapter will highlight the overarching goal to reduce code duplication while preserving the robust safety intrinsic to Go's strong typing system.

This chapter will also navigate the world of constraints, showcasing how Go fortifies generic algorithms against unintended mishaps, as well as help you understand when to use generic algorithms versus interfaces. Through practical examples and activities, you will grasp the art of designing generic algorithms and understand the superpowers of generic algorithms. By the end of the chapter, you will be equipped with a profound understanding of when, why, and how to wield the generic algorithm superpowers in Go. We'll also cover some best practices and provide clarity on when to use interfaces versus generics.

Technical requirements

For this chapter, you'll require Go version 1.21 or higher. The code for this chapter can be found at https://github.com/PacktPublishing/Go-Programming-From-Beginner-to-Professional-Second-Edition-/tree/main/Chapter08.

Introduction

The Go team at Google is always thinking about how to make the lives of Go developers easier and what tools, packages, and support we need for the future – always in a fully backward-compatible way. In this chapter, we will expand upon our knowledge gained so far and discuss Go generics.

Generics officially became a part of the language in Go version 1.18. Go generics provide a powerful means of developing code that removes duplication, simplifies readability, and enables developers a way to use multiple types within a function. However, with great power comes great responsibility. Let's discuss generics further.

When to use generics?

The decision to finally incorporate generics into the Go programming language was not a trivial one. As they are such a large change to the language, it is important to remember our roots as developers and not to allow support such as generics to change *how* we write our code. In other words, you should continue writing normal Go code and not overly design types right from the get-go. These are fundamental Go philosophies rooted in simplicity and readability, which are the core tenets of the language.

The following is a synopsis of insights to consider when incorporating Go generics into a code base:

- **Write normal Go code, and don't design types**: Start with your typical concrete types and straightforward functions, leveraging Go's strong static typing and simplicity. Generics were never meant to replace the fundamental principles guiding the use of the language but, rather, be a tool to be applied judiciously.

- **Avoid boilerplate code**: This was one of the main motivating factors behind introducing generics to the language. When you find yourself writing repetitive and nearly identical code for different types, then it is a signal that generics can help streamline your implementation. Instead of duplicating logic for various data structures and types, you can create generic functions or types that work seamlessly with different types. This removes code redundancy and improves developer maintainability of the logic.

- **Code complexity considerations**: If your project involves intricate data structures or algorithms, generics can help abstract away the complexity and make your code more comprehensible. However, be cautious to not over-engineer; only introduce generics when they genuinely simplify your code.

- **Enhance code flexibility**: Generics allow functions and data structures to work with various types. If your code needs to accommodate diverse data types without sacrificing performance or safety, then generics can be a valuable addition.

- **Future-proofing code**: If you anticipate changes or expansion where introducing new types is likely, incorporating generics early on can future-proof your code and reduce the need for extensive refactoring down the line.

To take a look at what generics look like in action in Go, let's first look at a regular implementation for a function, finding the maximum value for integer values passed into a function using a naive approach:

```go
package main
import "fmt"

func findMaxInt(nums []int) int {
    if len(nums) == 0 {
        return -1
    }
    max := nums[0]
    for _, num := range nums {
        if num > max {
            max = num
        }
    }
    return max
}
func main() {
    max := findMaxInt([]int{1, 32, 5, 8, 10, 11})
    fmt.Printf("max integer value: %v\n", max)
}
```

If we wanted to now find the maximum value for a different type of input, such as floating-point values, then we'd have to add a new function containing duplicate logic:

```go
func findMaxFloat(nums []float64) float64 {
    if len(nums) == 0 {
        return -1
    }
    max := nums[0]
    for _, num := range nums {
        if num > max {
            max = num
        }
    }
    return max
}
```

You can see how this is already repetitive. If we wanted to check for the max value for additional types, then so far, we'd have a lot of repeated logic. However, now we can take a look at how having a generic maximum function can be beneficial here:

```
func findMaxGeneric[Num int | float64](nums []Num) Num {
    if len(nums) == 0 {
        return -1
    }
    max := nums[0]
    for _, num := range nums {
        if num > max {
            max = num
        }
    }
    return max
}
```

Albeit, this is a simple example to find a maximum, we've made progress by moving from expanded code to adding generics to it and removing code duplication, making for cleaner code. You can also see that the preceding function signature uses a different notation utilizing generics in Go that allows for integer input or float-point input to the function. Now, let's introduce type parameters, a fundamental aspect of generics that helps developers enhance code clarity and maintainability, which will explain the different notations in the function signature on our preceding generic function.

Type parameters

Type parameters for Go functions give you the ability to parameterize a function with types that support generic input. It's a way to specify to the compiler the types allowed when invoking a generic function and represents a placeholder for a type within a given function. Type parameter lists look like normal parameter lists but are encompassed by square brackets. For example, [T any] declares a T type parameter that can be any type. The any keyword was touched on in the previous chapter.

To continue to understand type parameters, let's return to our maximum generic function signature from the earlier example code:

```
func findMaxGeneric[Num int | float64](nums []Num) Num {
```

This indicates that our function, titled findMaxGeneric, includes a type parameter, Num, that can be instantiated by an integer or float64 type. It will take in a slice of Num and return the resulting maximum integer or float64 value.

An interesting concept associated with type parameters is type sets. In the preceding example function signature, we discussed how Num can be instantiated by an integer or float64 type. This means that the type set for the Num type parameter is the union of integer and float64 types. So, our findMaxGeneric function may be called with those constrained allowed types for Num. Type constraints will be discussed further in this chapter.

> **Note**
>
> Type parameters are usually uppercase to emphasize that they are indeed types.

We can call the generic function and pass in our input with the following code:

```
maxGenericInt := findMaxGeneric([]int{1, 32, 5, 8, 10, 11})
```

The numbers we pass into the function are called our type arguments. Providing type arguments to a function is called instantiation. Instantiation is important in generics when you provide type arguments for type parameters. The type argument is the actual type that is provided or inferred when using generic functions. It is the concrete type that replaces the type parameter when the generic code is instantiated or called upon.

Furthermore, if we were to pass in an invalid type argument for our type parameter, then the Go compiler would complain. For example, if we tried to pass in string values, then we'd see an error:

```
string does not satisfy int | float64 (string missing in int |
float64)
```

Our code did not compile properly, as the Go type system prevented us from passing in an invalid type argument for our type parameter.

Activity 8.01 – a minimum value

In this activity, we write a simple function to calculate a minimum value, where the input can be of the integer or float64 type:

1. Create a findMinGeneric function that calculates the minimum value of a slice of input.

    The input can only be of integer or float64 type.

2. Print the resulting minimum value for both integers and floating-point values.

For input using []int{1, 32, 5, 8, 10, 11}, your output should look like this:

```
min value: 1
```

For input using [] float64{1.1, 32.1, 5.1, 8.1, 10.1, 11.1}, your output should look like this:

```
min value: 1.1
```

> **Note**
>
> The solution for this activity can be found in the GitHub repository folder for this chapter: https://github.com/PacktPublishing/Go-Programming-From-Beginner-to-Professional-Second-Edition-/tree/main/Chapter08/Activity08.01.

Type parameters are useful when working with functions that operate on slices, maps, and channels of any element type. Furthermore, when the function has parameters with those types and doesn't make assumptions based on the element type, it can be generalized– for example, returning keys in any map type. This is also useful when working with general-purpose data structures such as linked lists or binary trees. Replacing an element type with a type parameter can provide a more general data structure that is far more reusable. You should not make use type parameters prematurely. Wait until you're about to write boilerplate code. Premature abstractions can lead to unnecessary complexity and make code harder for others to understand. It is recommended to wait until you encounter a specific need for generic solutions, especially when faced with repetitive patterns or boilerplate code. This approach aligns well with Go's philosophy of simplicity and incremental design, ensuring that the introduction of generics to a code base is purposeful and justified.

Now, let's explore type constraints and how they give us a way to specify capabilities or properties that a type parameter must have, in order to be used with a generic function.

Type constraints

Type constraints are a sort of meta-type for the function type parameter. Type constraints dictate the allowed type arguments for any given type parameter of a function.

Type constraints in Go generics refer to interfaces that define sets of types. These interfaces play a powerful role in specifying the requirements or capabilities that a type parameter must satisfy when working with generic functions or types. To use these interfaces effectively, they must be placed in what is known as the "constraint position" within the syntax, specifically in the type parameter list where the type parameter is declared.

In this constraint position, when declaring a generic function or type, the constraints are expressed using an interface type to define the expected behavior of the type parameter. This ensures that the provided types adhere to the specified constraints, allowing the generic code to operate on them safely. By enforcing these constraints, the Go compiler can perform thorough type checking at compile time, enhancing code reliability and maintainability.

When dealing with more complex types, oftentimes you will declare constraints as an interface. The constraint allows any type that implements the interface to be used with the function. Constraint interfaces can refer to specific and more basic types. Using constraint interfaces can help pull out the type constraints into a more readable form.

Containing a distinct set of logic for constraints for the added generics in the Go programming language, a standard library package called `constraints` has been added experimentally that you can explore for more insights on defining constraints when working with type parameters.

Exercise 8.01 – calculate the maximum value using interfaces

Let's take a look at expanding our maximum logic from earlier into a more readable form, using interfaces for our type constraints. We will continue only allowing integer and float64 values for now:

1. Create a new folder and add a `main.go` file.

2. In `main.go`, add the main package name to the top of the file:

    ```
    package main
    ```

3. Now, add the imports that we'll use in this file:

    ```
    import (
      "fmt"
    )
    ```

4. Create a `Number` interface that will represent the types of values we allow as input:

    ```
    type Number interface {
        int | float64
    }
    ```

5. Create a function that takes a slice of numbers and returns the maximum value:

    ```
    func findMaxGeneric[Num Number](nums []Num) Num {
    ```

6. Ensure valid input by verifying that there are inputs passed into the function:

    ```
    if len(nums) == 0 {
        return -1
    }
    ```

7. Get the first value to have a placeholder maximum value, before checking the remaining values:

    ```
    max := nums[0]
    ```

8. Traverse the numbers:

    ```
    for _, num := range nums {
    ```

9. Check whether the current number is greater than the placeholder maximum value, and reset the maximum to the current value as needed:

```
if num > max {
        max = num
}
```

10. Close the `for` loop:

```
}
```

11. Return the maximum:

```
return max
```

12. Close the function:

```
}
```

13. Define the main function:

```
func main() {
```

14. Call our function and print out the results for integer and float64 input:

```
maxGenericInt := findMaxGeneric([]int{1, 32, 5, 8, 10, 11})
fmt.Printf("max generic int: %v\n", maxGenericInt)

maxGenericFloat := findMaxGeneric([]float64{1.1, 32.1, 5.1,
8.1, 10.1, 11.1})
fmt.Printf("max generic float: %v\n", maxGenericFloat)
```

15. Close the main function:

```
}
```

Running the preceding code shows the following output:

```
max generic int: 32
max generic float: 32.1
```

We have now seen what it looks like to make our type constraint interface more readable, by defining a `Number` interface to find the maximum value. You can see the benefits of defining one function that can be used for integer and float64 values.

In the last chapter, we learned a lot about interfaces and how they define a set of methods that a type must implement. When working with generics, you can express constraints on the types that can be used as type parameters, by specifying that they must satisfy certain interface requirements.

For type parameters, you might see constraints such as comparable or custom interfaces that define specific methods. Let's take a peek at leveraging a more complex example using comparable.

Exercise 8.02 – calculate the largest stock of items on a ranch

Let's say that there is a ranch with different items in stock. We can use generics to calculate the largest stock of different items on the ranch:

1. Create a new folder and add a main.go file.

2. In main.go, add the main package name at the top of the file:

   ```
   package main
   ```

3. Now, add the imports that we'll use in this file:

   ```
   import (
     "fmt"
   )
   ```

4. Define the function to find the largest ranch stock using generics:

   ```
   func FindLargestRanchStock[K comparable, V int | float64](m
   map[K]V) K {
   ```

5. Define variables to save the largest stock found so far and the name of the stocked item:

   ```
   var stock V
   var name K
   ```

6. Loop over the map, and if the new value found is greater than the largest stock at the time, then update the values to the largest and save the item name:

   ```
   for k, v := range m {
       if v > stock {
           stock = v
           name = k
       }
   }
   ```

7. Return the name of the item with the largest stock on the ranch:

   ```
   return name
   ```

8. Close the function:

   ```
   }
   ```

9. Define the `main` function:

```
func main() {
```

10. Define our ranch items in stock:

```
animalStock := map[string]int{
    "Chicken": 5,
    "Cattle": 20,
    "Horses": 4,
}
miscStock := map[string]float64{
    "Hay": 5.5,
    "Feed": 1.2,
    "Fertilizer": 4.5,
}
```

11. Call our function, and print out the results for the largest stocked items in the ranch:

```
largestStockOnRanchInt := FindLargestRanchStock(animalStock)
fmt.Printf("The largest stocked item on the ranch is %s\n",
largestStockOnRanchInt)

largestStockOnRanchFloat := FindLargestRanchStock(miscStock)
fmt.Printf("The largest stocked item on the ranch is %s\n",
largestStockOnRanchFloat)
```

12. Close the `main` function:

```
}
```

Running the preceding code shows the following output:

```
The largest stocked item on the ranch is Cattle
The largest stocked item on the ranch is Hay
```

We've now seen a generics example using `comparable`. The constraint on our K type parameter in the function was `comparable`. This is thanks to the type of the commonly used constraint, enabled by helpers from Go using the `comparable` standard library. `comparable` allows any type whose value can be used as an operand of the comparison operators, such as `==` and `!=`. Go requires the keys of maps to be comparable, so the `comparable` declaration is necessary on our map key type to use K as the key in the ranch map. If we didn't declare K to be `comparable`, then the Go compiler would reject the reference to map [K] V in our function's argument.

As you can see, Go allows a very powerful form of interface type to express constraints. We can easily expand this example to work on even more complex interfaces and constraints.

It is noteworthy to mention that replacing an interface type with a type parameter can make the underlying storage of data more efficient. It can also mean that code can avoid type assertions and be fully type-checked at compile time.

Now that we've discussed type parameters and type constraints, let's take a peek at what's going on when it comes to type inference.

Type inference

The Go compiler infers the types we want to use from the function arguments. This is called type inference. The compiler will deduce type arguments from type parameter constraints.

Type inference either succeeds or fails. The compiler will complain, and we are provided the type arguments that need correcting upon finding an issue. Using generics is meant to be easy; however, the underlying details of type inference are highly complicated. It is also something the authors are iterating on to improve.

At this point, when it comes to calling generic functions, we've covered how you can specify type arguments in square brackets as type names. This allows the compiler to know to replace the type parameters within the function you're invoking. However, you can omit the type arguments, as most of the time Go can infer them. However, it is not always possible to simplify your code by dropping type arguments. As the compiler runs your code, it replaces each type parameter with the concrete types.

A concrete example of this can be seen in many of our function signatures where we've allowed the compiler to infer our types. For example, in the last exercise, we discussed ranch item stocks. Our function signature in the code was as follows:

```
largestStockOnRanchInt := FindLargestRanchStock(animalStock)
```

This invocation allows the compiler to infer the type of `animalStock`. However, it is also identical to the following:

```
largestStockOnRanchInt := FindLargestRanchStock[string, int]
(animalStock)
```

Here, we explicitly state the types for our key and values getting passed in. There are a few scenarios where it may not be possible or advisable to rely on the compiler to infer types when working with generic functions:

- **Ambiguous types**: There may be multiple types that satisfy the constraints. For example, imagine you have a `PrintType` function that prints the type of a value. If you pass in a string, it should recognize it as a string; if you pass in an integer, it should recognize it as an integer. When calling this function, you explicitly state the types using `PrintType("Hello")`, `PrintType(42)`, `PrintType(3.14)`, and so on.

- **Multiple type parameters**: Consider a `PrintTwoTypes` function that takes two parameters of potentially different types. When calling this function, you might specify the types explicitly for various reasons. Then, `PrintTwoTypes` could be defined with an integer and string parameter and used as such – `PrintTwoTypes(42, "Hello)`.

- **Chained calls**: This is where types need to flow multiple calls. Envision a scenario where you have a function, `ChainCalls`, that processes a value and then calls another function, `AnotherFunction`. Here, you might explicitly state the types of chained calls to ensure a smooth flow.

You can also add explicit types to add clarity in complex scenarios or to enhance readability, reducing time spent debugging when it comes to type inference.

When to use generics versus interfaces

The question of when to use generics versus interfaces in Go often depends on the nature of the problem you're solving and the specific requirements of your code.

Generics in Go allow you to write functions or data structures that can operate on a variety of types, without sacrificing type safety. With generics, you can create functions or structures that work with different types, without the need for code duplication and while maintaining compile-time safety checks.

Interfaces in Go define a set of method signatures. Any type that implements all the methods of an interface is said to satisfy the interface. Interfaces provide a way to achieve polymorphism in Go, enabling code to work with different types that share a common set of behaviors. Interfaces are technically a form of generic programming by allowing developers to capture common aspects of different types and express them as methods. This allows for not only a nice abstraction layer but also duplicate logic.

You should use interfaces when your work requires an abstraction layer that others may implement, or you have distinct behavior you want captured. Generics are good for maintaining compilation type safety in a statically typed language when writing type-agnostic functions and methods. Other considerations such as performance and optimizations benchmarking can be considered for different use cases.

What are some best practices?

The following are a few best practices to consider when working with generic code:

- **Use functions over methods**: A method is a function associated with a type and is called with a receiver; therefore, a function in the context of generics is more flexible, as it is not tied to a specific type. This allows for easier reuse and the ability to compose functions with different types.

- **Ease of transformation**: It is easier to turn methods into functions than it is to add a function to a type. Functions can be defined independently of specific types. In the context of generics, you can use generic functions with any type that satisfies the required constraints. If it later makes sense to convert to a method, then you can do so without modifying the original function more easily.

- **Prefer functions over constraints that require methods**: Instead of defining constraints that specifically require a method on a type, prefer using functions that work with types that satisfy more general constraints, such as `comparable`. This allows flexibility in the future when working with type parameters and a broader range of types to be used with the function.

When working with generics in Go, it is also best to be mindful of the complexity that can be involved. They are a tool in our toolbelt to be used wisely and properly. By doing so, you can leverage the power of generics without compromising the simplicity and readability that define the Go programming language.

Summary

In this chapter, we explored the world of Go generics, a groundbreaking enhancement to the language that provides key features such as type parameters, constraints, and type inference. Type parameters, encapsulated within square brackets, emerged as versatile placeholders, enabling the creation of functions and data structures without prior knowledge of the specific types they are to interact with. The incorporation of constraints such as `comparable` bolstered type safety and clarity, ensures that the generic constructs adhere to specific rules or interfaces. Moreover, the compiler's type inference unveiled a new era of concise and streamlined code, where developers can leverage static typing without the burden of explicit type annotations.

While Go generics is still being smoothened out and added to, it is a powerful addition that aims to empower developers to write efficient, reusable code with unprecedented ease. Now that we know how to write optimal and reusable code thanks to generics, we can look at expanding this knowledge in the next chapter. There, we will enhance our understanding by covering Go modules and seeing how to reuse code at a much larger scale and collaborative effort.

Part 3:
Modules

A module serves as a repository for reusable code utilized by various applications. Whether large or small, a module enables efficient code organization and enhances reusability. In this section, you'll learn how to create and manage modules effectively, leveraging packages and external modules to streamline your development process.

This part has the following chapters:

- *Chapter 9, Using Go Modules to Define a Project*
- *Chapter 10, Package Keep Projects Manageable*
- *Chapter 11, Bug-Busting Debugging Skills,*
- *Chapter 12, About Time*

9

Using Go Modules to Define a Project

Overview

This chapter dives into the use of Go modules for structuring and managing Go projects. We will start by introducing the concept of modules and their significance in organizing code. This chapter will also cover creating your first module while discussing the essential go.mod and go.sum files.

Moreover, we will cover how to use third-party modules as dependencies and offer insights into managing these dependencies effectively. This chapter will provide hands-on experience through exercises and activities that will empower you to develop more structured and manageable Go projects, promoting code reusability and simplifying the development process.

Technical requirements

For this chapter, you'll require Go version 1.21 or higher. The code for this chapter can be found at: https://github.com/PacktPublishing/Go-Programming-From-Beginner-to-Professional-Second-Edition-/tree/main/Chapter09.

Introduction

In the previous chapter, we learned about the importance of creating maintainable, reusable, and modular software using Go packages. We learned how packages are structured, the principles of proper package naming, and the distinctions between executable and non-executable packages. The concept of exportable and unexportable code was also discussed.

In this chapter, we will expand upon this knowledge and explore the utilization of Go modules to define projects, advancing our software development capabilities. We will understand what Go modules are, how they are helpful, and even create our own module. We will understand the different files required for working with Go modules to maintain the integrity of our project dependencies, and then learn how to consume third-party modules and manage them. Lastly, we will look at how to create a project containing multiple modules, and when that is useful.

What is a module?

In the world of Go programming, a module is a fundamental concept that serves as a cornerstone for organizing, versioning, and managing your projects and their dependencies. Think of it as a self-contained, encapsulated unit that simplifies the complexities of dependency management while fostering code reusability and maintainability.

A Go module represents a discrete collection of Go packages, all neatly bundled together under a common, versioned umbrella. This isolation ensures that your code base remains cohesive and well-structured, making it easier to share, collaborate on, and maintain. Modules are designed to put you in control of your project's external dependencies and provide a structured mechanism for versioning and managing them.

Key components when working with Go modules

There are a few key components that are associated with working Go modules. Let's take a look at some of the aspects that help us with Go dependency management for our projects:

- **The** go.mod file: At the core of a Go module is the go.mod file. This file serves as the blueprint for your module and contains essential information such as the module's path and version, as well as a comprehensive list of its dependencies. This detailed map ensures that all required packages are clearly defined and that their specific versions are recorded.

- **The** go.sum file: The go.sum file, working in tandem with go.mod, is a vital component in Go module management. It contains cryptographic checksums, such as SHA-256 hashes, for all the dependencies listed in go.mod. These checksums serve as security measures, ensuring that the downloaded dependencies have not been tampered with or corrupted.

- **Versioning**: Go modules introduce a robust versioning system that plays a pivotal role in dependency management. Each module is assigned a unique version identifier, typically through tags or commit hashes in the version control system. This meticulous approach guarantees that your project consistently uses a known and verified set of dependencies. A released module is published with a version number using the semantic versioning model, which you can find more information about on their website: https://semver.org.

These three aspects of Go modules help us with project dependency management. With Go modules, you no longer need to worry about manually tracking and managing your project's dependencies. As you import packages, they are automatically added to the go.mod file with version information, simplifying the process of ensuring that your code remains compatible with the exact set of dependencies it was designed for.

The go.mod file

The go.mod file is the main configuration file for a Go module. It contains the following information:

- **Module path**: This is the path at which the module is expected to be found. As an example, module mymodule specifies the module path as mymodule.

- **Dependencies**: The go.mod file lists the dependencies required by the module, including their module paths and specific versions or version ranges.

- **Replace directives (optional)**: These directives allow you to specify replacements for certain dependencies, which can be useful for testing or resolving compatibility issues.

- **Exclude directives (optional)**: These directives allow you to exclude specific versions of a dependency that may have known issues.

Here's an example of a simple go.mod file:

```
module mymodule
require (
  github.com/some/dependency v1.2.3
  github.com/another/dependency v2.0.0
)
replace (
  github.com/dependency/v3 => github.com/dependency/v4
)
exclude (
  github.com/some/dependency v2.0.0
)
```

The preceding code shows how the go.mod file can be easily read, lists the dependencies of a project, and makes adjustments when working locally with the replace directive, or excludes certain dependencies as needed.

The go.sum file

The go.sum file contains a list of checksums for the specific versions of the dependencies used in the project. These checksums are used to verify the integrity of downloaded package files.

The go.sum file is automatically generated and maintained by the Go toolchain. It ensures that the downloaded packages have not been tampered with and that the project always uses the correct versions of the dependencies.

Here's a simplified example of a go.sum file:

```
github.com/some/dependency v1.2.3 h1:abcdefg...
github.com/some/dependency v1.2.3/go.mod h1:hijklm...
github.com/another/dependency v2.0.0 h1:mnopqr...
github.com/another/dependency v2.0.0/go.mod h1:stuvwx...
```

The sample go.sum file's contents in the preceding example demonstrate how to verify the integrity of downloaded package files for Go projects. This was a very simple example; however, in reality, the go.sum file can become quite large, depending on the size and amount of dependencies that a project may have.

How are modules helpful?

Go modules offer many benefits that enhance the Go development experience. Let's take a closer look at how Go modules are helpful.

Precise and simplified dependency management

One of the most significant advantages of Go modules is their ability to provide precise control over dependencies. When specifying dependencies in your go.mod file, you can define the exact versions you need, which eliminates the guesswork and potential compatibility issues associated with less rigorous dependency management methods.

Go modules have streamlined the process of adding, updating, and managing dependencies. In the past, Go developers had to rely on the GOPATH and vendor directories, which could lead to version conflicts and make it challenging to manage dependencies. Go modules replace these practices with a more intuitive and efficient approach.

Versioning and reproducibility

Go modules introduce a robust versioning system. Each module is tagged with a specific version identifier or commit hash. This meticulous version control ensures that your project relies on a consistent and known set of dependencies. It promotes reproducibility, meaning that you and your collaborators can recreate the same development environment effortlessly, reducing the "it works on my machine" problem.

Improved collaboration

With well-defined modules, collaborating on Go projects becomes more accessible. Modules provide a clear boundary for your code, ensuring that it remains cohesive and self-contained. This makes it easier for you to share your work with others and for others to contribute to your projects without worrying about breaking existing functionality.

Dependency safety

Go modules incorporate security measures through the go.sum file. By incorporating cryptographic checksums for all your project's dependencies, as mentioned previously in this chapter, you can see how this safeguards against potential tampering or corruption of downloaded packages.

Ease of use while promoting isolation and modularity

It is easy to see the benefits in which Go modules help our programs. Modules lead to easier maintenance on the development team through ease of use to understand, update, and track project dependencies. As projects evolve, it is easy to keep up with changes in external packages.

Go modules promote isolation and modularity. They also provide a natural mechanism for isolating your project from the global workspace. This isolation fosters modularity, allowing you to focus on building self-contained, reusable components that are easy to manage and share. This builds on the idiomatic nature of Go and promotes best practices for development teams for their Go projects.

Go modules were officially introduced in Go 1.11, and they provide a more sophisticated, structured, and version-aware way of managing project dependencies. Developers are encouraged to migrate to Go modules for modern Go project development.

Exercise 09.01 – creating and using your first module

In this exercise, we will see how to create our first Go module with ease:

1. Create a new directory called bookutil and navigate into it:

    ```
    mkdir bookutil
    cd bookutil
    ```

2. Initialize a Go module named bookutil:

    ```
    go mod init bookutil
    ```

3. Verify that go.mod is created within your project directory with the module path set as bookutil.

> **Note**
> No go.sum file is created after running go mod init. It will be generated and updated as you interact with your module and add to its dependencies.

4. Now, let's create a Go package for the author information while focusing on functions related to book chapters by creating a directory named author within our module's project directory.

5. Inside the author directory, create a file named author.go to define the package and functions.

   Here is the starting code for author.go:

   ```go
   package author
   import "fmt"
   // Author represents an author of a book.
   type Author struct {
       Name string
       Contact string
   }
   ```

6. Now, we can add the necessary functions to create our author and define actions that our author can perform:

   ```go
   func NewAuthor(name, contact string) *Author {
       return &Author{Name: name, Contact: contact}
   }
   func (a *Author) WriteChapter(chapterTitle string, content
   string) {
       fmt.Printf("Author %s is writing a chapter titled   '%s'\n",
   a.Name, chapterTitle)
       fmt.Println(content)
   }
   func (a *Author) ReviewChapter(chapterTitle string, content
   string) {
       fmt.Printf("Author %s is reviewing a chapter titled '%s'\n",
   a.Name, chapterTitle)
       fmt.Println(content)
   }
   func (a *Author) FinalizeChapter(chapterTitle string) {
       fmt.Printf("Author %s has finalized the chapter titled
   '%s'.\n", a.Name, chapterTitle)
   }
   ```

7. With the author package defined, we can create a Go file in our module to demonstrate how to use it. Let's name this file main.go at the root of our directory:

   ```go
   package main
   import "bookutil/author "
   ```

```
func main() {
    // Create an author instance.
    authorInstance := author.NewAuthor("Jane Doe",    "jane@
example.com")
    // Write and review a chapter.
    chapterTitle := "Introduction to Go Modules"
    chapterContent := "Go modules provide a structured way to
manage dependencies and improve code maintainability."
    authorInstance.WriteChapter(chapterTitle, chapterContent)
    authorInstance.ReviewChapter(chapterTitle, "This chapter
looks great, but let's add some more examples.")
    authorInstance.FinalizeChapter(chapterTitle)
}
```

8. Save the file in the folder and run the following command:

```
go run main.go
```

Running the preceding code results in the following output:

```
Author John Doe is writing a chapter titled 'Introduction to Go
Modules':
Go modules provide a structured way to manage dependencies and improve
code maintainability.
Author John Doe is reviewing a chapter titled 'Introduction to Go
Modules':
This chapter looks great, but let's add some more examples.
Author John Doe has finalized the chapter titled 'Introduction to Go
Modules'.
```

In this exercise, we learned how to create a Go module and run a program using it.

> **Note**
>
> Your Go module does not have to be named the same as your Go package since you can have many packages to one Go module and project. It is good practice to name your module based on the main purpose of the project.
>
> In this case, the primary purpose of the module is to manage and work with book chapters and authors, so the module's name reflects the broader context. The name `bookutil` provides flexibility to include multiple packages related to book-related operations, including the `author` package.

In addition, there are best practices for module naming, such as `<prefix>/<descriptive-text>` and `github.com/<project-name>/`, that you can read more about in the Go documentation: `https://go.dev/doc/modules/managing-dependencies#naming_module`.

Now that you have successfully created a Go module named bookutil with an author package focused on book chapters, let's explore the importance of using external Go modules and how they can enhance your project.

When should you use external modules, and why?

In Go development, leveraging external modules is a frequent practice that can benefit your projects. External modules, also known as third-party dependencies, offer many advantages when used judiciously. In this section, we will explore when to use external modules and the compelling reasons behind their adoption.

You should use external modules to do the following:

- Promote code reusability and efficiency
- Expand project functionality
- Offload dependency management
- Enable collaborative development with the open source community
- Utilize proven reliability, community support, and documentation by open source code

However, always exercise caution and select dependencies and modules that align with your project's goals and long-term sustainability plans.

Exercise 09.02 – using an external module within our module

Sometimes, in code, you need a unique identifier for an identity you provide to something. This unique identifier is often called a **universally unique identifier** (UUID). Google provides a package to create such a UUID. Let's look at how to use it:

1. Create a new directory called myuuidapp and navigate into it:

   ```
   mkdir myuuidapp
   cd myuuidapp
   ```

2. Initialize a Go module named myuuidapp:

   ```
   go mod init myuuidapp
   ```

3. Verify that the go.mod file is created within your project directory with the module path set as myuuidapp.

4. Add a main.go file.

5. In `main.go`, add the main package name to the top of the file:

    ```
    package main
    ```

6. Now, add the imports we will use in this file:

    ```
    import (
        "fmt"
        "github.com/google/uuid"
    )
    ```

7. Create the `main()` function:

    ```
    func main() {
    ```

8. Generate a new UUID using the external module package:

    ```
    id := uuid.New()
    ```

9. Print the generated UUID:

    ```
    fmt.Printf("Generated UUID: %s\n", id)
    ```

10. Close the `main()` function:

    ```
    }
    ```

11. Save the file and then run the following command to fetch the external dependencies, thereby updating your `go.mod` file with the dependency information:

    ```
    go get github.com/google/uuid
    ```

12. Verify that our `go.mod` file has now been updated with the package dependency with a new `require` line. Your version number may be different for the package, depending on what release version they are on:

    ```
    require github.com/google/uuid v1.3.1
    ```

13. Verify that our `go.sum` file has now been updated with the new dependencies. Again, your version numbers may be different for the package, depending on what release version they are on:

    ```
    github.com/google/uuid v1.3.1
    h1:KjJaJ9iWZ3jOFZIf1Lqf4laDRCasjl0BCmnEGxkdLb4=
    github.com/google/uuid v1.3.1/go.mod
    h1:TIyPZe4MgqvfeYDBFedMoGGpEw/LqOeaOT+nhxU+yHo=
    ```

14. Run the code:

    ```
    go run main.go
    ```

Running the preceding code results in the following output, with a random UUID:

```
Generated UUID: 7a533339-58b6-4396-b7f7-d0a50216bf88
```

With that, you've learned how to use an external module's package within your module by generating a unique identifier using Google's open source code. In this example, we trusted that Google has well-tested code and that it meets the standards we set for our code base. If we ever want to upgrade or downgrade the version of the external package, then that is offloaded to our Go module. Next, we'll look at expanding our understanding of modules by looking at when to use multiple modules within their project.

> **Note**
>
> More information on the UUID module and package can be found on GitHub at `https://github.com/google/uuid/tree/master`.

Consuming multiple modules within a project

You can consume multiple Go modules within a project. Just as you saw with the Google module example earlier, you can use that module alongside other Go modules that you may need in your project.

Activity 9.01 – consuming multiple modules

In this activity, we will use multiple Go modules within our code:

1. Create a new UUID and print the UUID.
2. Fetch and print a random quote using the `rsc.io/quote` module.

Your output should look like this, with a different UUID and a different random sentence for your second line:

```
Generated UUID: 3c986212-f12d-415e-8eb5-87f61a6cbfee
Random Quote: Do not communicate by sharing memory, share memory by
communicating.
```

> **Note**
>
> The solution for this activity can be found in the GitHub repository folder for this chapter: `https://github.com/PacktPublishing/Go-Programming-From-Beginner-to-Professional-Second-Edition-/tree/main/Chapter09/Activity09.01`.

Defining multiple modules within a project

The Go module system is designed to manage dependencies and versions for the entire module, not for subsets or subprojects within a module. However, there might be situations where you have multiple distinct components or subprojects within your main project, and each of these components or subprojects has dependencies and version requirements. In such cases, you can structure your project in a way that each component is its own module, separate from the main project module. These submodules can be maintained as separate Go modules, each with its own go.mod file.

For example, if you have a project with a main component and two other components, and each component has unique dependencies, you can structure your project like this:

```
myproject/
├── mainmodule/
│   ├── main.go
│   ├── go.mod
│   ├── go.sum
│   ├── ...
├── secondmodule/
│   ├── othermain.go
│   ├── go.mod
│   ├── go.sum
│   ├── ...
├── thirdmodule/
│   ├── othermain.go
│   ├── go.mod
│   ├── go.sum
│   ├── ...
```

Each subcomponent/module (that is, secondmodule and thirdmodule) is treated as a separate Go module with its own go.mod file and dependencies.

It makes sense to create submodules in the following situations:

- **Components have different dependencies**: When different components within your project have distinct sets of dependencies, creating submodules allows you to manage these dependencies separately

- **There are separate versioning requirements**: If different components need different versions of the same dependency, using submodules can help manage these version conflicts more effectively

- **There's component reusability**: When you intend to reuse a component across multiple projects, structuring it as a separate module can facilitate its reuse in various contexts

- **There's maintainability**: Submodules can enhance code organization and maintainability as each component can be developed, tested, and maintained separately

While you can technically create submodules within a project, it is not a customary practice, and it should be done when there is a clear need for separate dependency management, versioning, or code organization for distinct components within your project. Each submodule should have its own go.mod file that defines its specific dependencies and version requirements.

Go workspaces

In Go 1.18, the *Go workspaces* feature was released, which improved the experience of working with multiple Go modules within the same project locally. Originally, when working with multiple Go modules in the same project, you would need to manually edit the Go module files for each module with the replace directive to use your local changes. Now, with Go workspaces, we can define a go.work file, specifying to use our local changes, and not have to worry about managing several go.mod files manually ourselves. This is particularly useful when working with larger projects, or projects that span multiple repositories.

Exercise 09.03 – working with workspaces

In this exercise, we will look at what it used to be like when working with projects that had multiple Go modules that needed their dependencies to be replaced so that they could use local changes. We will then update the example code so that it uses Go workspaces to show the improvements:

1. Create a new folder called printer and add a printer.go file.

2. In printer.go, add the printer package name to the top of the file:

    ```
    package printer
    ```

3. Now, add the imports we will use in this file:

    ```
    import (
        "fmt"
        "github.com/google/uuid"
    )
    ```

4. Create the exported PrintNewUUID() function, returning a string:

    ```
    func PrintNewUUID() string {
    ```

5. Generate a new UUID using the external module package:

    ```
    id := uuid.New()
    ```

6. Create and return a string to print the generated UUID:

    ```
    return fmt.Sprintf("Generated UUID: %s\n", id)
    ```

7. Close the `PrintNewUUID()` function:

```
}
```

8. Create a Go module and install the necessary dependencies:

```
go mod init github.com/sicoyle/printer
go mod tidy
```

9. Go back a folder and create a new folder sitting side-by-side with the `printer` folder called `othermodule` and add a `main.go` file.

10. In `main.go`, add the `main` package name to the top of the file:

```
package main
```

11. Now, add the imports we will use in this file:

```
import (
    "fmt"
    "github.com/sicoyle/printer"
)
```

12. Create the `main()` function:

```
func main() {
```

13. Use the `PrintNewUUID()` function we defined in our `printer` module:

```
msg := printer.PrintNewUUID()
```

14. Print the generated UUID message string:

```
fmt.Println(msg)
```

15. Close the `main()` function:

```
}
```

16. Initialize a Go module named `othermodule`:

```
go mod init othermodule
```

17. Add the module's requirements:

```
go mod tidy
```

18. View the error message when Go tries to retrieve the module dependencies; the `printer` package includes only local changes that are not published externally on GitHub:

```
go: finding module for package github.com/sicoyle/printer
go: othermodule imports
        github.com/sicoyle/printer: cannot find module...
```

19. The old way of addressing this before Go workspaces included editing the Go module with a replacement inside the `othermodule` directory:

```
go mod edit -replace github.com/sicoyle/printer=../printer
```

20. Verify that the `othermodule/go.mod` file was updated to include the following contents:

```
module othermodule
go 1.21.0
replace github.com/sicoyle/printer => ../printer
```

21. Now, we can successfully tidy our dependencies:

```
go mod tidy
```

22. Run the code:

```
go run main.go
```

23. Running the preceding code shows the following output, with a random UUID:

```
Generated UUID: 5ff596a2-7c0e-41fe-b0b1-256b28a35b76
```

We've just seen what the flow was like before Go workspaces were introduced. Now, let's see what changes with this new feature.

1. Replace the entirety of `othermodule/go.mod` with the following contents:

```
module othermodule
go 1.21.0
```

2. Run the tidying command; you'll see that the error finds the `printer` module:

```
go mod tidy
```

3. Run the following command in the `printer` directory to initialize a Go workspace:

```
go work init
```

4. Use your local changes within the workspace:

```
go work use ./printer
```

5. Run the code:

    ```
    go run othermodule/main.go
    ```

6. Running the preceding code shows the following output, with a random UUID:

    ```
    Generated UUID: 5ff596a2-7c0e-41fe-b0b1-256b28a35b76
    ```

This exercise demonstrated the flow both before and after the Go workspaces feature was introduced. This feature gives developers a way to better manage local changes among larger projects and across different repositories that include multiple go.mod files that might need updating.

We've covered a lot of ground in this chapter. Let's take a look at everything that we covered.

Summary

In this chapter, we explored the world of Go modules, beginning with an understanding of what modules are and how they provide structured project organization and management of project dependencies. We introduced the two key module files – go.mod and go.sum – that handle dependencies. We also delved into external modules, emphasizing their role in expanding project functionality and their impact on maintainability. We discussed using and consuming multiple modules in a single project, and the concept of Go workspaces for managing multiple modules within a project directory. Hands-on exercises and activities reinforced our understanding.

In the next chapter, we will enhance our module understanding by covering how packages help keep projects more manageable for teams as they iterate, reuse, and maintain projects using packages.

10

Packages Keep Projects Manageable

Overview

This chapter aims to demonstrate the importance of the use of packages in our Go programs. We will discuss how packages can be used to assist our code in being more maintainable, reusable, and modular. In this chapter, you will see how they can be used to bring structure and organization to our code. This will also be seen in our exercises, activities, and some examples from the Go standard library.

By the end of the chapter, you will be able to describe a package and its structure and declare a package. You will learn to evaluate exported and unexported names in a package, create your own package, and import your custom package. You will also be able to distinguish between executable packages and non-executable packages and create an alias for a package.

Technical requirements

For this chapter, you'll require Go version 1.21 or higher. The code for this chapter can be found at: `https://github.com/PacktPublishing/Go-Programming-From-Beginner-to-Professional-Second-Edition-/tree/main/Chapter10`.

Introduction

In the previous chapter, we looked at interfaces. We saw how we can use interfaces to describe the behavior of a type. We also discovered that we can pass different types to functions that accept an interface, as long as the type satisfies the interface's method sets. We also saw how we can achieve polymorphism using interfaces.

In this chapter, we will look at how Go organizes its code into packages. We will see how we can hide or expose different Go constructs such as structs, interfaces, functions, and more, using packages. Our programs have been rather small in the number of lines of code and in complexity to a certain extent. Most of our programs have been contained in a single code file, often named `main.go`, and inside a single package named `main`. Later in this chapter, we will explore the significance of `package main`, so do not be worried at this juncture if you do not understand it. This will not always be the case when you are working on a development team. Often, your code base can become rather large, with multiple files, multiple libraries, and multiple members of the team. It would be rather restrictive if we could not break our code into smaller, manageable parts. The Go programming language solves the complexity of managing large code bases with the ability to modularize similar concepts into packages. The creators of Go use packages for their own standard libraries to tackle this problem. In this book, you have been working with many Go packages, such as `fmt`, `string`, `os`, and so on.

Let's look at an example of a package structure from the Go standard library. The Go `strings` package encapsulates string functions that manipulate strings. By keeping the `strings` package focused on only the functions that manipulate strings, we, as Go developers, know that this function should contain all that we need for string manipulation.

The Go `strings` package is structured as follows (`https://pkg.go.dev/strings#section-sourcefiles`):

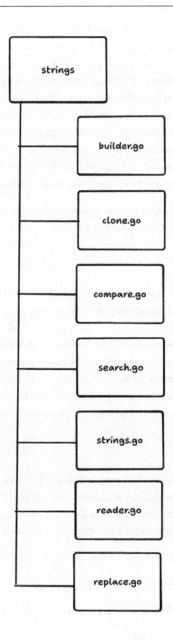

Figure 10.1: The strings package along with the files contained within it as of Go 1.21

The preceding diagram shows the `strings` package and the files that are in the package. Each file in the `strings` package is named after the functionality it is supporting. The logical organization of the code goes from package to file. We can easily conclude that the `strings` package contains code for manipulating strings. We can then further conclude that the `replace.go` file contains functions for replacing strings. You can already see that the conceptual structure of packages can organize your code into modular chunks. You start with code that is working together to serve a purpose, string manipulation, and it gets stored in a package called `strings`. You can then further organize the code into `.go` files and name them according to their purpose. The next step is keeping functions in there that perform a single purpose that reflects the name of the file and the name of the package. We will discuss these conceptual ideas later in the chapter when we discuss structuring code.

It is important to develop software that is maintainable, reusable, and modular. Let's briefly discuss each of these core components of software development.

Maintainable

For code to be maintainable, it must be easy to change, and any changes must have a low risk of having an adverse impact on the program. Maintainable code is easy to modify and extend and is readable. As code progresses through the different stages of the **software development life cycle** (SDLC), the cost of changes to the code increases. These changes can be due to bugs, enhancements, or a change in requirements. Costs also increase when code is not easily maintainable. Another reason that code needs to be maintainable is the need to be competitive in the industry. If your code is not easily maintainable, it may be hard to react to a competitor who is releasing a software feature that could be used to outsell your application. These are just some of the reasons for code needing to be maintainable.

Reusable

Reusable code is code that can be used in new software. For example, I have code in my existing application that has a function that returns an address for my mailing application; that function may be used in a new piece of software. That function that returns the address could be used in my new software that returns a customer address for an order the customer has placed.

The advantages of having reusable code are as follows:

- It decreases future project costs by using existing packages
- It decreases the time it takes to deliver an application, due to not having to reinvent the wheel
- The quality of the program will increase through increased testing and more usage
- More time can be spent on other areas of innovation during the development cycle
- As your packages grow, it becomes easier to lay the foundations for future projects in a timely manner

It is easy to see the many benefits of making reusable code for our projects.

Modular

Modular and reusable code is related to a certain extent, in the sense that having modular code makes it more likely that it will be reusable. One of the prominent problems when developing code is the organization of the code. Finding code that performs a certain function in a large program that is unorganized would be near to impossible, and even finding out whether there is code that performs a certain task would be difficult to ascertain without some code organization. Modularization aids in that area. The idea is that each discrete task that your code performs has its own section of code located in a specific spot.

Go encourages you to develop maintainable, reusable, and modular code by using packages. It was designed to encourage good software practices. We will be diving into how Go utilizes packages to accomplish those tasks:

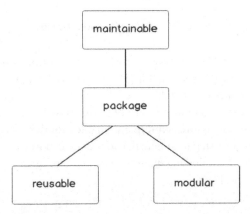

Figure 10.2: The types of code packages can provide

In the next topic, we are going to discuss what a package is and what the components that make up a package are.

What is a package?

Go follows the **Don't Repeat Yourself** (**DRY**) principle. This means that you should not write the same code twice. Refactoring your code into functions is the first step of the DRY principle. What if you had hundreds or even thousands of functions that you used regularly? How would you keep track of all those functions? Some of those functions might even have common characteristics. You could have a group of functions that perform math operations, string manipulations, printing, or file-based operations. You may be thinking of breaking them up into individual files:

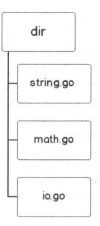

Figure 10.3: Group functions by files

That could alleviate some of the issues. However, what if your string's functionality started to grow further? You would then have a ton of string functions in one file or even multiple files. Every program you build would also have to include all of the code for `string`, `math`, and `io`. You would be copying code to every application that you built. Bugs in one code base would have to be fixed in multiple programs. That kind of code structure is not maintainable, nor does it encourage code reusability. The packages in Go are the next step to organizing your code in a way that makes it easy to reuse the components of your code. The following diagram shows the progression of organizing code from functions to source files to packages:

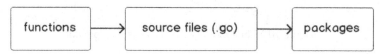

Figure 10.4: Code progression organization

Go organizes its code for reusability into directories called packages. A package is essentially a directory inside your workspace that contains one or more Go source files, which is used for grouping code that performs a task. It exposes only the necessary parts in order for those using your package to get a job done. The package concept is akin to using directories to organize files on a computer.

Package structure

It does not matter to Go how many different files are in a package. You should separate code into as many files as makes sense for readability and logic grouping. However, all the files that are in a package must live in the same directory. The source files should contain code that is related, meaning that if the package is for configuration parsing, you should not have code in there for connecting to a database. The basic structure of a package consists of a directory and contains one or more Go files and related code. The following diagram summarizes the core components of a package structure:

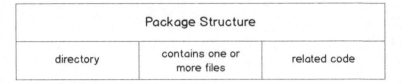

Figure 10.5: Package structure

One of the commonly used packages in Go is the `strings` package. It contains several Go files that are referred to in the Go documentation as package files. Package files are `.go` source files that are part of the package; for example:

- `builder.go`
- `compare.go`
- `reader.go`
- `replace.go`
- `search.go`
- `strings.go`

The files in the preceding list all play their part in sharing related code for string operations within the standard library. Before we discuss how to declare a package, we need to discuss proper Go naming conventions for a package.

Package naming

The name of your package is significant. It represents what your package contains and identifies its purpose. You can think of a package name as self-documentation. Careful consideration needs to go into naming a package. The name of the package should be short and concise. It should not be verbose. Simple nouns are often chosen for a package name. The following would be poor names for a package:

- `stringconversion`
- `synchronizationprimitives`
- `measuringtime`

Better alternatives would be the following:

- `strconv`
- `sync`
- `time`

> **Note**
>
> `strconv`, `sync`, and `time` are actual Go packages found in the standard library.

Also, the styling of a package is something to take into consideration. The following would be poor style choices for a Go package name:

- `StringConversion`
- `synchronization_primitives`
- `measuringTime`

In Go, package names should be all lowercase with no underscores. Don't use camel-case or snake-case styling. There are multiple packages with pluralized names.

Abbreviations are encouraged, just as long as they are familiar or common in the programming community. The user of the package should easily understand what the package is used for just from its name; for example:

- `strconv` (string conversion)
- `regexp` (regular expression search)
- `sync` (synchronization)
- `os` (operating system)

Avoid package names such as `misc`, `util`, `common`, or `data`. These package names make it harder for the user of your package to understand its purpose. In some cases, there is a deviation from these guidelines, but for the most part, it is something we should strive for:

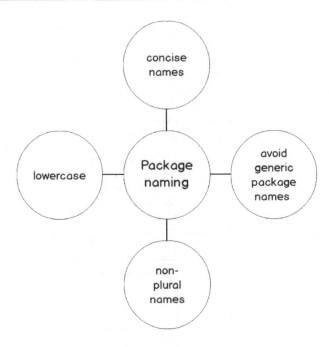

Figure 10.6: Package naming conventions

You can see how there is almost an art to making a good package name. You want to be concise, descriptive, and clear on the package usage when picking package names. Now that we've discussed package names, let's take a peek at package declarations.

Package declarations

Every Go file starts with a package declaration. The package declaration is the name of the package. The first line of each file in a package must be the package declaration:

```
package <packageName>
```

Recall that the `strings` package from the standard library has the following Go source files:

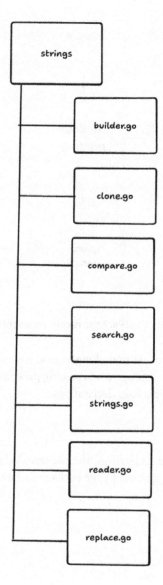

Figure 10.7: The strings package along with the files contained within it as of Go 1.21

Each one of those files starts with a package declaration, even though they are all separate files. We will look at an example from the Go standard library. In the Go standard library, there is a package called `strings\`. It is made up of multiple files. We will only be looking at a snippet of code from the files in the package: `builder.go`, `compare.go`, and `replace.go`. We have removed comments and some code just to demonstrate that the package files start with the package name. There will be no output from the code snippet. This is an example of how Go organizes code into multiple files but in the same package (`https://golang.org/src/strings/builder.go`):

```
package strings
import (
    "unicode/utf8"
    "unsafe"
)
type Builder struct {
    addr *Builder // of receiver, to detect copies by value
    buf []byte
}
// https://golang.org/src/strings/compare.go
package strings
func Compare(a, b string) int {
    if a == b {
        return 0
    }
    if a < b {
        return -1
    }
    return +1
}
```

The full code is available at `https://github.com/PacktPublishing/Go-Programming-From-Beginner-to-Professional-Second-Edition-/blob/main/Chapter10/Example10.01/strings.go`.

All functions, types, and variables that are defined in the Go source file are accessible within that package. Though your package could spread across multiple files, it is all part of the same package. Internally, all code is accessible across the files. Simply stated, the code is visible within the package. Notice that not all of the code is visible outside of the package. The preceding snippet is from the official Go libraries. For a further explanation of the code, visit the links in the preceding Go snippet.

Exported and unexported code

Go has a very simple way to determine whether code is exported or unexported. Exported means that variables, types, functions, and so on are visible from outside of the package. Unexported means it is only visible from inside the package. If a function, type, variable, and so on starts with an uppercase letter, it is exportable; if it starts with a lowercase letter, it is unexportable. There are no access modifiers to be concerned with in Go. If the function name is capitalized, then it is exported, and if it is lowercase, then it is unexported.

> **Note**
>
> It is good practice to only expose code that we want other packages to see. We should hide everything else that is not needed by external packages.

Let's look at the following code snippet:

```
package main
import (
    "strings"
    "fmt"
)
func main() {
    str := "found me"
    if strings.Contains(str, "found") {
        fmt.Println("value found in str")
    }
}
```

This code snippet uses the `strings` package. We are calling a `strings` function called `Contains`. The `strings.Contains` function searches the `str` variable to see whether it has the value `"found"` within it. If `"found"` is within the `str` variable, the `strings.Contains` function will return `true`; if `"found"` is not within the `str` variable, the `strings.Contains` function will return `false`:

```
strings.Contains(str, "found")
```

To call the function, we prefix it with the package name and then the function name.

This function is exportable and thus is accessible to others outside of the `strings` package. We know it is an exported function because the first letter of the function is capitalized.

When you import a package, you only have access to the exported names.

We can validate whether the function exists in the `strings` package by looking at the `strings.go` file:

```
// https://golang.org/src/strings/strings.go
// Contains reports whether substr is within s.
func Contains(s, substr string) bool {
    return Index(s, substr) >= 0
}
```

The next code snippet will attempt to access an unexported function in the `strings` package:

```
package main
import (
    "fmt"
    "strings"
)
func main() {
    str := "found me"
    slc := strings.explode(str, 3)
    fmt.Println(slc)
}
```

The function is unexported because it starts with a lowercase letter. Only code within the package can access the function; it is not visible outside of the package.

The code is attempting to call an unexported function in the `strings.go` package file:

```
prog.go:10:9: cannot refer to unexported name strings.explode
prog.go:10:9: undefined: strings.explode

Go build failed.
```

Figure 10.8: Program output

The following code snippet is from the Go standard library `strings` package and from the `strings.go` file inside of that package (`https://packt.live/2RMxXqh`). You can see that the `explode()` function is unexportable because the function name starts with a lowercase letter:

main.go

```
1   // https://golang.org/src/strings/strings.go
2   // explode splits s into a slice of UTF-8 strings,
3   // one string per Unicode character up to a maximum of n (n < 0
    means no limit).
4   // Invalid UTF-8 sequences become correct encodings of U+FFFD.
5   func explode(s string, n int) []string {
6       l := utf8.RuneCountInString(s)
7       if n < 0 || n > l {
8           n = l
9       }
10      a := make([]string, n)
11      for i := 0; i < n-1; i++ {
12          ch, size := utf8.DecodeRuneInString(s)
13          a[i] = s[:size]
```

```
14              s = s[size:]
15              if ch == utf8.RuneError {
16                  a[i] = string(utf8.RuneError)
```

The full code is available at https://github.com/PacktPublishing/Go-Programming-From-Beginner-to-Professional-Second-Edition-/blob/main/Chapter10/Example10.02/strings.go.

Package alias

Go also has the ability to alias package names. There are a few reasons that you may want to use alias names:

- The package name may not make it easy to understand its purpose. For clarity, it might be better to alias (use) a different name for the package.

- The package name might be too long. In this case, you want the alias to be more concise and less verbose.

- There could be scenarios where the package path is unique but both package names are the same. You would need to then use aliasing to differentiate between the two packages.

The package-aliasing syntax is very simple. You place the alias name before the import package path:

```
import "fmt"
```

Here is a simple example showing how to use package aliasing:

```
package main
import (
    f "fmt")
func main() {
    f.Println("Hello, Gophers")
```

We are aliasing the fmt package as f:

```
    f.Println("Hello, Gophers")
```

In the main() function, we are now able to call the Println() function using the f alias.

Main package

The main package is a special package. There are two basic types of packages in Go: executable and non-executable. The main package is an executable package in Go. Logic that resides in this package may not be consumed by other packages. The main package requires there to be a main() function in its package. The main() function is the entry point for a Go executable. When you perform go build on the main package, it will compile the package and create a binary. The binary is created inside the directory where the main package is located. The name of the binary will be the name of the folder it resides in:

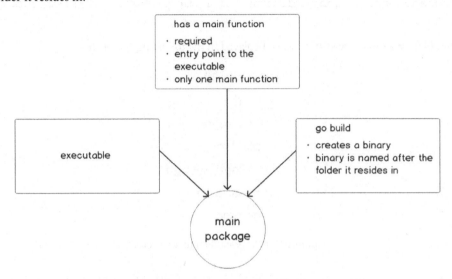

Figure 10.9: Why main package is special

Here's a simple example of the main package code:

```
package main
import (
    "fmt"
)
func main() {
    fmt.Println("Hello Gophers!")
}
```

The expected output is as follows:

```
Hello Gophers!
```

Exercise 10.01 – Creating a package to calculate areas of various shapes

In *Chapter 7, Getting Flexible with Interfaces*, we implemented code to calculate areas of different shapes. In this exercise, we will move all the code about shapes into a package called shape. We will then update the code in the shape package to be exportable. Then, we will update main to import our new shape package. However, we want it to still perform the same functionality in the main() function of the main package.

Here is the code that we will be converting into packages:

`https://github.com/PacktPublishing/Go-Programming-From-Beginner-to-Professional-Second-Edition-/blob/main/Chapter07/Exercise07.02/main.go`

You should have a directory structure, as displayed in the following screenshot:

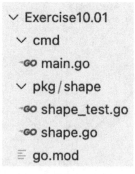

Figure 10.10: Program directory structure

The `shape.go` file should contain the entire code: `https://github.com/PacktPublishing/Go-Programming-From-Beginner-to-Professional-Second-Edition-/blob/main/Chapter10/Exercise10.01/pkg/shape/shape.go`.

We will only be going over changes that are relevant to making this code a package; for details on the parts of the code that we have gone over in a previous chapter, please see *Chapter 7, Getting Flexible with Interfaces*:

1. Create a directory called `Exercise10.01` inside `Chapter10`.

2. Create a new Go module within the `Exercise10.01` directory:

    ```
    go mod init exercise10.01
    ```

3. Create two more directories called `cmd` and a nested directory of `pkg/shape` inside the `Exercise10.01` directory.

4. Create a file called `main.go` inside the `Exercise10.01/cmd` directory.

5. Create a file called `shape.go` inside the `Exercise10.01/pkg/shape` directory.

6. Open the `Exercise10.01/pkg/shape.go` file.

7. Add the following code:

    ```
    package shape
    import "fmt"
    ```

The first line of code in this file tells us this is a non-executable package called `shape`. A non-executable package, when compiled, does not result in binary or executable code. Recall that the `main` package is an executable package.

8. Next, we need to make the types exportable. For each `struct` type, we have to capitalize on the type name and its fields to make it exportable. Exportable means that it is visible outside of this package:

```go
type Shape interface {
    area() float64
    name() string
}
type Triangle struct {
    Base float64
    Height float64
}
type Rectangle struct {
    Length float64
    Width float64
}
type Square struct {
    Side float64
}
```

9. We also have to make the methods non-exportable by changing the method name to lowercase. There is no need at the moment to make those methods visible outside of the package.

10. The `shape.go` file contents should now include the following:

```go
func PrintShapeDetails(shapes ...Shape) {
    for _, item := range shapes {
        fmt.Printf("The area of %s is: %.2f\n", item.name(),
item.area())
    }
}
func (t Triangle) area() float64 {
    return (t.Base * t.Height) / 2
}
func (t Triangle) name() string {
    return "Triangle"
}
func (r Rectangle) area() float64 {
    return r.Length * r.Width
}
func (r Rectangle) name() string {
```

```
        return "Rectangle"
    }
func (s Square) area() float64 {
        return s.Side * s.Side
    }
func (s Square) name() string {
        return "Square"
    }
```

11. The full code for this step is available at `https://github.com/PacktPublishing/Go-Programming-From-Beginner-to-Professional-Second-Edition-/blob/main/Chapter10/Exercise10.01/pkg/shape/shape.go`.

12. The `PrintShapeDetails()` function also needs to be capitalized:

```
func PrintShapeDetails(shapes ...Shape) {
    for _, item := range shapes {
        fmt.Printf("The area of %s is: %.2f\n", item.name(),
item.area())
    }
}
```

13. Perform a build to ensure that there are no compilation errors:

```
go build
```

14. Here is the listing for the `main.go` file. By having a package as `main`, we know that this is executable:

```
package main
```

15. The `import` declaration only has one import. It is the `shape` package. We can see the name of the package is `shape` since it is the last directory name in the path declaration. The path for where my package is located may differ from yours:

```
import  "exercise10.01/pkg/shape"
```

16. In the `main()` function, we are initializing the `shape` package's exportable types:

```
func main() {
    t := shape.Triangle{Base: 15.5, Height: 20.1}
    r := shape.Rectangle{Length: 20, Width: 10}
    s := shape.Square{Side: 10}
```

17. We then call the `shape()` function, `PrintShapeDetails`, to get the area of each shape:

```
    shape.PrintShapeDetails(t, r, s)
}
```

18. At the command line, go to the `Exercise10.01/cmd` directory structure.

19. Type the following:

```
go build
```

20. The `go build` command will compile your program and create an executable named after the directory, `cmd`.

21. Type the executable name and hit *Enter*:

```
./cmd
```

The expected output is as follows:

```
The area of Triangle is: 155.78
The area of Rectangle is: 200.00
The area of Square is 100.00
```

We now have the functionality that we previously had in the interface chapter's implementation of `shape`. We have the `shape` functionality now encapsulated in the `shape` package. We exposed or made visible only functions or methods that are needed to maintain the previous implementation. The `main` package has less clutter and imports the local `shape` package to provide the functionality that was in the previous implementation.

The init() function

As we have discussed, every Go program (executable) starts in the `main` package and the entry point is the `main()` function. There is another special function that we should be aware of, called `init()`. Each source file can have an `init()` function, but for now, we will look at the `init()` function in the context of the `main` package. When you start writing packages, you might need to provide some initialization (the `init()` function) for the package. The `init()` function is used to set up states or values. The `init()` function adds initialization logic for your package. Here are some examples of uses of the `init()` function:

- Setting database objects and connections
- The initialization of package variables
- Creating files
- Loading configuration data
- Verifying or repairing the program state

The init () function requires the following:

- Imported packages are initialized first
- Package-level variables are initialized
- The package's init () function is called
- main () is executed

The following diagram shows the execution order that a typical Go program follows:

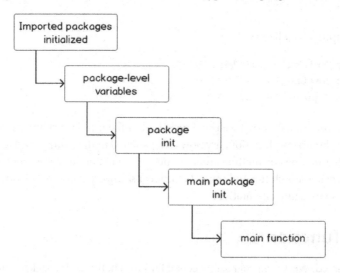

Figure 10.11: Order of execution

Here is a simple example that demonstrates the package main order of execution:

```
package main
import (
    "fmt"
)
var name = "Gopher"
func init() {
    fmt.Println("Hello,", name)
}
func main() {
    fmt.Println("Hello, main function")
}
```

The output of the code is as follows:

```
Hello, Gopher
Hello, main function
```

Let's understand the code in parts:

```
var name = "Gopher"
```

Based on the output of the code, the package-level variable declaration gets executed first. We know this because the name variable is printed in the init () function:

```
func init() {
    fmt.Println("Hello,", name)
}
```

The init () function then gets called and prints out "Hello, Gopher":

```
func main() {
    fmt.Println("Hello, main function")
}
```

Finally, the main () function is executed:

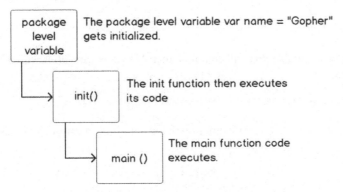

Figure 10.12: Execution flow of the code snippet

The init () function cannot have any arguments or return values:

```
package main
import (
    "fmt"
)
var name = "Gopher"
func init(age int) {
```

```
    fmt.Println("Hello, ", name)
}
func main() {
    fmt.Println("Hello, main function")
}
```

Running this code snippet will result in the following error:

```
prog.go:8:6: func init must have no arguments and no return values
Go build failed.
```

Figure 10.13: Program output

Exercise 10.02 – Loading budget categories

Write a program that will load budget categories into a global map, before the main() function runs. The main() function should then print out the data on the map:

1. Create a main.go file.

2. The code file will belong to package main and will need to import the fmt package:

    ```
    package main
    import "fmt"
    ```

3. Create a global variable that will contain a map of budget categories with a key of int and a value of string:

    ```
    var budgetCategories = make(map[int]string)
    ```

4. We will need to use an init() function to load our budget categories before main() runs:

    ```
    func init() {
        fmt.Println("Initializing our budgetCategories")
        budgetCategories[1] = "Car Insurance"
        budgetCategories[2] = "Mortgage"
        budgetCategories[3] = "Electricity"
        budgetCategories[4] = "Retirement"
        budgetCategories[5] = "Vacation"
        budgetCategories[7] = "Groceries"
        budgetCategories[8] = "Car Payment"
    }
    ```

5. Since our budget categories have been loaded, we can now iterate over the map and print them:

```
func main() {
    for k, v := range budgetCategories {
        fmt.Printf("key: %d, value: %s\n", k, v)
    }
}
```

We will get the following output:

```
Initializing our budgetCategories
key: 5, value: Vacation
key: 7, value: Groceries
key: 8, value: Car Payment
key: 1, value: Car Insurance
key: 2, value: Mortgage
key: 3, value: Electricity
key: 4, value: Retirement
```

> **Note**
>
> The output may differ in terms of the order displayed; Go maps do not guarantee the order of data.

The aim here was to demonstrate how the init() function can be used to perform data initialization and loading before the main() function executes. Data that generally needs to be loaded before main() runs is static data, such as picklist values or some sort of configuration. As demonstrated, after the data gets loaded through the init() function, it can be used by the main() function. In the next topic, we will see how multiple init() functions get executed.

Executing multiple init() functions

There can be more than one init() function in a package. This enables you to modularize your initialization for better code maintenance. For example, suppose you need to set up various files and database connections and repair the state of the environment your program will be executed in. Doing all that in one init() function would make it complicated for maintaining and debugging. The order of execution of multiple init() functions is the order in which the functions are placed in the code:

```
package main
import (
    "fmt"
)
var name = "Gopher"
func init() {
    fmt.Println("Hello,", name)
```

```
}
func init() {
    fmt.Println("Second")
}
func init() {
    fmt.Println("Third")
}
func main() {
    fmt.Println("Hello, main function")
}
```

Let's break the code into parts and evaluate it:

```
var name = "Gopher"
```

Go initializes the name variable first, before the init() function gets executed:

```
func init() {
    fmt.Println("Hello,", name)
}
```

This prints out first since it is the first init in the function:

```
func init() {
    fmt.Println("Second")
}
```

The preceding gets printed out second since it is the second init in the function:

```
func init() {
    fmt.Println("Third")
}
```

The preceding gets printed out third since it is the third init in the function:

```
func main() {
    fmt.Println("Hello, main function")
}
```

Finally, the main() function gets executed.

The results would be as follows:

```
Hello, Gopher
Second
Third
Hello, main function
```

Exercise 10.03 – Assigning payees to budget categories

We are going to expand our program from *Exercise 10.02, Loading budget categories*, to now assign payees to budget categories. This is similar to many budgeting applications that try to match payees to commonly used categories. We will then print the mapping of a payee to a category:

1. Create a `main.go` file.

2. Copy the code from *Exercise 10.02, Loading Budget Categories*, (`https://github.com/PacktPublishing/Go-Programming-From-Beginner-to-Professional-Second-Edition-/blob/main/Chapter10/Exercise10.02/main.go`) into the `main.go` file.

3. Add a `payeeToCategory` map after `budgetCategories`:

    ```
    var budgetCategories = make(map[int]string)
    var payeeToCategory = make(map[string]int)
    ```

4. Add another `init()` function. This `init()` function will be used to populate our new `payeeToCategory` map. We will assign payees to the key value of the categories:

    ```
    func init() {
        fmt.Println("Initializing our budgetCategories")
        budgetCategories[1] = "Car Insurance"
        budgetCategories[2] = "Mortgage"
        budgetCategories[3] = "Electricity"
        budgetCategories[4] = "Retirement"
        budgetCategories[5] = "Vacation"
        budgetCategories[7] = "Groceries"
        budgetCategories[8] = "Car Payment"
    }
    ```

5. The full code for this step is available at `https://github.com/PacktPublishing/Go-Programming-From-Beginner-to-Professional-Second-Edition-/blob/main/Chapter10/Exercise10.03/main.go`.

6. In the `main()` function, we will print out the payees to categories. We iterate over the `payeeToCategory` map, printing the key (payee). We print the category by passing the value of the `payeeToCategory` map as a key to the `budgetCategories` map:

    ```
    func main() {
        fmt.Println("In main, printing payee to category")
        for k, v := range payeeToCategory {
            fmt.Printf("Payee: %s, Category: %s\n", k,
        budgetCategories[v])
        }
    }
    ```

Here's the expected output:

```
Initializing our budgetCategories
Assign our Payees to categories
In main, printing payee to category
Payee: Walt Disney World, Category: Vacation
Payee: Wal Mart, Category: Groceries
Payee: Chevy Loan, Category: Car Payment
Payee: Nationwide, Category: Car Insurance
Payee: BBT Loan, Category: Mortgage
Payee: First Energy Electric, Category: Electricity
Payee: Ameriprise Financial, Category: Retirement
Payee: ALDI, Category: Groceries
Payee: Martins, Category: Groceries
```

Figure 10.14: Assigning a payee to budget categories

You have now created a program that executes multiple init() functions before the execution of the main() function. Each of the init() functions loaded data into our global map variables. We have determined the order of init() functions executing because of the print statements that get displayed. This demonstrates that the init() functions print in the order they are present in the code. It is important to be aware of the order of your init() functions as you may have unforeseen results based on the order of the code execution.

In the upcoming activity, we will be using all these concepts that we have looked at with packages and see how they all work together.

Activity 10.01 – Creating a function to calculate payroll and performance review

In this activity, we are going to take *Activity 7.01, Calculating pay and performance review*, from *Chapter 7* and modularize it using packages. We will be refactoring the code from https://github.com/PacktPublishing/Go-Programming-From-Beginner-to-Professional-Second-Edition-/blob/main/Chapter07/Activity7.01/main.go:

1. Move the types and methods of Developer, Employee, and Manager into their own package under pkg/payroll. Types, methods, and functions must be properly exported or unexported.

2. Name the package payroll.

3. Logically separate the types and their methods into different package files. Recall that good code organization involves separating similar functionality into separate files.

4. Create a main() function as an alias to the payroll package.

5. Introduce two `init()` functions in the `main` package under the `cmd` directory. The first `init()` function should simply print a greeting message to `stdout`. The second `init()` function should initialize/set up key-value pairs.

The expected output would be as follows:

```
Welcome to the Employee Pay and Performance Review
++++++++++++++++++++++++++++++++++++++++++++++++++
Initializing variables
Eric Davis got a review rating of 2.80
Eric Davis got paid 84000.00 for the year
Mr. Boss got paid 160500.00 for the year
```

In this activity, we have seen how to use packages to separate our code and then logically separate the code into individual files. We can see that each of those files makes up a package. Each file of the package has internal access to the other files regardless of the fact that they are in separate files. This activity demonstrates how to create a package with multiple files and how those separate files can be used to further organize our code.

> **Note**
>
> The solution for this activity can be found in the GitHub repository folder for this chapter: `https://github.com/PacktPublishing/Go-Programming-From-Beginner-to-Professional-Second-Edition-/tree/main/Chapter10/Activity10.01`.

Summary

In this chapter, we looked at the importance of developing software that is maintainable, reusable, and modular. We discovered how Go's packages play an important part in meeting those criteria for developing software. We looked at the overall structure of a package. It is made up of a directory, can contain one or more files, and has code that is related. A package is essentially a directory inside of your workspace that contains one or more files that are used for grouping code that is to perform a task. It exposes only the necessary parts to those using your package to get a job done. We discussed the importance of naming packages properly. We also learned how to name a package; that is, concisely, in lowercase, descriptively, using non-plural names, and avoiding generic names. Packages can be executable or non-executable. If a package is the `main` package, then it is an executable package. The `main` package must have a `main()` function, and that is where the entry point is for our package.

We also talked about what is exportable and unexportable code. When we capitalize the name of a function, type, or method, it is visible to others using our package. Lowercasing a function, type, or method makes it not visible to other users from outside our package. We learned that `init()` functions can perform the following duties: initializing variables, loading configuration data, setting database connections, or verifying that our program state is ready for execution. `init()` functions have certain rules when they get executed and on how to utilize them. This chapter will help you to write highly manageable, reusable, and modular code.

In the next chapter, we will start exploring debugging skills, a crucial aspect of software development. This will include learning about effective troubleshooting to enable a robust development experience.

11

Bug-Busting Debugging Skills

Overview

In this chapter, we will look at basic debugging methodologies. We will look at some proactive measures we can take to reduce the number of bugs we introduce into our program. Once we understand these measures, we will investigate the ways in which we can locate a bug.

You will be able to acquaint yourself with debugging in Go and implement various ways to format printing. You will evaluate various techniques of basic debugging and find the general location of a bug in code. By the end of the chapter, you will know how to print out variable types and values using Go code and log the state of an application for debugging purposes. You will also see what debugging measures are available in different or restricted environments that your code may eventually be deployed to.

Technical requirements

For this chapter, you'll require Go version 1.21 or higher. The code for this chapter can be found at: https://github.com/PacktPublishing/Go-Programming-From-Beginner-to-Professional-Second-Edition-/tree/main/Chapter11.

Introduction

As you develop software programs, there are going to be times when your program behaves in an unintended way. For instance, the program could throw an error and might crash. A crash is when our code stops functioning midway and then exits abruptly. Perhaps the program has given us unexpected results. For example, we request a video-streaming service for the movie *Rocky 1* but instead get *Creed 1!* Or you deposited a check into your bank account but, instead of being credited, the bank software debited your account. These examples of software programs behaving in an unintended way are called bugs. Sometimes, "bug" and "error" are used interchangeably. In *Chapter 6, Don't Panic! Handle Your Errors*, in the *What are errors?* section, we discussed how there are three different types of errors or bugs: syntax errors, runtime errors, and logic errors. We also examined examples and saw the difficulty of discovering the location of each type of error.

The process of determining the cause of unintended behavior is called debugging. There are various causes of bugs that get released into production:

- **Testing is performed as an afterthought**: During the development life cycle, it is tempting to not perform testing incrementally. For instance, we are creating multiple functions for an application, and once we finish all the functions, they then get tested. A possibly better way of testing our code would be to test each function as we complete it. This is known as incrementally testing or delivering code in smaller chunks. This gives us better code stability. This is accomplished by testing a function to ensure it works before continuing to the next function. The function that we just completed could be used by other functions. If we do not test it before we continue, the other functions that use our function could be using a buggy function. Depending on the bug and the change to our function, it could impact other users of our function. Later in the chapter, we will discuss more benefits of testing incrementally.

- **Application enhancements or changes to requirements**: Our code often changes between the development phase and when we release it to production. Once in production, we receive feedback from the users; the feedback could be additional requirements or even enhancements to the code. Changing the production-level code in one area could have a negative impact on another area. If the development team uses unit tests, then this would aid in mitigating some of the bugs introduced in a change to the code base. By using unit tests, we could run our unit test before we deliver the code to see whether our change had a negative impact. We will discuss what a unit test is later.

- **Unrealistic development timeframe**: There are times when functionality is requested to be delivered in very tight timeframes. This can lead to taking shortcuts in best practices, shortening the design phase, performing less testing, and receiving unclear requirements. All of those can increase the chance of introducing bugs.

- **Unhandled errors**: Some developers may choose not to handle errors as they occur; for example, a file that is needed for the application to load configuration data is not found, not handling an error return for an invalid mathematical operation such as dividing by zero, or perhaps a connection to a server could not be established. If your program does not properly handle these and other types of errors, this can cause bugs.

These are just a few causes of bugs. Bugs have a negative impact on our programs. The results of a bug that causes a miscalculation can be life-threatening. In the medical industry, a machine is used to administer a drug called heparin; this drug is a blood thinner and is used to prevent blood clots. If the code that determines the calculation of how often and how much heparin can be administered has a bug that causes it to malfunction, the machine could deliver too much or too little of the drug. This could have an adverse effect on the patient. As you can see, it is critical to deliver software that is as bug-free as possible. In this chapter, we are going to look at some ways to minimize the number of bugs that are introduced and ways of isolating the location of bugs.

Methods for bug-free code

We will briefly look at some methods that will help us to minimize the number of bugs that could be introduced into our code. These methods will also aid in giving us confidence as to the portions of the code that introduced the bug:

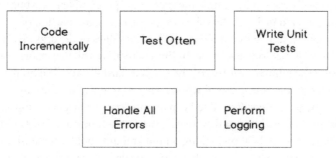

Figure 11.1: Different methods to debug code

Let's look at these methods in more detail.

Coding incrementally and testing often

Let's consider the approach of developing incrementally. This means developing the program incrementally and testing it often after adding an incremental piece of code. This pattern will help you to track bugs easily because you are testing every small snippet of code as opposed to one large program.

Writing unit tests

When a test is written and code changes occur, the unit test protects the code from potential bugs being introduced. A typical unit test takes a given input and validates that a given result is produced. If the unit test is passing before the code change but is now failing after the code change, then we can conclude that we introduced some unintended behavior. The unit test needs to pass before we push our code to a production system. In other words, development teams verify that tests pass and that the code still works as expected before accepting new changes to the code base.

Handling all errors

This was discussed in *Chapter 6, Don't Panic! Handle Your Errors.* Ignoring errors can lead to potentially unintended results in our program. We need to handle errors properly to make the debugging process easier.

Performing logging

Logging is another technique that we can use to determine what is occurring in the program. There are various types of logging; some common logging types are debug, info, warn, error, fatal, and trace. We will not go into the details of each type; we will focus instead on performing debug-type logging. This type of logging is typically used to determine the state of the program before a bug occurs. Some of the information that is gathered includes the values of the variables, the portion of the code that is being executed (one example would be the function name), the values of the arguments being passed, the output of the function or method, and more. In this chapter, we will be performing our own custom debug logging using the built-in features of the Go standard library. The built-in `log` package of Go can provide timestamps. This is useful when trying to understand the timing of various events. When you perform logging, you will need to keep in mind the performance implications. Depending on the application and the load it is under (that is, the number of users interacting with the system around the same time), the application logging output amount could be extensive during peak times and may have a negative impact on the performance of the application. Depending on the number of logs added to the application, the more the users that interact with the system the more logs it will generate, and the more of a negative impact on the performance of the application this could create. In certain circumstances, it could cause it to be unresponsive.

Formatting using fmt

One of the uses of the `fmt` package is to display data to the console or to the filesystem, such as a text file, that will contain information that could be helpful in debugging the code. We have used the `fmt.Println()` function on numerous occasions. Let's take a slightly deeper look at the functionality of `fmt.Println()`. The `fmt.Println()` function places spaces between arguments passed to the function and then appends a newline character at the end of the string.

Each type in Go has a default way that it is formatted when printed. For example, strings are printed as they are, and integers are printed in decimal format. The `fmt.Println()` function prints the default formats of arguments.

Exercise 11.01 – Working with fmt.Println

In this exercise, we will print a `hello` statement using `fmt.Println`:

1. Import the `fmt` package:

```
package main
import (
    "fmt"
)
```

2. Declare the `fname` and `lname` variables in a `main()` function and assign two strings to a variable:

```
func main() {
    fname:= "Edward"
    lname:= "Scissorhands"
```

3. Call the `Println` method from the `fmt` package. It will print `Hello:` and then the value of both variables followed by a space. Then, it will print a `\n` (newline character) to the standard output:

```
fmt.Println("Hello:", fname, lname)
```

4. The following statement prints `Next Line` plus `\n` to the standard output:

```
fmt.Println("Next Line")
}
```

The output is as follows:

```
Hello: Edward Scissorhands
Next Line
```

We have demonstrated the basics of printing out messages. In the next topic, we will look at how we can format the data that we want to print.

Formatting using fmt.Printf()

The `fmt` package also has numerous ways of formatting the output of our various `print` statements. We will look next at the `fmt.Printf()` function.

`fmt.Printf()` formats the string according to the verb and prints it to `stdout`. The standard output (`stdout`) is a stream for output. By default, the standard output is pointed to the terminal. The function uses something called format verbs, sometimes called a format specifier. The verbs tell the `fmt` function where to insert the variable. For example, `%s` prints a string; it is a placeholder for a string. These verbs are based on the C language:

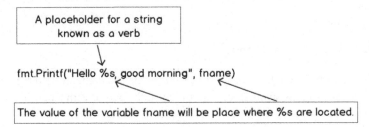

Figure 11.2: Explanation of Printf

Consider the following example:

```
package main
import (
    "fmt"
)
func main() {
    fname := "Edward"
    fmt.Printf("Hello %s, good morning", fname)
}
```

The fname variable is assigned as Edward. When the fmt.Printf() function runs, the %s verb will have the value of fname.

The output is as follows:

```
Hello Edward, good morning
```

But what happens when we have more than one variable that we want to print? How can we print more than one variable in the fmt.Printf() function? Let's take a look:

```
package main
import (
    "fmt"
)
func main() {
    fname := "Edward"
    lname := "Scissorhands"
    fmt.Printf("Hello Mr. %s %s", fname, lname)
}
```

As you see in the preceding code, we now have fname and lname assigned to a string. The fmt.Printf() function has two verb strings and two variables. The first variable, fname, is assigned to the first %s instance. The second variable, lname, is assigned to the second %s instance. The variables replace the verbs in the order they are placed in the fmt.Printf() function.

The output is as follows:

```
Hello Mr. Edward Scissorhands
```

The fmt.Printf() function does not add a new line to the end of the string that it prints. We must add a newline character in the string if we want to return the output with a new line:

```
package main
import (
    "fmt"
```

```
)
func main() {
    fname := "Edward"
    lname := "Scissorhands"
    fmt.Printf("Hello my first name is %s\n", fname)
    fmt.Printf("Hello my last name is %s", lname)
}
```

In Go, you can escape characters using \. If you ever wanted to print the \ character, then you'd put `fmt.Println("\\")` to escape the character. This tells us that a character should not be printed because it has a special meaning. When you use \n, it denotes a newline. We can place a newline anywhere within the string.

The output is as follows:

```
Hello my first name is Edward
Hello my last name is Scissorhands
```

The following would be the result if we did not place \n in the string:

```
Hello my first name is EdwardHello my last name is Scissorhands
```

The Go language has several printing verbs. We will introduce some basic verbs that are frequently used. We will introduce others as they become pertinent to performing basic debugging:

Verb	Meaning
%d	Prints an integer in base-10
%f	Prints a floating point number, default width, default precision
%t	Prints a bool type
%s	Prints a string type
%v	Prints the value in default format
%b	Prints the base two\binary representation
%x	Prints the hex representation

Figure 11.3: Table representing verbs and their meanings

> **Note**
>
> A full list of verbs available with the `fmt` package can be found at `https://pkg.go.dev/fmt#hdr-Printing`.

Let's look at an example of using verbs for printing out various data types:

```
package main
import (
    "fmt"
)
func main() {
    fname := "Joe"
    gpa := 3.75
    hasJob := true
    age := 24
    hourlyWage := 45.53
    fmt.Printf("%s has a gpa of %f.\n", fname, gpa)
    fmt.Printf("He has a job equals %t.\n", hasJob)
    fmt.Printf("He is %d earning %v per hour.\n", age, hourlyWage)
}
```

- We initialize various variables of different types that will be used in our `Printf()` function:

  ```
  fmt.Printf("%s has a gpa of %f.\n", fname, gpa)
  ```

- `%s` is the placeholder for a string; when the `Printf()` function runs, the value from the `fname` variable will replace `%s`. `%f` is the placeholder for a float; when the `Printf()` statement runs, the value in the `gpa` variable will replace `%f`.

- Check whether the person has a job as follows:

  ```
  fmt.Printf("He has a job equals %t.\n", hasJob)
  ```

- `%t` is the placeholder for a `bool` type. When the `Printf()` statement runs, the value in the `hasJob` variable will replace `%t`.

- Print the age of the person and their wage per hour:

  ```
  fmt.Printf("He is %d earning %v per hour.\n", age, hourlyWage)
  ```

- `%d` is the placeholder for an `int` base-10. When the `Printf` statement runs, the value in the `age` variable will replace `%d`.

- `%v` is the placeholder for the value in a default format.

The following is the expected output:

```
Joe has a gpa of 3.750000.
He has a job equals true.
He is 24 earning 45.53 per hour.
```

Next, we will demonstrate how to format verbs, such as `gpa`, to make them round to a specific number of decimal places.

Additional options for formatting

Verbs can also be formatted by adding additional options to the verb. In our previous example, the gpa variable printed out some erroneous zeros. In this topic, we are going to demonstrate how to control the printing of certain verbs. If we want to round to a certain precision when using the %f verb, we can do so by placing a decimal and a number following the % symbol: %.2f. That would specify two decimal places, with the second one being rounded. Given the following examples, notice how the *n*th number is rounded to what is specified by the number (n) used in the %.nf verb:

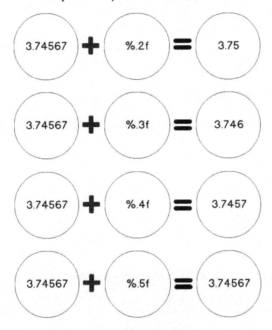

Figure 11.4: Rounding off decimals

You can also specify the overall width of a number. The width of a number refers to the total characters of the number you are formatting, including the decimal point. You can specify the width of the number you are formatting by putting a number before the decimal point. %10.0f states the format will be a total width of 10; this includes the decimal point. It will pad with spaces if the width is less than what is being formatted, and it will be right aligned.

Let's look at an example of formatting various numbers using the width and %.f verb together:

```
package main
import (
    "fmt"
)
func main() {
    v := 1234.0
```

```
v1 := 1234.6
v2 := 1234.67
v3 := 1234.678
v4 := 1234.6789
v5 := 1234.67891
fmt.Printf("%10.0f\n", v)
fmt.Printf("%10.1f\n", v1)
fmt.Printf("%10.2f\n", v2)
fmt.Printf("%10.3f\n", v3)
fmt.Printf("%10.4f\n", v4)
fmt.Printf("%10.5f\n", v5)
}
```

Now, let's understand this code in detail:

- In the main() function, we declared variables with different decimal places:

```
func main() {
    v := 1234.0
    v1 := 1234.6
    v2 := 1234.67
    v3 := 1234.678
    v4 := 1234.6789
    v5 := 1234.67891
```

- %10.0f states that the total width is ten with a precision of zero:

```
fmt.Printf("%10.0f\n", v)
```

- %10.1f states that the total width is ten with a precision of one:

```
fmt.Printf("%10.1f\n", v1)
```

- %10.2f states that the total width is ten with a precision of two:

```
fmt.Printf("%10.2f\n", v2)
```

- %10.3f states that the total width is ten with a precision of three:

```
fmt.Printf("%10.3f\n", v3)
```

- %10.4f states that the total width is ten with a precision of four:

```
fmt.Printf("%10.4f\n", v4)
```

- `%10.5f` states that the total width is ten with a precision of five:

```
fmt.Printf("%10.5f\n", v5)
}
```

The result is as follows:

```
   1234
 1234.6
1234.67
1234.678
1234.6789
1234.67891
```

Figure 11.5: Output after formatting verbs

- To make the results left align your fields, you can use the – flag after the `%` symbol as follows:

```
fmt.Printf("%-10.0f\n", v)
fmt.Printf("%-10.1f\n", v1)
fmt.Printf("%-10.2f\n", v2)
fmt.Printf("%-10.3f\n", v3)
fmt.Printf("%-10.4f\n", v4)
fmt.Printf("%-10.5f\n", v5)
```

Using the same variables as before, the results would be as follows:

```
1234
1234.6
1234.67
1234.678
1234.6789
1234.67891
```

Figure 11.6: Output after left aligning the formatted verbs

We have just skimmed the surface of Go's support for using verbs. You should, by now, have a fundamental understanding of how verbs work. We will continue to build on using verbs and the various ways to format `print` in the upcoming topics. This topic laid the groundwork for the techniques that we will be using to do basic debugging.

Exercise 11.02 – Printing decimal, binary, and hex values

In this exercise, we will be printing decimal, binary, and hex values from 1 to 255. The results should be right aligned. The decimal width should be set to 3, the binary or base 2 width set to 8, and the hex width set to 2. The aim of this exercise is to properly format the output of our data by using a Go standard library package:

1. Create a directory called `Exercise11.02` inside the `Chapter11` directory.

2. Create a file called `main.go` inside the `Chapter11/Exercise11.02/` directory.

3. Open the `main.go` file.

4. Import the following packages:

```
package main
import (
    "fmt"
)
```

5. Add a `main()` function:

```
func main() {
}
```

6. In the `main()` function, use a `for` loop that will loop up to 255 times:

```
func main() {
    for i := 1; i <= 255; i++ {
    }
}
```

7. Next, we want to print the variable in three different ways, formatted to the following specifications:

Display i as a decimal value with a width of 3 and right aligned.

Display i as a base 2 value with a width of 8 and right aligned.

Display i as a hex value with a width of 2 and right aligned.

This code should be placed inside of the `for` loop:

```
func main() {
    for i := 1; i <= 255; i++ {
        fmt.Printf("Decimal: %3.d Base Two: %8.b Hex: %2.x\n",
i, i, i)
    }
}
```

8. At the command line, change the directory using the following code:

```
cd Chapter11/Exercise11.02/
```

9. At the command line, type the following:

```
go build main.go
```

10. Type the executable that was created from the `go build` command and hit *Enter*.

Here are the expected results of the program:

```
Decimal:  16 Base Two:   10000 Hex:  10
Decimal:  17 Base Two:   10001 Hex:  11
Decimal:  18 Base Two:   10010 Hex:  12
Decimal:  19 Base Two:   10011 Hex:  13
Decimal:  20 Base Two:   10100 Hex:  14
Decimal:  21 Base Two:   10101 Hex:  15
Decimal:  22 Base Two:   10110 Hex:  16
Decimal:  23 Base Two:   10111 Hex:  17
Decimal:  24 Base Two:   11000 Hex:  18
Decimal:  25 Base Two:   11001 Hex:  19
Decimal:  26 Base Two:   11010 Hex:  1a
Decimal:  27 Base Two:   11011 Hex:  1b
Decimal:  28 Base Two:   11100 Hex:  1c
Decimal:  29 Base Two:   11101 Hex:  1d
Decimal:  30 Base Two:   11110 Hex:  1e
Decimal:  31 Base Two:   11111 Hex:  1f
Decimal:  32 Base Two:  100000 Hex:  20
Decimal:  33 Base Two:  100001 Hex:  21
Decimal:  34 Base Two:  100010 Hex:  22
Decimal:  35 Base Two:  100011 Hex:  23
```

Figure 11.7: Expected output after printing the decimal, binary, and hex values

We have seen how to format our data using the `Printf()` function from the Go standard library `fmt` package. We will use this knowledge to perform some basic debugging of printing code markers in our programs. We will learn more about this in the following section.

Basic debugging

We have been happily coding along. The big moment has arrived; it is time to run our program. We run our program and find the results are not as we expected them to be. In fact, something is grossly wrong. Our inputs and outputs are not matching up. So, how do we figure out what went wrong? Well, having bugs appear in our programs is something that we all face as developers. However, there is some basic debugging that we can perform to aid us in remediating or, at the very least, gathering information about these bugs:

- **Printing out code markers in the code:**

  Markers in our code are `print` statements that help us to identify where we are in the program when the bug occurred:

  ```
  fmt.Println("We are in function calculateGPA")
  ```

- **Printing out the type of the variable**:

  While debugging, it might be useful to know the variable type that we are evaluating:

  ```
  fmt.Printf("fname is of type %T\n", fname)
  ```

- **Printing out the value of the variable**:

  Along with knowing the type of the variable, it is sometimes valuable to know the value that is stored in the variable:

  ```
  fmt.Printf("fname value %#v\n", fname)
  ```

- **Performing debug logging**:

  At times, it might be necessary to print debug statements to a file: maybe there is an error that only occurs in a production environment, or perhaps we would like to compare the results of data printed in a file for different inputs to our code. This log-formatted message adjusting the message from the standard logger can help in this case:

  ```
  log.Printf("fname value %#v\n", fname)
  ```

> **Note**
>
> Formatting directives such as %T and %#v will be discussed a bit more later in this chapter.

Here are some basic debugging methods:

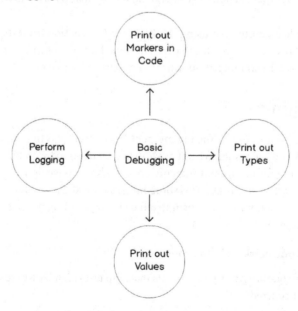

Figure 11.8: Basic debugging methods

One of the first steps in debugging is to identify the general location of where the bug is in the code. Before you can start to analyze any data, we need to know where this bug is occurring. We do this by printing out markers in our code. Markers in our code are typically nothing more than `print` statements that help us to identify where we were in the program when the bug occurred. They are also used to narrow the scope of the location of the bug. Generally, this process involves placing a `print` statement with a message that shows us where we are in the code. If our code reaches that point, we can then determine, based on some conditions, whether that area is where the bug is. If we find that it is not, we potentially remove that `print` statement and place it in other spots in the code.

Given the following trivial example, here is a bug that returns some output:

```
Incorrect value
Program exited: status 1.
```

The code is reporting an error, but we do not know where the error is coming from. This code generates a random number, and that random number is passed to `func  a` and `func  b`. The value of the random number will depend on which function the error occurs in. The following code demonstrates the importance of having properly placed `debug` statements to help determine the area of code where a potential bug is located:

`main.go`

```go
func main() {
    r := random(1, 20)
    err := a(r)
    if err != nil {
        fmt.Println(err)
        os.Exit(1)
    }
    err = b(r)
    if err != nil {
        fmt.Println(err)
        os.Exit(1)
    }
}
```

The full code is available at `https://github.com/PacktPublishing/Go-Programming-From-Beginner-to-Professional-Second-Edition-/blob/main/Chapter11/Example01/main.go`.

- We are using the `rand` package to generate a random number.
- `rand.Seed()` is used so that each time you run the program with `rand.Intn`, it lowers the possibility of returning the same number. `rand.Seed()` is deprecated as of Go 1.20 as there is no reason to call `Seed` with a random value. Programs that call `Seed` with a known

value to get a specific sequence of results should use `New(NewSource(seed))` to obtain a local random value in future versions of Go. However, if you use the same seed each time, the random number generator will return the same number the first time you run the code. To minimize the probability of the same number being generated, we need to provide the seed function with a unique number each time. We use `time.Now().UTC.UnixNano()` to help our program get a more random number. It should be noted, though, that if you put this in a loop, the loop could iterate at a speed that `time.Now().UTC.UnixNano()` could generate the same time value. However, for our program, this is not as likely; rather, it is just something to consider in future code.

- `rand.Intn((max-min)+1)+min` is starting to generate a random number between two other numbers. In our program, it is 1 and 20:

```go
func a(i int) error {
    if i < 10 {
        fmt.Println("Error is in func a")
        return errors.New("Incorrect value")
    }
    return nil
}
func b(i int) error {
    if i >= 10 {
        fmt.Println("Error is in func b.)
        return errors.New("Incorrect value")
    }
    return nil
}
```

- The preceding two functions evaluate i to see whether it falls within a given range. If the value that falls within that range returns an error, it also prints a `debug` statement to let us know where the error occurred.

By strategically placing `print` statements in our code, we can see which function an error is in.

The output should look something like this:

```
Error is in func a
Incorrect value
Program exited: status 1.
```

This section covered debugging basics. We were introduced to using `print` statements for debugging. In the next topic, we will build on our knowledge of printing and look at how to print the variable type.

> **Note**
>
> Due to the randomness of the value of `r`, it can be different, which will impact the results of the program to be either `func a` or `func b`.
>
> Additionally, if you run the preceding program in the Go playground, it will give you the same result every time. This is due to the fact that the playground caches, so it does not adhere to the randomness of the answer.

Printing Go variable types

It is often useful to know the type of a variable when debugging. Go provides this functionality through the use of a `%T` verb. Go is case-sensitive. A capital `%T` means the type of the variable, and a lowercase `%t` means the `bool` type:

```go
package main
import (
    "fmt"
)
type person struct {
    lname string
    age int
    salary float64
}
func main() {
    fname := "Joe"
    grades := []int{100, 87, 67}
    states := map[string]string{"KY": "Kentucky", "WV": "West
Virginia", "VA": "Virginia"}
    p := person{lname:"Lincoln", age:210, salary: 25000.00}
    fmt.Printf("fname is of type %T\n", fname)
    fmt.Printf("grades is of type %T\n", grades)
    fmt.Printf("states is of type %T\n", states)
    fmt.Printf("p is of type %T\n", p)
}
```

Here are the results of the preceding code snippet:

```
fname is of type string
grades is of type []int
states is of type map[string]string
p is of type main.person
```

The %T verb is used in each print statement to print the concrete type of the variable. In a previous topic, we printed out values. We can also print out a Go syntax representation of the type using %#v. It is useful to be able to print out the Go representation of a variable. The Go representation of a variable is the syntax that can be copied and pasted into the Go code:

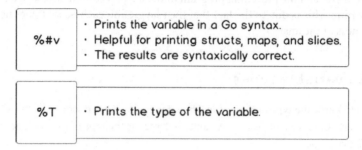

Figure 11.9: Syntax representation of the type using %T and the Go syntax representation, %#v

Exercise 11.03 – Printing the Go representation of a variable

In this exercise, we will create a simple program that will demonstrate how to print out the Go representation of various variables. We will use various types (such as a string, slice, map, and a struct) and print the Go representations of those types:

1. Create a directory called `Exercise11.03` inside the `Chapter11` directory.

2. Create a file called `main.go` inside the `Chapter11/Exercise11.03/` directory.

3. Open the `main.go` file.

4. Add the following code to `main.go`:

```
package main
import (
    "fmt"
)
```

5. Next, create a `person` struct with the same fields listed as follows:

```
type person struct {
    lname string
    age int
    salary float64
}
```

6. Inside the `main` function, assign a value to the `fname` variable:

```
func main() {
    fname := "Joe"
```

7. Create a `slice` literal and assign it to a `grades` variable:

   ```
   grades := []int{100, 87, 67}
   ```

8. Create a `map` literal of a key string and a value string and assign it to a variable of states. This is a map of state abbreviations and their respective names:

   ```
   states := map[string]string{"KY": "Kentucky", "WV": "West
   Virginia", "VA": "Virginia"}
   ```

9. Create a `person` literal and assign it to p:

   ```
   p := person{lname:"Lincoln", age:210, salary: 25000.00}
   ```

10. Next, we will be printing out the Go representation of each of our variables using `%#v`:

    ```
    fmt.Printf("fname value %#v\n", fname)
    fmt.Printf("grades value %#v\n", grades)
    fmt.Printf("states value %#v\n", states)
    fmt.Printf("p value %#v\n", p)
    }
    ```

11. At the command line, change the directory using the following code:

    ```
    cd Chapter11/Exercise11.03/
    ```

12. At the command line, type the following:

    ```
    go build main.go
    ```

13. Type the executable that was created from the `go build` command and hit *Enter*:

    ```
    ./main
    ```

You will get the following output:

```
fname value "Joe"
grades value []int{100, 87, 67}
states value map[string]string{"KY":"Kentucky", "VA":"Virginia", "WV":"West Virginia"}
p value main.person{lname:"Lincoln", age:210, salary:25000}
```

Figure 11.10: Go representation of the types

In this exercise, we saw how we can print the Go representation of simple types (the `fname` string) to more complex types such as a `person` struct. This is another tool in our toolbox that we can use for debugging; it allows us to see the data the way Go sees it. In the next topic, we will be looking at another tool to help us debug our code. We will be looking at how we log information that can be used to further aid in debugging.

Logging

Logging can be used to help debug a bug in our program. Operating systems log various information such as access to resources, what an application is doing, the overall health of the system, and much more. It is not doing this because there is an error; rather, it is logging to make it easier for the system administrator to determine what is going on with the operating system at various times. It allows for easier debugging when the operating system acts in an unusual way or performs a certain task that was not expected. This is the same attitude we should take when logging our application. We need to think about the information that we gather and how that would help us to debug the application if something is not performing the way we think it should.

We should be performing logging regardless of whether the program needs debugging. Logging is useful for understanding events that happen, the health of the application, any potential issues, and who is accessing our application or data. Logging is an infrastructure to your program that can be utilized when an abnormality occurs in the application. Logging helps us to track abnormalities that we would otherwise miss. In production, our code could be executed in different conditions compared to a development environment, such as an increase in the number of requests to the server.

If we do not have the ability to log this information and how our code performs, we could spend endless hours trying to figure out why our code behaves the way it does in production but not in development environments. Another example would be that we get some malformed data as a request in production, and our code does not handle the format properly and causes undesired behavior. Without proper logging, it could take an extraordinary amount of time to determine that we received data that we were not adequately handling.

The Go standard library provides a package called `log`. It includes basic logging that can be used by our programs. We will investigate how the package can be used to log various information.

Consider the following example:

```
package main
import (
    "log"
)
func main() {
    name := "Thanos"
    log.Println("Demo app")
    log.Printf("%s is here!", name)
    log.Print("Run")
}
```

The `Println()`, `Printf()`, and `Print()` log functions perform the same functionality as their `fmt` counterparts, with one exception. When the log functions execute, it gives additional details such as the date and time of the execution, as follows:

```
2019/11/10 23:00:00 Demo app
2019/11/10 23:00:00 Thanos is here!
2019/11/10 23:00:00 Run
```

This information can be useful when investigating and reviewing the logs later and for understanding the order of events. We can even get more details to be logged by our logger. The Go `log` package has a `SetFlags` function that allows us to be more specific.

Here is a list of options for logging provided by the Go package that we can set in the function (`https://go.dev/src/log/log.go?s=8483:8506#L28`):

```go
// These flags define which text to prefix to each log entry generated by the Logger.
// Bits are or'ed together to control what's printed.
// There is no control over the order they appear (the order listed
// here) or the format they present (as described in the comments).
// The prefix is followed by a colon only when Llongfile or Lshortfile
// is specified.
// For example, flags Ldate | Ltime (or LstdFlags) produce,
//     2009/01/23 01:23:23 message
// while flags Ldate | Ltime | Lmicroseconds | Llongfile produce,
//     2009/01/23 01:23:23.123123 /a/b/c/d.go:23: message
const (
    Ldate         = 1 << iota // the date in the local time zone: 2009/01/23
    Ltime                     // the time in the local time zone: 01:23:23
    Lmicroseconds             // microsecond resolution: 01:23:23.123123.  assumes Ltime.
    Llongfile                 // full file name and line number: /a/b/c/d.go:23
    Lshortfile                // final file name element and line number: d.go:23. overrides Llongfile
    LUTC                      // if Ldate or Ltime is set, use UTC rather than the local time zone
    LstdFlags     = Ldate | Ltime // initial values for the standard logger
)
```

Figure 11.11: List of flags in Go

Let's set some of the flags in *Figure 11.11* and observe the difference in behavior from what we had before.

Consider the following example:

```go
package main
import (
    "log"
)
func main() {
    log.SetFlags(log.Ldate | log.Lmicroseconds | log.Llongfile)
    name := "Thanos"
    log.Println("Demo app")
    log.Printf("%s is here!", name)
    log.Print("Run")
}
```

Let's break down the code to understand it better:

```
log.SetFlags(log.Ldate | log.Lmicroseconds | log.Llongfile)
```

`log.Ldate` is the date of the local time zone. This is the same information that was logged before.

`log.Lmicroseconds` will give the microseconds of the formatted date. Note that we have not discussed time yet; for further details on time, please refer to *Chapter 12, About Time.*

`log.LlongFile` will give us the full filename and line number that the log comes from.

The output is as follows:

```
2019/04/30 08:15:57.835521 /go/src/myprojects/scratch/main.go:10: Demo app
2019/04/30 08:15:57.835754 /go/src/myprojects/scratch/main.go:11: Thanos is here!
2019/04/30 08:15:57.835769 /go/src/myprojects/scratch/main.go:12: Run
```

Figure 11.12: Output

Logging fatal errors

Using the `log` package, we can also log fatal errors. The `Fatal()`, `Fatalf()`, and `Fatalln()` functions are similar to `Print()`, `Printf()`, and `Println()`. The difference is after logging, `Fatal()` functions are followed by an `os.Exit(1)` system call. The `log` package also has the following functions: `Panic`, `Panicf`, and `Panicln`. The difference between the `Panic` functions and the `Fatal` functions is that the `Panic` functions are recoverable. When using the `Panic` functions, you can use the `defer()` function, whereas when using the `Fatal` functions, you cannot. As stated earlier, the `Fatal` functions call `os.Exit()`; a `defer` function will not be called when `os.Exit()` gets called. There may be some instances where you want to abort the program immediately with no possibility of recovery. For example, the application may have gotten to a state where it is best to exit it before data corruption or undesired behavior results. Or, you may have developed a command-line utility that is used by others and you need to provide an exit code to the callers of your executable to signal it has completed its tasks.

In the following code example, we will look at how `log.Fataln` is used:

```
package main
import (
    "log"
    "errors"
)
func main() {
    log.SetFlags(log.Ldate | log.Lmicroseconds | log.Llongfile)
    log.Println("Start of our app")
    err := errors.New("Application Aborted!")
    if err != nil {
```

```
        log.Fatalln(err)
    }
    log.Println("End of our app")
}
```

Let's break down the code to understand it better:

```
log.Println("Start of our app")
```

The statement prints to `stdout` with the date, time, and line number of the log message:

```
err := errors.New("We crashed!")
```

We create an error to test the logging of `Fatal()` errors:

```
log.Fatalln(err)
```

We log the error, and then it exits the program:

```
log.Println("End of our app")
```

The line did not execute because we logged the error as `fatal`, and that caused the program to exit.

Here are the results. Notice that even though it was an error, it still logs the same details about the error as it does the print functionality, and then it exits:

```
2009/11/10 23:00:00.000000 /tmp/sandbox182690719/prog.go:10: Start of our app
2009/11/10 23:00:00.000000 /tmp/sandbox182690719/prog.go:13: Application Aborted!
```

Figure 11.13: Logging a fatal error

Activity 11.01 – Building a program to validate Social Security Numbers

In this activity, we are going to be validating **Social Security Numbers** (**SSNs**). Our program will be accepting SSNs without the dashes. We will want to log the validation process for the SSNs so that we can trace the entire process. Logging real SSNs in production applications is not a recommended practice as it includes sensitive information and would violate security measures; however, it is useful for a fun book activity. We do not want our application to stop if an SSN is invalid; we want it to log the invalid number and continue to the next one:

1. Create a custom error called `ErrInvalidSSNLength` for invalid SSN length.

2. Create a custom error called `ErrInvalidSSNNumbers` for SSNs that have non-numeric digits.

3. Create a custom error called `ErrInvalidSSNPrefix` for an SSN that has three zeros as the prefix.

4. Create a custom error called `ErrInvalidDigitPlace` for SSNs that start with a 9 if it requires 7 or 9 in the fourth place.

5. Create a function that returns an error if the SSN length is not 9.

6. Create a function that checks whether the SSN is a length of 9. The function returns an error that has the SSN that was invalid and a custom error, `ErrInvalidSSNLength`.

7. Create a function that checks whether the SSN contains all numbers. The function returns an error that has the SSN that was invalid and a custom error, `ErrInvalidSSNNumbers`.

8. Create a function that checks whether the SSN does not have a prefix of 000. The function returns an error that has the SSN that was invalid and a custom error, `ErrInvalidSSNPrefix`.

9. Create a function that checks that if the SSN starts with a 9, then it requires a 7 or 9 in the fourth place. The function returns an error that has the SSN that was invalid and a custom error, `ErrInvalidDigitPlace`.

10. In the `main()` function, create a slice of SSNs so that your program will validate each of them.

11. For each SSN that you are validating, if errors are returned from your functions that are being used to validate, then log those errors and continue processing the slice.

12. An example slice to validate is as follows:

```
validateSSN := []string{"123-45-6789", "012-8-678", "000-12-
0962", "999-33- 3333", "087-65-4321","123-45-zzzz"}
```

The preceding slice should have the following output:

```
2024/02/12 07:09:14.015902 /Users/samcoyle/go/src/github.com/packt-
book/Go-Programming---From-Beginner-to-Professional-Second-Edition-/
Chapter11/Activity11.01/main.go:21: Checking data []string{"123-45-
6789", "012-8-678", "000-12-0962", "999-33-3333", "087-65-4321", "123-
45-zzzz"}
2024/02/12 07:09:14.016070 /Users/samcoyle/go/src/github.com/packt-
book/Go-Programming---From-Beginner-to-Professional-Second-Edition-/
Chapter11/Activity11.01/main.go:23: Validate data "123-45-6789" 1 of 6
2024/02/12 07:09:14.016085 /Users/samcoyle/go/src/github.com/packt-
book/Go-Programming---From-Beginner-to-Professional-Second-Edition-/
Chapter11/Activity11.01/main.go:23: Validate data "012-8-678" 2 of 6
2024/02/12 07:09:14.016089 /Users/samcoyle/go/src/github.com/packt-
book/Go-Programming---From-Beginner-to-Professional-Second-Edition-/
Chapter11/Activity11.01/main.go:31: the value of 0128678 caused an
error: ssn is not nine characters long
2024/02/12 07:09:14.016092 /Users/samcoyle/go/src/github.com/packt-
book/Go-Programming---From-Beginner-to-Professional-Second-Edition-/
Chapter11/Activity11.01/main.go:23: Validate data "000-12-0962" 3 of 6
2024/02/12 07:09:14.016127 /Users/samcoyle/go/src/github.com/packt-
book/Go-Programming---From-Beginner-to-Professional-Second-Edition-/
Chapter11/Activity11.01/main.go:35: the value of 000120962 caused an
error: ssn has three zeros as a prefix
```

```
2024/02/12 07:09:14.016132 /Users/samcoyle/go/src/github.com/packt-
book/Go-Programming---From-Beginner-to-Professional-Second-Edition-/
Chapter11/Activity11.01/main.go:23: Validate data "999-33-3333" 4 of 6
2024/02/12 07:09:14.016139 /Users/samcoyle/go/src/github.com/packt-
book/Go-Programming---From-Beginner-to-Professional-Second-Edition-/
Chapter11/Activity11.01/main.go:39: the value of 999333333 caused an
error: ssn starts with a 9 requires 7 or 9 in the fourth place
2024/02/12 07:09:14.016141 /Users/samcoyle/go/src/github.com/packt-
book/Go-Programming---From-Beginner-to-Professional-Second-Edition-/
Chapter11/Activity11.01/main.go:23: Validate data "087-65-4321" 5 of 6
2024/02/12 07:09:14.016201 /Users/samcoyle/go/src/github.com/packt-
book/Go-Programming---From-Beginner-to-Professional-Second-Edition-/
Chapter11/Activity11.01/main.go:23: Validate data "123-45-zzzz" 6 of 6
2024/02/12 07:09:14.016204 /Users/samcoyle/go/src/github.com/packt-
book/Go-Programming---From-Beginner-to-Professional-Second-Edition-/
Chapter11/Activity11.01/main.go:27: the value of 12345zzzz caused an
error: ssn has non-numeric digits
```

> **Note**
>
> The solution for this activity can be found in the GitHub repository folder for this chapter:
> `https://github.com/PacktPublishing/Go-Programming-From-Beginner-to-Professional-Second-Edition-/tree/main/Chapter11/Activity11.01`.

In this activity, we used the `log` package to capture information to trace the process of validating an SSN. If we ever need to debug the validation process for our SSN, then we can look at the logging messages and follow the validation failures of the SSN. We also demonstrated how to format logging messages to contain information that would be needed for debugging.

Debugging in live or restricted environments

Debugging is an indispensable skill in software development, especially when dealing with elusive bugs that only manifest in certain environments. In real-world scenarios, modifying code on the fly might not be feasible, making it crucial to master techniques that work seamlessly in live or restricted environments.

To best debug in those kinds of environments, you should consider the following points:

- **Understand the environment**: Before diving into debugging, take a step back. Understand the deployment setup, network configurations, and any security constraints. This information helps to anticipate potential issues and streamline debugging.

- **Remote debugging with proper tools**: Delve is a powerful debugger for Go that supports remote debugging. By using Delve, you can connect to a running Go process and inspect variables, set breakpoints, and step through code. This is an invaluable debugging tool.

- **Observability of the code**: Go's built-in profiling tools, such as `pprof`, allow you to gather runtime statistics and profile your application's performance. By exposing a profiling endpoint in your code, you can collect data from live systems without modifying the code after it's deployed. The same can be said if you add metrics and additional observability to your application. There are also tools available to capture application logs and aggregate them to be searchable in the future. This provides additional context that can assist the debugging process.

- **Utilize log levels**: Utilizing the different log levels available in the language is useful in different environments. However, you should be cautious to not over-share information via logging – especially in the event of dealing with private data.

- **Set up integrated development environment (IDE) debuggers**: Modern IDEs such as Visual Studio Code or JetBrains GoLand provide robust debugging capabilities. You can use breakpoints, watch expressions, and walk-through code using your debugger in the IDE. This is extremely efficient in pinpointing problems but is not something you can do in every deployment environment.

- **Feature flags and canary releases**: Leveraging feature flags and/or canary releases enables you to selectively enable or disable specific functionalities in production. By gradually rolling out changes, you can observe the impact on a subset of users. This makes it easier to identify and address issues before a widespread release.

Overall, it's important to note that debugging can be an art. What works in some environments may not work in others. For example, you cannot set up an IDE debugger on code already running in a production environment, but you can leverage this approach easily in developing your code. You may also only have issues that plague certain environments. This is the classic tale of "it works locally for me," but you are plagued with dealing with the issue and could end up spending several hours/days testing code commits by committing against your **continuous integration** (**CI**) environment. It happens to the best of us and is also a fair approach to debugging, trying out changes in small increments until it's fixed.

At the end of the day, knowledge is power, and knowing the tools available to best debug an issue can drastically reduce your debugging time. In addition, practicing debugging in different environments and forcing issues/incidents sometimes upon a team in planned scenarios can be a great way to prepare teams for production-level incidents where speed is key.

Summary

In this chapter, we studied various methodologies for easing the debugging process such as coding incrementally and testing the code often, writing unit tests, handling all errors, and performing logging on the code.

Looking at the `fmt` package, we discovered various ways to output information to help us to find bugs. The `fmt` package offered different print formatting, verbs, and ways to control the output of verbs by the use of various flags.

With the usage of logging from Go's standard library, we were able to see details of how our application was executed. The `log` package allowed us to see the file path and line number on which the log event took place. The `log` package came with various print functions that mimic some of the `fmt` print functions, which provided us with various insights into the usage of the verbs we learned in this chapter. We were able to perform basic debugging by using the standard library that is provided by Go. We looked at the `log` package and were introduced to the `time` type. We did not go into the details of Go's implementations of time. We also saw various additional methodologies to debug code in live or restricted environments.

In the next chapter, we will be looking at how time is represented in Go. We will be discussing the various functions used with the `time.Time` type. We will also demonstrate how to convert time to various time constructs (such as nanoseconds, microseconds, milliseconds, seconds, minutes, hours, and so on). Then, we will finally learn about the underlying type of time.

12
About Time

Overview

This chapter demonstrates how Go handles variables representing time data, which is a very important aspect of the language.

By the end of this chapter, you will be able to create your own time format, compare and manage time, calculate the duration of time series, and format time according to user requirements.

Technical requirements

For this chapter, you'll require Go version 1.21 or higher. The code for this chapter can be found at: `https://github.com/PacktPublishing/Go-Programming-From-Beginner-to-Professional-Second-Edition-/blob/main/Chapter12`.

Introduction

The previous chapter introduced you to basic debugging in Go. The more you develop code in Go, the better you get; however, developing and deploying code may come with corner cases that need to be debugged. The previous chapter showed you how to use the `fmt` package, how to log in to files, and how to use printing verbs for string formatting.

This chapter is dedicated to teaching you all you need to know about handling variables that represent time data. You will learn how to do it the "Go way." First, we will start out with basic time creation, timestamps, and more; then, we will learn how to compare and manipulate time, calculate the duration between two dates, and create timestamps. Finally, we will learn how to format time according to our needs. So, let's not waste any more time and jump right in.

Making time

Making time means declaring a variable that holds the time formatted in a specific way. Formatting time will be covered at the end of this chapter; so, for now, we will use the default formatting that is provided by Go. In this topic, we will be executing everything in the `main()` function of our script, so the skeleton should look like this:

```
package main
import (
    "fmt"
    "time"
)
func main(){
    // this is where the code goes.
}
```

Let's look at our skeleton first and learn how to create and manipulate `time` variables. Our skeleton has the standard `package main` definition that is necessary. We use the `fmt` package to print the output to the console. Since we'll be using the `time` package, we'll need to import that as well.

Whenever we issue `go run <script>.go`, the `main()` function gets called and executes whatever is declared in it.

One of the most common jobs for the `time` package is to measure the duration of the execution of the script. We can do this by capturing the current time in a variable, at the beginning, and at the end so that we can calculate the difference and know how long the specific action took to complete. The time difference will be shown later in the book chapter. The very first example is as follows:

```
start := time.Now()
fmt.Println("The script has started at: ", start)
fmt.Println("Saving the world...")
time.Sleep(2 * time.Second)
end := time.Now()
fmt.Println("The script has completed at: ", end)
```

The output from our script should look like this:

```
The script has started at: 2023-09-27 08:19:33.8358274 +0200 CEST
m=+0.001998701
Saving the world...
The script has completed at: 2023-09-27 08:19:35.8400169 +0200 CEST
m=+2.006161301
```

As you can see, this does not look very fancy; however, by the end of this chapter, you will have learned how to make it more readable.

Consider the following scenario: your employer gives you a task to develop a small Go application that tests a web application based on the day of the week. Your employer has the main release of a new web app every Monday at 12:00 A.M. CEST. With a downtime window from 12:00 A.M. CEST to 2:00 P.M. CEST, and the deployment being about 30 minutes, you have 1.5 hours to test the app. This is where Go's time package comes to your rescue. The script performs a hit-n-run test on the other days of the week, but on release day, you are required to perform a full-blown functionality test. The first version of the script took the argument to see which test to perform, but the second script version made the decision based on the day and the hour:

Days	Testing strategy
Monday	full-blown
Rest of the week	hit-n-run

Figure 12.1: Testing strategies

Consider the following code:

```
day := time.Now().Weekday()
hour := time.Now().Hour()
fmt.Println("Day: ", day, "Hour: ", hour)
if day.String() == "Monday"{
  if hour >= 1{
    fmt.Println("Performing full blown test!")
  } else {
    fmt.Println("Performing hit-n-run test!")
  }
} else { fmt.Println("Performing hit-n-run test!")}
```

The current day of the week is captured in the variable called day. The hour of execution is also captured in the variable called hour. When this script is executed, there are two types of output.

The first one is a simple hit-n-run output, as follows:

```
Day: Thursday Hour: 14
Performing hit-n-run test!
```

The second one is the full blown output, as follows:

```
Day: Thursday Hour: 14
Performing full blown test!
```

In this example, we have seen how the day of execution modifies the behavior of the application.

> **Note**
>
> The actual test was left out intentionally as this is not part of the chapter's topic. However, the output clearly shows which part was responsible for the control of the test.

Another example would be to create the log filenames for scripts in Go. The basic idea is to collect a log per day and have a timestamp concatenated with the name of the log file. The skeleton looks like this:

```
Application_Action_Year_Month_Day
```

In Go, there is an elegant and simple way to do it within your main function:

```go
package main
import (
  "fmt"
  "strconv"
  "time"
)
func main() {
  appName := "HTTPCHECKER"
  action := "BASIC"
  date := time.Now()
  logFileName := appName + "_" + action + "_" + strconv.Itoa(date.
Year()) + "_" + date.Month().String() + "_" + strconv.Itoa(date.Day())
+ ".log"
  fmt.Println("The name of the logfile is ", logFileName)
}
```

The output appears as follows:

```
The name of the logfile is: HTTPCHECKER_BASIC_2024_March_16.log
```

However, there is a catch. If you want to concatenate strings with time types, which are not implicitly convertible, use the strconv package, which needs to be imported on top of your script:

```go
import "strconv"
```

In turn, this allows you to call the strconv.Itoa() function, which converts your Year and Day values and, finally, lets you concatenate them into a single string.

Now that we have learned how to make time variables, let's learn to compare them.

Exercise 12.01 – Creating a function to return a timestamp

In this exercise, we will create a function called whatstheclock. The goal of this function is to demonstrate how you can create a function that wraps a nice, formatted time.Now() function and returns the date in an ANSIC format. The ANSIC format will be explained in further detail in the *Formatting time* section:

1. Create a new folder and add a main.go file.

2. Initialize the script with package and import statements:

    ```
    package main
    import "time"
    import "fmt"
    ```

3. Define a function called whatstheclock():

    ```
    func whatstheclock() string {
       return time.Now().Format(time.ANSIC)
    }
    ```

4. In the main() function, define a call to the whatstheclock() function and print the result to the console:

    ```
    func main(){
       fmt.Println(whatstheclock())
    }
    ```

5. Save the file and run the code:

    ```
    go run main.go
    ```

    You should see the following output:

    ```
    Thu Oct 17 13:56:03 2023
    ```

In this exercise, we demonstrated how you can create a small function that returns the current time in an ANSIC format.

> **Note**
>
> Any type of operating system that you work with will provide two types of clocks to measure the time; one is called the "monotonic clock," and the other is called the "wall clock." The wall clock is what you see on a Windows machine in the taskbar; it's subject to change and is usually synchronized with a public or corporate **Network Time Protocol** (**NTP**) server based on your current location. NTP is used to tell clients the time based on an atomic clock or from a satellite reference.

Comparing time

Most of the time, when working with Go on smaller scripts, it is very important for your statistics to know when a script should run, or between what hours and minutes a script should be completed. By statistics, we mean knowing how much time the app saves by executing a specific operation compared to what time cost it would have if we had to perform these manually. This allows us to measure the improvement of the script over time when we develop the functionality further. In this topic, we will look at some live examples demonstrating how you can solve this problem.

Let's look at the logic for the first script, which was intended not to run before or after a specified time. This time can arrive either via another automation or when a trigger file is manually placed there; every day, the script needs to run at different times –specifically, after the specified time as soon as possible.

The time was in the following 2023-09-27T22:08:41+00:00 format:

```
now := time.Now()
onlAafter, err := time.Parse(time.RFC3339,"2020-11-
01T22:08:41+00:00")
if err != nil {
  fmt.Println(err)
}
fmt.Println(now, onlyAfter)
fmt.Println(now.After(onlyAfter))
if now.After(onlyAfter){
  fmt.Println("Executing actions!")
} else {
  fmt.Println("Now is not the time yet!!")
}
```

The output of the script when we are not yet at the deadline is as follows:

```
Now is not the time yet!!
```

When we meet the criteria, the output looks like this:

```
Executing actions!
```

Let's examine what is happening here. We create a now variable, which is crucial for the execution. We have the time string parsed based on RFC3339. RFC3339 specifies the format that should be used for the date and time strings. This function returns two values: one value is the output if the conversion succeeds, and the other is the error if there is one. We capture the output in the onlyAfter variable, along with the error, err. We could use a standard variable such as onlyAfterError, but unless we use that variable later in time, the compiler will throw an error that the variable was declared but never used. This is circumvented using the _ variable. Based on this logic, we could implement the onlyBefore argument or variable very simply. The time package has two particularly useful functions: one is called After(), and the other is called Before(). They allow us to simply compare two time variables.

There is a third function in the package called Equal(). This function allows you to compare two time variables and returns true or false depending on whether they are equal.

Let us look at an example of the Equal () function in action:

```
now := time.Now()
nowToo := now
time.Sleep(2*time.Second)
later := time.Now()
if now.Equal(nowTtoo){
  fmt.Println("The two time variables are equal!")
} else {
  fmt.Println("The two time variables are different!")
}
if now.Equal(later) {
  fmt.Println("The two time variables are equal!")
}else{
  fmt.Println("The two time variables are different!")
}
```

The output looks like this:

```
The two time variables are equal!
The two time variables are different!
```

Let's see what happens here. We have three time variables, which are called now, now_too, and later. The time module's Sleep() function is used to simulate the latency of 2 seconds. This function takes an integer argument and waits for the given time to pass and then continues the execution. The result of this is that the later variable holds different time values and allows us to demonstrate the Equal() function's purpose, which you can see in the output.

Now, the time has come to check what facilities are provided to calculate the duration or difference between the two time variables.

Duration calculation

The ability to calculate the duration of an execution comes in handy during many aspects of programming. In our everyday lives, we can monitor discrepancies and performance bottlenecks that our infrastructure might face. For example, if you have a script that takes only 5 seconds to complete on average and the monitoring execution time shows you a huge bump during certain hours of a day or certain days, it might be wise to investigate. The other aspect is related to web applications. Measuring the duration of request-response in your scripts can give you an insight into how well invested you are in your apps to serve high loads, and it even allows you to expand your capacity on certain days or weeks of the year. For example, if you have an online shop dealing with products, it might be wise to size your capacity according to patterns such as Black Friday or Christmas.

You may do well with a lower capacity during most of the year, but those holidays can result in revenue loss if the infrastructure is not sufficiently well sized. There is very little coding required to add such functionality to your scripts. Let's now look at how to do it:

```go
start := time.Now()
fmt.Println("The script started at: ", start)
sum := 0
for i := 1; i < 10000000000; i++ {
  sum += i
}
end := time.Now()
duration := end.Sub(start)
fmt.Println("The script completed at: ", end)
fmt.Println("The task took", duration.Hours(), "hour(s) to
complete!")
fmt.Println("The task took", duration.Minutes(), "minutes(s) to
complete!")
fmt.Println("The task took", duration.Seconds(), "seconds(s) to
complete!")
fmt.Println("The task took", duration.Nanoseconds(), "nanosecond(s)
to complete!")
```

If you execute this script, the result will be something like this, depending on the PC's performance:

```
The script started at:  2023-12-17 22:58:46.45057 -0600 CST m=+0.000111835
The script completed at:  2023-12-17 22:58:50.754004 -0600 CST m=+4.303461543
The task took 0.001195374918888889 hour(s) to complete!
The task took 0.07172249513333333 minutes(s) to complete!
The task took 4.303349708 seconds(s) to complete!
The task took 4303349708 nanosecond(s) to complete!
```

Figure 12.2: Measuring the execution time

All that needs to be done is to capture the time when the script starts and ends. Then, we can calculate the duration by subtracting the start time and the end time. After that, we can utilize the Duration variable's functions to get the Hours(), Minutes(), Seconds(), and Nanoseconds() values of the time it took to complete the task.

There are four resolutions you will be provided with – namely, the following:

- Hours
- Minutes
- Seconds
- Nanoseconds

If you need, for example, days, weeks, or months, then you can calculate it from the resolutions provided.

Back in the day, we had a requirement to measure the duration of transactions, and we had a **service-level agreement (SLA)** that needed to be met. This meant that there were applications that needed to process a request in, let's say, 1,000 ms or 5 s depending on the criticality of the product. The next script will show you how this was implemented. There are six different resolutions that you have the option to choose from:

- Hour

- Minute

- Second

- Millisecond

- Microsecond

- Nanosecond

Let's consider the following example:

```
deadlineSeconds := time.Duration((600 * 10) * time.Millisecond)
start := time.Now()
fmt.Println("Deadline for the transaction is", deadlineSeconds)
fmt.Println("The transaction has started at:", start)
sum := 0
for i := 1; i < 25000000000; i++ {
   sum += i
}
end := time.Now()
duration := end.Sub(start)
transactionTime := time.Duration(duration.Nanoseconds()) * time.
Nanosecond
fmt.Println("The transaction has completed at:", end, duration)
if transactionTime <= deadlineSeconds{
   fmt.Println("Performance is OK transaction completed in",
transactionTime)
} else{
   fmt.Println("Performance problem, transaction completed in",
transactionTime,"second(s)!")
}
```

When we don't meet the deadline, the output is as follows:

```
Deadline for the transaction is  6s
The transaction has started at:  2023-12-17 23:05:39.024446 -0600 CST m=+0.000108251
The transaction has completed at:  2023-12-17 23:05:47.688939 -0600 CST m=+8.664585417 8.664477166s
Performance problem, transaction completed in 8.664477166s second(s)!
```

Figure 12.3: Transaction deadline not met

When we meet the deadline, it looks like this:

```
Deadline for the transaction is  1m40s
The transaction has started at:  2023-12-17 23:09:23.879401 -0600 CST m=+0.000130501
The transaction has completed at:  2023-12-17 23:09:34.478346 -0600 CST m=+10.599057043 10.598926542s
Performance is OK transaction completed in 10.598926542s
```

Figure 12.4: Transaction deadline met

Let's dissect our example. First, we define a deadline for the transaction with the `time.Duration()` variable. In my experience, the `Millisecond` resolution is optimal; however, it does take some time to get used to calculating it. Feel free to use whichever resolution you prefer. We mark the beginning with the `start` variable, do some calculations, and mark the completion with the `end` variable. The magic happens after this. We would like to calculate the difference between the deadline and the transaction duration, but we cannot do it directly. We need to convert the `duration` value to `transaction` time. This was done the same way when we created our deadline. We simply use the `Nanosecond` resolution, which is the lowest resolution we should go to. However, in this case, you can use the resolution you would like. After conversion, we can easily compare and decide whether the transaction is fine or not.

Now, let's see how we can manipulate time.

Managing time

The Go programming language's `time` package provides two functions that allow you to manipulate time. One of them is called `Sub()`, and the other one is called `Add()`. There have not been many cases, in my experience, where this has been used. Mostly, when calculating the elapsed time of a script's execution, the `Sub()` function is used to tell the difference.

Let's see what the addition looks like:

```
    timeToManipulate := time.Now()
    toBeAdded := time.Duration(10 * time.Second)
    fmt.Println("The original time:", timeToManipulate)
    fmt.Printf("%v duration later %v", toBeAdded, timeToManipulate.
Add(toBeAdded))
```

After execution, the following output welcomes us:

```
The original time: 2023-10-18 08:49:53.1499273 +0200 CEST
m=+0.001994601
10s duration later: 2023-10-18 08:50:03.1499273 +0200 CEST
m=+10.001994601
```

Let's inspect what happened here. We created a variable to hold our time, which requires some manipulation. The `toBeAdded` variable represents a duration of 10 seconds, which we would like to add. The `Add()` function of the `time` package expects a variable of the `time.Duration()`

type. Then, we simply call the `Add()` function of our date, and the result is visible on the console. The functionality of the `Sub()` function is rather cumbersome, and it is not really intended to remove a specific duration from the time we have. It can be done, but you need many more lines of code to achieve this. What you can do is craft your duration with a negative value. Swap out the second line for this:

```
toBeAdded := time.Duration(-10 * time.Minute)
```

It will work just fine and output you this:

```
The original time: 2023-10-18 08:50:36.5950116 +0200 CEST
m=+0.001994401
-10m0s duration later: 2023-10-18 08:40:36.5950116 +0200 CEST
m=+599.998005599
```

This works as we expected; we have successfully calculated what time it was 10 minutes ago.

Exercise 12.02 – Duration of execution

In this exercise, we will craft a function that allows you to calculate the duration of the execution between two `time.Time` variables and return a string that tells you how long the execution took to complete.

Perform the following steps in order:

1. Create a new folder and add a `main.go` file.

2. Initialize the script with the following `package` and `import` statements:

    ```
    package main
    import (
      "time"
      "fmt"
      "strconv"
    )
    ```

3. Let's now define our `elapsedTime()` function:

    ```
    func elapsedTime(start time.Time, end time.Time) string {
      elapsed := end.Sub(start)
      hours := strconv.Itoa(int(elapsed.Hours()))
      minutes := strconv.Itoa(int(elapsed.Minutes()))
      seconds := strconv.Itoa(int(elapsed.Seconds()))



      return "The total execution time elapsed is: " + hours +
    " hour(s) and " + minutes + " minute(s) and " + seconds + "
    ```

```
    second(s)!"
}
```

4. Now, we are ready to define our `main()` function:

```
func main(){
    start := time.Now()
    time.Sleep(2 * time.Second)
    end := time.Now()
    fmt.Println(elapsedTime(start, end))
}
```

5. Run the code:

```
go run main.go
```

The following should appear as the output:

```
The total execution time elapsed is: 0 hour(s) and 0 minute(s) and 2
second(s)!
```

In this exercise, we created a function that shows us how many hours, minutes, and seconds it took to execute the action. This is useful because you can reuse this function in other Go apps.

Now, let's turn our eyes toward the formatting of time.

Formatting time

So far in this chapter, you may have noticed that the dates are pretty ugly. I mean, take a look at the following lines:

```
The transaction has started at: 2023-09-27 13:50:58.2715452 +0200 CEST
m=+0.002992801
```

These were intentionally left there to force you to think about whether this is all that Go can do. Is there a way to format these lines to make them more convenient and easier to read? If so, what are those extra lines?

Here, we will answer those questions. When we talk about time formatting, there are two main concepts we are referring to. The first option is for instances when we would like our `time` variable to output a desirable-looking string when we use it in print, and the second option is for when we would like to take a string and parse it to a specific format. Both have their own use cases; we are going to look at them in more detail as I teach you how to use both.

First, we are going to learn about the `Parse()` function. This function has essentially two arguments. The first one is the format string to parse against, and the second one is the string that needs to be parsed. The end of this parse will result in a `time` variable that can utilize built-in Go functions. Go uses a POSIX-based date format, where **POSIX** stands for **Portable Operating System Interface**, thus allowing Go applications to run on any Unix flavor. Parse() is very useful when you have an application that is working with time values from different time zones and you would like to convert them, for example, to the same time zone for better understanding and easier comparison:

```
Mon Jan 2 15:04:05 -0700 MST 2006
 0  1  2  3  4  5  6
```

This date format is equal to "123456" in POSIX, which can be decoded from the preceding example. There are constants provided in the language to help you deal with parsing different time strings.

There are three main time formats against which we can parse:

- RFC3339

- UnixDate

- ANSIC

Let's look at how Parse() works:

```
t1, err := time.Parse(time.RFC3339, "2019-09-27T22:18:11+00:00")
if err != nil {
  fmt.Println(err)
}
t2, err := time.Parse(time.UnixDate, "2019-09-27T22:18:11+00:00")
if err != nil {
  fmt.Println(err)
}
t3, err := time.Parse(time.ANSIC, "2019-09-27T22:18:11+00:00")
if err != nil {
  fmt.Println(err)
}
fmt.Println("RFC3339:", t1)
fmt.Println("UnixDate", t2)
fmt.Println("ANSIC", t3)
```

The output is as follows:

```
parsing time "2019-09-27T22:18:11+00:00" as "Mon Jan _2 15:04:05 MST
2006": cannot parse "2019-09-27T22:18:11+00:00" as "Mon"
parsing time "2019-09-27T22:18:11+00:00" as "Mon Jan _2 15:04:05
2006": cannot parse "2019-09-27T22:18:11+00:00" as "Mon"
RFC3339: 2019-09-27 22:18:11 +0000 +0000
UnixDate 0001-01-01 00:00:00 +0000 UTC
ANSIC 0001-01-01 00:00:00 +0000 UTC
```

What happens behind the scenes is as follows. We have the `t1`, `t2`, and `t3` variables that hold the time, which is parsed against the specified format. The `err` variables hold the error results if there are any during the conversion. The output from the `t1` variable is the only one that makes sense; `UnixDate` and `ANSIC` are wrong because the wrong string is parsed against the format. `UnixDate` expects something that they call `epoch`. The epoch is a very unique date; on Unix systems, it marks the beginning of time, which starts at January 1, 1970. It expects a huge integer, which is the number of seconds elapsed since this date. The format expects something like this as the input: `Mon Sep _27 18:24:05 2019`. Providing such time allows the `Parse()` function to provide the correct output.

Now that we have clarified the `Parse()` function, it's time to look at the `Format()` function.

Go allows you to craft your own `time` variables. Let's learn how we can do that and, afterward, we will format them:

```
date := time.Date(2019, 9, 27, 18, 50, 48, 324359102, time.UTC)
fmt.Println(date)
```

The preceding code demonstrates how you can craft the time for yourself; however, we are going to look at what all those numbers are. The skeleton syntax for that is as follows:

```
func Date(year int, month Month, day, hour, min, sec, nsec int, loc
*Location) Time
```

Essentially, we need to specify the year, month, day, hour, and so on. We would like to reformat our output based on the input variables; this should appear as follows:

```
2019-09-27 18:50:48.324359102 +0000 UTC
```

Time zones were not important until people started working in big enterprise environments. When you have a global fleet of interconnected devices, it is important to be able to differentiate between time zones. If you want to have an `AddDate()` function, which can be used to add `Year`, `Month`, and `Day` to your current time, then this must enable you to dynamically add to your dates. Let's look at an example. Given our previous date, let's add 1 year, 2 months, and 3 days:

```
date := time.Date(2019, 9, 27, 18, 50, 48, 324359102, time.UTC)
next Date := date.AddDate(1, 2, 3)
fmt.Println(next Date)
```

You will get the following output upon execution of this program:

```
2020-11-30 18:50:48.324359102 +0000 UTC
```

The `AddDate()` function takes three arguments: the first is `years`, the second is `months`, and the third is `days`. This gives you the opportunity to fine-tune the scripts you have. To properly understand how formatting works, you need to know what is under the hood.

One last important aspect of time formatting is to understand how you can utilize the LoadLocation() function of the time package to convert your local time to the local time of another time zone. Our reference time zone will be the Los Angeles time zone. The Format() function is used to tell Go how we would like to see our output formatted. The In() function is a reference to a specific time zone we want our formatting to be present in.

Let's find out what the time is in Los Angeles:

```
current := time.Now()
losAngeles, err := time.LoadLocation("America/Los_Angeles")
if err != nil {
  fmt.Println(err)
}
fmt.Println("The local current time is:", current.Format(time.
ANSIC))
  fmt.Println("The time in Los Angeles is:", current.In(losAngeles).
Format(time.ANSIC))
```

Depending on your day of execution, you should see the following output:

```
The local current time is: Fri Oct 18 08:14:48 2019
The time in Los Angeles is: Thu Oct 17 23:14:48 2019
```

The key here is that we get our local time in a variable, and then we use the In() function of the time package to, say, convert that value to a specific time zone's value. It's simple, yet useful.

Exercise 12.03 – What is the time in your zone?

In this exercise, we will create a function that tells the difference between the current time zone and the specified time zone. The function will utilize the LoadLocation() function to specify the location based on which a variable will be set to a specific time. The In() location will be used to convert a specific time value to a given time zone value. The output format should be in the ANSIC standard.

Perform the following steps in order:

1. Create a new folder and add a main.go file.

2. Initialize the script with the following package and import statements:

```
package main
import (
  "time"
  "fmt"
)
```

3. Now is the time to create our function called `timeDiff()`, which will also return the `current` and the `remoteTime` variable formatted with `ANSIC`:

```
func timeDiff(timezone string) (string, string) {
    current := time.Now()
    remoteZone, err := time.LoadLocation(timezone)
    if err != nil {
        fmt.Println(err)
    }
    remoteTime := current.In(remoteZone)
    fmt.Println("The current time is:", current.Format(time.
ANSIC))
    fmt.Println("The timezone:", timezone, "time is:", remoteTime)
    return current.Format(time.ANSIC), remoteTime.Format(time.
ANSIC)
}
```

4. Define a `main()` function:

```
func main(){
    fmt.Println(timeDiff("America/Los_Angeles"))
}
```

5. Run the code:

```
go run main.go
```

The output looks as follows:

```
The current time is: Thu Oct 17 15:37:02 2023
The timezone: America/Los_Angeles time is: 2023-10-17 06:37:02.2440679
-0700 PDT
Thu Oct 17 15:37:02 2023 Thu Oct 17 06:37:02 2023
```

> **Note**
>
> The time printed out will be different depending on the time you run your code. In this exercise, we saw how easy it is to navigate between different time zones.

Activity 12.01 – Formatting a date according to user requirements

In this activity, you need to create a small script that takes the current date and outputs it in the following format: `02:49:21 31/01/2023`. You need to utilize what you have learned so far regarding the conversion of an integer to a string. This will allow you to concatenate different parts of your `time` variable. Remember that the `Month()` function omits the name and not the number of the month.

You must perform the following steps to get the desired output:

1. Use the `time.Now()` function to capture the current date in a variable.

2. Dissect the captured date to `day`, `month`, `year`, `hour`, `minute`, and `seconds` variables by converting them into strings.

3. Print out the concatenated variables in order.

    Once the script is complete, the output should appear as follows (note that this depends on when you run the code):

    ```
    15:32:30 2023/10/17
    ```

    By the end of this activity, you should have learned how you can craft your custom `time` variables and use `strconv.Itoa()` to convert a number to a string and concatenate the result.

> **Note**
>
> The solution for this activity can be found in the GitHub repository of the book: GitHub repository folder for this chapter: `https://github.com/PacktPublishing/Go-Programming-From-Beginner-to-Professional-Second-Edition-/tree/main/Chapter12/Activity12.01`.

Activity 12.02 – Enforcing a specific format of date and time

This activity requires you to use the knowledge you have accumulated in this chapter about time. We would like to create a small script that prints out a date with the following format: `02:49:21 31/01/2023`.

First, you need to create a `date` variable by utilizing the `time.Date()` function. You then need to recall how we accessed the `Year`, `Month`, and `Day` properties of the variable, and create a concatenation with an appropriate order. Remember that you cannot concatenate string and integer variables. The `strconv()` function is there to help you. You also need to remember that when you omit the `date.Month()` command, it prints the name of the month, but it also needs to be converted into an integer and then back into a string with a number.

You must perform the following steps to get the desired output:

1. Capture the current date with the `time.Now()` function in a variable.

2. Use the `strconv.Itoa()` function to save the appropriate parts of the captured `date` variable into the following variables: `day`, `month`, `year`, `hour`, `minute`, and `second`.

3. Finally, print these out using the appropriate concatenation.

The expected output should look like this:

```
2:49:21 2023/1/31
```

By the end of this activity, you should have learned how to format the current date to a specific custom format.

> **Note**
>
> The solution for this activity can be found in the https://github.com/PacktPublishing/ Go-Programming-From-Beginner-to-Professional-Second-Edition-/ tree/main/Chapter12/Activity12.02.

Activity 12.03 – Measuring elapsed time

This activity requires you to measure the duration of sleep. You should use the time.Sleep() function to sleep for 2 seconds, and once the sleep is complete, you need to calculate the difference between the start and end times and show how many seconds it took.

First, you mark the start of the execution, sleep for 2 seconds, and then capture the end of the execution time in a variable. By utilizing the time.Sub() function, we can use the Seconds() function to output the result. The output will be a bit strange as it will be slightly longer than expected.

You must perform the following steps to get the desired output:

1. Capture the start time in a variable.

2. Craft a sleep variable that is 2 seconds long.

3. Capture the end time in a variable.

4. Calculate the length by subtracting the start time from the end time.

5. Print out the result.

Depending on the speed of your PC, you should expect the following output:

```
The execution took exactly 2.0016895 seconds!
```

By the end of this activity, you should have learned how to measure the elapsed time for a specific activity.

> **Note**
>
> The solution for this activity can be found in the GitHub repository folder for this chapter: https://github.com/PacktPublishing/Go-Programming-From- Beginner-to-Professional-Second-Edition-/tree/main/Chapter12/ Activity12.03.

Activity 12.04 – Calculating the future date and time

In this activity, we are going to calculate the date that is 6 hours, 6 minutes, and 6 seconds from Now(). You will need to capture the current time in a variable. Then, utilize the Add() function on the given date to add the previously mentioned length. Please use the time.ANSIC format for convenience. There is a catch, however. Because the Add() function expects a duration, you need to pick a resolution such as Second and craft the duration before you can add it.

You must perform the following steps to get the desired output:

1. Capture the current time in a variable.

2. Print out this value as a reference in ANSIC format.

3. Calculate the duration with seconds as input.

4. Add the duration to the current time.

5. Print out the future date in ANSIC format.

Make sure your output looks like this, with the string formatting:

```
The current time: Thu Oct 17 15:16:48 2023
6 hours, 6 minutes and 6 seconds from now the time will be: Thu Oct 17
21:22:54 2023
```

By the end of this activity, you should have learned how you can calculate specific dates in the future by utilizing the time.Duration() and time.Add() functions.

> **Note**
>
> The solution for this activity can be found in the GitHub repository folder for this chapter: https://github.com/PacktPublishing/Go-Programming-From-Beginner-to-Professional-Second-Edition-/tree/main/Chapter12/Activity12.04.

Activity 12.05 – Printing the local time in different time zones

This activity requires you to utilize what you learned in the *Formatting time* section. You need to load an east coast city and a west coast city. Then, print out the current time for each city.

The key here is the LoadLocation() function, and you need to use the ANSIC format for the output. Remember that the LoadLocation() function returns two values!

You must perform the following steps to get the desired output:

1. Capture the current time in a variable.
2. Create reference time zone variables for `NyTime` and `LaTime` using the `time.LoadLocation()` function.
3. Print out, in `ANSIC` format, the current time in the respective time zones.

Depending on your day of execution, the following could be your expected output:

```
The local current time is: Thu Oct 17 15:16:13 2023
The time in New York is: Thu Oct 17 09:16:13 2023
The time in Los Angeles is: Thu Oct 17 06:16:13 2023
```

By the end of this activity, you should have learned how to convert your time variables to a specific time zone.

> **Note**
>
> The solution for this activity can be found in the GitHub repository folder for this chapter: `https://github.com/PacktPublishing/Go-Programming-From-Beginner-to-Professional-Second-Edition-/tree/main/Chapter12/Activity12.05`.

Summary

This chapter introduced you to the `time` package of Go, which allows you to reuse code that has been invented by other programmers and incorporated into the language. The goal was to teach you how to create, manipulate, and format `time` variables, and, in general, make you familiar with what you can do with the help of the `time` package. If you would like to further improve or dig deeper into what the package has to offer, you should check out the following link: `https://golang.org/pkg/time/`.

Timestamps and time manipulation are essential skills for every developer. Whether you have a big or small script put into production, the `time` module helps you to measure the elapsed time of actions and provide you with the logging of actions that happen during the execution. The most important thing about it, if used correctly, is that it helps you to easily trace back production problems to their roots.

Part 4: Applications

Applications come in various sizes and functionalities, ranging from small tools with a single purpose to extensive systems with numerous features. Regardless of their complexity, all applications feature interfaces, whether for human interaction (user interface/UI) or for communication with other applications (Application Programming Interface/API).

In this section, you'll explore the development of applications, from command-line tools to systems interacting with files, databases, and more.

This part has the following chapters:

- *Chapter 13, Programming from the Command Line*
- *Chapter 14, Files and Systems*
- *Chapter 15, SQL and Databases*

13

Programming from the Command Line

Overview

In this chapter, we will look at programming from the command line. We will see how Go is an excellent choice for creating powerful command-line utilities and applications, as well as discuss the many tools available for working with the command line using Go.

By reading this chapter, you will acquaint yourself with developing powerful command-line utilities and applications in Go. We will start with the basics of reading in command-line arguments and employing those flag values to control application behavior, take a peek at dealing with larger amounts of data inside and outside the application, and evaluate exit codes and best practices along the way. Then, we will dive a bit deeper and discuss strategies for gracefully handling interrupts, initiating external commands from our application, and using `go install`. Finally, we will learn how to create **terminal user interfaces** (**TUIs**), which allow us to craft robust, user-friendly command-line tools in Go.

Technical requirements

For this chapter, you'll require Go version 1.21 or higher. The code for this chapter can be found at `https://github.com/PacktPublishing/Go-Programming-From-Beginner-to-Professional-Second-Edition-/tree/main/Chapter13`.

Introduction

In the previous chapter, we looked at how Go provides powerful constructs when dealing with time data. We will be shifting gears a bit in this chapter to discuss one of the many ways that Go is beneficial in creating a powerful interface for applications.

UIs don't always have to be a web application frontend web page. End users can interact with software through engaging command-line interfaces, as well as by using a **command-line interface** (CLI).

Go provides many packages that allow us to program for the command line. We'll look at some of these packages, see where Go is at in terms of creating powerful command-line utilities, and learn about some of the current efforts in this space.

Reading arguments

Command-line arguments are a fundamental aspect of building versatile and interactive command-line applications. Reading arguments allow developers to make their applications more dynamic and adaptable to user input. Command-line arguments serve as a means for users to customize the behavior of a program without modifying its source code. By capturing input parameters from the command line, developers can create versatile applications that cater to different use cases and scenarios.

In Go, the os package serves as a straightforward way to access these arguments. The os.Args slice provides a convenient way to access command-line arguments. This allows developers to retrieve information such as file paths, configuration parameters, or any other input relevant to the application's functionality. The ability to read command-line arguments enhances the user experience by making applications more interactive and user-friendly.

Moreover, command-line arguments enable automation and scripting, allowing users to pass inputs programmatically. This flexibility is particularly valuable in scenarios where the same program needs to be executed with different parameters, making it a powerful tool for scripting and automation tasks.

Let's dive into the process of reading command-line arguments and illustrate this with a simple example that greets users with a personalized message.

Exercise 13.01 – saying hello using a name passed as an argument

In this exercise, we will print a hello statement using arguments that have been passed in from the command line:

1. Import the fmt and os packages:

    ```
    package main
    import (
      "fmt"
      "os"
    )
    ```

2. Utilize the args slice mentioned previously to capture the command-line arguments:

    ```
    func main() {
      args := os.Args
    ```

3.   Perform validation on the number of arguments supplied, excluding the executable name provided:

```
if len(args) < 2 {
    fmt.Println("Usage: go run main.go <name>")
    return
}
```

4.   Extract the name from the arguments supplied:

```
name := args[1]
```

5.   Display a personalized greeting message:

```
greeting := fmt.Sprintf("Hello, %s! Welcome to the command
line.", name)
    fmt.Println(greeting)
}
```

6.   Run the following command to execute the code:

```
go run main.go Sam
```

The output is as follows:

```
Hello, Sam! Welcome to the command line.
```

With that, we have demonstrated the basics of capturing a command-line argument using Go, and seen some of the benefits of capturing input data in an easy way for our program. While we used the os package in this example, other packages can assist in achieving the same goal of reading the input provided to the application, such as using the flags package. Let's look at how useful flags can be in programming for the command line.

Using flags to control behavior

The flags package provides a higher-level and more structured approach to reading arguments compared to directly using the os package. Flags simplify the process of parsing and handling command-line input, making it easier for developers to create robust and user-friendly command-line applications.

The flags package allows you to define flags with associated types and default values, making it clear what kind of input a user is expected to provide. It also automatically generates help messages, making your program more self-documenting. Here's a brief overview of how the flags package can help in reading and handling command-line arguments:

- **Define flags**: You can define flags, along with their types and default values. This provides a clear and structured way to specify expected inputs.

- **Parse flags**: After defining flags, you can parse the command-line arguments. This initializes flag variables with the values provided by a user.

- **Access flag values**: Once you have parsed the flag values that have been passed in, you can access the defined flags through variables and continue to work with them throughout the application.

Flags allow you to customize the behavior of your program without the need to modify the source code. For example, you can create flags that allow you to toggle behavior based on if a flag value is set. You can also use basic conditional logic pending the values set for certain flags. Let's complete an exercise and utilize the flags package to say hello.

Exercise 13.02 – using flags to say hello conditionally

In this exercise, we will print a hello statement using the flags package:

1. Import the fmt and os packages:

```
package main
import (
  "flag"
  "fmt"
)
```

2. Create our flags for the utility and set the default values:

```
var (
  nameFlag = flag.String("name", "Sam", "Name of the person to say hello to")
  quietFlag = flag.Bool("quiet", false, "Toggle to be quiet when saying hello")
)
Parse the flags and conditionally say hello pending the value of
the quiet flag:
func main() {
  flag.Parse()
  if !*quietFlag {
    greeting := fmt.Sprintf("Hello, %s! Welcome to the command line.", *nameFlag)
    fmt.Println(greeting)
  }
}
```

Here's the output you'll receive if you run go run main.go. This is because quietFlag defaults to false and nameFlag defaults to Sam:

```
Hello, Sam! Welcome to the command line.
```

However, you can set values for the flags. For this, you can use `nameFlag` and set the `quietFlag` value. The output of running `go run main.go --name=Cassie --quiet=false` is listed here. This is because `quietFlag` is set to false and `nameFlag` is set to Sam:

```
Hello, Cassie! Welcome to the command line.
```

Alternatively, you will get no output if you use `quietFlag` with a value of `true`. So, if you run `go run main.go --quiet=true`, then you'll see no output as we have just used flags to control the expected output behavior of our program.

This code demonstrated how you can use flags to control the behavior of a program. If you are working with someone else's command-line interface, then you can seamlessly use the `help` flag to list the defined flags available. The `flag` package in Go automatically generates a help message based on the flags in the program. To see the available help message for the preceding code, you can run `go run main.go --help`. That will provide the following output:

```
Usage of /var/folders/qt/5jjdv1bj3h33t2rl40tpt56w0000gn/T/
go-build1361710947/b001/exe/main:
-name string
Name of the person to say hello to (default "Sam")
-quiet
Toggle to be quiet when saying hello
```

By utilizing the `flags` package, you enhance the readability and maintainability of your code, as well as provide a more user-friendly experience. It simplifies the process of handling various types of input and automates the generation of usage information, making it easier for users to understand and interact with your command-line application. Now, let's see what it looks like to stream data in and out of the application.

Streaming large amounts of data in and out of your application

In command-line applications, it is crucial to handle large amounts of data efficiently for performance and responsiveness purposes. Often, command-line applications may be a small part of a larger pipeline processing data. Most people are not going to want to sit around typing out a large amount of data, such as a dataset, piece by piece.

Go allows you to stream data to your applications so that you can process information in chunks, rather than all at once. This allows you to effectively process large amounts of data, reduce memory overhead, and provide better scalability in the future.

When dealing with large amounts of data, it's often stored in files. This can range from financial CSV files, analysis Excel files, or machine learning datasets. There are a few main benefits of streaming data with Go:

- **Memory efficiency**: The program can read and process data line by line, reducing memory consumption, as you then don't have to read the entire data into memory

- **Real-time analysis**: Users can observe a real-time analysis of the results of processing their data

- **Interactive interface**: You can enhance the command-line interface so that it accepts dynamic information or displays additional details when processing large amounts of data

Data confidentiality might be top of mind, depending on the type of data you may be streaming to your command-line application. For this reason, different encoding mechanisms may be employed to hide text without providing real security on the data, or as a first step toward securing the data.

Rot13, or rotate by 13 places, is a simple letter substitution cipher that replaces a letter with the 13th letter after it in the alphabet. For example, the letter A would become N, and B would become C, and so forth. It is a symmetric key algorithm that is often used as a trivial form of encryption to obscure text. This algorithm provides no significant security and is mainly used for fun, typically never used in a production-level environment to secure data. It is also fully self-reversible, meaning that applying Rot13 twice would result in the same originating data. This can be useful for sending and receiving text in environments where the receiving end may or may not know if the data has been encoded.

Let's expand our new Rot13 knowledge so that we can work on a fun streaming data example for a command-line application.

Exercise 13.03 – using pipes, stdin, and stdout to apply a Rot13 encoding to a file

In this exercise, we will work with the Rot13 encoding for some input data:

1. Import the required packages:

```
package main
import (
    "bufio"
    "fmt"
    "io"
    "os"
)
```

2. Define the rot13 function to apply Rot13 encoding to a given string:

```
func rot13(s string) string {
    result := make([]byte, len(s))
```

```
   for i := 0; i < len(s); i++ {
     char := s[i]
     switch {
     case char >= 'a' && char <= 'z':
       result[i] = 'a' + (char-'a'+13)%26
     case char >= 'A' && char <= 'Z':
       result[i] = 'A' + (char-'A'+13)%26
     default:
       result[i] = char
     }
   }
   return string(result)
}
```

3. Define the function to read data from `stdin`, apply the Rot13 encoding, and write the output to `stdout`:

```
func processStdin() {
  reader := bufio.NewReader(os.Stdin)
  for {
    input, err := reader.ReadString('\n')
    if err == io.EOF {
      break
    } else if err != nil {
      fmt.Println("Error reading stdin:", err)
      return
    }
    encoded := rot13(input)
    fmt.Print(encoded)
  }
}
```

4. Define the function to process file or user input, apply the Rot13 encoding, and write the output to `stdout`:

```
func processFileOrInput() {
  var inputReader io.Reader
  // Check if a file path is provided
  if len(os.Args) > 1 {
    file, err := os.Open(os.Args[1])
    if err != nil {
      fmt.Println("Error opening file:", err)
      return
    }
    defer file.Close()
```

```
        inputReader = file
    } else {
        // No file provided, read user input
        fmt.Print("Enter text: ")
        inputReader = os.Stdin
    }
    // Process input and apply rot13 encoding
    scanner := bufio.NewScanner(inputReader)
    for scanner.Scan() {
        // Apply rot13 encoding to the input line
        encoded := rot13(scanner.Text())
        fmt.Println(encoded)
    }
    if err := scanner.Err(); err != nil {
        fmt.Println("Error reading input:", err)
    }
}
```

5. Define the main function:

```
func main() {
    // Check if data is available on stdin
    stat, _ := os.Stdin.Stat()
    if (stat.Mode() & os.ModeCharDevice) == 0 {
        // Data available on stdin, process it
        processStdin()
    } else {
        // No data on stdin, process file or user input
        processFileOrInput()
    }
}
```

If you run go run main.go and enter some text when prompted, you'll receive the following output:

```
Enter text: enjoy
rawbl
the
gur
book
obbx
```

To exit the program, you can type Ctrl + C. Also, the program can be used in a pipeline, where the output of one command becomes the input of the command-line application if you use cat data. txt | go run main.go. cat is a command that you can use to concatenate files together (For

Windows, the `type` command is used for concatenation). In the event you use it on a single file, then it gives you an easy way of printing out the contents of the file. If you declare a `data.txt` file and pipe the contents of the file to the command-line application with the following command, then you will see a similar output:

```
cat data.txt | go run main.go
```

Here's the resulting output:

```
rawbl
gur
obbx
```

The preceding exercise demonstrated a few things. First, we saw how we could process `stdin` data line by line using `bufio.NewReader` until an end-of-file error is encountered. We also saw how to process files or input data and Rot13 encode it. Lastly, we saw how we could use the same code and pipe large amounts of data into the program to encode it. This code demonstrated Go's capabilities to stream large data in and out of a command-line application. The program had to be *Ctrl + C* terminated to interrupt the reading from `stdin` and exit the program. That's a perfect segway into exploring exit codes and best practices in more detail before we explore interrupts, where we'll learn more about terminating programs using interrupts such as *Ctrl + C*.

Exit codes and command line best practices

Ensuring proper exit codes and following best practices is essential for a seamless user experience. Exit codes provide a way for command-line applications to communicate their status to the calling application. A well-defined exit code system allows users and the other scripts to understand whether the application executed successfully or encountered an issue when running.

In Go, the `os` package provides a straightforward way to set exit codes using the `ox.Exit` function. Conventionally, an exit code of 0 indicates success, while any non-zero code signals an error.

For example, you can check the status code of the previous exercise and verify the successful status code. To do this, run `echo $?` in the terminal. `$?` Is a special shell variable that holds the exit status of the last command that was executed, and the `echo` command prints it out. You'll see the 0 exit code printout denoting a successful execution status, and no error. You can manually catch errors in the program and return non-zero code signals to denote errors. You can even create custom exit codes, such as the following:

```
const (
    ExitCodeSuccess = 0
    ExitCodeInvalidInput = 1
    ExitCodeFileNotFound = 2
)
```

These can easily be used using `os.Exit`, by placing `os.Exit(ExitCodeSuccess)` in successful cases you want to exit, and by using one of the other error codes when you want to exit in certain circumstances.

While using proper exit codes is an important command line best practice, there are a few others to keep in mind:

- **Consistent logging**: Use meaningful messages to aid troubleshooting.

- **Clear usage information**: Provide clear and concise usage information, including flags and arguments. Also, some packages allow you to provide example commands. Those should be used to let others see how to use the commands easily.

- **Handle help and versioning**: Implement flags to display help and version information. This is good for making your application more user-friendly and providing a means to ensure they are on the latest version by checking the version information.

- **Graceful termination**: Exit codes should be considered and terminated gracefully, ensuring proper cleanup tasks are performed as needed.

You are now well on your way when it comes to command-line application best practices and exit code considerations. However, there are times when end users will provide interrupts to cancel an application. Let's learn what to do and consider when that happens.

Knowing when to stop by watching for interrupts

When building robust applications, it's crucial to handle interrupts gracefully, ensuring the software can respond appropriately to signals indicating it should stop or perform a specific action. In Go, the standard way to achieve this is by monitoring interrupt signals, allowing the application to shut down or clean up resources in an orderly manner.

Graceful shutdown, or termination, is an important concept in computer science in general. Unforeseen events, server maintenance, or external factors might require your application to stop gracefully. This could involve releasing resources, saving state, or notifying connected clients. A graceful shutdown ensures your application remains reliable and predictable, minimizing the risk of data corruption or loss.

Abruptly terminating an application without proper cleanup can lead to various issues, such as incomplete transactions, resource leaks, corrupted data, and more. Graceful shutdowns mitigate these risks by providing an opportunity to finish ongoing tasks and release acquired resources.

The operating systems communicate with running processes through signals. A process is simply a program running on a computer. The `os/signal` package provides a convenient way to handle these signals within Go programs. There are common interrupt signals, such as **SIGINT** (*Ctrl + C*) and **SIGTERM**, that provide a comprehensive strategy for graceful terminations. We saw the SIGINT interrupt in *Exercise 13.03*. That program had to be *Ctrl + C* terminated to interrupt the reading from `stdin` and exit the program.

The `signal.Notify` function allows you to register channels to receive specified signals. This sets the foundation for creating a mechanism to gracefully shut down your application upon receiving an interrupt signal. There are also effective shutdown patterns and best practices to keep in mind, such as ensuring closed network connections, saving state, and signaling goroutines, to finish up their tasks before exiting. Additionally, using timeouts and the `context` package enhances your application's responsiveness during shutdown, preventing it from getting stuck indefinitely.

Gracefully handling interrupt signals is a fundamental skill for building robust and reliable command-line applications in Go. By following best practices and patterns to ensure graceful termination, you can ensure that your software behaves predictably, even in the face of unexpected interruptions.

Not only can you stop programs gracefully with different interrupts, but you can also start other commands from the command-line application.

Starting other commands from your application

Launching external commands from your Go application opens opportunities for interaction with other programs, processes, and system utilities. The `os/exec` package in Go provides functionalities for starting and interacting with external processes. You can run basic commands, capture their output, and handle errors seamlessly with this package. It serves as a foundation for more advanced command execution scenarios.

For example, the `os/exec` package allows you to customize the execution of commands by configuring attributes such as the working directory, environment variables, and more. You can also provide inputs to the subcommand through standard input streams from the originating command-line application.

By running other commands from within your command-line application, you can run some processes in the background, allowing the application to continue its execution while monitoring or interacting with parallel processes. You can even establish bidirectional communication with commands, enabling real-time interaction and data exchange between the command-line application and the external processes.

When starting other applications, cross-platform considerations must be kept in mind. There are differences in shell behavior and command paths across different operating systems. So, when executing subcommands from a command-line application, it is important to keep a consistent and reliable command execution in mind, regardless of the compute an end user may be using. Thankfully, the `os/exec` package provides a cross-platform solution for executing external commands in Go, making it easier to write code across different operating systems.

Now that we've discussed how useful it can be to execute other commands from a Go command-line application, let's see an example in action.

Exercise 13.04 – creating a stopwatch with a time limit

In this exercise, we will create a stopwatch with a time limit and start another command from the application:

1. Import the necessary packages:

```
package main
import (
    "fmt"
    "os"
    "os/exec"
    "time"
)
```

2. Within the main function, set the time limit for the stopwatch and allow user input to start the clock:

```
func main() {
    timeLimit := 5 * time.Second
    fmt.Println("Press Enter to start the stopwatch...")
    _, err := fmt.Scanln() // Wait for user to press Enter
    if err != nil {
        fmt.Println("Error reading from stdin:", err)
        return
    }
    fmt.Println("Stopwatch started. Waiting for", timeLimit)
```

3. Sleep for the time limit, execute the other command from within the command-line application, and close the main function:

```
    time.Sleep(timeLimit)
    fmt.Println("Time's up! Executing the other command.")
    cmd := exec.Command("echo", "Hello")
    cmd.Stdout = os.Stdout
    cmd.Stderr = os.Stderr
    err = cmd.Run()
    if err != nil {
        fmt.Println("Error executing command:", err)
    }
}
```

If you run go run main.go and press Enter to start the timer when prompted, you will receive the following output:

```
Press Enter to start the stopwatch...
Stopwatch started. Waiting for 5s
Time's up! Executing the other command.
Hello
```

Executing external commands is a powerful capability that allows your Go applications to interact with the broader system environment. While this was a simple echo command, it shows how strong this capability is if you expand this code to start other applications, run commands in parallel or in the background, and more.

Terminal UIs

Some of the latest updates to command-line programming with Go have included **terminal UIs**, or **TUIs** for short. Creating a TUI in Go opens a world of possibilities for building interactive command-line applications. There are a few fundamental concepts that are involved with building UIs for the terminal:

- **Components**: TUIs are composed of various components, such as buttons, input fields, and/or lists

- **Layouts**: Arranging components in a structured layout is crucial for a clean and intuitive design

- **User input handling**: Processing user input from keyboard events is fundamental to interactive interfaces

Some TUI packages provide support for event handling, such as mouse events and key presses, dynamic updates based on input data, or customizing the appearance of UI components. There are several popular TUI packages available. We will look at one in the following exercise, where we'll build on a previous exercise in this chapter.

Exercise 13.05 – creating a wrapper for our Rot13 pipeline

In this exercise, we will create a TUI wrapper for the Rot13 pipeline that we created in *Exercise 13.03*:

1. Import the necessary packages:

```
package main
import (
  "bufio"
  "fmt"
  "io"
  "os"
  "strings"
  tea "github.com/charmbracelet/bubbletea"
)
```

2. Denote TUI choices and model specifics:

```go
var choices = []string{"File input", "Type in input"}
type model struct {
  cursor int
  choice string
}
func (m model) Init() tea.Cmd {
  return nil
}
```

3. Define the function to handle model updates:

```go
func (m model) Update(msg tea.Msg) (tea.Model, tea.Cmd) {
  switch msg := msg.(type) {
  case tea.KeyMsg:
    switch msg.String() {
    case "ctrl+c", "q", "esc":
      return m, tea.Quit
    case "enter":
      m.choice = choices[m.cursor]
      return m, tea.Quit
    case "down", "j":
      m.cursor++
      if m.cursor >= len(choices) {
        m.cursor = 0
      }
    case "up", "k":
      m.cursor--
      if m.cursor < 0 {
        m.cursor = len(choices) - 1
      }
    }
  }
  return m, nil
}
```

4. Define the TUI view:

```go
func (m model) View() string {
  s := strings.Builder{}
  s.WriteString("Select if you would like to work with file
input or type in input:\n\n")
  for i := 0; i < len(choices); i++ {
    if m.cursor == i {
      s.WriteString("(•) ")
```

```
      } else {
        s.WriteString("( ) ")
      }
      s.WriteString(choices[i])
      s.WriteString("\n")
    }
    s.WriteString("\n(press q to quit)\n")
    return s.String()
  }
```

5. Define the same Rot13 encoding function from earlier:

```
  func rot13(s string) string {
    result := make([]byte, len(s))
    for i := 0; i < len(s); i++ {
      char := s[i]
      switch {
      case char >= 'a' && char <= 'z':
        result[i] = 'a' + (char-'a'+13)%26
      case char >= 'A' && char <= 'Z':
        result[i] = 'A' + (char-'A'+13)%26
      default:
        result[i] = char
      }
    }
    return string(result)
  }
```

6. Define the function to read in data from stdin to apply Rot13 encoding to:

```
  func processStdin() {
    reader := bufio.NewReader(os.Stdin)
    for {
      input, err := reader.ReadString('\n')
      if err == io.EOF {
        break
      } else if err != nil {
        fmt.Println("Error reading stdin:", err)
        return
      }
      encoded := rot13(input)
      fmt.Print(encoded)
    }
  }
```

7. Define the modified function to handle file input:

```go
func processFile(filename string) {
  var inputReader io.Reader
  file, err := os.Open(filename)
  if err != nil {
    fmt.Println("Error opening file:", err)
    return
  }
  defer file.Close()
  inputReader = file
  // Process input and apply rot13 encoding
  scanner := bufio.NewScanner(inputReader)
  for scanner.Scan() {
    encoded := rot13(scanner.Text())
    fmt.Println(encoded)
  }
  if err := scanner.Err(); err != nil {
    fmt.Println("Error reading input:", err)
  }
}
```

8. Define the main function to start the TUI:

```go
func main() {
  p := tea.NewProgram(model{})
  m, err := p.Run()
  if err != nil {
    fmt.Println("Error running program:", err)
    os.Exit(1)
  }
  if m, ok := m.(model); ok && m.choice != "" {
    fmt.Printf("\n---\nYou chose %s!\n", m.choice)
  }
  if m, ok := m.(model); ok && m.choice != "" && m.choice ==
"File input" {
    processFile("data.txt")
  }
  if m, ok := m.(model); ok && m.choice != "" && m.choice ==
"Type in input" {
    processStdin()
  }
}
```

You'll receive the following output if you run go run main.go and select File input:

```
Select if you would like to work with file input or type in input:
(•) File input
( ) Type in input
(press q to quit)
---
You chose File input!
rawbl
gur
obbx
```

You'll receive the following output if you run go run main.go and select Type in input:

```
Select if you would like to work with file input or type in input:
( ) File input
(•) Type in input
(press q to quit)
---
You chose Type in input!
enjoy
rawbl
the
gur
book
obbx
```

The preceding example expanded upon our previous exercise. Here, we provided a very simple wrapper for the entrance to the Rot13 coding exercise, providing a nice UI to input if you are going to use the default data file for input or provide your own input. This TUI was simple on purpose to demonstrate that quite a bit is involved when it comes to defining the model interface so that it can work with the terminal UI.

Now, let's see what it looks like to consume other people's command-line applications using go install.

go install

You can install Go command-line applications using the go install command. This command is a powerful tool that's provided (among the many) by the Go toolchain to compile and install Go applications in your workspace's bin directory. This allows you to run your applications globally from any terminal window. To install a Go application, you can simply navigate to the project's root directory and run go install.

This command considers cross-platform compilation by providing the GOOS flag, where you can specify which operating system to target, as well as the GOARCH flag, where you can specify the underlying architecture to target.

An example of a common Go package that you can use to generate command-line interfaces in Go is the cobra package. This is also a tool you can use to bootstrap application scaffolding to rapidly develop Cobra-based applications if you would like to dive further into developing your programming in terms of command-line skills. This package provides a simple example of using the go install command:

```
go install github.com/spf13/cobra-cli@latest
```

The preceding command installs all of the dependencies to use the Cobra CLI. As a result, my machine knows about the tool, and you can easily work with the command-line program that you just installed, as shown here:

```
cobra-cli -help
```

Cobra is a CLI library for Go that empowers applications.

It can generate the necessary files to quickly create a Cobra application:

```
Usage:
  cobra-cli [command]
Available Commands:
  add Add a command to a Cobra Application
completion Generate the autocompletion script for the specified shell
help Help about any command
init Initialize a Cobra Application
Flags:
-a, --author string author name for copyright attribution (default
"YOUR NAME")
--config string config file (default is $HOME/.cobra.yaml)
-h, --help help for cobra-cli
-1, --license string name of license for the project
--viper use Viper for configuration
Use "cobra-cli [command] --help" for more information about a command.
```

With that, you know how to install someone else's command-line application. Now, let's summarize what we learned in this chapter.

Summary

In this chapter, we studied various methodologies of programming via the command line. We uncovered how Go is an excellent choice for creating command-line applications with ease, as well as how to use the native Go toolchain.

Starting with the os and flag packages, we looked at how to read arguments from the command line for our application. Then, we looked at flags to control the behavior of our program and looked at how streaming large amounts of data in and out of an application can shed light on how command-line applications in Go can be part of a bigger programmatic pipeline.

We also took a peak at handling the CLI shutdown process gracefully by discussing exit codes and interrupts, as well as invoking other commands from within our command-line application. We ended this chapter by looking at terminal UIs, taking our CLI to the next level, and installing other CLIs using the native Go toolchain.

In the next chapter, we will look at files and systems using Go. While we did touch on that in this chapter so that we could read input data for our CLI application, we will do a deep dive into reading and writing files next.

14

File and Systems

Overview

We will see in this chapter how to interact with the filesystem, which means we will read files, manipulate them, store them for later use, and get information about them. We will also cover how to read folders so that we can search for the files we need, and will examine some specific file formats such as CSV, which is commonly used to share information in tabular form.

Another thing you will learn in this chapter is how to send some information to your application in the form of flags.

Technical requirements

For this chapter, you'll require Go version 1.21 or higher. The code for this chapter can be found at: `https://github.com/PacktPublishing/Go-Programming-From-Beginner-to-Professional-Second-Edition-/tree/main/Chapter14`.

Introduction

In the previous chapter, we looked at how to write simple command-line applications. We will carry on with this here, introducing ways to pass parameters to our application so that it behaves differently depending on the values we send.

After that, we will interact with the filesystem. The levels we are going to be working with the filesystem at are the file, directory, and permission levels. We will tackle everyday issues that developers face when working with the filesystem.

We will learn how to create a command-line application that will read and write files. Along with discussing what happens when we get a signal interrupt from the OS, we will demonstrate how to perform cleanup actions before our application stops running. We will also handle a scenario of receiving an interrupt to our application and handling how the application exits. There are times when your application is running, and a signal comes from the OS to shut down the application.

In such instances, we may want to log information at the time of the shutdown for debugging purposes; this will help us to understand why the application shuts down. We will look at how we can do that in this chapter. However, before we start tackling these issues, let's get a basic understanding of the filesystem.

Filesystem

A filesystem controls how data is named, stored, accessed, and retrieved on a device such as a hard drive, USB, DVD, or another medium. There is no one filesystem, and how it behaves largely depends on what OS you are using. You must have heard of FAT, FAT32, NFTS, and so on, which are all different filesystems and are used normally by Windows. Linux can read and write to them, but it generally uses a different family of filesystems that have names starting with ext, which stands for *extended*. You do not need to have a deep understanding of filesystems, but, as a software engineer, it is good to at least have a basic understanding of the subject.

What interests us in this chapter, however, is that each filesystem has its conventions for naming files, such as the length of the filename, the specific characters that can be used, how long the suffix or file extension can be, and so on. Each file has information or metadata, data embedded within a file or associated with it that describes or provides information about the file. This metadata about a file can contain information such as file size, location, access permissions, date created, date modified, and more. This is all the information that can be accessed by our applications.

Files are generally placed in some sort of hierarchal structure. This structure typically consists of multiple directories and sub-directories. The placement of the files within the directories is a way to organize your data and get access to the file or directory:

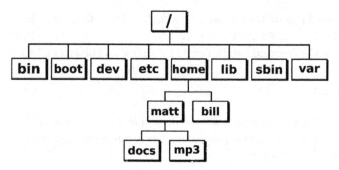

Figure 14.1 – The Linux filesystem

As shown in *Figure 14.1*, directories can be nested. In a normal Linux filesystem, we will see that there is a root directory, which is defined by the name /, and everything else is a subdirectory of it. The **home** directory generally holds data for each user of the system, and in the case shown above, **matt** is a directory holding a **docs** and an **mp3** directory, which are subdirectories of **matt**, but **matt** itself is a subdirectory of **home**.

In the next topic, we will be looking at file permissions.

File permissions

Permissions are an important aspect that you need to understand when dealing with file creation and modifications.

We need to look at various permission types that can be assigned to a file. We also need to consider how those permission types are represented in symbolic and octal notation.

Go uses the Unix nomenclature to represent permission types. They are represented in symbolic notation or octal notation. The three permission types are *Read*, *Write*, and *Execute*.

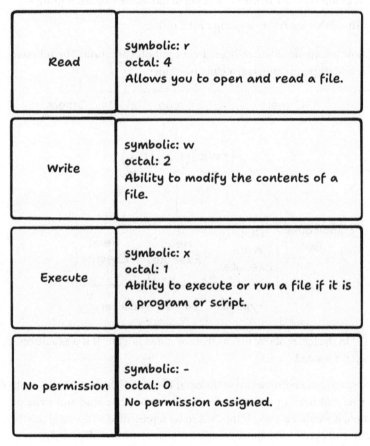

Figure 14.2 – File permissions

Permissions for every file are assigned to three different entities that can be individuals or groups. This means that a user can be part of a group that has access to some files, as a result of which the user inherits access to those files. It is not possible to assign permissions for a file to a specific user; rather, we add the user to a group and then assign permissions to that group. That said, it is possible to assign permission for a file to the following:

- **Owner**: This is an individual, a single person such as John Smith, or the root user who is the owner of the file. In general, it is the individual who created the file.

- **Group**: A group typically consists of multiple individuals or other groups.

- **Others**: Those that are not in a group or the owner.

Let's see now, how permissions are indicated via symbolic notation. The following diagram is an example of a file and its permissions on a Unix machine:

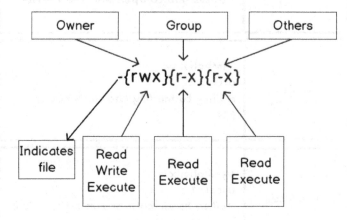

Figure 14.3 – Permissions notation

The first dash (-) in the figure above means that the entity is a file. If it was a directory, it would have been the character d instead.

Another way to specify the permissions is the octal notation, which expresses multiple permissions types with a single number. For example, if you want to indicate read and write permissions using symbolic notation, it would be rw-. If this was to be represented as an octal number, it would be 6, because 4 means read permission and 2 means write permission. Full permission would be 7, which means *4+2+1* or *read+write+execute* (rwx).

The following recaps the permissions and their explanations:

Permission Type	Octal	Symbolic
No Permission	0	---
Execute	1	--x
Write	2	-w-
Execute+Write	3	-wx
Read	4	r--
Read+Execute	5	r-x
Read+Write	6	rw-
Read+Write+Execute	7	Rwx

Figure 14.4 – Groups and permission examples

As you can see, each permission can be expressed with a number <=7, which is in one digit. Permissions for owner, group, and others can then be expressed in octal notation with three digits, as we can see in the following:

File Permission	Octal	Symbolic
Owner: Read Group: Read Others: Read	0444	-r--r--r--
Owner: Write Group: Write Others: Write	0222	--w--w--w-
Owner: Execute Group: Execute Others: Execute	0111	--x—x—x
Owner: Read Write Execute Group: Read Write Others: Write Execute	0763	-rwxrw-wx
Owner: Read Write Execute Group: Read Write Execute Others: Read Write Execute	0777	-rwxrwxrwx

Figure 14.5 – Permission representations examples

You might notice that in octal representation all numbers start with a *0*. When working with the filesystem via the command line you can omit the leading zero. However, in many cases, when programming, you need to pass it so that the compiler will understand that you are writing something in octal notation. You might argue that 0777 and 777 are the same number, but the leading zero is just a *convention* that tells the compiler that you are using an octal notation and the number is octal and not decimal. In other words, 777 is interpreted as the decimal number 777, while 0777 is interpreted as the octal number 0777, which is the decimal number 511.

Flags and arguments

Go provides support for creating command-line interface tools. Often, when we write Go programs that are executables, they need to accept various inputs. These inputs could include the location of a file, a value to run the program in the debug state, getting help to run the program and more. All of this is made possible by a package in the Go standard library called flag. It is used to allow the passing of arguments to the program. A flag is an argument that is passed to a Go program. The order of the flags being passed to the Go program using the flag package does not matter to Go.

To define your flag, you must know the flag type you will be accepting. The flag package provides many functions for defining flags. Here is a sample list:

```
func Bool(name string, value bool, usage string) *bool
func Duration(name string, value time.Duration, usage string) *time.
Duration
func Float64(name string, value float64, usage string) *float64
func Int(name string, value int, usage string) *int
func Int64(name string, value int64, usage string) *int64
```

These are some of the functions allowing you to create flags and accept parameters, and there is one for each default type in Go.

The parameters of the preceding functions can be explained as follows:

- **name**: This parameter is the name of the flag; it is a string type. For example, if you pass *file* as an argument, you would access that flag from the command line with the following:

    ```
    ./app -file
    ```

- **value**: This parameter is the default value that the flag is set to.

- **usage**: This parameter is used to describe the flag's purpose. It will often show up on the command line when you incorrectly set the value. Passing the wrong type for a flag will stop the program and cause an error; the usage will be printed.

- **return value**: This is the address of the variable that stores the value of the flag.

Let's take a look at a simple example:

```
package main
import (
    "flag"
    "fmt"
)
func main() {
    v := flag.Int("value", -1, "Needs a value for the flag.")
    flag.Parse()
    fmt.Println(*v)
}
```

Let's go over the preceding code block and analyze it:

1. First, we define the `main` package.

2. Then we import the `flag` and `fmt` packages.

3. The `v` variable will reference the value for either `-value` or `--value`.

4. The initial value of `*v` is the default value of `-1` before calling `flag.Parse()`

5. After defining the flags, you must call `flag.Parse()` to parse the defined flags into the command line.

6. Calling `flag.Parse()` places the argument for `-value` into `*v`.

7. Once you have called the `flag.Parse()` function, the flags will be available.

8. On the command line, execute the following command and you will get the executable in the same directory:

   ```
   go build -o flagapp main.go
   ```

To get the executable on Windows, run:

```
go build -o flagapp.exe main.go
```

There is another way, however, to define these flags. It can be done using the following functions:

```
func BoolVar(p *bool, name string, value bool, usage string)
func DurationVar(p *time.Duration, name string, value time.Duration,
usage string)
func Float64Var(p *float64, name string, value float64, usage string)
func Int64Var(p *int64, name string, value int64, usage string)
func IntVar(p *int, name string, value int, usage string)
```

As you can see, for each type, there is a function similar to those we've already seen, whose names end with `Var`. They all accept a pointer to the type of the flag as the first argument, and can be used as in the following code snippet:

```
package main
import (
    "flag"
    "fmt"
)
func main() {
    var v int
    flag.IntVar(&v, "value", -1, "Needs a value for the flag.")
    flag.Parse()
    fmt.Println(v)
}
```

This code does the same as the previous snippet, however, here's a quick breakdown:

- First, we define an integer variable v
- Use its reference as the first parameter of the `IntVar` function
- Parse the flags
- Print the v variable, which now does not need to be dereferenced as it is not the flag but an actual integer

If we compile our application, using any of the preceding snippets, as an executable called `flagapp`, with the following call in the same directory as the executable, we will see that it will print the number 5:

```
flagapp -value=5
```

If we call it without the parameter with the following call in the same directory as the executable, we will see that it will just print -1:

```
flagapp
```

This is because -1 is the default value.

Signals

A signal is an interrupt that is sent to our program or a process by the OS. When a signal is delivered to our program, the program will stop what it is doing; either it will handle the signal or, if possible, ignore it.

The following is a list of the top three most often used interrupt signals for Go programs:

- SIGINT (interrupt):

  - Situation: This signal is commonly used when a user presses *Ctrl + C* in the terminal to interrupt the execution of a program.

  - Definition: SIGINT is the interrupt signal. It is used to gracefully terminate a program and perform cleanup operations before exiting.

- SIGTERM (termination):

  - Situation: This signal is often used to request the termination of a program in a controlled manner. It is a generic signal to terminate a process.

  - Definition: SIGTERM is the termination signal. It allows a program to perform cleanup operations before exiting, similar to SIGINT, but it can be caught and handled differently.

- SIGKILL (kill):

  - Situation: This signal is used to forcefully terminate a program. It doesn't allow the program to perform any cleanup operations.

  - Definition: SIGKILL is the kill signal. It immediately terminates a process without giving it a chance to clean up resources. It is a more forceful way of ending a program compared to SIGTERM.

We have seen other Go commands that change the flow of the program; you may be wondering which one to use.

We use defer statements in our applications to perform various cleanup activities, such as the following:

- The release of resources
- The closing of files
- The closing of database connections
- Performing the removal of configuration or temporary files

In some use cases, it is important that these activities are completed. Using a defer function will execute it just before returning to the caller. However, this does not guarantee that it will always run. There are certain scenarios in which the defer function won't execute; for example, an OS interrupt to your program:

- os.Exit(1)
- *Ctrl + C*
- Other instructions from the OS

The preceding scenarios indicate where it may warrant using signals. Signals can help us control the exit of our program. Depending on the signal, it could terminate our program. For example, the application is running and encounters an OS interrupt signal after executing `employee.CalculateSalary()`. In this scenario, the `defer` function will not run, thus, `employee.DepositCheck()` does not execute and the employee does not get paid. A signal can change the flow of the program. The following diagram goes over the scenario we discussed previously:

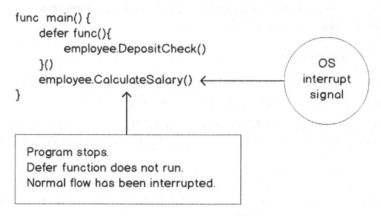

Figure 14.6 – Example program with signals

Support for handling signals is built into the Go standard library; it is in the `os/signal` package. This package will allow us to make our programs more resilient. We want to gracefully shut down when we receive certain signals. The first thing to do when handling signals in Go is to trap or catch the signal that you are interested in. This is done by using the following function:

```
func Notify(c chan<- os.Signal, sig ...os.Signal)
```

This function accepts an `os.Signal` data type on a channel, `c`. The `sig` argument is a variadic variable of `os.Signal`; we specify zero or more `os.Signal` data types that we are interested in. Let's see a code snippet showing how we can use this function to stop the execution of an application:

```
package main
import (
    "fmt"
    "os"
    "os/signal"
    "syscall"
)
func main() {
    sigs := make(chan os.Signal, 1)
```

```
    done := make(chan struct{})
    signal.Notify(sigs,syscall.SIGINT)
    go func() {
    for {
        s := <-sigs
        switch s {
            case syscall.SIGINT:
                fmt.Println()
                fmt.Println("My process has been interrupted. Someone
might of pressed CTRL-C")
                fmt.Println("Some clean up is occuring")
                done <-struct{}{}
            }
        }
    }()
    fmt.Println("Program is blocked until a signal is caught")
    done <- struct{}{}
    fmt.Println("Out of here")
}
```

After the definition of the package and importing the packages, we do the following:

- Define a channel to send signals

- Define a channel that we can use as a flag to stop the execution

- Use Notify to send a SIGINT signal

- Create a goroutine that listens indefinitely to signals and if the signal is SIGINT, it does some printouts and sends a message to the done channel with the true value

- Print a message stating we are waiting for the done message to be received

- Wait for the done message

- Print the final message

When we run the application, we will actually see the application terminate quite quickly, because we manually send the SIGINT signal. In a real-world scenario, the application would just wait for the SIGKILL signal, which we can manually send with *Ctrl + X*.

Let's see now how we can simulate a cleanup.

Exercise 14.01 – simulating a cleanup

In this exercise, we will be catching two signals: SIGINT and SIGTSTP. Once those signals have been caught, we will simulate a cleanup of the files. We have not gone over how to remove files yet, so, in this example, we will simply create a delay to demonstrate how we can run a function after a signal is caught. This is the desired output from this exercise:

1. Create a file called main.go.

2. Add to this file the main package and the following import statements:

    ```go
    package main
    import (
        "fmt"
        "os"
        "os/signal"
        "syscall"
        "time"
    )
    ```

3. In the main() function, create a channel of the os.Signal type. The sigs channel is used to receive these notifications from the Notify method:

    ```go
    func main() {
        sigs := make(chan os.Signal, 1)
    ```

4. Next, add a done channel. The done channel is used to let us know when the program can exit:

    ```go
    done := make(chan struct{})
    ```

5. We will then add a signal.Notify method. The Notify method works by sending values of the os.Signal type to a channel.

6. Recall that the last parameter of the signal.Notify method is a variadic parameter of the os.Signal type.

7. The signal.Notify method will receive notifications on the sigs channel that are of the syscall.SIGINT and syscall.SIGTSTP types.

8. Generally speaking, the syscall.SIGINT type can occur when you press *Ctrl* + *C*.

9. Generally speaking, the syscall.SIGTSTP type can occur when you press *Ctrl* + *Z*:

    ```go
    signal.Notify(sigs, syscall.SIGINT, syscall.SIGTSTP)
    ```

10. Create an anonymous function as a goroutine:

    ```go
    go func() {
    ```

11. Inside the goroutine, create an infinite loop. Inside the infinite loop, we will receive a value from the sigs channel and store it in the s variable, s := <-sigs:

```
for {
    s := <-sigs
```

12. Create a switch statement that evaluates what is received from the channel.

13. We will have two case statements that will check for the syscall.SIGINT and syscall.SIGTSP types.

   Each case statement will have a message being printed.

14. We will also call our cleanup() function.

15. The last statement in the case statement is sending true to the done channel to stop the blocking:

```
    switch s {
    case syscall.SIGINT:
      fmt.Println()
      fmt.Println("My process has been interrupted. Someone
might have pressed CTRL-C")
      fmt.Println("Some clean up is occuring")
      cleanUp()
      done <- struct{}{}
    case syscall.SIGTSTP:
      fmt.Println()
      fmt.Println("Someone pressed CTRL-Z")
      fmt.Println("Some clean up is occuring")
      cleanUp()
      done <- struct{}{}
    }
  }
}()
  fmt.Println("Program is blocked until a signal is
caught(ctrl-z, ctrl-c)")
  done <- struct{}{}
  fmt.Println("Out of here")
}
```

16. Create a simple function to mimic a process performing a cleanup:

```
func cleanUp() {
  fmt.Println("Simulating clean up")
  for i := 0; i <= 10; i++ {
    fmt.Println("Deleting Files.. Not really.", i)
```

```
        time.Sleep(1 * time.Second)
    }
}
```

17. You can try running this program and pressing *Ctrl* + *Z* and *Ctrl* + *C* to examine the different results of the program. This only works on Linux and macOS:

18. Now run the code:

```
go run main.go
```

19. The following is the output:

```
Program is blocked until a signal is caught(ctrl-z, ctrl-c)
^Z
Someone pressed CTRL-Z
Some clean up is occuring
Simulating clean up
Deleting Files.. Not really. 0
Deleting Files.. Not really. 1
Deleting Files.. Not really. 2
Deleting Files.. Not really. 3
Deleting Files.. Not really. 4
Deleting Files.. Not really. 5
Deleting Files.. Not really. 6
Deleting Files.. Not really. 7
Deleting Files.. Not really. 8
Deleting Files.. Not really. 9
Deleting Files.. Not really. 10
Out of here
```

Figure 14.7 – Example output

In this exercise, we have demonstrated the ability to intercept an interrupt and perform a task before the application closes. We have the ability to control our exit. This is a powerful feature that allows us to perform cleanup actions that include removing files, performing a last-minute log, freeing up memory, and more. In the next topic, we are going to be creating and writing to files. We will be using functions that come from the Go standard package, os.

Create and write to files

The Go language provides support in various ways to create and write to new files. We will examine some of the most common ways in which this is performed.

The os package provides a simple way in which to create a file. For those who are familiar with the touch command from the Unix world, it is similar to this. Here is the signature of the function:

```
func Create(name string(*File, error)
```

The function will create an empty file much as the `touch` command does. It is important to note that if the file already exists, then it will truncate the file.

The `os` package's `Create` function has an input parameter, which is the name of the file to create and its location. If successful, it will return a `File` type. It is worth noting that the `File` type satisfies the `io.Write` and `io.Read` interfaces. This is important to know for later in the chapter:

```
package main
import (
    "os"
)
func main() {
    f, err := os.Create("test.txt")
    if err != nil {
        panic(err)
    }
    defer f.Close()
}
```

The preceding code simply defines the imports and then, in the `main` function, tries to create a file called `test.txt`. If there is an error as a result, it panics. The last line before the closing brackets makes sure that whenever the application is interrupted, either because it terminates successfully or it panics, the file will be closed. We want to make sure we never keep files in an open state.

Creating an empty file is straightforward, but let's continue with `os.Create` and write to the file we just created. Recall that `os.Create` returns an `*os.File` type. There are two methods of interest that can be used to write to the file:

- `Write`
- `WriteString`

Let's see some examples of how to use them:

```
package main
import (
    "os"
)
func main() {
    f, err := os.Create("test.txt")
    if err != nil {
        panic(err)
    }
    defer f.Close()
    f.Write([]byte("Using Write function.\n"))
```

```
        f.WriteString("Using Writestring function.\n")
}
```

This code is pretty similar to the previous one. We just added two lines where we write two sentences to the file.

The first function call is the following:

```
f.Write([]byte("Using Write function.\n"))
```

Here, we can see that the function needs bytes to be sent, hence we convert a string into a slice of bytes with the following:

```
[]byte("Using Write function.\n")
```

The second function just accepts a string and is straightforward to use.

We can, however, use the package to write to the file directly without having to open it first. We can do this using the os.WriteFile function:

```
func WriteFile(filename string, data []byte, perm os.FileMode) error
```

The method writes the data to the file specified in the filename parameter, with the given permissions. It will return an error if one exists. Let's take a look at this in action:

```
package main
import (
    "fmt"
    "os
)
func main() {
    message := []byte("Look!")
    err := os.WriteFile("test.txt", message, 0644)
    if err != nil {
        fmt.Println(err)
    }
}
```

As we can see, we can create a file, send a string transformed into a slice of bytes, and assign the permission to it, all in one line. It is important to also send the permission level and note that we need to use the octal notation with the leading zero (this is because without the leading zero, the permission will not work as expected).

One important thing that we haven't seen till now is how to check whether a file exists or not. This is important because if a file does exist, we might not want to truncate it and override it with new content. Let's see how we can do that:

```go
package main
import (
    "fmt"
    "s"
    "flag"
)
func main() {
    var name tring
    flag.StringVar(&name, "name", "", "File name")
    flag.Parse()
    file, err := os.Stat(name)
    if err != nil {
        if os.IsNotExist(err) {
            fmt.Printf("%s: File does not exist!\n", name)
            fmt.Println(file)
            return
        }
        fmt.Println(err)
        return
    }
    fmt.Printf("file name: %s\nIsDir: %t\nModTime: %v\nMode: %v\nSize: %d\n", file.Name(),
        file.IsDir(), file.ModTime(), file.Mode(), file.Size())
}
```

Let's review what the preceding code does:

1. Firstly, we import all the needed packages.

2. We then define a string flag that represents the filename:

    ```go
    flag.StringVar(&name, "name", "", "File name")
    ```

3. Next, we parse the flags; in this case, the only one is the one we created.

4. We then get the stats for the file:

    ```go
    file, err := os.Stat(name)
    ```

5. If there is an error, we check whether this is because the file does not exist:

    ```go
    if os.IsNotExist(err) {
    ```

6. If the file does not exist, we print a message and we then terminate the application.

7. If the error is different from `IsNotExist`, we just then print the error.

8. If, finally, the file exists, we then print a set of information related to it. The file implements the `FileInfo` interface, which includes in its details the modification time, the size, the octal permissions (*mode*), the name, and whether it is a directory or not.

You can try to run this application and pass the name of any file. If it exists in the directory from which you run the application, you will see all this information printed out for you.

Let's now see how can we read a whole file.

Reading the whole file at once

In this topic, we will look at two methods that read all the contents of the file. These two functions are good to use when your file size is small. While these two methods are convenient and easy to use, they have one major drawback. That is, if the file size is too large, then it could exhaust the memory available on the system. It is important to keep this in mind and understand the limitations of the two methods we will be going over in this topic. Even though these methods are some of the quickest and easiest ways to load data, it is important to understand that they should be limited to small files and not large ones. The method's signature is as follows:

```
func ReadFile(filename string) ([]byte, error)
```

The `ReadFile` function reads the contents of the file and returns it as a slice of bytes along with any reported errors. We will look at the error return when the `ReadFile` method is used:

- A successful call returns `err == nil`.

- In some of the other read methods for files, **end of file** (**EOF**) is treated as an error. This is not the case for functions that read the entire file into memory.

Let's see a code snippet that explains how to use this function:

```
package main
import (
    "fmt"
    "os"
)
func main() {
    content, err := os.ReadFile("test.txt")
    if err != nil {
        fmt.Println(err)
    }
    fmt.Println("File contents: ")
```

```
    fmt.Println(string(content))
}
```

As we can see, what we do in this code is as follows:

- We do our imports
- We read the contents of the whole `test.txt` file
- We print an error if it occurs
- Else, we print the content of the file:

```
    fmt.Println("File contents: ")
    fmt.Println(string(content))
```

As the content is retrieved as a slice of bytes, we need to convert it to a string to visualize it. Let's see how to read, instead, the file character by character in the next snippet:

```
package main

import (
    "fmt"
    "io"
    "log"
    "os"
)

func main() {
    f, err := os.Open("test.txt")
    if err != nil {
        log.Fatalf("unable to read file: %v", err)
    }
    buf := make([]byte, 1)
    for {
        n, err := f.Read(buf)
        if err == io.EOF {
            break
        }
        if err != nil {
            fmt.Println(err)
            continue
        }
    if n > 0 {
            fmt.Print(string(buf[:n]))
    }
```

```
    }
}
```

Let's analyze this snippet in more detail as it is a bit complicated. In this case, after importing the required packages, we do the following:

1. Open the file using the Open function:

    ```
    f, err := os.Open("test.txt")
    ```

2. We check whether the error is nil, and if is not, we print the error and exit:

    ```
    if err != nil {
        log.Fatalf("unable to read file: %v", err)
    }
    ```

3. We then create a slice of bytes of size 1:

    ```
    buf := make([]byte, 1)
    ```

4. We then make an infinite loop, and inside it, we read the file into the buffer:

    ```
    n, err := f.Read(buf)
    ```

5. We then check whether there is an error, which also means that we reached the end of the file, in which case we stop the loop:

    ```
    if err == io.EOF {
        break
    }
    ```

6. If the error is not nil but is not end of file, we carry on with the loop, ignoring the error.

7. If there is no error and the content has been read, then we display the content:

    ```
    if n > 0 {
        fmt.Print(string(buf[:n]))
    }
    ```

Notice that we read one character at a time, as we made a buffer (slice of bytes) of size one. This might be resource intensive, so you might change this value to any other value for your particular case and needs.

Exercise 14.02 – backing up files

Oftentimes, when working with files, we need to back up a file before making changes to it. This is for instances where we might make mistakes or want the original file for auditing purposes. In this exercise, we will take an existing file called note.txt and back it up to backupFile.txt. We will then open note.txt and add some additional notes to the end of the file. Our directory will contain the following files:

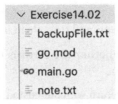

Figure 14.8 – Backing up files to the directory

1. We must first create the note.txt file in the same directory as our executable. This file can be blank or contain some sample data such as this:

```
Notes:
1. Get better at coding.
```

Figure 14.9 – Example of the notes.txt file content

2. Create a Go file called main.go.

3. This program will be part of the main package.

4. Include the imports, as seen in the following code:

```
package main
import (
    "errors"
    "fmt"
    "io"
    "os"
    "strconv"
)
```

5. Create a custom error that will be used when the working file (note.txt) is not found:

```
var (
    ErrWorkingFileNotFound = errors.New("The working file is not
found.")
)
```

6. Create a function to perform the backup. This function is responsible for taking the working file and storing its content in the backup file. This function accepts two arguments. The working parameter is the file path of the file that you currently are working on:

```
func createBackup(working, backup string) error {
}
```

7. Inside this function, we will need to check to see whether the working file exists. It must first exist before we can read its contents and store them in our backup file.

   We are able to check to see whether the error is one where the file does not exist by using os.IsNotExist(err).

   If the file does not exist, we will return with our custom error, ErrWorkingFileNotFound:

   ```
   // check to see if our working file exists,
   // before backing it up
   _, err := os.Stat(working)
   if err != nil {
   if os.IsNotExist(err) {
       return ErrWorkingFileNotFound
   }
   return err
   }
   ```

8. Next, we need to open the working file and store the os.File returned by the function to the workFile variable:

   ```
   workFile, err := os.Open(working)
   if err != nil {
       return err
   }
   ```

9. We need to read the contents of workFile. We will be using the io.ReadAll method to get all the contents of workFile. workFile is of the os.File type, which satisfies the io.Reader interface; this allows us to pass it to ioutil.ReadFile.

10. Check to see whether there is an error:

    ```
    content, err := io.ReadAll(workFile)
    if err != nil {
      return err
    }
    ```

11. The content variable contains the data of the workFile represented as a slice of bytes. That data needs to be written to the backup file. We will implement the code that will write the data of the content variable to the backup file.

12. The content stores the []byte data that gets returned from the function. This is the entire contents of the file stored in the variable.

13. We can use the `os.Writefile` method. If the backup file does not exist, it will create the file. If the backup file does exist, it will overwrite the file with the content variable data:

```
err = os.WriteFile(backup, content, 0644)
if err != nil {
    fmt.Println(err)
}
```

14. We need to return nil, indicating that, at this juncture, we have not encountered any errors:

```
    return nil
}
```

15. Create a function that will append data to our working file.

16. Name the function `addNotes`; this will accept the location of our working file and a string argument that will be appended to the working file. The function will need to return an error:

```
func addNotes(workingFile, notes string) error {
//...
    return nil
}
```

17. Inside the `addNotes` function, add a line that will append a new line to each note's string. This will place each note on a separate line:

```
func addNotes(workingFile, notes string) error {
    notes += "\n"
    //...
    return nil
}
```

18. Next, we will open the working file and allow for appending to the file. The `os.OpenFile()` function will create the file if it does not exist. Check for any errors:

```
func addNotes(workingFile, notes string) error {
    notes += "\n"
    f, err := os.OpenFile(
        workingFile,
        os.O_APPEND|os.O_CREATE|os.O_WRONLY,
        0644,
    )
    if err != nil {
        return err
    }
```

```
    // ...
    return nil
}
```

19. After opening a file and checking for an error, we should make sure that it closes when the function exits by using the defer function, f.Close():

```go
func addNotes(workingFile, notes string) error {
    notes += "\n"
    f, err := os.OpenFile(
        workingFile,
        os.O_APPEND|os.O_CREATE|os.O_WRONLY,
        0644,
    )
    if err != nil {
        return err
    }
    defer f.Close()
//...
    return nil
}
```

20. The final step of the function is to write the contents of the note to the workingFile variable. We can use the Write method to accomplish this:

```go
func addNotes(workingFile, notes string) error {
    notes += "\n"
    f, err := os.OpenFile(workingFile, os.O_APPEND|os.O_
CREATE|os.O_WRONLY, 0644)
    if err != nil {
        return err
    }
    defer f.Close()
    if _, err := f.Write([]byte(notes)); err != nil {
        return err
    }
    return nil
}
```

21. In the `main()` function, we will initialize three variables; the `backupFile` variable contains the name of the file for backing up our `workingFile` variable, while the `data` variable is what we will be writing to our `workingFile` variable:

```
func main() {
    backupFile := "backupFile.txt"
    workingFile := "note.txt"
    data := "note"
```

22. Call our `createBackup()` function to back up our `workingFile`. Check for errors after calling the function:

```
err := createBackup(workingFile, backupFile)
if err != nil {
    fmt.Println(err)
os.Exit(1)
}
```

23. Create a `for` loop that will iterate `10` times.

    With each iteration, we set our `note` variable to the `data` variable plus the `i` variable of our loop.

    Since our `note` variable is a string and our `i` variable is an `int`, we will need to convert `i` to a string using the `strconv.Itoa(i)` method.

    Call our `addNotes()` function and pass the `workingFile` and our `note` variables.

    Check for any errors returned from the function:

```
for i := 1; i <= 10; i++ {
note := data + " " + strconv.Itoa(i)
err := addNotes(workingFile, note)
if err != nil {
    fmt.Println(err)
    os.Exit(1)
    }
    }
}
```

24. Run the program:

```
go run main.go
```

25. Evaluate the changes to the files after running the program.

The following are the results after running the program:

```
Notes:
1. Get better at coding.
note 1
note 2
note 3
note 4
note 5
note 6
note 7
note 8
note 9
note 10
```

Figure 14.10 – Result of backup

Let's see next how to handle CSV files with Go.

CSV

One of the most common ways a file is structured is as a comma-separated value. This is a clear-text file that contains data, which is basically represented as rows and columns. Frequently, these files are used to exchange data. A CSV file has a simple structure. Each piece of data is separated by a comma and then a new line for another record. An example of a CSV file is as follows:

```
firstName, lastName, age
Celina, Jones, 18
Cailyn, Henderson, 13
Cayden, Smith, 42
```

You will, at some point in your life, come across CSV files as they are very common. The Go programming language has a standard library that is used for handling CSV files: `encoding/csv`:

```go
package main
import (
    "encoding/csv"
    "fmt"
    "io"
    "log"
    "strings"
)
func main() {
    in := `firstName, lastName, age
```

```
Celina, Jones, 18
Cailyn, Henderson, 13
Cayden, Smith, 42
`

    r := csv.NewReader(strings.NewReader(in))
    for {
        record, err := r.Read()
        if err == io.EOF {
            break
        }
        if err != nil {
            log.Fatal(err)
        }
        fmt.Println(record)
    }
}
```

Here we are defining a string with the content of our CSV file:

```
func main() {
    in := `firstName, lastName, age
Celina, Jones, 18
Cailyn, Henderson, 13
Cayden, Smith, 42`
```

And then we use the following line to read the content of the whole CSV:

```
    r := csv.NewReader(strings.NewReader(in))
```

The following code line creates a string reader that can be used by the csv.NewReader function. We cannot, in fact, pass just a string to the CSV reader as it needs an io.Reader instance, which in this case is provided by strings.NewReader:

```
strings.NewReader(in)
```

We then make an infinite loop, which gets terminated when we reach the end of the CSV:

```
if err == io.EOF {
    break
}
```

As we did earlier in this chapter, we then check for another error and we exit if we find it; otherwise, we print the record, which is retrieved via the Read() method of the CSV reader.

In the previous example, we saw how to get a whole record at once, meaning one row of our CSV. However, there is a way to access each column in the returned row, that is, each single element of the row.

If you look back at the previous snippet of code, you will see that the rows are returned with the following:

```
record, err := r.Read()
```

We then just printed the content, but this is an actual slice of strings, so we can get each item with its index. Let's say we are just interested in visualizing the names of the people in the CSV. To do so, we can modify the `fmt.Println(record)` line as follows:

```
fmt.Println(record[0])
```

With this, we will only see a list of names.

Embedding

Often, you will need to present to the user some complex text, maybe an HTML page, and it might be impractical to define the whole file as a string. You might read the file, as we learned in this chapter, and then use it as a template. You might want to display an image, again by opening and reading the file containing the image. One of the great features of Go is that even if you can build your application as a single binary, you will also have external dependencies that need to be distributed with your binary. Another issue is that reading from a file might be slow, so it would be great if we could embed files inside our Go application. This will allow us to just distribute one binary including all our assets. In the past, this required external libraries, but now Go includes a package called `embed` that allows you to easily embed any file into your binary so that you do not need to share other dependencies. Let's see an example of how we can do that.

In the next snippet, we will create a very simple template file and will read and parse it. Then we will use it to display some greetings. Let's start with the template. We need a folder structure like this: `embedding_example/main.go` and `templates/template.txt`.

The content of the `template.txt` file is `Hello {{.Name}}`, which is pretty simple. This simply means that when we use this template and pass a variable called `Name`, the engine will substitute the variable with anything we pass as a value. You do not need, at this stage, to understand much more about the templating system.

Let's see now how we can make use of this template written in an external file, without having to read it every time we run the application:

```go
package main

import (
    "embed"
    "os"
    "text/template"
)
```

```go
type Person struct {
    Name string
}

var (
    //go:embed templates
    f embed.FS
)

func main() {
    p := Person{"John"}
    tmpl, err := template.ParseFS(f, "templates/template.txt")
    if err != nil {
        panic(err)
    }
    err = tmpl.Execute(os.Stdout, p)
    if err != nil {
        panic(err)
    }
}
```

1. We start importing all the necessary packages. After that, we define a struct called `Person` that will hold the name of the person to greet. The next part is the important bit:

    ```go
    var (
        //go:embed templates
        f embed.FS
    )
    ```

This defines an `f` variable of type `embed.FS`, which stands for *embedded file system* and will work as a virtual filesystem for us. The directive on top of the declaration needs to be just above the variable we define, otherwise the compiler will prompt us with an error. This directive tells the Go compiler that it needs to read and embed whatever is inside the `templates` folder and make it available. Be careful if you add a folder with too many big files, as your final binary will increase in size.

1. Inside the `main` function, we then instantiate a struct of type `Person` where the `Name` attribute has the value `John`.

2. After that, we use the `ParseFS` function of the `template` package, and we use it to read from the embedded file system, represented by the variable `f`, the file called `template.txt` from inside the `templates` folder.

3. Next, we just execute the templating engine, passing the previously created struct. If you run the application, you will see the message printed out as follows:

    ```
    Hello John
    ```

4. Now, this does not seem much, but try running the following command:

    ```
    go build -o embtest main.go
    ```

5. Then, copy your executable to a different location where the `template` folder is not available. If you now run from that new folder, you will still see the exact same message:

    ```
    ./embtest
    ```

The key takeaway here is that the directive takes the whole filesystem from the point you specify, in this case, the `templates` folder, and creates a virtual filesystem. From this virtual filesystem, you can read all the files, but the content of the whole folder will actually be stored inside the final binary of your application. This feature is very powerful but should be used wisely, as the final binary could easily become very big.

Summary

In this chapter, we gained an understanding of how Go views and uses file permissions. We learned that file permissions can be represented as symbolic and octal notations. We discovered that the Go standard library has built-in support for opening, reading, writing, creating, deleting, and appending data to a file. We looked at the `flag` package and how it provides functionality to create command-line applications to accept arguments.

Using the `flag` package, we could also print out `usage` statements that pertained to our command-line application.

Then, we demonstrated how OS signals can impact our Go program; however, by using the Go standard library, we can capture OS signals and, if applicable, control how we want to exit our program.

We also learned that Go has a standard library for working with CSV files. In our previous work with files, we saw that we can also work with files that are structured as CSV files. That Go CSV package provides the ability to iterate over the contents of the file. The CSV file can be viewed as rows and columns similar to database tables.

Finally, we saw how to embed files inside the final binary of the application and how to use this feature to speed up the application and avoid shipping external dependencies with the binary. In the next chapter, we will look at how to connect to databases and execute SQL statements against a database. This will demonstrate the ability of Go to be used for applications that require a backend for storing data.

15

SQL and Databases

> **Overview**
>
> This chapter will introduce you to databases – specifically relational databases – and how to access them via the Go programming language.
>
> This chapter will guide you through how to connect to the SQL database engine, how to create a database, how to create tables in a database, and how to insert and retrieve data in and from tables. By the end of this chapter, you will be able to update and delete data in specific tables, as well as truncate and drop tables.

Technical requirements

For this chapter, you'll require Go version 1.21 or higher. The code for this chapter can be found at https://github.com/PacktPublishing/Go-Programming-From-Beginner-to-Professional-Second-Edition-/tree/main/Chapter15.

Introduction

In the previous chapter, you learned how to interact with the filesystem your Go app is running on. You learned about the importance of exit codes and how to customize your scripts to take arguments, thus adding flexibility to your applications. You also learned how to handle different signals that your application receives.

In this chapter, you will further master your Go skills by learning how to use SQL and databases in Go. As a developer, it is impossible to get by without a proper understanding of persistent data storage and databases. Our applications process input and produce output, but most of the time, if not in all cases, a database is involved in the process. This database can be in-memory (stored in the computer's RAM) or file-based (a single file in a directory), and it can live on local or remote storage. A database engine can be installed locally, as we will do later in this chapter, but it is also possible to use cloud providers, which allow you to use a database as a service; some of the cloud providers that offer several different database engine options are Azure, AWS, and Google Cloud.

What we aim to do in this chapter is make you fluent in talking to these databases and understanding the basic concepts of what a database is. Finally, you will have extended your skillset to make you a better Go developer as you progress through this chapter.

Let's say your boss wants you to create a Go app that can communicate with a database. By *communicate*, we mean that any transaction that is INSERT, UPDATE, DELETE, or CREATE can and should be handled by the application. This chapter will show you how to do that.

Understanding the database

We commonly use the word database in different ways, but let's be a bit more formal here:

> *A database is where we store our data, where we persist it (if we want), and where we can run some queries to insert new data and retrieve or modify existing data.*

You might think that a filesystem fits this description, but actually, this is not the case; a real database allows us to perform very complex and precise queries to gather data based on very specific conditions. To do so, we will have a language to perform these queries or other operations. In our case, we will focus on a language called SQL.

We've stated what a database is, but this is still quite abstract. To create a database and fill it with data, we need an engine – essentially, an application – that will allow us to perform all these operations. In this section, we'll learn how to use a database engine called **Postgres SQL**. As its name suggests, this engine will allow us to perform operations using the SQL language.

Installing and configuring Postgres SQL

As a first step, you need to install Postgres SQL and configure it for yourself so that you can try out the following examples.

First, you need to grab the installer from https://www.postgresql.org/download/. Select the one that is appropriate for your system; we will go through the Windows installer here, but things are pretty similar for other systems. The installer is very easy to use, and I suggest that you accept the defaults:

1. Run the installer:

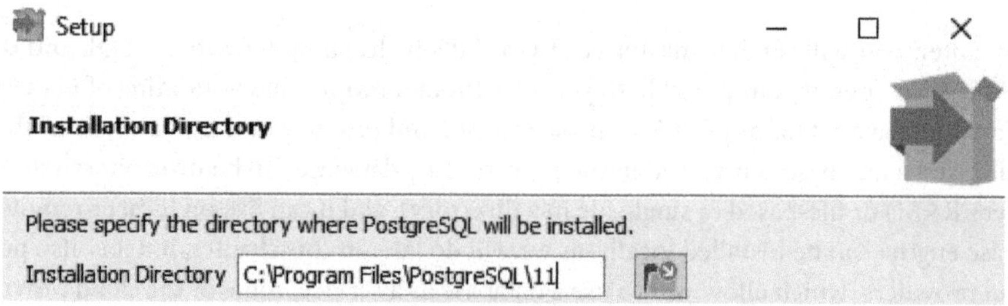

Figure 15.1: Selecting the installation directory

2. Leave the default components as-is:

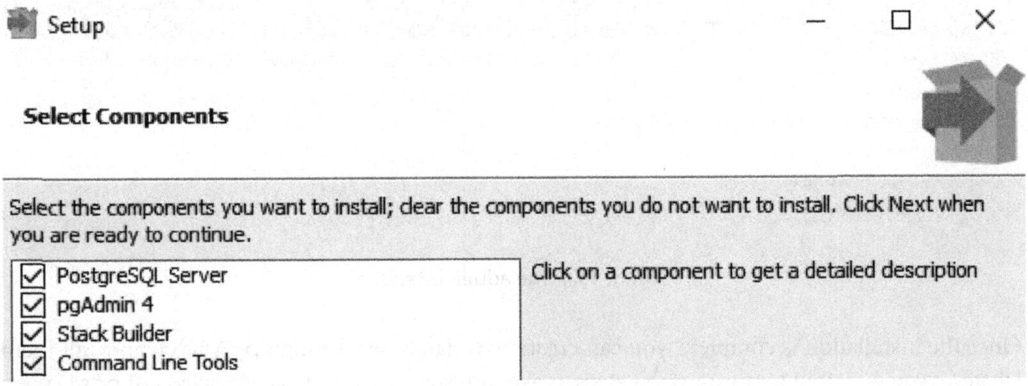

Figure 15.2: Selecting components to install

3. Leave the default data directory:

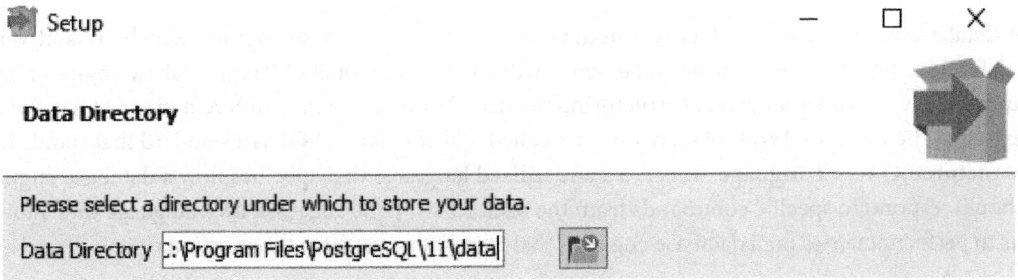

Figure 15.3: Selecting the data directory

> **Note**
>
> You will be asked for a password. You need to remember this because this is the master password for your database.

Start!123 is the password for this example. The database is running on local port 5432. The pgAdmin GUI tool will also be installed, and, once the installer completes, you can start pgAdmin to connect to the database.

In your browser, go to `https://packt.live/2PKWc5w` to access the admin interface:

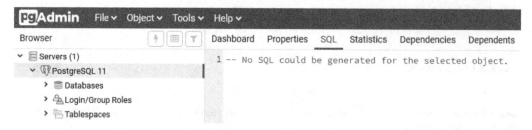

Figure 15.4: The admin interface

Once the installation is complete, you can create new databases through pgAdmin and call them whatever you want, but for the next few steps, make sure you have one database called just postgres to which we will connect via Go. We are now ready to proceed to the next part and connect to the database via Go.

Database API and drivers

A database is a place where data is stored; we normally use database engines, which are software applications that allow us to create and interact with databases. A lot of different database engines exist, and they give us different ways of structuring the data. Nowadays, many different kinds of databases exist, but the most used and solid are the ones called *SQL databases*. **SQL** is a standard that stands for **Structured Query Language**. This is a standardized language that specifies how a database engine should respond to specific commands from the user. As its name suggests, it's a language that allows us to perform queries on a database engine – that is, ask it to perform those actions.

To work with databases, there is something called the *pure* Go approach, which means Go has an API that allows you to use different drivers to connect to databases. The API comes from the database/sql package, and the drivers can be of two types. There is native support for a wide variety of drivers, all of which can be found on the official GitHub page (`https://packt.live/2LMzcC4`), and there are third-party drivers that need additional packages to function, such as the SQLlite3 package, which requires you to have GCC installed because it is a pure C implementation.

> **Note**
> GCC is a compiler system produced by the GNU Project. It takes your source code and translates it into machine code so that your computer can run the application.

Here is a list of a couple of drivers:

- **MySQL** (`https://packt.live/38zk9Fw`)
- **Oracle** (`https://packt.live/34cxwrP`)

- **ODBC** (`https://packt.live/2EfETV8`)

- **Postgres** (`https://packt.live/35jKEwL`)

The idea behind the API and driver approach is that Go provides a unified interface that allows developers to talk to different types of databases. All you need to do is import the API and the necessary driver and you can talk to the database. You don't need to learn driver-specific implementations or how that driver works because the API's sole purpose is to create an abstraction layer that accelerates development.

Let's consider an example. Let's say we would like to have a script that queries a database. This database is MySQL. One approach is to take the driver and learn how to code in its language, and then you are good to go. Some time passes by, and you build lots of small scripts that do their job properly. Now, the time has come for a management decision that will make you unhappy. They decide that MySQL is not good enough, and they are going to replace the database with AWS Athena, a cloud-based database.

Now, since you wrote your scripts specifically for a certain driver, you will be busy rewriting your scripts for them to work properly. The safeguard here is to use a unified API and driver combination. This means writing the scripts against the API and not the driver. The API will translate your wishes for the specific driver. This way, all you need to do is swap out the driver, and the scripts are guaranteed to work. You just saved yourself many hours of scripting and rewriting code, even though the underlying database has been completely replaced.

When we are working with databases in Go, we can differentiate between the following types of databases:

- Relational databases

- NoSQL databases

- Search and analytic databases

In our case, we will focus on relational databases, which mostly use the SQL language.

Connecting to databases

Connecting to a database is by far the easiest thing to do; however, we need to keep a few things in mind. To connect to any database, we need at least four things to be in place:

- We need a host to connect to

- We need a database to connect to that is running on a port

- We need a username

- We need a password

The user needs to have appropriate privileges because we not only want to connect but we would like to perform specific operations, such as query, insert, or remove data, create or delete databases, and manage users and views. Let's imagine that connecting to a database is like walking up to a door as a specific person with a specific key. Whether the door opens or not depends on the key, but what we can do after we have crossed the threshold will depend on the person (which is defined by their privileges).

In most cases, the database server supports multiple databases, and the databases hold one or more tables:

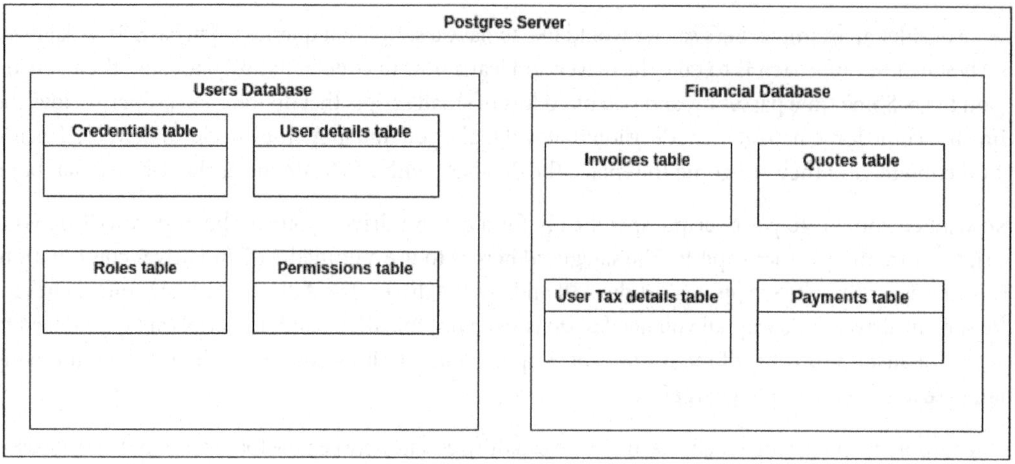

Figure 15.5 – Databases in a server

Imagine that the databases are logical containers that belong together.

Creating a new project

First, let's create a new project. To do so, create a folder called database1 and go to this folder with your terminal. Inside the folder, write the following:

```
go mod init
```

Let's take a look at how we can connect to a database in Go. To connect, we need to get the appropriate module from GitHub, which needs internet connectivity. We need to issue the following command to get the package needed to interact with the Postgres instance:

```
go get github.com/lib/pq
```

> **Note**
>
> This chapter uses the pq package to connect to the database. However, alternative packages are available that can be used here instead.

Remember to run it from within your project's folder. Once this is completed, you are ready to start scripting. First, we will initialize our script:

```
package main
import "fmt"
import "database/sql"
import _ "github.com/lib/pq"
// import _ <package name> is a special import statement that
tells Go to import a package solely for its side effects.
```

> **Note**
>
> If you would like further information, please visit https://packt.live/2PByusw.

Now that we have initialized our script, we can connect to our database:

```
db, err := sql.Open("postgres", "user=postgres password=Start!123
host=127.0.0.1 port=5432 dbname=postgres sslmode=disable")
```

This topic is special because the API gives us an Open() function, which takes a variety of arguments. There are shorthand ways of doing this, but I would like you to know about all the components that are involved in making the connections, so I will use the longer way. Later, you can decide which one to use.

The postgres string, used as the first parameter in the Open function call, tells the function to use the Postgres driver to make the connection. The second argument is a so-called connection string, which holds the user, password, host, port, dbname, and sslmode arguments; these will be used to initialize the connection. In this example, we're connecting to the local host marked by 127.0.0.1 on the default port of 5432, and we don't use ssl. For production systems, people tend to change the default port and enforce encrypted traffic via ssl toward the database server; you should always follow the best practices concerning the type of database you're working with.

As you can see, the Open() function returns two values. One is for the database connection and the other is for the error, if one occurred during initialization. How do we check whether the initialization was successful? Well, we can check whether there were any errors by writing the following code:

```
if err != nil {
  panic(err)
}else{
  fmt.Println("The connection to the DB was successfully
initialized!")
}
```

The panic() function in Go is used to indicate that something went wrong unexpectedly, and we are not prepared to handle it gracefully, thus stopping the execution. If the connection succeeds, we print out a message stating The connection to the DB was successfully initialized!. When you have a long-running application, it is worth incorporating a way to check whether the database is still reachable because due to intermittent network errors, you could lose the connection and fail to execute whatever you want to execute. This can be checked with the following small code snippet:

```
connectivity := db.Ping()
if connectivity != nil{
    panic(err)
}else{
    fmt.Println("Good to go!")
}
```

You can run this check constantly on a different Go routine every few seconds. It will check if the database is on but also help keep the connection open; otherwise, it will go idle. This is a proactive solution as you check the status of the database connection.

In this case, we used the panic() function to indicate that the connection has been lost. Finally, once our job is done, we need to terminate our connection to the database to remove user sessions and free up resources. This can happen either if you are building a script that will run as a job, hence will run and finish, or if you are building a long-running service. In the first case, you can use the following command at the end of the script:

```
db.Close()
```

This ensures that before terminating the script, the connection will be dropped. If you are building a long-running service, you don't have a specific point in your code where you know that the script will terminate, but it can happen at any time. You can use the following code to ensure the connections are dropped:

```
defer db.Close()
```

The difference is the scope. db.Close() will terminate the connection to the database once the execution arrives at the specific line, while defer db.Close() indicates that the database connection should be executed once the function in which it was called goes out of scope. The idiomatic way to do this is with defer db.Close().

In the next section, we will start using the connection for something more purposeful, and we will start by creating tables.

> **Note**
>
> The official Postgres library for Go can be found at https://packt.live/35jKEwL.

Creating tables

The act of creating tables aims to make logical containers that persistently hold data that belongs together. You will need to create tables for many reasons – for example, tracking employee attendance, revenue tracking, and statistics. The common goal is to provide a service for applications that make sense of it. How do these database engines control who can access what data? There are two approaches:

- The first one is **access control lists** (**ACLs**), which is a simple yet powerful approach. ACL security logic tells us which user has which permissions, such as CREATE, UPDATE, and DELETE.

- The second approach involves inheritance and roles. This is more robust and is better suited for big enterprises.

Postgres uses the second approach, and in this section, we will learn how to create a SQL table and how to create one specifically in Postgres.

The general syntax for table creation looks like this:

```
CREATE TABLE table_name (
  column1 datatype constrain,
  column2 datatype constrain,
  column3 datatype constrain,
  ....
);
```

When we talk via SQL to the Postgres, mysql, or mssql server, they all respond in the same way to a CREATE TABLE or INSERT command because they are SQL compliant. The idea of the standard is not to specify how the engine works internally but how the interaction with it should happen. These database engines usually differ in terms of functionality, speed, and storage approaches; that's where the variety comes from. This is not, however, a full SQL or database engine tutorial, so we just gave you a brief introduction to what SQL is without going into a lot of details.

Let's see some of the general statements of the SQL language, with which we will then experiment a bit later. The statement for table creation is CREATE TABLE. This command is understood in the context of the database you are connected to. One server can host multiple databases, and connecting to the wrong one can cause headaches when issuing a command that modifies the structure. The command usually takes a column name, which is column1 in our case, and the type of data in our column, which is datatype. Finally, we can set constraints on our columns, which will imbue them with special properties. The supported data types for our columns depend on the database engine.

Here are some common data types:

- INT
- DOUBLE

- FLOAT

- VARCHAR, which is a string with a specific length

The constraints also depend on the database engine, but some of them are as follows:

- NOT NULL

- PRIMARY KEY

- Named function

The named function is executed every time a new record is inserted or an old one is updated and, based on the evaluation of the transaction, is either allowed or denied.

We are not only able to create a table, but we can also empty the table – that is, remove all of its contents, or remove the table itself from the database. To empty a table, we can use the following command:

```
TRUNCATE TABLE table_name
```

To remove the table, we can use the following:

```
DROP TABLE table_name
```

Now, create a new table. In Postgres, you have a default database you can use; we are not going to create a separate database for the examples in this chapter.

We would like to initialize our script, which you can find in the examples folder, and it's called DBInit.go:

```
package main
import (
    "fmt"
    "database/sql"
    _ "github.com/lib/pq"
)
```

Now, we are ready to define our main() function:

DBInit.go

```
func main(){
    db, err := sql.Open("postgres", "user=postgres password=Start!123
host=127.0.0.1 port=5432 dbname=postgres sslmode=disable")
    if err != nil {
        panic(err)
    }else{
        fmt.Println("The connection to the DB was successfully
initialized!")
```

```
    }
    DBCreate := `
    CREATE TABLE public.test (
        id integer,
        name character varying COLLATE pg_catalog."default"
    )
    WITH (
        OIDS = FALSE
    )
    `

    _, err = db.Exec(DBCreate),
    if err != nil {
        panic(err)
    } else{
        fmt.Println("The table was successfully created!")
    }
    db.Close()
```

The full code is available at `https://github.com/PacktPublishing/Go-Programming-From-Beginner-to-Professional-Second-Edition-/blob/main/Chapter15/Examples/DBInit.go`.

Let's dissect what is happening here. We initialize our connection to the database without the default username and password that was previously mentioned, and now, we have the db variable to interact with the database. Unless there was an error upon execution, the following output will be visible in our console:

```
The connection to the DB was successfully initialized!
The table was successfully created!
```

Figure 15.6 – The desired output, as visible in the console

If we were to rerun the script, the following error would occur:

```
The connection to the DB was successfully initialized!
panic: pq: relation "test" already exists

goroutine 1 [running]:
main.main()
        /home/delio/goproj/packt/rest/example1/cmq/main.go:29 +0x12a

Process finished with the exit code 2
```

Figure 15.7 – Output of failure after consecutive execution

This says that the table already exists. We created a multiline string called `DBCreate` that holds all the table creation information. In this, we have a table called `test`, which has an integer column called `id` and a string column called `name`. The rest of it is Postgres-specific configuration. The tablespace defines where our table lives. The `_, err` line with `db.Exec()` is responsible for executing the query.

The table we are creating will have an ID (unique identifier) per row, which will be of the integer type, and a name column, which will be of the character type. The names have a few characteristics; for example, *COLLATE* defines how the data will be ordered, or better, what comes first or after when requesting data in ascending or descending order. We are taking the default collate for `postgres`, which is defined by the localization currently in the database.

As we've just said, we are going to create a table with an ID, and we will use that to identify the rows. `Postgres` provides a unique identifier for each row automatically, which is called **oid** (**Object Identifier**), but we don't need this as we are handling it manually. Note that not all other database engines provide the oid.

Since our goal now is to create the table, we only care whether there are any errors; otherwise, we can use a throwaway variable to capture the output. If `err` is not `nil`, there was an error, as we saw previously. Otherwise, we assume the table was created as expected. Finally, the connection to the database is closed.

Now that we can connect to the database and we have a table, we can insert some data.

Inserting data

Long ago, when the era of web applications backed by SQL databases started to bloom, some gutsy people invented the SQL injection attack. Here, a type of authentication is done against a database via SQL queries and, for example, after converting the password with mathematical magic into hash functions, the web app executes the query with the username and password coming from the input of the form. Many servers executed something like this:

```
"SELECT password FROM Auth WHERE username=<input from user>"
```

Then, the password gets rehashed; if the two hashes match, the password is good for the user.

The problem with this came from the `<input from user>` part because if the attacker was smart enough, they could reformulate the query and run additional commands. Here's an example:

```
"SELECT password FROM Auth WHERE username=<input from user> OR
'1'='1'"
```

The problem with this query is that `OR '1' = '1'` always evaluates to `true`, and it does not matter what the username is; the user's password hash would be returned. This can be further reused to formulate an additional attack. To prevent this, Go uses something called the `Prepare()` statement, which protects against these attacks.

Go has two types of substitutions:

- We use WHERE col = $1 in the case of queries
- We use VALUES ($1, $2) in the case of inserts or updates

Let's add some values to our tables. We are going to initialize our script in the usual way. This script can be found under the examples folder and is called DBInsert.go:

```
package main
. . . . . . . . . . . . . . .
  insert, err := db.Prepare("INSERT INTO test VALUES ($1, $2)")


  if err != nil {
    panic(err)
  }
  _, err = insert.Exec(2, "second")
  if err != nil {
    panic(err)
  }
  fmt.Println("The value was successfully inserted!")

  defer db.Close()
}
```

Upon successful execution, we'll get the following output:

```
The connection to the DB was successfully initialized!
The value was successfully inserted!
```

Let's see what's happening with the insert part. db.Prepare() takes a SQL statement and imbues it with protection against SQL injection attacks. It works by restricting the values of the variable substitutions. In our case, we have two columns, so for the substitution to work, we use $1 and $2. You can use any number of substitutions; you only need to make sure they result in a valid SQL statement when evaluated. When the insert variable is initialized without errors, it will be responsible for executing the SQL statement. It finds out how many arguments the prepared statement expects, and its sole purpose is to call the statement and perform the operation. insert.Exec(2, "second") inserts a new element with id=2 and name='second'. If we were to check what we have in our database, we would see the results.

Now that we have some data in our table, we can query it.

Exercise 15.01 – creating a table that holds a series of numbers

In this exercise, we are going to write a script that is going to create a table called Numbers, in which we are going to store numbers. These numbers will be inserted at a later time.

Create two columns, Number and Property. The Number column will hold numbers, while the Property column will be Odd or Even when it's created.

Use the default Postgres database for the connection. The numbers should range from 0 to 99.

Perform the following steps to complete this exercise:

1. Create a file called main.go.

2. Initialize the package with the following lines:

```
package main
import "fmt"
import "database/sql"
import _ "github.com/lib/pq"
func main(){
```

3. Create a property string variable for later use:

```
var property string
```

4. Initialize the database connection:

```
db, err := sql.Open("postgres", "user=postgres
password=Start!123 host=127.0.0.1 port=5432 dbname=postgres
sslmode=disable")
    if err != nil {
      panic(err)
    }else{
      fmt.Println("The connection to the DB was successfully
initialized!")
    }
```

5. Create a multiline string to create the table:

```
    TableCreate := `
CREATE TABLE Number
(
    Number integer NOT NULL,
    Property text COLLATE pg_catalog."default" NOT NULL
)
WITH (
    OIDS = FALSE
```

```
    )
TABLESPACE pg_default;
ALTER TABLE Number
  OWNER to postgres;
`
```

6. Create the table:

```
    _, err = db.Exec(TableCreate)
  if err != nil {
    panic(err)
  } else{
    fmt.Println("The table called Numbers was successfully
created!")
  }
```

7. Insert the numbers:

```
    insert, insertErr := db.Prepare("INSERT INTO Number
VALUES($1,$2)")
  if insertErr != nil{
    panic(insertErr)
  }
  for i := 0; i < 100; i++ {
    if i % 2 == 0{
      prop = "Even"
    }else{
      prop = "Odd"
    }
    _, err = insert.Exec(i,prop)
    if err != nil{
      panic(err)
    }else{
      fmt.Println("The number:",i,"is:",prop)
    }
  }
  insert.Close()
  fmt.Println("The numbers are ready.")
```

8. Close the database connection and function:

```
    db.Close()
  }
```

When you execute the script, you should see the following output:

```
The connection to the DB was successfully initialized!
The table called Messages was successfully created!
The number: 0 is: Even
The number: 1 is: Odd
The number: 2 is: Even
The number: 3 is: Odd
The number: 4 is: Even
......
The number: 98 is: Even
The number: 99 is: Odd
The numbers are ready.
```

Figure 15.8 – Output of the successful property update

> **Note**
> Part of the output has been omitted from *Figure 15.8* due to its length.

In this exercise, we saw how to create a new table in our database and how to insert new records with the help of a `for` loop and a `Prepare()` statement.

Retrieving data

SQL injection does not only concern the data being inserted. It also concerns any data that is manipulated in the database. Retrieving data and, most importantly, retrieving it safely is also something we must prioritize and handle with proper caution. When we query data, our results depend on the database we connect to and the table we would like to query. However, we must also mention that the security mechanisms that are implemented by the database engine may also prevent a successful query unless the user has appropriate privileges.

We can differentiate between two types of queries:

- Some queries do not take an argument, such as `SELECT * FROM table`
- Some queries require you to specify filter criteria

Go provides two functions that allow you to query data. One is called `Query()` and the other is called `QueryRow()`. As a rule of thumb, you should remember that `Query()` is used to return any number of results, while `QueryRow` is used when you expect to retrieve at most one row. You can also wrap them with the `Prepare()` statement, though we won't cover this here as it was demonstrated before. Instead, we want to see how these functions work.

Let's create a script for `Query()`. As always, we'll initialize the script. It can be found in the examples and is called `DBQuery.go`:

```go
package main
import "fmt"
import "database/sql"
import _ "github.com/lib/pq"
```

Our `main()` function will be a little bit different because we would like to introduce the `Scan()` function:

```go
func main(){
  var id int
  var name string
  db, err := sql.Open("postgres", "user=postgres password=Start!123
host=127.0.0.1 port=5432 dbname=postgres sslmode=disable")
  if err != nil {
    panic(err)
  }else{
    fmt.Println("The connection to the DB was successfully
initialized!")
  }
  rows, err := db.Query("SELECT * FROM test")
  if err != nil {
    panic(err)
  }
  for rows.Next() {
    err := rows.Scan(&id, &name)
    if err != nil {
      panic(err)
    }
    fmt.Printf("Retrieved data from db: %d %s\n", id, name)
  }
  err = rows.Err()
  if err != nil {
    panic(err)
  }
  err = rows.Close()
  if err != nil {
    panic(err)
  }

  db.Close()
}
```

The output should look like this:

```
The connection to the DB was successfully initialized!
Retrieved data from db: 2 second
```

> **Note**
> A `SELECT *` query string is not likely to be seen in professional environments due to performance and security concerns. You will typically have more specific query strings for the specific data.

As we inserted this data into our database previously, feel free to add some more data based on the previous example. We have defined the `id` and `name` variables, which will help our `Scan()` function. We connect to the database and create our `db` variable. After that, we fill our `rows` variable with the result of the `Query()` function, which will hold all the elements from the table.

Here comes the tricky part: we use `for rows.Next()` to iterate over the resulting rows. But that is not enough; we would like to assign the results of the query to the corresponding variable, which is returned by `rows.Scan(&id, &name)`. This allows us to refer to the current row's ID and NAME, which makes it easier to do whatever we would like to do with the value. Finally, the rows and the database connections are gracefully closed.

Let's query a single row with `Prepare()`. The initialization looks the same as before:

DBPrepare.go

```go
package main
import "fmt"
import "database/sql"
import _ "github.com/lib/pq"
```

The full code is available at `https://github.com/PacktPublishing/Go-Programming-From-Beginner-to-Professional-Second-Edition-/blob/main/Chapter15/Examples/DBPrepare.go`.

The main difference is at the beginning of the `main()` function:

```go
func main(){
  var name string
  var id int
  id = 2
  db, err := sql.Open("postgres", "user=postgres password=Start!123
host=127.0.0.1 port=5432 dbname=postgres sslmode=disable")
  if err != nil {
    panic(err)
  }else{
    fmt.Println("The connection to the DB was successfully
```

```
initialized!")
  }
  qryrow, err := db.Prepare("SELECT name FROM test WHERE id=$1")
  if err != nil{
    panic(err)
  }
  err = qryrow.QueryRow(id).Scan(&name)
  if err != nil {
    panic(err)
  }
  fmt.Printf("The name with id %d is %s", id, name)
  err = qryrow.Close()
  if err != nil {
    panic(err)
  }
  db.Close()
}
```

The output, if you did everything correctly, should look something like this:

```
The connection to the DB was successfully initialized!
The name with id 2 is second
```

Let's inspect our main function closely. We defined two variables: the name variable, which will be used when we process the query result, and the id variable, which serves as a flexible input for the query we execute. The usual connection initialization toward our database happens as before.

Then comes the SQL Injection proof part. We prepare a query that is dynamic in the sense that it accepts a parameter that will be the ID we are looking for. Then, qryrow is used to execute the QueryRow() function, which, in turn, takes the id variable we specified previously and returns the result in the name variable. Then, we output the string with an explanation that the value of the column is based on the id variable that was specified. In the end, the qryrow and db resources are closed.

Now that we know how to retrieve data from the database, we need to see how to update existing data in our database.

Updating existing data

When you are updating a row or multiple rows with Go, you are in trouble. The sql package does not provide any function called Update(); however, there is the Exec() function, which serves as a universal executor for your queries. You can execute SELECT, UPDATE, DELETE, or whatever you need to execute with this function. This section will show you how you can do this safely.

We would like to start our script in the usual way. It can be found in the examples folder and is called DBUpdate.go:

```
package main
import "fmt"
import "database/sql"
import _ "github.com/lib/pq"
```

Then the magic comes. The idea is to update the name column's value for a specific id variable that we give as an argument. So, the main() function looks like this:

```
func main(){
  db, err := sql.Open("postgres", "user=postgres password=Start!123
host=127.0.0.1 port=5432 dbname=postgres sslmode=disable")
  if err != nil {
    panic(err)
  }else{
    fmt.Println("The connection to the DB was successfully
initialized!")
  }
  UpdateStatement :=`
  UPDATE test
  SET name = $1
  WHERE id = $2
  `

  updateResult, updateResultErr := db.Exec(updateStatement,"well",2)
  if updateResultErr != nil {
    panic(updateResultErr)
  }
  updatedRecords, updatedRecordsErr := updateResult.RowsAffected()
  if updatedRecordsErr != nil {
    panic(UpdatedRecordsErr)
  }
  fmt.Println("Number of records updated: ",UpdatedRecords)
  db.Close()
}
```

If everything has gone well, we'll see the following output:

```
The connection to the DB was successfully initialized!
Number of records updated: 1
```

Note that you can and should experiment with different inputs and see how the script reacts to different problems/errors.

Let's dissect what's happening here. We initialize our database connection as we did before. We create the `UpdateStatement` variable, which is a multiline string, and it is crafted so that it can be fed to the `Exec()` function, which takes arguments. We want to update the name of the column that has the specified ID. This function either runs the specified statement on its own or can be used to pass arguments that are substituted in the appropriate place. This would be perfectly fine and would do the job for us, but we would like to make sure that the `UPDATE` command updates at least one record.

To this end, we could use `RowsAffected()`. It will return the number of rows that were updated and any errors that were faced along the way. Finally, we print how many rows were updated to the console and close the connection.

The time has come to delete data from our database.

Deleting data

Data can be deleted for multiple reasons: we don't need the data anymore, we are migrating to another database, or we are replacing the current solution. We are in luck because the current Go facilities provide a very nice way to do this. The analogy is the same as for the `UPDATE` statement of our records. We formulate a `DELETE` statement and execute it; we can technically modify the action of our `UPDATE` script to delete it from the database.

For the sake of simplicity, we'll only modify the relevant lines. Our `DELETE` statement will replace the `UPDATE` statement, like this:

`DBDelete.go`

```
12   DeleteStatement :=`
13   DELETE FROM test
14   WHERE id = $1
15   `
```

The full code is available at `https://github.com/PacktPublishing/Go-Programming-From-Beginner-to-Professional-Second-Edition-/blob/main/Chapter15/Examples/DBDelete.go`. We'll update the line with the `Exec()` statement:

```
deleteResult, deleteResultErr := db.Exec(deleteStatement,2)
if deleteResultErr != nil {
  panic(deleteResultErr)
}
```

Also, we must update the line with the calculation of updated records:

```
deletedRecords, deletedRecordsErr := deleteResult.RowsAffected()
if deletedRecordsErr != nil {
  panic(deletedRecordsErr)
}
fmt.Println("Number of records deleted: ",deletedRecords)
```

Our result should look like this:

```
The connection to the DB was successfully initialized!
Number of records deleted: 1
```

That's it. With a little modification, we have a script that can either update or delete records with verification.

Now, let's see how we can create a table that holds prime numbers.

Exercise 15.02 – holding prime numbers in a database

In this exercise, we will build on *Exercise 15.01 – creating a table that holds a series of numbers*. We would like to create a script that will tell us how many prime numbers are in our table and give them to us in order of appearance. We would like to see the sum of prime numbers in the output. Then, we would like to remove every even number from the table and see how many were removed. We would like to add the sum of prime numbers to the remaining odd numbers and update the table with the records, changing the property if necessary. Use the `math/big` package for the primality test.

Follow these steps:

1. Create a script called `main.go`.

2. Initialize our script to perform the specific actions:

    ```go
    package main
    import "fmt"
    import "database/sql"
    import _ "github.com/lib/pq"
    import "math/big"
    func main(){
    ```

3. Define four variables for later use:

    ```go
    var number int64
    var prop string
    var primeSum int64
    var newNumber int64
    ```

4. Initialize the database connection:

    ```go
    db, err := sql.Open("postgres", "user=postgres
    password=Start!123 host=127.0.0.1 port=5432 dbname=postgres
    sslmode=disable")
    if err != nil {
      panic(err)
    }else{
      fmt.Println("The connection to the DB was successfully
    initialized!")
    ```

```
  }
```

5. Get a list of all the prime numbers:

```
allTheNumbers := "SELECT * FROM Number"
numbers, err := db.Prepare(allTheNumbers)
if err != nil {
  panic(err)
}
primeSum = 0
result, err := numbers.Query()
fmt.Println("The list of prime numbers:")
for result.Next(){
  err = result.Scan(&number, &prop)
  if err != nil{
    panic(err)
  }
  if big.NewInt(number).ProbablyPrime(0) {
    primeSum += number
    fmt.Print(" ",number)
  }
}
err := numbers.Close()
if err != nil{
  panic(err)
}
```

6. Print the sum of the prime numbers:

```
fmt.Println("\nThe total sum of prime numbers in this range
is:", primeSum)
```

7. Remove the even numbers:

```
remove := "DELETE FROM Number WHERE Property=$1"
removeResult, err := db.Exec(remove,"Even")
if err != nil {
  panic(err)
}
modifiedRecords, err := removeResult.RowsAffected()
fmt.Println("The number of rows removed:",ModifiedRecords)
fmt.Println("Updating numbers...")
```

8. Update the remaining records with `primeSum` and print a closing sentence:

```
update := "UPDATE Number SET Number=$1 WHERE Number=$2 AND
Property=$3"
allTheNumbers = "SELECT * FROM Number"
numbers, err = db.Prepare(allTheNumbers)
if err != nil {
  panic(err)
}
result, err = numbers.Query()
for result.Next(){
    err = result.Scan(&number, &prop)
    if err != nil{
      panic(err)
    }
    newNumber = number + primeSum
    _, err = db.Exec(update,newNumber,number,prop)
    if err != nil {
      panic(err)
    }
}
numbers.Close()
if err != nil{
  panic(err)
}

fmt.Println("The execution is now complete...")
```

9. Close the database connection:

```
db.Close()
}
```

Once the script has been executed, the following output should be visible:

```
The connection to the DB was successfully initialized!
The list of prime numbers:
 2 3 5 7 11 13 17 19 23 29 31 37 41 43 47 53 59 61 67 71 73 79 83 89 97
The total sum of prime numbers in this range is: 1060
The number of rows removed: 50
Updating numbers...
The execution is now complete...
```

Figure 15.9 – Output of the calculations

In this exercise, we saw how to utilize a built-in Go function to find prime numbers. We also manipulated the table by removing numbers, and then we performed update actions.

> **Note**
> Closing the database is important because once our job is done, we do want to release unused resources.

Truncating and deleting table

In this section, we want to empty a table and get rid of it. To empty the table, we can simply formulate DELETE statements that match every record in our table and thus remove every single record from our table. However, there is a more elegant way to do this: we can use the TRUNCATE TABLE SQL statement. The result of this statement is an empty table. We can use the Exec() function from our sql package for this. You already know how to initialize the package with imports. You also know how to connect to the database. This time, we'll only focus on the statements.

The following statement will achieve a full TRUNCATE:

```
emptyTable, emptyTableErr := db.Exec("TRUNCATE TABLE test")
if emptyTableErr != nil {
  panic(emptyTableErr)
}
```

The result of this is an empty table called test. To get rid of the table completely, we can modify our statement as follows:

```
dropTable, dropTableErr := db.Exec("DROP TABLE test")
if dropTableErr != nil {
  panic(dropTableErr)
}
```

If you need a table but do not need any more old data, you might want to truncate it and carry on adding new data to the existing table. If you do not need the table anymore because you changed your schema, you might want to just delete it using the DROP command.

If we inspect our database engine, we won't find any trace of the test table. This eradicated the whole table from the very face of the database.

This section was all about interacting with databases via the Go programming language. Now, you have a decent understanding of how to get started.

> **Note**
> For further information and extra details, you should check out the official documentation of the SQL API: https://packt.live/2Pi5oj5.

Activity 15.01 – holding user data in a table

In this activity, we are going to create a table that is going to hold user information such as ID, Name, and Email. We'll build on the knowledge you gathered in the *Creating tables* and *Inserting data* sections.

Follow these steps to complete this activity:

1. Create a small script that will create a table called Users. This table must have three columns: ID, Name, and Email.

2. Add the details of two users, along with their data, to the table. They should have unique names, IDs, and email addresses.

3. Then, you need to update the email of the first user to user@packt.com and remove the second user. Make sure that none of the fields are NULL. Since the ID is the primary key, it needs to be unique.

4. When you are inserting, updating, and deleting from the table, please use the Prepare() function to protect against SQL injection attacks.

5. You should use a struct to store the user information you would like to insert, and when you are inserting, iterate over the struct with a for loop.

6. Once the insert, update, and delete calls are complete, make sure you use Close() when appropriate and close the connection to the database.

    Upon successful completion, you should see the following output:

```
The connection to the DB was successfully initialized!
Good to go!
The table called Users was successfully created!
The user with name: Szabo Daniel and email: daniel@packt.com was successfully added!
The user with name: Szabo Florian and email: florian@packt.com was successfully added!
The user's email address was succesfully updated!
The second user was succeesfully removed!
```

Figure 15.10 – Possible output

> **Note**
>
> The solution to this activity can be found on https://github.com/PacktPublishing/ Go-Programming-From-Beginner-to-Professional-Second-Edition-/ blob/main/Chapter15/Activity15.01/main.go.

By the end of this activity, you should have learned how to create a new table called users and how to insert data into it.

Activity 15.02 – finding the messages of specific users

In this activity, we will build on *Activity 15.01 – holding user data in a table.*

We need to create a new table called `Messages`. This table will have two columns, both of which should have a 280-character limit: one is `UserID` and the other is `Message`.

When your table is ready, you should add some messages with user IDs. Make sure you add `UserID`, which is not present in the `users` table.

Once you have added the data, write a query that returns all the messages a specified user has sent. Use the `Prepare()` function to protect against SQL injection.

If the specified user cannot be found, print `The query returned nothing, no such user: <username>`. You should take the username as input from the keyboard.

Perform these steps to complete this activity:

1. Define a struct that holds `UserID` and its messages.

2. Messages should be inserted with a `for` loop that iterates over the previously defined struct.

3. When the user input is received, make sure you use the `Prepare()` statement to craft your query.

    If everything has gone well, you should get the following output, depending on how you fill your database with usernames and messages:

```
The connection to the DB was sucessfully initialized!
Good to go!
The table called Messages was successfully created!
The UserID: 1 with message: Hi Florian, when are you coming home? was successfully added!
The UserID: 1 with message: Can you send some cash? was successfully added!
The UserID: 2 with message: Hi can you bring some bread and milk? was successfully added!
The UserID: 7 with message: Well... was successfully added!
Give me the user's name: Szabo Daniel
Looking for all the messages of user with name: Szabo Daniel ##
The user: Szabo Daniel with email: user@packt.com has sent the following message: Hi Florian, when are you coming home?
The user: Szabo Daniel with email: user@packt.com has sent the following message: Can you send some cash?
```

Figure 15.11: Expected output

> **Note**
>
> The solution to this activity can be found on `https://github.com/PacktPublishing/Go-Programming-From-Beginner-to-Professional-Second-Edition-/blob/main/Chapter15/Activity15.02/main.go`.

If you want, you can tweak the script so that you don't recreate the database on consecutive runs.

By the end of this activity, you should have learned how to create a new table called `Messages`, then take input from the user and search for related users and messages based on the input.

Adding users with GORM

So far, we've interacted with the database by writing some SQL queries directly. What we've done is create and run Go code, which was used to then run SQL code. This is perfectly fine, but there is also a way to run just Go code to interact with a SQL database. On top of this, the data that we are storing in the database will then be unwrapped into Go variables, and the content of a row might define the values of an instance of a Go struct. What we can do to improve and simplify the whole process is abstract the database even more and use an **object-relational mapper** (**ORM**). This is a library that matches the tables and their relations as Go structs so that you can insert and retrieve data the same way you would instantiate and delete any instance of a Go struct. An ORM is not generally part of a language, and Go does not provide one by itself. There is, however, a set of third-party libraries, one of which is the de facto ORM for Go, and this is GORM. You can find all the details of this package at `https://gorm.io/`, but we will briefly learn how to use it to add and search for data in our database.

To use GORM, we must import it. Here's how:

```
import (
    "gorm.io/gorm"
    "gorm.io/driver/postgres"
)
```

As you can see, we do not have just one line but two. The first loads the GORM library, while the second specifies the driver to use. GORM can be used to interact with a lot of different database engines, including MySQL, Postgres, and SQLite. While the library itself is available from `gorm.io/gorm`, the specific way to interact with the engine is handled by the driver – in this case, the Postgres driver.

The next step will be to define a schema – that is, a Go struct representing what's inside a table. Let's define a struct representing a user:

```
type User struct {
    gorm.Model
    FirstName  string
    LastName   string
    Email      string
}
```

This is pretty straightforward – we define a struct called `User` and we add some fields that will hold the first and last name of a user, together with their email address. The first important thing, however, is that we embed the `gorm.Model` struct into our struct, making it effectively a GORM model. This struct will add some fields, such as an ID, and set it as a primary key, as well as some other fields, such as creation and update date, and will also add some methods that will be used by the library to make it interact with a database.

Now that we have a struct defining a user, let's see how we can insert a user into the database. To interact with the database, we must connect to it. Earlier, we saw how to connect to PostgreSQL; we will do something similar here:

```
connection_string = "user=postgres password=Start!123 host=127.0.0.1
port=5432 dbname=postgres sslmode=disable"
db, err := gorm.Open(postgres.Open(connection_string), &gorm.Config{})
if err != nil {
    panic("failed to connect database")
}
```

As you can see, we can use the same connection string as earlier, but we will do so inside the gorm. Open call, which allows GORM to interact with the underlying database engine.

So far, we haven't created a table for the users, and we've seen how to create one using SQL and call it via Go. With GORM, we do not need to do that. After defining the type that will go inside the table that will hold users, we can have GORM create that table for us, if it does not exist already. We can do this with the following code:

```
db.AutoMigrate(&User{})
```

This call ensures that there is a table holding users that contains all the required columns, and by default will call it *users*. There are ways to change the name of the table, but in general, it is better to follow the conventions. So, a table holding users' data will be called *users*, while a struct holding the details of a user will be called User.

What remains now is just to add an actual user – we will call him John Smith and use john.smith@ gmail.com as his email address. This is how we can instantiate the struct with his details:

```
u := &User{FirstName: "John", LastName: "Smith", Email: "john.smith@
gmail.com"}
```

Finally, we can insert it into the database:

```
db.Create(u)
```

As you can see, this is pretty straightforward and allows us to write just Go code and model our data as Go structs.

GORM has quite a few functionalities; in this section, we learned how to create structs and use them to match a schema in a database, as well as add data to a specific table. Now, let's learn how to find users with GORM.

Finding Users with GORM

Once we've added users, we would like to retrieve them. Let's add a few other users using what we learned in the previous section:

```
db.Create(&User{FirstName: "John", LastName: "Doe", Email: "john.doe@
gmail.com"
db.Create(&User{FirstName: "James", LastName: "Smith", Email: "james.
smith@gmail.com"})
```

Let's assume that we had already inserted the record for John Smith. So, starting from a clean database and clean table, we should have users with IDs of 1, 2, and 3, respectively.

Now, we want to retrieve details about the first user we inserted. We can do that with the following command:

```
var user User
db.First(&user, 1)
```

This will return the first user matching the condition where the user's ID is equal to 1. The returned record is un-marshaled into the `user` variable, which is an instance of the `User` struct. We can search for every other user via their ID and substitute the number 1 with 2 or 3. This, however, is not very interesting, as we might not know the user's ID but only their name or surname. Let's see how to retrieve John Doe from his surname:

```
db.First(&user, "last_name = ?", "Doe")
```

Note that we did not use "LastName" but `last_name` as GORM automatically transforms every attribute of the struct that's camel case into snake case; this is the usual convention for database column names. The other important thing to notice is that we use two parameters:

```
"last_name = ?" and "Doe"
```

The first one represents the column we want to search in, and we have a question mark after the equals sign. The question mark is a placeholder and will be replaced by the next parameter, which is *Doe*. As we have two people with the surname Smith, the function we just used will retrieve the first person with that surname, but this is not necessarily the one we are looking for. We could use the `Last` function, which returns the last result that matches the query, but we could have more users with the same surname. The solution for this is as follows:

```
db.First(&user, "last_name = ? AND first_name= ?", "Smith", "James")
```

Here, we created a query that includes more conditions – the first few parameters express the condition, while the following parameters fill the values with placeholders.

The issue we could face here is that we might get confused with the names of the struct's attributes and the actual column names. If we need to do a simple matching query, we can substitute the previous code with the following:

```
db.First(&user, &User{FirstName: "James", LastName: "Smith"})
```

Here, we just pass an instance of the User struct with a few attributes set, leaving the other ones to the default values.

These examples allow us to search for a specific record, but often, we need a list of objects. Of course, the First and Last functions return only one item, but GORM also gives us a function to return all the records that match our criteria. If the criteria is simply an ID, or if the field we search for is unique, we are better off sticking with First, but if our criteria are not unique, we should use the following function:

```
var users []User
db.Find(&users, &User{LastName: "Smith"})
```

The Find function returns all the matching records, but we cannot just un-marshal it into a single user instance. So, we must define a users variable, which is a slice of User instances, rather than using the previously seen user, which was an instance of a User struct.

This gives us an idea of how to use GORM to insert and retrieve data, but we've forgotten one important thing: errors. These functions are contacting the database, but the queries might somehow error for several reasons, and we need to control that. The previously seen function does not return an error but a pointer to the database struct, which we can use to get the errors:

```
tx := db.Find(&users, &User{LastName: "Smith"})
if tx.Error != nil {
  fmt.Println(tx.Error)
}
```

Here, the tx variable stands for *transaction* and returns a set of values with a potential error among them. We can check if there is an error by comparing the tx.Error value with nil. When we use a transaction, whatever we do to the database is not definitive; it does not affect the state of the database that's accessed by any other client, so any change is temporary. To make any change effective, we need to commit the transaction. In this case, we are just returning results, and not modifying the database, so we do not need to commit. We are using the transactions because GORM returns a transaction from the Find call.

This gives us a starting point to use GORM to model and use data while storing it in a database.

Summary

This chapter made you efficient in interacting with SQL databases. You learned how to create, delete, and manipulate database tables. You also become aware of all the different types of databases Go is suited to interact with. As this chapter was made with the PostgreSQL engine in mind, you should familiarize yourself with its Go module too.

With this knowledge, you will now be able to step foot into the realm of database programming with the Go language and be self-sufficient in the sense that you know where to look for solutions to problems and extra knowledge. The most common use case for this knowledge is when you must build automated reporting apps that pull data from a database and report it as an email. The other use case is when you have an automated app for pushing data to the database server that processes a CSV file or an XML file. This depends on the situation you are in.

This chapter also introduced you to the concept of ORM and has given you an introduction to the most famous ORM for the Go language: GORM.

In the next chapter, you will learn how to interact with web interfaces via HTTP clients, which is one of the most interesting topics in Go.

Part 5:
Building For The Web

The modern world has been profoundly influenced by the Internet and the World Wide Web. Go, born in the internet age, was meticulously crafted to thrive in this digital landscape.

This section delves into the realm of web development with Go, empowering you to create robust and efficient web applications.

This section includes the following chapters:

- *Chapter 16, Web Servers*
- *Chapter 17, Using the Go HTTP Client*

16

Web Servers

> **Overview**
>
> This chapter introduces you to different ways of creating an HTTP server to accept requests from the internet. You will be able to understand how a website can be accessed and how it can respond to a form. You will also learn how to respond to requests from another software program.
>
> By the end of this chapter, you'll be able to create an HTTP server that renders a simple message. You will also know how to create an HTTP server that renders complex data structures that serve local static files. Further, you know how to create an HTTP server that renders dynamic pages and works with different ways of routing. Finally, you will know how to create a REST service, accept data through a form, and accept JSON data.

Technical requirements

To complete and run the examples in this chapter, you will need your favorite IDE and the latest version of the Go compiler. At the time of writing, this is 1.21. All the examples will use the standard Go library. You can refer to this book's GitHub repository for the code in this chapter: `https://github.com/PacktPublishing/Go-Programming-From-Beginner-to-Professional-Second-Edition-/tree/main/Chapter16`.

Introduction

In this chapter, we will dig into how a remote server is created, so if you already know how to request information, you will see how to reply to these requests.

A web server is a program that uses the HTTP protocol – hence, the HTTP server – to accept requests from any HTTP client (web browser, another program, and so on) and respond to them with an appropriate message. When we browse the internet with our browser, it will be an HTTP server that will send an HTML page to our browser and we will be able to see it. In some other cases, a server will not return an HTML page but a different message that's appropriate to the client.

Some HTTP servers provide an API that can be consumed by another program. Think of when you want to register with a website, and you are asked if you want to sign up through Facebook or Google. This means that the website you want to register with will consume a Google or Facebook API to get your details. These APIs generally respond with structured text, which is a piece of text representing a complex data structure. The way these servers expect the requests can be different. Some expect the same type of structured messages they return, while some provide what is called a REST API, which is quite strict with the HTTP methods that are used and expects inputs in the form of URL parameters or values, similar to the ones in a web form.

How to build a basic server

The simplest HTTP server that we can create is a Hello World server. This is a server that returns a simple message stating `Hello World` and will not do anything else. It is not very useful, but it is a starting point to see what default Go packages give us and is the basis for any other more complex server. The aim is to have a server that runs on a specific port on your machine's local host and accepts any path under it. Accepting any path means that when you test the server with your browser, it will always return the `Hello World` message and a status code of `200`. Of course, we could return any other message, but, for historical reasons, the simplest project you learn when you study programming is always some sort of software that returns a message stating `Hello World`. In this case, we will see how this can be done and then visualized in a normal browser, before perhaps being put on the internet and shared with billions of users, although users may, in practice, prefer a more useful server. Let's say this is the most basic HTTP server you can create.

HTTP handler

To react to an HTTP request, we need to write something that, we usually say, handles the request; hence, we call this something a handler. In Go, we have several ways to do that, and one way is to implement the handler interface of the `http` package. This interface has one pretty self-explanatory method, and this is as follows:

```
ServeHTTP(w http.ResponseWriter, r *http.Request)
```

So, whenever we need to create a handler for HTTP requests, we can create a struct that includes this method and we can use it to handle an HTTP request. Here's an example:

```
type MyHandler struct {}
func(h MyHandler) ServeHTTP(w http.ResponseWriter, r *http.Request) {}
```

This is a valid HTTP handler and you can use it like so:

```
http.ListenAndServe(":8080", MyHandler{})
```

Here, `ListenAndServe()` is a function that will use our handler to serve the requests; any struct that implements the handler interface will be fine. However, we need to let our server do something.

As you can see, the `ServeHTTP` method accepts `ResponseWriter` and a `Request` object. You can use them to capture parameters from the request and write messages to the response. The simplest thing, for example, is to let our server return a message:

```go
func (h MyHandler) ServeHTTP(w http.ResponseWriter, r *http.Request) {
  _, err := w.Write([]byte("HI"))
  if err != nil {
    log.Printf("an error occurred: %v\n", err)
    w.WriteHeader(http.StatusInternalServerError)
  }
}
```

The `ListenAndServe` method might return an error. If this happens, we will want the execution of our program to halt. One common practice is to wrap this function call with a fatal log:

```go
log.Fatal(http.ListenAndServe(":8080", MyHandler{}))
```

This will halt the execution and print the error message that's returned by the `ListenAndServe` function.

Exercise 16.01 – creating a Hello World server

Let's start by building a simple `Hello World` HTTP server based on what you learned in the previous section.

The first thing you need to do is create a folder called `hello-world-server`. You can do this via the command line or you can create it with your favorite editor. Inside the folder, create a file called `main.go`. We will not use any external library here:

1. Add the package's name, as shown here:

    ```go
    package main
    ```

    This tells the compiler that this file is an entry point for a program that can be executed.

2. Import the necessary packages:

    ```go
    import (
      "log"
      "net/http"
    )
    ```

3. Now, create `handler`, the struct that will handle the requests:

    ```go
    type hello struct{}
    func (h hello) ServeHTTP(w http.ResponseWriter, r *http.Request)
    {
      msg := "<h1>Hello World</h1>"
    ```

```
        w.Write([]byte(msg))
    }
```

4. Now that we have our handler, create the `main()` function. This will start the server and produce a web page with our message:

```go
func main() {
    log.Fatal(http.ListenAndServe(":8080", hello{}))
}
```

The entire file should look like this:

```go
package main
import (
    "log"
    "net/http"
)
type hello struct{}
func(h hello) ServeHTTP(w http.ResponseWriter, r *http.Request)
{
    msg := "<h1>Hello World</h1>"
    w.Write([]byte(msg))
}
func main() {
    log.Fatal(http.ListenAndServe(":8080", hello{}))
}
```

5. Now, go to your Terminal, inside your `hello-world-server` folder, and type in the following command:

```
go run .
```

You shouldn't see anything; the program has started.

6. Now, open your browser at the following address:

```
http://localhost:8080
```

You should see a page with a big message:

Hello World

Figure 16.1: Hello World server

Now, if you try to change path and go to /page1, you will see the following message:

Hello World

Figure 16.2: Hello World server sub-pages

Congratulations! This is your first HTTP server.

In this exercise, we created a basic Hello World server that returns a message stating Hello World in response to any request on any sub-address.

Simple routing

The server we built in the previous exercise doesn't do much – it just responds with a message; we cannot ask anything else. Before we can make our server more dynamic, let's imagine we want to create an online book and we want to be able to select a chapter just by changing the URL. At the moment, if we browse the following pages, we'll always see the same message:

```
http://localhost:8080
http://localhost:8080/hello
http://localhost:8080/chapter1
```

Now, we want to associate different messages with these different paths on our server. We will do this by introducing some simple routing to our server.

A path is what you see after 8080 in the URL, where 8080 is the port number we chose to run the server on. This path can be one number, a word, a set of numbers, or character groups separated by a /. To do this, we will use another function of the net/http package:

```
HandleFunc(pattern string, handler func(ResponseWriter, *Request))
```

Here, the pattern is the path we want to be served by the handler function. Note how the handler function signature has the same parameters as the ServeHTTP method, which you added to the hello struct in the previous exercise.

As an example, the server we built in *Exercise 16.01* is not very useful, but we can transform it into something much more useful with the addition of pages other than the Hello World one. To do so, we need to do some basic routing. The aim here is to write a book, and the book must have a welcome page that contains a title and a first chapter. The book title is Hello World, so we can keep what we did before. The first chapter will have a heading stating Chapter 1. The book is a work in progress, so it doesn't matter that the content is still poor; what we require is the ability to select the chapter; we will add the content later.

Exercise 16.02 – routing our server

We are going to modify the code in *Exercise 16.01* so that it supports different paths. If you haven't gone through the previous exercise, do so now so that you have a basic framework for this exercise:

1. Create a new folder and a `main.go` file, and add the code from the previous exercise to the definition of the `main` function:

```
package main
import (
  "log"
  "net/http"
)
type hello struct{}
    func(h hello) ServeHTTP(w http.ResponseWriter, r *http.
Request) {
        msg := "<h1>Hello World</h1"
        w.Write([]byte(msg))
    }
```

2. Create the `main()` function:

```
func main() {
```

3. Then, use `handle` to route `/chapter1` through a `handlefunc()` function:

```
    http.HandleFunc("/chapter1", func(w http.ResponseWriter, r
*http.Request) {
        msg := "Chapter 1"
        w.Write([]byte(msg))
    })
```

This means that we associate the path, `/chapter1`, with a function that returns a specific message.

4. Finally, set the server so that it listens to a port; then, run the following command:

```
        log.Fatal(http.ListenAndServe(":8080", hello{}))
    }
```

5. Now, save your file and run the server again with the following command:

```
go run .
```

6. Then, go to your browser and load the following URLs:

- `http://localhost:8080`
- `http://localhost:8080/chapter1`

- The output for the home page is shown in the following screenshot:

Hello World

Figure 16.3: Multi-page server – home page

The output for page 1 is shown in the following screenshot:

Hello World

Figure 16.4: Multi-page server – page 1

Note that they both still display the same message. This happens because we are setting `hello` as the handler for our server, and this overrides our specific path. We can modify our code so that it looks like this:

```go
func main() {
  http.HandleFunc("/chapter1", func(w http.ResponseWriter, r *http.
Request) {
    msg := "<h1>Chapter 1</h1>"
    w.Write([]byte(msg))
})
    http.Handle("/", hello{})
    log.Fatal(http.ListenAndServe(":8080", nil))
}
```

Here, we removed the `hello` handler so that it's no longer the main handler for our server and we associated this handler with the main / path:

```go
http.Handle("/", hello{})
```

Then, we associated a `handler` function with the specific /`chapter1` path:

```go
http.HandleFunc("/chapter1", func(w http.ResponseWriter, r *http.
Request) {
    msg := "Chapter 1"
    w.Write([]byte(msg))
})
```

Now, if we stop and then run our server again, we will see that the `/chapter1` path now returns the new message:

Chapter 1

Figure 16.5: Multi-page server repeated – chapter 1

In the meantime, all the other paths return the old **Hello World** message:

Hello World

Figure 16.6: Multi-page server – base page

The default page for the server is also displayed for another route:

Hello World

Figure 16.7: The page that is not set returns the default setting

With that, we made a basic Hello World web server with specific routes for different pages. During the process, we used several functions from the go `http` package, some of which are used to achieve the same result. We will see why there are multiple ways to do the same thing and why we need all of them shortly.

Handler versus handler function

As you may have noticed, we used two different functions before, `http.Handle` and `http.HandleFunc`, both of which have a path as their first parameter, but which differ in terms of the second parameter. These two functions both ensure that a specific path is handled by a function. `http.Handle`, however, expects `http.Handler` to handle the path, while `http.HandleFunc` expects a function to do the same.

As we've seen before, `http.Handler` is any struct that has a method with this signature:

```
ServeHTTP(w http.ResponseWriter, r *http.Request)
```

So, in both cases, there will always be a function with `http.ResponseWriter` and `*http.Request` as parameters that will handle the path. When one or the other might be chosen may just be a matter of personal preference in many cases, but it might be important – when creating a complex project, for example – to choose the right method. Doing so will ensure that the structure of the project is optimal. Different routes may appear better organized if they're handled by handlers that belong to different packages, or might have to perform very few actions, as in our previous case; and a simple function might prove to be the ideal choice.

In general, for simple projects where you have a handful of simple pages, you may opt for `HandleFunc`. For example, let's say you want to have static pages and there is no complex behavior on each page. In this case, it would be overkill to use an empty struct just for returning static text. The handler is more appropriate whenever you need to set some parameters, or if you want to keep track of something. As a general rule, let's say that if you have a counter, `Handler` is the best choice because you can initialize a struct with a count of 0 and then increment it, but we will see this in *Activity 16.01*.

Activity 16.01 – adding a page counter to an HTML page

Imagine that you own a website with, say, three pages, where you are writing your book. You earn money based on how many visits your website receives. To understand how popular your website is, and how much money you are earning, you need to keep track of the visits.

In this activity, you will build an HTTP server with three pages that contain some content, and display, on each page, how many visits that page has had so far. You will use the `http.Handler` method, which, in this case, will help you generalize your counter.

To display the dynamic value, you can use the `fmt.Sprintf` function in the `fmt` package, which prints and formats a message to a string. With this function, you can build a string containing characters and numbers. You can find more information about this method online in the Go documentation.

You will use everything you've learned so far, including how a struct is instantiated, how to set the attributes of a struct, pointers, how to increase an integer, and, of course, everything you've learned about HTTP servers so far.

Observing the following steps will provide an elegant and effective solution:

1. Create a folder called `page-counter`.
2. Create a file called `main.go`.
3. Add the necessary imports to the `http` and `fmt` packages.
4. Define a struct called `PageWithCounter` with `counter` as an integer attribute, `content`, and `heading` as a text attribute.
5. Add a `ServeHTTP` method to the struct that's capable of displaying the content, the heading, and a message with the total number of views.

6. Create your `main` function and, inside, implement the following:

    - Instantiate three handlers of the `PageWithCounter` type, with `Hello World`, `Chapter 1`, and `Chapter 2` headings and some content.
    - Add the three handlers to the `/`, `/chapter1`, and `/chapter2` routes.

7. Run the server on port `8080`.

When you run the server, you should see the following:

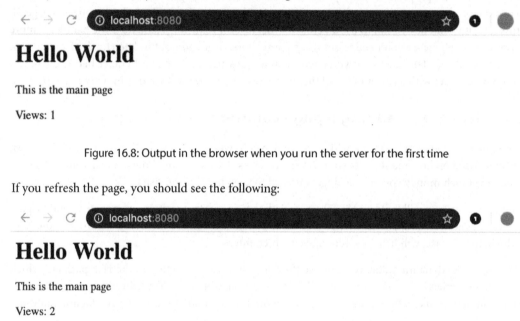

Figure 16.8: Output in the browser when you run the server for the first time

If you refresh the page, you should see the following:

Figure 16.9: Output in the browser when you run the server for the second time

Next, navigate to `chapter1` by typing `localhost:8080/chapter1` in the address bar. You should be able to see something along the lines of the following:

Figure 16.10: Output in the browser when you visit the chapter1 page for the first time

Similarly, navigate to `chapter2`; you should be able to see the following increment in terms of the number of views:

Chapter 2

This is the second chapter

Views: 1

Figure 16.11: Output in the browser when you visit the chapter2 page for the first time

When you revisit `chapter1`, you should see an increase in the number of views, as follows:

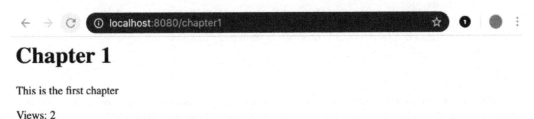

Chapter 1

This is the first chapter

Views: 2

Figure 16.12: Output in the browser when you visit the chapter1 page for the second time

> **Note**
>
> The solution for this activity can be found in this book's GitHub repository at `https://github.com/PacktPublishing/Go-Programming-From-Beginner-to-Professional-Second-Edition-/blob/main/Chapter16/Activity16.01/main.go`.

In this activity, you learned how to create a server that responds to different requests on different pages with a specific static text, along with a counter on each page, with each counter independent from the others.

Adding middleware

Sometimes, you will need to create a lot of functions to handle HTTP requests, maybe serving different paths in a URL, all performing different actions. You might need to create a function to handle a server returning a list of users, one with a list of projects, a route for updating some details, and all the functions doing different things. It might happen, however, that although these functions perform different actions, they will also have something in common. A common example is when these functions have to be performed on a secured environment, which means only for users that have been logged in. Let's look at a very simple example and consider the following two functions:

```
http.HandleFunc(
  "/hello1",
  func(w http.ResponseWriter,
  r *http.Request,
){
    msg := "Hello there, this is function 1"
    w.Write([]byte(msg))
})
http.HandleFunc(
  "/hello2",
  func(w http.ResponseWriter,
  r *http.Request,
){
    msg := "Hello there, and now we are in function 2"
    w.Write([]byte(msg))
})
```

Both functions will display a sentence that starts with Hello there,. Let's find a way to extract this part of the behavior of these functions and create a third function that will be used to perform the act of writing the initial cheering message:

```
func Hello(next http.HandlerFunc) http.HandlerFunc {
  return func(w http.ResponseWriter, r *http.Request) {
    msg := "Hello there,"
    w.Write([]byte(msg))
    next.ServeHTTP(w, r)
  }
}
```

This function has the following signature:

```
func Hello(next http.HandlerFunc) http.HandlerFunc
```

This means it is called Hello, accepts http.HandlerFunc as a parameter, and returns a result against http.HandlerFunc. This parameter is called next because it is the function that we will want to run next. Let's look at the body of the function:

```
  return func(w http.ResponseWriter, r *http.Request) {
    msg := "Hello there,"
    w.Write([]byte(msg))
    next.ServeHTTP(w, r)
  }
```

As you can see, it returns a function that implements the `http.HandlerFunc` type and has the correct arguments and return type. This function will write a message stating `Hello there,` to the response writer, w, and then call the `next` function with the same response writer and request that the function without a name receives.

Now, let's refactor our code to make it a bit easier to read. We'll create two functions for the actions we want to perform:

```
func Function1(w http.ResponseWriter,
  r *http.Request,
) {
  msg := " this is function 1"
  w.Write([]byte(msg))
}

func Function2(w http.ResponseWriter,
  r *http.Request,
) {
  msg := " and now we are in function 2"
  w.Write([]byte(msg))
}
```

Let's see what our file looks like so far:

```
package main

import (
  "log"
  "net/http"
)

func Hello(next http.HandlerFunc) http.HandlerFunc {
  return func(w http.ResponseWriter, r *http.Request) {
    msg := "Hello there,"
    w.Write([]byte(msg))
    next.ServeHTTP(w, r)
  }
}
func Function1(w http.ResponseWriter,
  r *http.Request,
) {
  msg := " this is function 1"
  w.Write([]byte(msg))
}
```

```
func Function2(w http.ResponseWriter,
  r *http.Request,
) {
  msg := " and now we are in function 2"
  w.Write([]byte(msg))
}
```

As you can see, we have our `Hello` function and two functions returning two different sentences to the response writer. The last step is to associate these functions with a path, like so:

```
func main() {

  http.HandleFunc(
    "/hello1", Function1)
  http.HandleFunc(
    "/hello2", Function2)
  log.Fatal(http.ListenAndServe(":8085", nil))
}
```

As you can see, we pass functions 1 and 2 to each route. If you run the code on your machine and go to `http://localhost:8085/hello1`, you will see a message stating `this is function 1`. What we have not used yet, though, is the `Hello` function. Let's rewrite the last block of code and make use of it:

```
func main() {

  http.HandleFunc(
    "/hello1", Hello(Function1))
  http.HandleFunc(
    "/hello2", Hello(Function2))
  log.Fatal(http.ListenAndServe(":8085", nil))
}
```

If you run this program again, you will see that the message has now changed to `Hello there, this is function 1`. The `Hello` function is essentially running before the `Function1` function and after doing its own work, it calls `Function` so that that function can also do its job. We call the `Hello` function `Middleware` as it acts as the man in the middle – it captures the request, does some work, and then calls the next function in line. By doing this, it is possible to chain many middleware by doing something like this:

```
Hello(Middleware2(Middleware3((Function2))))
```

You can use this pattern to perform many common actions before or after the actual function that needs to be associated with a path on the URL.

Dynamic content

A server that serves only static content is useful, but there is much more that can be done. An HTTP server can deliver content based on a more granular request, which is done by passing some parameters to the server. There are many ways to do so, but one simple way is to pass parameters to querystring. If the URL of the server is as follows:

```
http://localhost:8080
```

Then, we can add something like this:

```
http://localhost:8080?name=john
```

Here, ?name=john is called a querystring string as it is a string representing a query. In this case, querystring sets a variable called name with a value of john. This way of passing parameters is generally used with GET requests, while a POST request will generally make use of the body of the request to send parameters. We will begin by looking at how to accept parameters for a GET request since this request is made by simply opening our browser on a specific address. We will see how to handle a POST request through a form later.

In the next exercise, you will learn how to return different texts as responses to HTTP requests, where the text depends on what values the user puts in the querystring string in the address bar.

Exercise 16.03 – personalized welcome

In this exercise, we will create an HTTP server that can cheer us, but instead of a general hello world message, we will provide a message depending on our name. The idea is that, by opening the browser on the server's URL and adding a parameter called name, the server will welcome us with a message stating hello, followed by the value of the name parameter. The server is very simple and does not have sub-pages, but contains a dynamic element that constitutes a starting point for more complex situations:

1. Create a new folder called personalised-welcome and, inside the folder, create a file called main.go. Inside the file, add the package name:

    ```
    package main
    ```

2. Then, add the required imports:

    ```
    import (
      "fmt"
      "log"
      "net/http"
      "strings"
    )
    ```

3. These are the same imports we used in the previous exercises and activities, so there is nothing new. We will not use handlers in this exercise as it is much smaller, but we will make use of the `http.handleFunc` function.

4. Now, add the following code after the imports:

```
func Hello(w http.ResponseWriter, r *http.Request) {
```

5. This is the definition of a function that can be used as a handling function for an HTTP path.

6. Now, save the query to a variable using the `Query` method URL from the request:

```
v1 := r.URL.Query()
```

7. The `Query` method on the URL object of the request returns a `map[string][]string` string with all the parameters sent through `querystring` in the URL. We then assign this map to a variable, `v1`.

8. At this point, we need to get the value of a specific parameter called `name`, so we get the value from the name parameter:

```
name, ok := v1["name"]
```

9. As you can see, we have an assignment to two variables, but only one value comes from `v1["name"]`. The second variable, `ok`, is a Boolean that tells us whether the name key exists.

10. If the name parameter has not been passed and we want an error message to appear, we must add it if the variable is not found – in other words, if the `ok` variable is false:

```
if !ok {
    w.WriteHeader(400)
    w.Write([]byte("Missing name"))
    return
}
```

11. The conditional code gets called if the key does not exist in the slice, and it writes a `400` code (bad request) to the header, as well as a message to the response writer stating that the name has not been sent as a parameter. We stop the execution with a `return` statement to prevent further actions.

12. At this point, write a valid message to the response writer:

```
    w.Write([]byte(fmt.Sprintf("Hello %s", strings.Join(name,
",")))))
}
```

13. This code formats a string and injects the name into it. The `fmt.Sprintf` function is used to format, while `strings.Join` is used to transform the name slice into a string. Notice that the name variable is set to the value of `v1["name"]`, but `v1` is a `map[string][]`

string string, which means that it is a map with string keys whose values are slices of strings; hence, v1["name"] is a slice of strings and needs to be transformed into a single string. The strings.Join function takes all the elements of the slice and builds a single string using "," as a separator. Other characters could have also been used as separators.

14. The last part of the file you have to write is as follows:

```
func main() {
    http.HandleFunc("/", Hello)
    log.Fatal(http.ListenAndServe(":8080", nil))
}
```

15. As always, a main() function is created, and then the Hello function is associated with the "/" path and the server is started. Here is the output of three different URLs – two valid ones, and one with a missing parameter:

```
Hello john
```

Figure 16.13: The server's output when requesting the page with the name John

The preceding figure shows the output when we set the query parameter in the URL to the name John. If we change the name in the query parameter in the URL, we will see the new value:

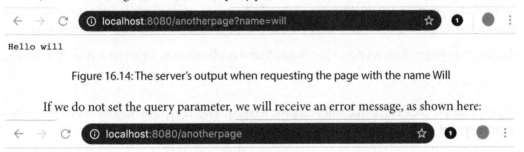

```
Hello will
```

Figure 16.14: The server's output when requesting the page with the name Will

If we do not set the query parameter, we will receive an error message, as shown here:

```
Missing name
```

Figure 16.15: The server outputting an error message when requesting a page without a name

Next, we'll explore the concept of templates.

Templating

Although JSON can be the best choice when complex data structures have to be shared across software programs, in general, this is not the case when the HTTP server is supposed to be consumed by humans. In the previous exercises and activities, the chosen way to format a piece of text has been the fmt.Sprintf function, which is good for formatting texts, but is simply insufficient when more dynamic and complex text is required. As you will have noticed in the previous exercise, the message that was returned in case a name was passed as a parameter to the URL observed a specific pattern, and this is where a new concept comes in – the template. A template is a skeleton from which complex entities can be developed. Essentially, a template is like text with some blanks. A template engine will take some values and fill in the blanks, as shown in the following diagram:

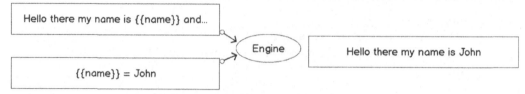

Figure 16.16: Templating example

As you can see, {{name}} is a placeholder, and, when a value is passed through to the engine, the placeholder is modified with that value.

We see templates everywhere. We have templates for Word documents, where we just fill in what is missing to produce new documents that all differ from one another. A teacher might have some templates for their lessons and will develop different lessons from that same template. Go provides two different templating packages – one for text and one for HTML. As we are working with HTTP servers and we want to produce a web page, we will use the HTML templating package, but the interface is the same for the text template library. Although the templating packages are good enough for any real-world application, several other external packages can be used to improve performance. One of these is the hero template engine, which is much faster than the standard Go templating package.

The Go templating package provides a placeholder language where we can use things such as the following:

```
{{name}}
```

This is a simple code block that will make the template engine replace the name variable with a provided value, but more complex situations can be handled via conditionals:

```
{{if age}} Hello {{else}} bye {{end}}
```

Here, if an age parameter is not null, the template will contain Hello; otherwise, it will contain bye. Each conditional needs an {{end}} placeholder to determine its ending.

Variables in a template, however, do not need to be simple numbers or strings; they can be objects. In this case, if we have a struct with a field called ID, we can reference this field in the template like so:

```
{{.ID}}
```

This is very handy as we can pass a struct to the template instead of many single parameters.

In the next exercise, you will learn how to use the basic templating functionalities of Go to create pages with custom messages, as you've done before, but just in a more elegant way.

Exercise 16.04 – templating our pages

This exercise aims to have you build a more structured web page, use a template, and fill it with parameters from the URL's querystring. In this scenario, we want to display basic information for a customer and hide some information when the data is missing. A customer has id, name, surname, and age values, and if any of these values are missing, they will not be displayed. Unless the data is the id value, as in this case, an error message will be displayed:

1. Begin by creating a server-template folder that contains a main.go file. Then, add the usual package and some imports:

```go
package main
import (
    "html/template"
    "log"
    "net/http"
    "strconv"
    "strings"
)
```

2. Here, we use two new imports: html/template for our templating and strconv to convert strings into numbers (this package could also work the other way around, but there are better solutions for formatting text).

3. Now, write the following:

```go
var tplStr = `
<html>
  <h1>Customer {{.ID}}</h1>
  {{if .ID }}
  <p>Details:</p>
  <ul>
  {{if .Name}}<li>Name: {{.Name}}</li>{{end}}
  {{if .Surname}}<li>Surname: {{.Surname}}</li>{{end}}
  {{if .Age}}<li>Age: {{.Age}}</li>{{end}}
  </ul>
  {{else}}
  <p>Data not available</p>
  {{end}}
</html>
`
```

4. This is a raw string that contains some HTML and templating code, which is wrapped by {{}}. We will analyze this now.

5. {{.ID}} is essentially a placeholder that tells the template engine that wherever this code is found, it will be substituted by a struct's attribute called ID. The Go templating engine works with structs, so essentially, a struct will be passed to the engine and its attributes' values will be used to fill the placeholders. {{if .ID}} is a conditional that tells the template that what happens next will depend on the value of ID. In this case, if ID is not an empty string, the template will display the customer's details; otherwise, it will display <p>Data not available</p>, which is wrapped between the {{else}} and {{end}} placeholders. As you can see, there are many more conditionals nested inside the first one. At each list item, there is a <li> tag, which is wrapped, for example, by {{if .Name}} and terminated with {{end}}.

6. Now that we have a string template, let's create a struct with the correct attributes. To fill in the template, write the following:

```go
type Customer struct {
    ID int
    Name string
    Surname string
    Age int
}
```

This struct is self-explanatory. It contains all the attributes needed by the template.

7. Define the handler function and set a variable to the map of values in querystring:

```go
func Hello(w http.ResponseWriter, r *http.Request) {
    vl := r.URL.Query()
```

8. Instantiate a cust variable of the Customer type:

```go
cust := Customer{}
```

9. The variable now has all its attributes set to the default values, and we need to grab the passed values from the URL. To do so, write the following:

```go
id, ok := vl["id"]
if ok {
    cust.ID, _ = strconv.Atoi(strings.Join(id, ","))
}
name, ok := vl["name"]
if ok {
    cust.Name = strings.Join(name, ",")
}
surname, ok := vl["surname"]
if ok {
    cust.Surname = strings.Join(surname, ",")
}
age, ok := vl["age"]
```

```
    if ok {
       cust.Age, _ = strconv.Atoi(strings.Join(age, ""))
    }
```

10. As you can see, the parameters are taken as they are from the values map, and if they exist, they are used to set the value of the related cust attribute. To check whether these parameters exist, we again used the ok variable, which is set to a Boolean with a value of true in case the map contains the requested key. The last attribute, Age, is handled slightly differently:

```
       cust.Age, _ = strconv.Atoi(strings.Join(age, ""))
```

11. This is because strconv.Atoi returns an error in case the parameter that's passed is not a number. In general, we should handle the errors but, in this case, we'll just ignore it and we won't display any age-related information if the age provided is not a number.

12. Next, write the following:

```
       tmpl, _ := template.New("test").Parse(tplStr)
```

13. This creates a template object called test that contains the content of the string that you created at the outset. Again, ignore the error as we are sure that the template we've written is a valid one. In production, however, all the errors should be dealt with.

14. You can now finish writing the function:

```
       tmpl.Execute(w, cust)
    }
```

15. Here, the template is executed using the cust struct; its content is sent directly to w ResponseWriter without the need to call the Write method manually.

16. What's missing now is the main method, which is fairly simple. Write the following:

```
    func main() {
       http.HandleFunc("/", Hello)
       log.Fatal(http.ListenAndServe(":8080", nil))
    }
```

17. Here, simply speaking, the main path is associated with the Hello function, and the server is then started.

18. The performance of this code is not very high as we create a template for every request. The template could be created in main and then passed to a handler, which could have a ServeHTTP method like the Hello function you've just written. The code has been kept simple here to focus on templating.

19. Now, if you start the server and visit the following pages, you should see some output similar to the following:

Customer 0

Data not available

Figure 16.17: Templated response with blank parameters

Now, you can add a query parameter called id and make it equal to 1 in the URL by visiting localhost:8080/?id=1:

Customer 1

Details:

Figure 16.18: Templated response with just the ID specified

Then, you can add a value for the name parameter by going to localhost:8080/?id=1&name=John:

Customer 1

Details:

- **Name: John**

Figure 16.19: Templated response with the ID and name specified

Finally, you also add an age by going to localhost:8080/?id=1&name=John&age=40:

Customer 1

Details:

- **Name: john**
- **Age: 40**

Figure 16.20: Templated response with the ID, name, and age specified

Here, each parameter in `querystring` is displayed, if valid, in the web application.

Static resources

Everything you've learned so far in this book, up to the previous exercise, is sufficient to build web applications and dynamic websites; you just need to put all the pieces together.

What you've been doing in this chapter is returning messages that are different but all hardcoded as strings. Even dynamic messages have been based on templates hardcoded in the source file of the exercises and activities. Now, let's consider something. In the case of the first `hello world` server, the message never changed. If we wanted to modify the message and return a `Hello galaxy` message, we would have to change the text in the code and then recompile and/or run the server again. What if you wanted to sell your simple "hello" server and give the option to everybody to specify a custom message? Of course, you should give the source code to everybody so that they can recompile and run the server.

Although you might want to embrace open source code, this might not be the ideal way to distribute an application, and we need to find a better way to separate the message from the server. A solution to that is to serve static files, which are files that are loaded by your program as external resources. These files do not change, do not get compiled, and are loaded and manipulated by your program. One such example may be templates, as seen previously, because they are just text and you can use template files instead of adding the templates as text to your code. Another simple example of static resources is if you want to include styling files such as CSS in your web page. You will see how to do that in the following exercises and activities. You'll learn how to serve a specific file or a specific folder, and then you'll learn how to serve dynamic files with a static template.

Exercise 16.05 – creating a Hello World server using a static file

In this exercise, you will create your Hello World server but with a static HTML file. What we want is to have a simple server with one handler function that looks for a specific file with a specific name, which will be served as the output for every path. In this case, you will need to create multiple files in your project:

1. Create a folder called `static-file` and, inside it, create a file called `index.html`. Then, insert the following code for a pretty simple HTML file with a title and an `h1` tag that states our welcome message:

```
<!DOCTYPE html>
<html lang="en">
<head>
  <meta charset="UTF-8">
  <title>Welcome</title>
</head>
<body>
```

```
    <h1>Hello World</h1>
  </body>
</html>
```

2. Now, create a file called main.go and start writing the necessary imports:

```
package main
import (
    "log"
    "net/http"
)
```

3. Now, write the main function:

```
func main() {
```

4. Next, write the handler function:

```
    http.HandleFunc("/", func (w http.ResponseWriter, r *http.
Request) {
      http.ServeFile(w, r, "./index.html")
    })
```

5. This is where the magic happens. Here a normal http.HandleFunc is being called with a "/" path as the first parameter, after which a handler function is passed, which contains a single instruction:

```
      http.ServeFile(w, r, "./index.html")
```

6. This sends the content of the index.html file to ResponseWriter.

7. Now, write the last part:

```
      log.Fatal(http.ListenAndServe(":8080", nil))
  }
```

8. As is always the case, this starts the server, logs in case of an error, and exits the program.

9. Now, save the file and run the program with the following command:

```
go run main.go
```

If you open your browser on the localhost:8080 page, you should see the following:

Hello World

Figure 16.21: Hello World with a static template file

10. Next, without stopping your server, just change the HTML file, index.html, and modify line 8, where you see the following:

```
<h1>Hello World</h1>
```

11. Change the text in the `<h1>` tag, like so:

```
<h1>Hello Galaxy</h1>
```

12. Save the index.html file and, without touching the terminal and without restarting your server, just refresh your browser on the same page. You should now see the following:

Hello Galaxy

Figure 16.22: Hello World server with the static template file modified

13. So, even if the server is running, it will pick up the new version of the file.

In this exercise, you learned how to use a static HTML file to serve a web page, as well as how detaching the static resources from your application allows you to change your served page without having to restart your application.

Getting some style

So far, you've seen how to serve one static page and you might consider serving a few pages with the same method, maybe creating a handler struct with the name of the file to serve as an attribute. This might be impractical for large numbers of pages, although, in some cases, it is necessary. A web page, however, does not include just HTML code – it may also include images and styles, as well as some frontend code.

It is not within the scope of this book to teach you how to build HTML pages, and even less how to write JavaScript code or CSS style sheets, but you need to know how to serve these documents as we use a small CSS file to build our example.

Serving static files and putting templates in different files, or generally using external resources, is a good way to separate concerns on our projects and make our projects more manageable and maintainable, so you should try to follow this approach in all your projects.

To add a style sheet to your HTML pages, you need to add a tag like this:

```
<link rel="stylesheet" href="file.css">
```

This injects the CSS file into the page as a "stylesheet," but this is reported here just by way of an example, in case you are interested in learning how to write HTML.

You have also seen that we have served files, reading them from the filesystem one by one, but Go provides us with an easy function to do the job for us:

```
http.FileServer(http.Dir("./public"))
```

Essentially, `http.FileServer` creates what its name says: a server serving external files. It takes it from the directory defined in `http.Dir`. Whatever file we put inside the `./public` directory will be automatically accessible in the address bar:

```
http://localhost:8080/public/myfile.css
```

This seems good enough. However, in a real-world scenario, you do not want to expose your folder names and instead specify a different name for your static resources. This can be achieved as follows:

```
http.StripPrefix(
    "/statics/",
    http.FileServer(http.Dir("./public")),
)
```

You may have noticed that the `http.FileServer` function is wrapped by an `http.StripPrefix` function, which we use to associate the requested path with the correct files on the filesystem. Essentially, we want the path of the `/statics` form to be available and to bind it to the content of the `public` folder. The `StripePrefix` function will remove the `"/statics/"` prefix from the request and pass it to the file server, which will just get the name of the file to serve and search for it in the `public` folder.

It is not necessary to use these wrappers if you do not want to change the name of the path and folder, but this solution is general and works everywhere, so you can utilize it in other projects without having to worry.

Exercise 16.06 – a stylish welcome

This exercise aims to help you display a welcome page while making use of some external static resources. We will adopt the same approach as in *Exercise 16.05*, but we will add some extra files and code. We will place some stylesheets in a `statics` folder, and we will serve them so that they can be used by other pages served by the same server:

1. By way of a first step, create a folder called `stylish-welcome` and, inside this folder, add a file called `index.html`. Then, incorporate the following content:

   ```
   <!DOCTYPE html>
   <html lang="en">
   <head>
     <meta charset="UTF-8">
     <title>Welcome</title>
   ```

```
      <link rel="stylesheet" href="/statics/body.css">
      <link rel="stylesheet" href="/statics/header.css">
      <link rel="stylesheet" href="/statics/text.css">
    </head>
    <body>
      <h1>Hello World</h1>
      <p>May I give you a warm welcome</p>
    </body>
    </html>
```

2. As you can see, there are few differences compared with the previous HTML; we have a paragraph with some more text, wrapped by the `<p>` tag, and, inside the `<head>` tag, we include three links to external resources.

3. Now, create a folder called `public` inside your `stylish-welcome` folder and create three files therein with the following names and content:

```
header.css
h1 {
   color: brown;
}
body.css
body {
   background-color: beige;
}
text.css
p {
   color: coral;
}
```

4. Now, go back to your main project folder, `stylish-welcome`, and create the `main.go` file. The content at the start corresponds exactly to that in one of the previous exercises:

```
package main
import (
  "log"
  "net/http"
)
func main() {
  http.HandleFunc("/", func (w http.ResponseWriter, r *http.
Request) {
    http.ServeFile(w, r, "./index.html")
  })
```

5. Now, add the following code to handle the static files:

```
http.Handle(
  "/statics/",
  http.StripPrefix(
  "/statics/",
  http.FileServer(http.Dir("./public")),
  ),
)
```

6. This code adds a handler to the /statics/ path and does so through an http.FileServer function, which returns a static file handler.

7. This function requires a directory to scrape, and we pass one to it as a parameter:

```
http.Dir("./statics")
```

8. This reads the local public folder that you created previously.

9. Now, add this final part to the file:

```
log.Fatal(http.ListenAndServe(":8080", nil))
}
```

10. Here, again, the server gets created and the main() function is closed. Now, run the server again:

```
go run main.go
```

11. You will see the following output:

Figure 16.23: Styled home page

Somehow, the HTML file is now getting the style from the style sheets you created at the beginning.

12. Now, let's examine how the files are injected. If you look back at the index.html file, you will see these lines:

```
<link rel="stylesheet" href="/statics/body.css">
<link rel="stylesheet" href="/statics/header.css">
<link rel="stylesheet" href="/statics/text.css">
```

13. So, essentially, we are looking for files under the `"/statics/"` path. The first address will display the content of the CSS for the body of the page:

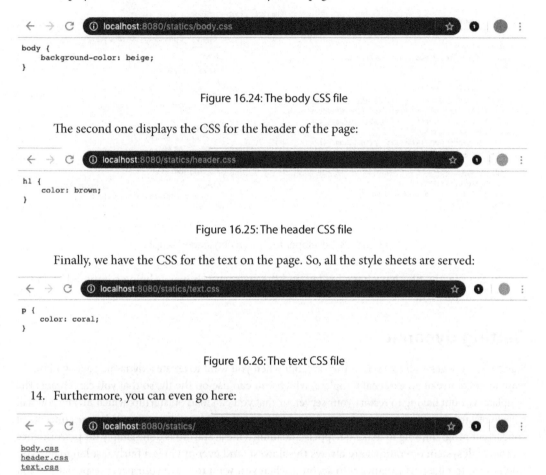

Figure 16.24: The body CSS file

The second one displays the CSS for the header of the page:

Figure 16.25: The header CSS file

Finally, we have the CSS for the text on the page. So, all the style sheets are served:

Figure 16.26: The text CSS file

14. Furthermore, you can even go here:

Figure 16.27: Static folder content visible in the browser

15. You'll see that all the files inside the `public` folder are served under the `/statics/` path. If you are looking for a simple static files server, Go allows you, with the help of a few lines of code, to create one, and, with a few more lines, you can make it production-ready.

16. If you use Chrome, you can inspect with your mouse by right-clicking, though you can do the same with any browser if you have developer tools. You will see something similar to the following:

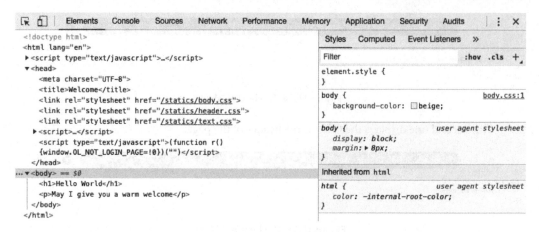

Figure 16.28: Developer tools showing loaded scripts

As you can see, the files have been loaded and the styles are shown as being computed from the stylesheet on the right.

Getting dynamic

Static assets are generally served as they are, but when you want to create a dynamic page, you might want to make use of an external template, which you can use on the fly, so that you can change the template without having to restart your server, or that you can load on startup, which means you will have to restart your server following any change (this is not strictly true, but we need some concepts of concurrent programming to make it happen). Loading a file at startup is done simply for performance reasons. Filesystem operations are always the slowest, and even if Go is a fairly fast language, you might want to take performance into account when you want to serve your pages, especially if you have many requests from multiple clients.

As you may recall, we used the standard Go templates to make dynamic pages. Now, we can use the template as an external resource, put our template code in an HTML file, and load it. The template engine can parse it and then fill in the blanks with the passed parameters. To do this, we can use the `html/template` function:

```
func ParseFiles(filenames ...string) (*Template, error)
```

As an example, this can be called with the following code:

```
template.ParseFiles("mytemplate.html")
```

In addition, the template is loaded in memory and is ready to be used.

So far, you have been the sole user of your HTTP servers, but in an actual scenario, that won't be the case. In the following examples, we will look at performance and will use a resource that's loaded at startup.

Activity 16.02 – external template

In this activity, you will create a welcome server, similar to the ones you created before, and you will have to use the template package, as you've done before. In this activity, however, we do not want you to create your template from a hardcoded string but from an HTML file, which will contain all the template placeholders.

You should be able to complete this activity by making use of what you've learned so far in this chapter and the previous one.

This activity returns a pointer to `template` and an error from a list of filenames. The error gets returned if any of the files does not exist or if the format of the template is wrong. In any case, do not concern yourself with the possibility of adding multiple files. Stick with one.

Here are the steps to complete this activity:

1. Create a folder for your project.
2. Create a template with a name such as `index.html` and fill it with standard HTML code, with a welcome message and a placeholder for the name. Make sure that if the name is empty, the message inserts the word `visitor` where the name is supposed to be.
3. Create your `main.go` file and add to it the right package and imports.
4. In the `main.go` file, create a struct holding a name that can be passed to a template.
5. Create a template from a file using your `index.html` file.
6. Create something that's able to handle the HTTP requests and use `querystring` to receive parameters and display the data through the template you created previously.
7. Set all the paths to the server so that you can use the function or handler you created in the previous step; then, create the server.
8. Run the server and check the result. The output will be as follows:

Hello visitor

May I give you a warm welcome

Figure 16.29: Anonymous visitor page

The visitor page, including the name that's displayed, will look something like this:

Hello Will

May I give you a warm welcome

Figure 16.30: Visitor page with the name "Will"

> **Note**
>
> The solution for this activity can be found in this book's GitHub repository at `https://github.com/PacktPublishing/Go-Programming-From-Beginner-to-Professional-Second-Edition-/tree/main/Chapter16/Activity16.02`.

In this activity, you learned how to create a templated HTTP handler as a struct that can be initialized with any external template. You can now create multiple pages, instantiating the same struct with different templates of your choice.

Embedding external files

In the previous sections, you learned about a very interesting technique, but having external files to read can be problematic when deploying something to production, especially with Go, where one of its strong features is building a single executable. Fortunately, there is a package in Go called `embed` that allows us to add external files to our final binary so that we need the original file when we develop, but we do not need to share this file with anybody else as it will be compiled and added to our final binary. Let's see how this works.

Let's imagine that you have a simple template file and want to use it on your web server:

```
mytemplate.html
<h1>{{.Text}}</h1>
```

Let's look at a small program that does exactly that, using what you've learned in the previous chapter:

```
package main

import (
  "html/template"
  "log"
  "net/http"
)
```

```go
func main() {
  t, _ := template.ParseFiles("mytemplate.html")
  http.HandleFunc(
    "/hello1", func(w http.ResponseWriter,
      r *http.Request,
    ) {
      data := struct {
        text string
      }{
        text: "Hello there",
      }

      t.Execute(w, data)
    })
  log.Fatal(http.ListenAndServe(":8085", nil))
}
```

If you run this code, the program will parse the file from your folder and use it as a template to display Hello there on the /hello1 path. If you build your application and you move your executable to a different folder, however, you will receive an error. Let's modify this software so that it uses the embed package:

```go
package main

import (
  _ "embed"
  "html/template"
  "log"
  "net/http"
)

//go:embed mytemplate.html
var s string

func main() {
  t, _ := template.New("mytemplate").Parse(s)
  http.HandleFunc(
    "/hello1", func(w http.ResponseWriter,
      r *http.Request,
    ) {
      data := struct {
        text string
      }{
```

```
        text: "Hello there",
      }

      t.Execute(w, data)
    })
  log.Fatal(http.ListenAndServe(":8085", nil))
}
```

The difference Is that we've just created a global variable, s, that holds the content of the mytemplate. html files and stores it in the binary when you compile your code using the //go:embed build tag directive:

```
_ "embed"
//go:embed mytemplate.html
var s string

t, _ := template.New("mytemplate").Parse(s)
```

Finally, we create a template with the New method and then parse the string. If you compile the code and run your application from a different folder, you won't have any errors.

Summary

In this chapter, you were introduced to the server side of web programming. You learned how to accept requests from HTTP clients and respond appropriately. You also learned how to separate the possible requests into different areas of an HTTP server via paths and sub-paths. For this, you used a simple routing mechanism with the standard Go HTTP package.

Then, you learned how to return your response to suit different consumers: JSON responses for synthetic clients, and HTML pages for human access.

Next, you learned how to use templates to format your plain text and HTML messages, using the standard templating package. You learned how to serve and use static resources, serving them directly through a default file server or a template object.

After that, you learned how to create a middleware and how to embed external files inside your binary for better portability. At this stage, you know all the basics for building production-grade HTTP servers, although you might want to use some external libraries to facilitate your Hello World example, facilitating better routing by using something such as gorilla mux or, generally, the entire gorilla package, which is a low-level abstraction on top of the http package. You could use hero as a template engine to make your page rendering faster.

One thing to mention is that you can make pretty much stateless services with what you've learned in this chapter, but you cannot create a production-grade stateful server at the moment as you do not know how to handle concurrent requests. This means that `views counter` is not suitable for a production server yet, but this will be the subject of another chapter.

In the next chapter, you will shift gears and learned how to use the Go HTTP client to talk to other systems over the internet.

17

Using the Go HTTP Client

> **Overview**
>
> This chapter will equip you to use the Go HTTP Client to talk to other systems over the Internet.
>
> You will start by learning to use the HTTP client to get data from a web server and to send data to a web server. By the end of the chapter, you will be able to upload a file to a web server and experiment with a custom Go HTTP Client to interact with web servers.

Technical requirements

For this chapter, you'll require Go version 1.21 or higher. The code for this chapter can be found at: `https://github.com/PacktPublishing/Go-Programming-From-Beginner-to-Professional-Second-Edition-/tree/main/Chapter17`.

Introduction

In the previous chapter, you looked at web APIs with REST. You learned what REST is, how to think about API design, resources, and errors in REST, as well as the problems with REST and some of its alternatives.

In this chapter, you will learn about the Go HTTP Client and how to use it. An HTTP client is something that is used to get data from or send data to a web server. Probably the most well-known example of an HTTP client is a web browser (such as Firefox, Chrome, and Microsoft Edge). When you enter a web address into a web browser, it will have an HTTP client built in that sends a request to the server for data. The server will gather the data and send it back to the HTTP client, which will then display the web page in the browser. Similarly, when you fill out a form in a web browser, for example, when you log in to a website, the browser will use its HTTP client to send that form data to the server and then take appropriate action, depending on the response.

This chapter looks at how you can use the Go HTTP Client to request data from a web server and send data to a server. You will examine the different ways you can use the HTTP client to interact with a web server and the various use cases for those interactions. The web browser example will be useful in explaining the different interactions. As part of this chapter, you will create your own Go programs that make use of the Go HTTP Client to send and receive data from a web server.

The Go HTTP Client and its uses

The Go HTTP Client is part of the Go standard library, specifically the `net/http` package. There are two main ways to use it. The first is to use the default HTTP client that is included in the `net/http` package. It's simple to use and allows you to get up and running quickly. The second way is to create your own HTTP client based on the default HTTP client. This allows you to customize the requests and various other things. It takes longer to configure, but it gives you much more freedom and control over the requests you send.

When using an HTTP client, you can send different types of requests. While there are many types of requests, we will discuss the two main ones: the GET request and the POST request. For instance, if you wanted to retrieve data from a server, you would send a GET request. When you enter a web address in your web browser, it will send a GET request to the server at that address and then display the data it returns. If you wanted to send data to the server, you would send a POST request. If you wanted to log into a website, you would POST your login details to the server.

In this chapter, there are a few exercises to teach you about the Go HTTP Client. They will teach you how to request data from a server in various formats using GET requests. They will also teach you how to POST form data to a web server, similar to how a web browser would send a POST request when you log in to a website. These exercises will also show you how to upload a file to a web server and how to use a customized HTTP client to have more control over the requests you send.

Sending a request to a server

When you want to retrieve data from a web server, you send a GET request to the server. When sending a request, the URL will contain information on the resource from which you want data. The URL can be broken down into a few key parts. These include the protocol, the hostname, the URI, and the query parameters. The format of it looks like this:

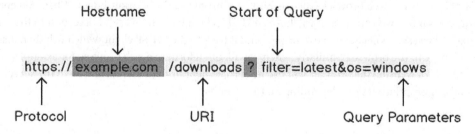

Figure 17.1: URL format breakdown

We can see the following in this example:

- `Protocol` tells the client how to connect to the server. The two most common protocols are HTTP and HTTPS. In this example, we have used `https`.

- `Hostname` is the address of the server we want to connect to. In this example, it is `example.com`.

- `URI` is the **uniform resource identifier** (**URI**), and this tells the server the path to the resource we want. In this example, it is `/downloads`.

- `Query Parameters` tells the server about any additional information it needs. In this example, we have two query parameters. These are `filter=latest` and `os=windows`. You will notice they are separated from the URI by `?`. This is so the server can parse them from the request. We join any additional parameters to the end of the URI with the & symbol, as seen with the `os` parameter.

Exercise 17.01 – sending a GET request to a web server using the Go HTTP Client

In this exercise, you will be getting data from a web server and printing out that data. You will send a GET request to `https://www.google.com` and display the data the web server returns:

1. Create a new directory, `Exercise17.01`. Within that directory, create a new Go file called `main.go`.

2. As this is a new program, you will want to set the package of the file to the `main()` function. Import the `net/http` package, the `log` package, and the `io` package. Type the following code:

    ```
    package main
    import (
      "io"
      "log"
      "net/http"
    )
    ```

    Now that you have the package set up and the imports you need, you can start creating a function to get data from a web server. The function you are going to create will request data from a web server.

3. Create a function that returns a string:

    ```
    func getDataAndReturnResponse() string {
    ```

4. Within that function, you can then use the default Go HTTP Client to request data from a server. In this exercise, you will request data from `https://www.google.com`. To request data from the web server, you use the `Get` function in the `http` package, which looks as follows:

```
r, err := http.Get("https://www.google.com")
if err != nil {
  log.Fatal(err)
}
```

5. The data the server sends back is contained within `r.Body`, so you just need to read that data. To read the data within `r.Body`, you can use the `ReadAll` function within the `io` package. The two together would look like this:

```
defer r.Body.Close()
data, err := io.ReadAll(r.Body)
if err != nil {
  log.Fatal(err)
}
```

6. After you have received the response from the server and read the data, you just need to return that data as a string, which looks like this:

```
  return string(data)
}
```

The function you have now created will now look like this:

```
func getDataAndReturnResponse() string {
  // send the GET request
  r, err := http.Get("https://www.google.com")
  if err != nil {
    log.Fatal(err)
  }
  // get data from the response body
  defer r.Body.Close()
  data, err := io.ReadAll(r.Body)
  if err != nil {
    log.Fatal(err)
  }
  // return the response data
  return string(data)
}
```

7. Create a `main` function. Within the `main` function, call the `getDataAndReturnResponse` function and log the string it returns:

```
func main() {
  data := getDataAndReturnResponse()
```

```
    log.Println(data)
}
```

8. To run the program, open your terminal and navigate to the directory that you created the `main.go` file in.

9. Run `go run main.go` to compile and execute the file:

```
go run main.go
```

The program will issue a GET request to `https://www.google.com` and log the response in your terminal.

While it may look like gibberish, if you were to save that data to a file called `response.html` and open it in your web browser, it would resemble the Google home page. This is what your web browser will do under the hood when you open a web page. It will send a GET request to the server and then display the data it returns. If we do this manually, it will look as follows:

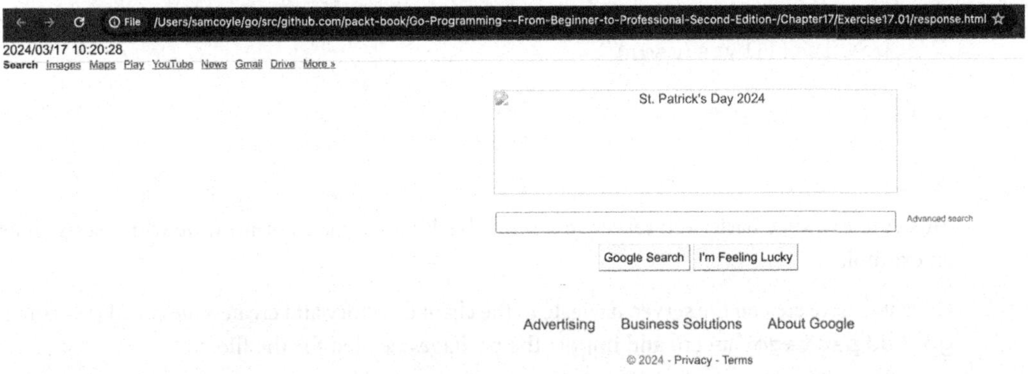

Figure 17.2: Request HTML response when viewed in Chrome

In this exercise, we saw how to send a GET request to a web server and get data back. You created a Go program that sent a request to `https://www.google.com` and got back the HTML data for the Google home page.

Structured data

Once you have requested data from a server, the data returned can come in various formats. For example, if you send a request to `packtpub.com`, it will return HTML data for the Packt website. While HTML data is useful for displaying websites, it isn't ideal for sending machine-readable data. A common data type used in web APIs is JSON. JSON provides a good structure for data that is both machine-readable and human-readable. Later, you will learn how to parse JSON and make use of it using Go.

Exercise 17.02 – using the HTTP Client with structured data

In this exercise, you will parse structured JSON data in Go. The server will return JSON data, and you will use the `json.Unmarshal` function to parse the data and put them into a struct:

1. Create a new directory, `Exercise17.02`. Within that directory, create two more directories, `server` and `client`. Then, within the `server` directory, create a file called `server.go` and write the following code:

    ```go
    package main
    import (
      "log"
      "net/http"
    )
    type server struct{}
    func (srv server) ServeHTTP(w http.ResponseWriter, r *http.Request) {
      msg := "{\"message\": \"hello world\"}"
      w.Write([]byte(msg))
    }
    func main() {
      log.Fatal(http.ListenAndServe(":8080", server{}))
    }
    ```

    This creates a very basic web server that sends back JSON data. For now, we will just use it as an example.

2. Once you have created the server, navigate to the client directory and create a file called `client.go`. Add `package main`, and import the packages needed for the file:

    ```go
    package main
    import (
      "encoding/json"
      "fmt"
      "io"
      "log"
      "net/http"
    )
    ```

3. Then, create a struct with a string parameter that can accept the response from the server. You must use the exported field to encode or decode JSON. Fields must start with capital letters to be exported. Then, add a struct tag to customize the encoded JSON key name. If the name of the JSON field is different from the field name in the Go struct, it allows us to link that JSON field to the field in the struct. In our case, the names are the same. We can omit the struct tag, but it is the best practice to use JSON tags explicitly to make it more clear:

    ```go
    type messageData struct {
    ```

```
        Message string `json:"message"`
    }
```

4. Next, create a function that you can call to get and parse the data from the server. Use the struct you just created as the return value:

    ```
    func getDataAndReturnResponse() messageData {
    ```

    When you run the web server, it will listen on http://localhost:8080. So, you need to send a GET request to that URL and then read the response body:

    ```
        r, err := http.Get("http://localhost:8080")
        if err != nil {
          log.Fatal(err)
        }
        defer r.Body.Close()
        data, err := io.ReadAll(r.Body)
        if err != nil {
          log.Fatal(err)
        }
    ```

5. This time, however, you will parse the response instead of simply returning it. To do that, you create an instance of the struct you created and then pass it along with the response data to json.Unmarshal:

    ```
        message := messageData{}
        err = json.Unmarshal(data, &message)
        if err != nil {
          log.Fatal(err)
        }
    ```

    This will populate the message variable with the data returned from the server.

6. You then need to return the struct to complete the function:

    ```
        return message
    }
    ```

7. Finally, call the function you just created from the main() function and log the message from the server:

    ```
    func main() {
      data := getDataAndReturnResponse()
      fmt.Println(data.Message)
    }
    ```

8. To run this, you need to do two steps. The first is to navigate to the server directory in your terminal and run the following command. This will start the web server:

```
go run server.go
```

9. In a second terminal window, navigate to the client directory and run go run main. go. This will start the client and connect to the server. It should output the following message from the server:

```
client [git::master] > go run main.go
hello world
```

Figure 17.3: Expected output

In this exercise, you sent a GET request to the server and received structured data in the JSON format. You then parsed that JSON data to get the message from it.

Activity 17.01 – requesting data from a web server and processing the response

Imagine you are interacting with a web API. You send a GET request for data and get back an array of names. You need to count those names to find out how many of each you have. In this activity, you will do just that. You will send a GET request to the server, get back structured JSON data, parse the data, and count how many of each name you got back in the response:

1. Create a directory called Activity17.01.

2. Create two subdirectories, one called client and another called server.

3. In the server directory, create a file called server.go.

4. Add the server code in server.go.

5. Start the server by calling go run server.go in the server directory.

6. In the client directory, create a file called client.go.

7. In client.go, add the necessary imports.

8. Create structs to parse the response data.

9. Create a function called getDataAndParseResponse that returns two integers.

10. Send a GET request to the server.

11. Parse the response into a struct. Here is an example of what the data will look like:

```
{"names":["Electric","Electric","Electric","Boogaloo","Booga-
loo","Boogaloo","Boogaloo"]}
```

12. Loop through the struct and count the occurrences of the names Electric and Boogaloo.

13. Return the counts.

14. Print the counts.

The expected output is as follows:

```
solution [git::master *] > go run main.go
Electric Count:  2
Boogaloo Count:  3
```

Figure 17.4: Possible output

> **Important note**
> The solution for this activity can be found in the GitHub repository at: `https://github.com/PacktPublishing/Go-Programming-From-Beginner-to-Professional-Second-Edition-/tree/main/Chapter17/Activity17.01`.

In this activity, we requested data from a web server and processed the data it returned using the Go HTTP Client.

Sending data to a server

In addition to requesting data from a server, you will also want to send data to a server. The most common way of doing this is via a POST request. A POST request comes in two main parts: the URL and the body. The body of a POST request is where you put the data you want to send to the server. A common example of this is a login form. When we send a login request, we POST the body to the URL. The web server then checks that the login details within the body are correct and updates our login status. It responds to the request by telling the client whether it succeeded or not. In this section, you will learn how to send data to a server using a POST request.

Exercise 17.03 – sending a POST request to a web server using the Go HTTP Client

In this exercise, you will send a POST request to a web server containing a message. The web server will then respond with the same message so you can confirm that it received it:

1. Create a new directory, `Exercise17.03`. Within that directory, create two more directories, `server` and `client`. Then, within the `server` directory, create a file called `server.go` and write the following code. We will ignore error handling to keep in mind brevity for the exercise code, but in real-world applications, be sure to handle errors:

```
package main
import (
```

```
    "encoding/json"
    "log"
    "net/http"
)
type server struct{}
type messageData struct {
  Message string `json:"message"`
}
func (srv server) ServeHTTP(w http.ResponseWriter, r *http.
Request) {
  jsonDecoder := json.NewDecoder(r.Body)
  messageData := messageData{}
  err := jsonDecoder.Decode(&messageData)
  if err != nil {
    log.Fatal(err)
  }
  jsonBytes, _ := json.Marshal(messageData)
  log.Println(string(jsonBytes))
  w.Write(jsonBytes)
}
func main() {
  log.Fatal(http.ListenAndServe(":8080", server{}))
}
```

This creates a very basic web server that receives a JSON POST request and returs the message sent to it back to the client.

2. Once you have the server created. Navigate to the client directory and create a file called `client.go`. Add `package main` and the imports needed for the file:

```
package main
import (
  "bytes"
  "encoding/json"
  "fmt"
  "io"
  "log"
  "net/http"
)
```

3. Next, you need to create a struct for the data we want to send and receive. This will be the same as the struct used by the server to parse the request:

```
type messageData struct {
  Message string `json:"message"`
}
```

4. You then need to create the function to POST the data to the server. It should accept a messageData struct parameter as well as return a messageData struct:

```
func postDataAndReturnResponse(msg messageData) messageData {
```

5. To post the data to the server, you need to marshal the struct into bytes that the client can send to the server. To do this, you can use the json.Marshal function. Note, we are intentionally ommitting error handling here, but normally you will handle errors:

```
jsonBytes, _ := json.Marshal(msg)
```

6. Now that you have the bytes, you can use the http.Post function to send the POST request. Within the request, you just need to tell the function what URL to post to, what kind of data you are sending, and the data you want to send. In this case, the URL is http://localhost:8080. The content you are sending is application/json, and the data are the jsonBytes variable you just created. Together, it looks like this:

```
r, err := http.Post("http://localhost:8080", "application/
json", bytes.NewBuffer(jsonBytes))
if err != nil {
  log.Fatal(err)
}
```

7. After that, the rest of the function is the same as in the previous exercise. You read the response, parse out the data, and then return the data, which looks like this:

```
defer r.Body.Close()
data, err := io.ReadAll(r.Body)
if err != nil {
  log.Fatal(err)
}
message := messageData{}
err = json.Unmarshal(data, &message)
if err != nil {
  log.Fatal(err)
}
return message
}
```

8. Then, you need to call the postDataAndReturnResponse function from your main function. This time, however, you need to pass the message you want to send to the function. You just need to create an instance of the messageData struct and pass that to the function when you call it, which looks like this:

```
func main() {
  msg := messageData{Message: "Hi Server!"}
```

```
        data := postDataAndReturnResponse(msg)
        fmt.Println(data.Message)
    }
```

9. To run this exercise, you need to carry out two steps. The first is to navigate to the server directory in your terminal and run go run server.go. This will start the web server. In a second terminal window, navigate to the client directory and run go run main. go. This will start the client and connect to the server. It should output the following message from the server:

```
client [git::master *] > go run main.go
Hi Server!
```

Figure 17.5: Expected output

In this exercise, you sent a POST request to the server. The server parsed the request and sent the same message back to you. If you change the message sent to the server, you should see the response from the server sending back the new message.

Uploading files in a POST request

Another common example of data you might want to post to a web server is a file from your local computer. This is how websites allow users to upload their photos and so on. As you can imagine, this is more complex than sending simple form data. To achieve this, the file needs to be read first and then wrapped in a format that the server can understand. It can then be sent in a POST request to the server in what's called a multipart form. You will learn how to read a file and upload it to a server using Go.

Exercise 17.04 – uploading a file to a web server via a POST request

In this exercise, you will read in a local file and then upload it to a web server. You can then check that the web server saved the file you uploaded:

Create a new directory, Exercise17.04. Within that directory, create two more directories, server and client. Then, within the server directory, create a file called server.go and write the following code:

```
func (srv server) ServeHTTP(w http.ResponseWriter, r *http.Request) {
    uploadedFile, uploadedFileHeader, err := r.FormFile("myFile")
    if err != nil {
        log.Fatal(err)
    }
    defer uploadedFile.Close()
    fileContent, err := io.ReadAll(uploadedFile)
```

```
if err != nil {
    log.Fatal(err)
}
```

1. The full code for this step is available at:`https://github.com/PacktPublishing/`
    `Go-Programming-From-Beginner-to-Professional-Second-Edition-/`
    `tree/main/Chapter17` .

    This creates a very basic web server that receives a multipart form POST request and saves the
    file within the form. A multipart form is a content type used for encoding files or binary data
    along with textual key-value pairs in HTTP requests. We are using this encoding to include
    files as part of the form data, as this is the standard way to handle file uploads in HTML forms.

2. Once you have created the server, navigate to the client directory and create a file called
    `client.go`. Add `package main` and the imports needed for the file:

    ```
    package main
    import (
        "bytes"
        "fmt"
        "io"
        "io"
        "log"
        "mime/multipart"
        "net/http"
        "os"
    )
    ```

3. You then need to create a function to call that you will give a filename to. The function will
    read in the file, upload it to the server, and return the server's response:

    ```
    func postFileAndReturnResponse(filename string) string {
    ```

4. You need to create a buffer that you can write the file bytes to and then create a writer to allow
    bytes to write into it:

    ```
    fileDataBuffer := bytes.Buffer{}
    multipartWriter := multipart.NewWriter(&fileDataBuffer)
    ```

5. Open the file from your local computer using the following command:

    ```
    file, err := os.Open(filename)
    if err != nil {
        log.Fatal(err)
    }
    ```

6. Once you have opened the local file, you need to create `formFile`. This wraps the file data in the right format to upload it to the server:

```
formFile, err := multipartWriter.CreateFormFile("myFile",
file.Name())
if err != nil {
  log.Fatal(err)
}
```

7. Copy the bytes from the local file into the form file and then close the form file writer so that it knows no more data will be added:

```
_, err = io.Copy(formFile, file)
if err != nil {
  log.Fatal(err)
}
multipartWriter.Close()
```

8. Next, you need to create the POST request that you want to send to the server. In the previous exercises, we used shortcut functions such as `http.Post`. However, in this exercise, we need more control over the data being sent. That means we'll need to create `http.Request`. In this case, you're creating a POST request that you will send to `http://localhost:8080`. As we are uploading a file, the bytes buffer also needs to be included in the request; this looks like the following:

```
req, err := http.NewRequest("POST", "http://localhost:8080",
&fileDataBuffer)
if err != nil {
  log.Fatal(err)
}
```

9. You then need to set the `Content-Type` request header. This tells the server about the content of the file so it knows how to handle the upload:

```
req.Header.Set("Content-Type", multipartWriter.
FormDataContentType())
```

10. Send the request as follows:

```
response, err := http.DefaultClient.Do(req)
if err != nil {
  log.Fatal(err)
}
```

11. After you have sent the request, we can read in the response and return the data within it:

```
defer response.Body.Close()
data, err := io.ReadAll(response.Body)
```

```go
    if err != nil {
       log.Fatal(err)
    }
    return string(data)
}
```

12. Finally, you just need to call the `postFileAndReturnResponse` function and tell it what file to upload:

```go
func main() {
    data := postFileAndReturnResponse("./test.txt")
    fmt.Println(data)
}
```

13. To run this, you need to carry out two steps. The first is to navigate to the `server` directory in your terminal and run `go run server.go`. This will start the web server:

```
go run server.go
```

14. Next, in the `client` directory, create a file named `test.txt` and put a few lines of text in it.

15. In a second terminal window, navigate to the `client` directory and run `go run client.go`. This will start the client and connect to the server:

```
go run client.go
```

16. The client will then read in `test.txt` and upload it to the server. The client should give the following output:

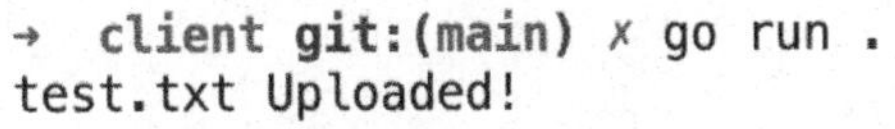

```
→  client git:(main) ✗ go run .
test.txt Uploaded!
```

Figure 17.6: Expected client output

Then, if you navigate to the `server` directory, you should see that the `test.txt` file has now appeared:

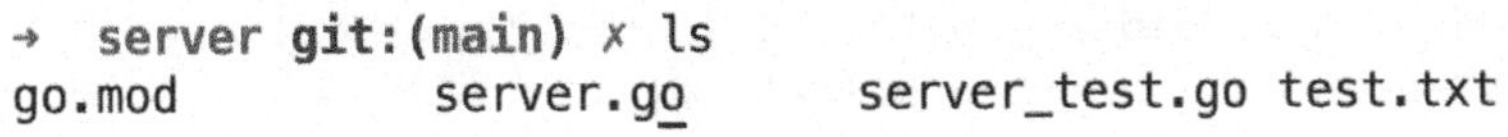

```
→  server git:(main) ✗ ls
go.mod          server.go       server_test.go test.txt
```

Figure 17.7: Expected text file present

In this exercise, you sent a file to a web server using the Go HTTP Client. This approach works well with small files but can lead to memory overflow in the case of big files. Therefore, you may have to adapt the code if using large files to use alternative methods, such as `os.Pipe()`. In this example, with a small file, you had the file read in from the disk, formatted it into a POST request, and sent the data to the server. You saw the use of multipart form file uploading. We also saw the use of Go `http.DefaultClient`. `DefaultClient` works great; however, it should never be used in a production environment as it does not set a default timeout for HTTP requests. When making HTTP requests, it is crucial to set timeouts to ensure that your application does not hang indefinitely in the case of network issues or unresponsive servers.

Custom request headers

Sometimes there is more to a request than simply requesting or sending data. This information is stored within the request headers. A very common example of this is authorization headers. When you log into a server, it will respond with an authorization token. In all future requests sent to the server, you would include this token in the request's headers so the server knows you are the one making the requests. You will learn how to add an authorization token to requests later.

Exercise 17.05 – using custom headers and options with the Go HTTP Client

In this exercise, you will create your own HTTP client and set custom options on it. You will also set an authorization token in the request headers so the server knows it is you requesting the data:

1. Create a new directory, `Exercise17.05`. Within that directory, create two more directories, `server` and `client`. Then, within the `server` directory, create a file called `server.go` and write the following code:

```go
package main
import (
  "log"
  "net/http"
  "time"
)
type server struct{}
func (srv server) ServeHTTP(w http.ResponseWriter, r *http.
Request) {
  auth := r.Header.Get("Authorization")
  if auth != "superSecretToken" {
    w.WriteHeader(http.StatusUnauthorized)
    w.Write([]byte("Authorization token not recognized"))
    return
  }
  time.Sleep(10 * time.Second)
  msg := "hello client!"
  w.Write([]byte(msg))
}
func main() {
```

```
    log.Fatal(http.ListenAndServe(":8080", server{}))
}
```

This creates a very basic web server that receives a request, checks the authorization header is correct, waits 10 seconds, and then sends back data.

2. Once you have created the server, navigate to the client directory and create a file called `client.go`. Add `package main` and the imports needed for the file:

```
package main
import (
  "fmt"
  "io"
  "log"
  "net/http"
  "time"
)
```

3. Then, you need to create a function that will create an HTTP client, set the timeout limitations, and set the authorization header:

```
func getDataWithCustomOptionsAndReturnResponse() string {
```

4. You need to create your own HTTP client and set the timeout to 11 seconds:

```
client := http.Client{Timeout: 11 * time.Second}
```

5. You also need to create a request to send it to the server. You should create a GET request with the URL `http://localhost:8080`. No data will be sent in this request, so the data can be set to nil. You can use the `http.NewRequest` function to do this:

```
req, err := http.NewRequest("POST", "http://localhost:8080",
nil)
if err != nil {
  log.Fatal(err)
}
```

6. If you look at the server code again, you will notice that it checks for the `Authorization` request header, and it expects its value to be `superSecretToken`. So, you need to set the `Authorization` header in your request as well:

```
req.Header.Set("Authorization", "superSecretToken")
```

7. You then get the client you created to enact the request:

```
resp, err := client.Do(req)
if err != nil {
```

```
        log.Fatal(err)
    }
```

8. Then, you need to read in the response from the server and return the data:

```
    defer resp.Body.Close()
    data, err := io.ReadAll(resp.Body)
    if err != nil {
        log.Fatal(err)
    }
    return string(data)
}
```

9. Finally, you need to call the function you just created from the `main` function and log the data it returns:

```
func main() {
    data := getDataWithCustomOptionsAndReturnResponse()
    fmt.Println(data)
}
```

10. To run this exercise, you need to carry out two steps. The first is to navigate to the `server` directory in your terminal and run `go run server.go`. This will start the web server.

11. In a second terminal window, navigate to the directory you created `client` in.

12. To execute the client, run the following command:

```
go run client.go
```

This will start the client and connect to the server. The client will send the request to the server, and after 10 seconds, it should output the following:

```
→  client git:(main) ✗ go run client.go
hello client!
```

Figure 17.8: Expected output

> **Important note**
>
> Change the timeout settings in the client to under 10 seconds and see what happens. You can also change or remove the authorization header on the request and see what happens.

In this exercise, you learned how to add custom headers to a request. You learned about the common example of adding an authorization header, which is required by many APIs when you want to interact with them.

Activity 17.02 – sending data to a web server and checking whether the data was received using POST and GET

Imagine you are interacting with a web API, and you wish to send data to a web server. You then want to check whether the data was added. In this activity, you will do just that. You will send a POST request to the server and then request the data back using a GET request, parse the data, and print it out.

Follow these steps to get the desired outcome:

1. Create a directory called `Activity17.02`.

2. Create two subdirectories, one called `client` and one called `server`.

3. In the `server` directory, create a file called `server.go`.

4. Add the server code to the `server.go` file.

5. Start the server by calling `go run server.go` in the server directory.

6. In the `client` directory, create a file called `client.go`.

7. In `client.go`, add the necessary imports.

8. Create structs to host the request data, which looks like the following: `{"name":"Electric"}`.

9. Create structs to parse the response data, which looks like the following: `{"ok":true}`.

10. Create an `addNameAndParseResponse` function that posts a name to the server.

11. Create a `getDataAndParseResponse` function that parses the server response.

12. Send a POST request to the server to add names.

13. Send a GET request to the server.

14. Parse the response into a struct.

15. Loop through the struct and print the names.

This is the expected output:

```
→  client git:(main) x go run client.go
2024/03/07 16:31:02 Electric
2024/03/07 16:31:02 Boogaloo
```

Figure 17.9: Possible output

> **Important note**
>
> The solution for this activity can be found at https://github.com/PacktPublishing/
> Go-Programming-From-Beginner-to-Professional-Second-Edition-/
> tree/main/Chapter17/Activity17.02.

In this activity, you saw how to send data to a web server using a POST request and then how to request data from the server to ensure it was updated using a GET request. Interacting with a server in this way is very common when programming professionally.

Summary

HTTP clients are used to interact with web servers. They are used to send different types of requests to a server (for example, GET or POST requests) and then react to the response returned by the server. A web browser is a type of HTTP client that will send a GET request to a web server and display the HTML data it returns. In Go, you created your own HTTP client and did the same thing, sending a GET request to `https://www.google.com` and then logging the response returned by the server. You also learned about the components of a URL and that you can control what you request from a server by changing the URL.

There is also more to web servers than simply requesting HTML data. You learned that they can return structured data in the form of JSON, which can be parsed and used in your code. Data can also be sent to a server using POST requests, allowing you to send form data to a server. However, the data sent to a server isn't limited to just form data: you can also upload files to a server using a POST request.

There are also ways to customize the requests you send. You learned about the common example of authorization, where you add a token to the header of HTTP requests so that a server can tell who is making that request.

Part 6: Professional

Having gained proficiency in utilizing Go for real-world tasks, it's time to equip you with the tools and techniques essential for professional programming in Go.

This section encompasses advanced topics and best practices aimed at elevating your programming skills to a professional level.

This section includes the following chapters:

- *Chapter 18, Concurrent Work*
- *Chapter 19, Testing*
- *Chapter 20, Using Go Tools*
- *Chapter 21, Go in the Cloud*

18

Concurrent Work

Overview

This chapter introduces you to Go features that will allow you to perform concurrent work, or, in other words, achieve concurrency. The first feature you will learn is called a Goroutine. You'll learn what a Goroutine is and how you can use it to achieve concurrency. Then, you'll learn how to utilize `WaitGroups` to synchronize the execution of several Goroutines. You will also learn how to implement synchronized and thread-safe changes to variables shared across different Goroutines using atomic changes. To synchronize more complex changes, you will work with mutexes.

Later in the chapter, you will experiment with the functionalities of channels and use message tracking to track the completion of a task. We will also cover the importance of concurrency, concurrency patterns, and more.

Technical requirements

For this chapter, you'll require Go version 1.21 or higher. The code for this chapter can be found at: `https://github.com/PacktPublishing/Go-Programming-From-Beginner-to-Professional-Second-Edition-/tree/main/Chapter18`.

Introduction

There is software that's meant to be used by a single user, and most of what you've learned so far in this book allows you to develop such applications. There is other software, however, that is meant to be used by several users at the same time. An example of this is a web server. You created web servers in *Chapter 16, Web Servers*. They are designed to serve websites or web applications that are generally used by thousands of users at the same time.

When multiple users are accessing a web server, it sometimes needs to perform a series of actions that are totally independent and whose result is the only thing that matters to the final output. All these situations call for a type of programming in which different tasks can be executed at the same time, independently from each other. Some languages allow parallel computation, where tasks are computed simultaneously.

In concurrent programming, when a task starts, all other tasks start as well, but instead of completing them one by one, the machine performs a bit of each task at the same time. While Go allows concurrent programming, tasks can also be performed in parallel when the machine has multiple cores. From the perspective of the programmer, however, this distinction is not that important, as tasks are created with the idea that they will be performed in parallel and in whatever way the machine will perform them. Let's find out more in this chapter.

Goroutines

Imagine several people have some nails to hammer into a wall. Each person has a different number of nails and a different area of the wall, but there is only one hammer. Each person uses the hammer for one nail, then passes the hammer to the next person, and so on. The person with the fewest nails will finish earlier, but they will all share the same hammer; this is how Goroutines work.

Using Goroutines, Go allows multiple tasks to run at the same time (they are also called coroutines). These are routines (read tasks) that can co-run inside the same process but are totally concurrent. Goroutines do not share memory, which is why they are different from threads. However, we will see how easy it is to pass variables across them in your code and how this might lead to some unexpected behavior.

Writing a Goroutine is nothing special; they are just normal functions. Each function can easily become a Goroutine; all we must do is write the word go before calling the function.

Let us consider a function called hello():

```
func hello() {
    fmt.Println("hello world")
}
```

To call our function as a Goroutine, we do the following:

```
go hello()
```

The function will run as a Goroutine. What this means can be understood better through the following code:

```
func main() {
    fmt.Println("Start")
    go hello()
    fmt.Println("End")
```

The code starts by printing `Start`, then it calls the `hello()` function. Then, the execution goes straight to printing End without waiting for the `hello()` function to complete. No matter how long it takes to run the `hello()` function, the `main()` function will not care about the `hello()` function as these functions will run independently. To better understand how this works, let's do some exercises.

> **Note**
>
> The important thing to remember is that Go is not a parallel language but concurrent, which means that Goroutines do not work in an independent manner, but each Goroutine is split into smaller parts and each Goroutine runs one of its subparts at a time.

Exercise 18.01 – using concurrent Goroutines

Let's imagine we want to make two calculations. First, we sum all numbers from 1 to 10, then numbers from 1 to 100. To save time, we want to make both calculations happen independently and see both results at the same time:

1. Create a new folder in your filesystem, and, inside it, create a `main.go` file and write the following:

    ```
    package main
    import "fmt"
    ```

2. Create a function to sum two numbers:

    ```
    func sum(from, to int) int {
      res := 0
      for i := from; i<=to; i++ {
        res += i
      }
      return res
    }
    ```

    This accepts two integers as extremes (the minimum and maximum of an interval) and returns the sum of all numbers in the range between these two extremes.

3. Create a `main()` function, which sums numbers 1 and 100, then print the result:

    ```
    func main() {
      s1 := sum(1, 100)
      fmt.Println(s1)
    }
    ```

4. Run the program:

    ```
    go run main.go
    ```

You will see the following output:

```
5050
```

5. Now, let's introduce some concurrency. Modify the main() function to look like this:

```
func main() {
   var s1 int
   go func() {
      s1 = sum(1, 100)
   }()
   fmt.Println(s1)
}
```

Here, we are running an anonymous function that assigns the value s1 to the sum as before, but if we run the code, the result will be 0. If you try to remove the term go before the func() part, you will see that the result is 5050. In this case, the anonymous function will run and start summing the numbers, but then there is a call to fmt.Println, which prints the value of s1. Here, the program waits for the sum() function to end before printing the value of s1, hence returning the correct result.

If we call the function and prepend the go word, the program prints the current value of s1 while the function is still computing the sum, which is still 0, and terminates.

Let's call the sum() function twice with two different ranges. Modify the main() function:

```
func main() {
   var s1, s2 int
   go func() {
      s1 = sum(1, 100)
   }()
   s2 = sum(1, 10)
   fmt.Println(s1, s2)
}
```

If you run this program, it will print numbers 0 and 55. This is because the concurrent function, go func(), does not have the time to return the result. The main() function is faster as it must count to 55 and not 5050, so the program terminates before the concurrent function is finished.

To solve this problem, we want to find a way to wait for the *concurrent* function to finish. There are some correct ways to do this, but for now, let's do something quite crude but effective, which is to wait for a fixed amount of time. To do so, just add this line before the fmt.Println command:

```
time.Sleep(time.Second)
```

6. Modify the import section, just below the package main instruction, to look as follows:

```
import (
    "log"
    "time"
)
```

If you run your program now, you should see 5050 55 printed on the screen.

7. In the main() function, write code for the log to be printed:

```
log.Println(s1, s2)
```

8. If you run your program now, you will see the same output again, 5050 55, but prepended by a timestamp representing when you ran the code:

```
2024/01/25 19:23:00 5050 55
```

As you can see, the calculations have happened concurrently, and we have received both outputs at the same time.

> **Note**
>
> The full code for this exercise is available at https://github.com/PacktPublishing/
> Go-Programming-From-Beginner-to-Professional-Second-Edition-/
> tree/main/Chapter18.

WaitGroup

In the previous exercise, we used a not-so-elegant method to ensure that the Goroutine ended by making the main Goroutine wait for a second. The important thing to understand is that even if a program does not explicitly use Goroutines via the go call, it still uses one Goroutine, which is the main routine. When we run our program and create a new Goroutine, we are running two Goroutines: the main one and the one we just created. In order to synchronize these two Goroutines, Go gives us a function called WaitGroup. You can define a WaitGroup using the following code:

```
wg := sync.WaitGroup{}
```

WaitGroup needs the sync package to be imported. Typical code using the WaitGroup will be something like this:

```
package main
import "sync"
func main() {
    wg := &sync.WaitGroup{}
    wg.Add(1)
```

```
.................. .
wg.Wait()
............ .
............ .
}
```

Here, we create a pointer to a new `WaitGroup`, then we mention that we are adding an asynchronous operation that adds `1` to the group using `wg.Add(1)`. This is essentially a counter holding the number of all concurrent Goroutines that are running. Later, we add the code that will run the concurrent call. At the end, we tell the `WaitGroup` to wait for the Goroutines to end using `wg.Wait()`.

How does the `WaitGroup` know that the routines are complete? Well, we need to explicitly tell the `WaitGroup` about it inside the Goroutine with the following:

```
wg.Done()
```

This must reside at the end of the called Goroutine. We will see this in the next exercise.

Exercise 18.02 – experimenting with WaitGroup

Let's say we calculate the addition in *Exercise 18.01, Using concurrent Goroutines*, again using a Goroutine that runs concurrently with the main process. However, this time, we want to use a `WaitGroup` to synchronize the results. We have a few changes to make. Essentially, the `sum()` function needs to accept a new parameter for the `WaitGroup`, and there is no need to use the `time` package. Many people new to concurrency add `time.Sleep` to wait for Goroutines to finish. This intentional delay is self-defeating and makes no practical sense outside of testing, as the purpose of Goroutines is to speed up the overall execution of things:

1. Create a new folder and a `main.go` file inside it. The package and import parts of your file will be as follows:

    ```
    package main
    import (
        "log"
        "sync"
    )
    ```

    Here, we define the package as the `main` package and then import the `log` and `sync` packages. `log` will be used again to print out messages, and `sync` will be used for the `WaitGroup`.

2. Next, write a `sum()` function:

    ```
    func sum(from,to int, wg *sync.WaitGroup, res *int) {
    ```

    Now, we add a parameter called `wg` with a pointer to `sync.WaitGroup` along with the result parameter. In the previous exercise, we wrapped the `sum()` function with an anonymous function that ran as a Goroutine. Here, we want to avoid that, but we need to somehow get the result of the sum() function. Hence, we pass an extra parameter as a pointer that will return the correct value.

3. Create a loop to increment the sum() function:

```
*res = 0
for i := from; i <=to ; i++ {
  *res += i
}
```

Here, we set the value of what is held by the res pointer to 0, and then we use the same loop that we saw earlier, but again associating the sum() function with the value pointed by the res parameter.

4. We can now complete this function:

```
wg.Done()}
```

Here, we tell the WaitGroup that this Goroutine is completed, and then we return.

5. Now, let's write a main() function, which will set up the variables and then run the Goroutine that calculates the sum. We will then wait for the Goroutine to finish and display the result:

```
func main() {
  s1 := 0
  wg := &sync.WaitGroup{}
```

Here, the main() function is defined, and then a variable called s1 is set to 0. Also, a pointer to the WaitGroup is created.

6. Add one to the count of the WaitGroup and then run the Goroutine:

```
wg.Add(1)
go sum(1,100, wg, &s1)
```

This code notifies the WaitGroup that there is one Goroutine running and then creates a new Goroutine calculating the sum. The sum() function will call the wg.Done() method to notify the WaitGroup of its completion.

7. We need to wait for the Goroutine to finish. To do so, write the following:

```
wg.Wait()
log.Println(s1)
}
```

This also logs the result to the standard output.

8. Run the program:

```
go run main.go
```

You will see the log output for the function using `WaitGroups`, as follows, with the timestamp:

```
2024/01/25 19:24:51 5050
```

With this exercise, we have explored the functionality of `WaitGroup` by synchronizing Goroutines in our code.

Race conditions

One important thing to consider is that whenever we run multiple functions concurrently, we have no guarantee in what order each instruction in each function will be performed. In many architectures, this is not a problem. Some functions are not connected in any way with other functions, and whatever a function does in its Goroutine does not affect the actions performed in other Goroutines. This is, however, not always true. The first situation we can think of is when some functions need to share the same parameter. Some functions will read from this parameter, while others will write to this parameter. As we do not know which operation will run first, there is a high likelihood that one function will override the value updated by another function. Let's see an example that explains this situation:

```
func next(v *int) {
    c := *v
    *v = c + 1
}
```

This function takes a pointer to an integer as a parameter. It is a pointer because we want to run several Goroutines with the `next()` function and update `v`. If we run the following code, we would expect that `a` will hold the value 3:

```
a := 0
next(&a)
next(&a)
next(&a)
```

This is perfectly fine. However, what if we run the following code:

```
a := 0
go next(&a)
go next(&a)
go next(&a)
```

In this case, we might see that `a` holds 3, or 2, or 1. Why would this happen? Because when a function executes the following statement, the value of `v` might be 0 for all functions running in independent Goroutines:

```
c := *v
```

If this happens, then each function will set v to c + 1, which means none of the Goroutines are aware of what the other Goroutines are doing and override any changes made by another Goroutine. This problem is called a **race condition** and happens every time we work with shared resources without taking precautions. Fortunately, we have several ways to prevent this situation and to make sure that the same change is made only once. We will look at these solutions in the next sections, and we will explore the situation we just described in more detail, with a proper solution and race detection.

Atomic operations

Let's imagine we want to run independent functions again. However, in this case, we want to modify the value held by a variable. We still want to sum the numbers from 1 to 100, but we want to split the work into two concurrent Goroutines. We can sum the numbers from 1 to 50 in one routine and the numbers from 51 to 100 in another routine. At the end, we will still need to receive the value of 5050, but two different routines can add a number at the same time to the same variable. Let's see an example with only four numbers where we want to sum 1, 2, 3, and 4, and the result is 10.

Think of it like having a variable called s := 0 and then making a loop where the value of s becomes the following:

```
s = 0
s = 1
s = 3 // (1 + 2)
s = 6
s = 10
```

However, we could also have the following loop. In this case, the order in which the numbers are summed is different:

```
s = 0
s = 1
s = 4 // 3 + 1, the previous value of 1
s = 6 // 2 + 4 the previous value of 4
s = 10
```

Essentially, this is just the commutative property of the sum, but this gives us a hint that we can split the sum into two or more concurrent calls. The problem that arises here is that all the functions need to manipulate the same variable, s, which can lead to race conditions and incorrect final values. A race condition happens when two processes change the same variable, and one process overrides the changes made by another process without considering the previous change. Thankfully, we have a package called atomic that allows us to safely modify variables across Goroutines.

We will look at how this package works soon, but, for now, all you need to know is that this package has some functions for executing simple concurrent safe operations on variables. Let's look at an example:

```
func AddInt32(addr *int32, delta int32) (new int32)
```

This code takes a pointer to int32 and modifies it by adding the value it points at to the value of delta. If addr holds a value of 2 and delta is 4, after calling this function, addr will hold 6.

Exercise 18.03 – an atomic change

In this exercise, we want to calculate the sum of all numbers between 1 and 100 but with more concurrent Goroutines – let's say 4. So, we have one function summing in the range of 1-25, one in the range of 26-50, then 51-75, and finally 76-100. We will use what we've learned about atomic operations and WaitGroups:

1. Create a new folder and a main.go file. Inside it, write the following code:

    ```
    package main
    import (
        "log"
        "sync"
        "sync/atomic"
    )
    ```

    This will import the same packages used for the previous exercises, in addition to the sync/atomic package.

2. The next step is to refactor the sum() function from *Exercise 19.02, Experimenting with WaitGroup*, to use the atomic package:

    ```
    func sum(from, to int, wg *sync.WaitGroup, res *int32) {
    ```

    Here, we just changed res from int to *int32. The reason for this is that the atomic operations available specifically for arithmetic operations only work on int32/64 and relative uint32/64.

3. At this point, write a loop to add each number to the total:

    ```
    for i := from; i <= to; i++ {
        atomic.AddInt32(res, int32(i))
    }
    wg.Done()
    return
    }
    ```

    As you can see, instead of assigning the value of res as 0, we are now adding i to the total value held by res. The rest of the code is unchanged.

4. The next step is to write a `main()` function to calculate the sum in four different Goroutines:

```go
func main() {
    s1 := int32(0)
    wg := &sync.WaitGroup{}
```

Here, we set `s1` to an `int32` type rather than `int` so that we can send it as a parameter to the `sum()` function. Then, we create a pointer to `WaitGroup`.

5. Now, tell the `WaitGroup` that we will have four Goroutines running:

```go
wg.Add(4)
```

6. Now, run four Goroutines performing the sum over four ranges: 1-25, 26-50, 51-75, and 76-100:

```go
go sum(1, 25, wg, &s1)
go sum(26, 50, wg, &s1)
go sum(51, 75, wg, &s1)
go sum(76, 100, wg, &s1)
```

7. Now, add the code that waits for the routines to complete and print the result:

```go
wg.Wait()
log.Println(s1)
}
```

8. Now, run the code with the following:

```go
go run main.go
```

You will then see something like this:

```
2024/01/25 19:26:04 5050
```

The actual date will be different because it depends on when you run this code.

9. Now, let's test the code. We will use it to show you what it means to have a race condition, why we use this `atomic` package, and what concurrency safety is. Here is the test code:

```go
package main
import (
    "bytes"
    "log"
    "testing"
)
func Test_Main(t *testing.T) {
    for i:=0; i < 10000; i++ {
        var s bytes.Buffer
        log.SetOutput(&s)
```

```
        log.SetFlags(0)
        main()
        if s.String() != "5050\n" {
          t.Error(s.String())
        }
      }
    }
```

We will run the same test 10,000 times.

10. Run your test:

```
   go test
```

The result of the test on atomic changes is as follows:

```
PASS
ok parallelwork 0.048s
```

11. And now, add the -race flag:

```
   go test -race
```

The output when running these tests with the -race flag is as follows:

```
PASS
ok parallelwork 3.417s
```

Again, everything is fine so far.

12. Let's now remove the sync/atomic import and modify the sum() function where you see this line:

```
   atomic.AddInt32(res, int32(i))
```

13. Change it to this:

```
   *res = *res + int32(i)
```

14. Now, run your program:

```
   go run main.go
```

15. The log output for a non-atomic change stays the same when using pointers:

```
2024/01/25 19:30:47 5050
```

16. But if you try running the test multiple times, you may see some different results, even though, in this case, that is quite unlikely. At this point, however, try running the tests with the -race flag:

```
go test -race
```

You will see the following output:

```
==================
WARNING: DATA RACE
Read at 0x00c00009a15c by goroutine 7:
  github.com/packt-book/Go-Programming---From-Beginner-to-Professional-Second-Edition-/Chapter18/Exercise18%2e03.sum()
      /Users/samcoyle/go/src/github.com/packt-book/Go-Programming---From-Beginner-to-Professional-Second-Edition-/Chapter18/Exercise18.03/main.go:10 +0x44
  github.com/packt-book/Go-Programming---From-Beginner-to-Professional-Second-Edition-/Chapter18/Exercise18%2e03.main.func1()
      /Users/samcoyle/go/src/github.com/packt-book/Go-Programming---From-Beginner-to-Professional-Second-Edition-/Chapter18/Exercise18.03/main.go:22 +0x48

Previous write at 0x00c00009a15c by goroutine 8:
  github.com/packt-book/Go-Programming---From-Beginner-to-Professional-Second-Edition-/Chapter18/Exercise18%2e03.sum()
      /Users/samcoyle/go/src/github.com/packt-book/Go-Programming---From-Beginner-to-Professional-Second-Edition-/Chapter18/Exercise18.03/main.go:10 +0x54
  github.com/packt-book/Go-Programming---From-Beginner-to-Professional-Second-Edition-/Chapter18/Exercise18%2e03.main.func2()
      /Users/samcoyle/go/src/github.com/packt-book/Go-Programming---From-Beginner-to-Professional-Second-Edition-/Chapter18/Exercise18.03/main.go:23 +0x48

Goroutine 7 (running) created at:
  github.com/packt-book/Go-Programming---From-Beginner-to-Professional-Second-Edition-/Chapter18/Exercise18%2e03.main()
      /Users/samcoyle/go/src/github.com/packt-book/Go-Programming---From-Beginner-to-Professional-Second-Edition-/Chapter18/Exercise18.03/main.go:22 +0x104
  github.com/packt-book/Go-Programming---From-Beginner-to-Professional-Second-Edition-/Chapter18/Exercise18%2e03.Test_Main()
      /Users/samcoyle/go/src/github.com/packt-book/Go-Programming---From-Beginner-to-Professional-Second-Edition-/Chapter18/Exercise18.03/main_test.go:15 +0xd8
  testing.tRunner()
      /usr/local/go/src/testing/testing.go:1595 +0x194
  testing.(*T).Run.func1()
      /usr/local/go/src/testing/testing.go:1648 +0x40
```

Figure 18.1: Race conditions arise when using the pointer here

> **Note**
>
> GCC must be installed to run this code. Information on installation instructions can be found at https://go.dev/doc/install/gccgo.

1. Now, let's run the code without the `-race` flag:

```
--- FAIL: Test_Main (0.02s)
    main_test.go:18: 2850

    main_test.go:18: 4856

    main_test.go:18: 4780

    ...

    main_test.go:18: 4516

    main_test.go:18: 2850

    main_test.go:18: 4555

    main_test.go:18: 4555

    main_test.go:18: 4803

    main_test.go:18: 4100

    main_test.go:18: 4100

    main_test.go:18: 4756

    main_test.go:18: 4516

    main_test.go:18: 4901
FAIL
exit status 1
FAIL    parallelwork    0.249s
```

Figure 18.2: Stack trace with racing conditions

> **Note**
>
> ... in *Figure 18.2* denotes some lines of output that I removed to make the visual more digestible.

By running the code several times, you can see different results because each routine can change the value of `s1` at any time and in any order, which we cannot know in advance.

In this exercise, you've learned how to use the `atomic` package to safely modify variables shared by multiple Goroutines. You've learned how direct access to the same variable from different Goroutines can be dangerous and how to use the `atomic` package to avoid this situation. We also saw how to work with tests in Go. This topic will be covered more thoroughly in the next chapter.

> **Note**
>
> The full code for this exercise is available at `https://github.com/PacktPublishing/`
> `Go-Programming-From-Beginner-to-Professional-Second-Edition-/`
> `tree/main/Chapter18/Exercise18.03`.

Invisible concurrency

We've seen in the previous exercise the effects of concurrency through race conditions, but we want to see them in practice. It is easy to understand that concurrency problems are difficult to visualize as they do not manifest in the same way every time we run a program. That's why we are focusing on finding ways to synchronize concurrent work. One easy way to visualize it, however, but that is difficult to use in tests, is to print out each concurrent routine and see the order in which these routines are called. In the previous exercise, for example, we could have sent another parameter with a name and printed the name of the function at each iteration in the `for` loop.

If we want to see the effects of concurrency and still be able to test it, we could use the `atomic` package again, this time with strings so that we can build a string containing a message from each Goroutine. For this scenario, we will use the `sync` package again, but we will not make use of atomic operations. Instead, we will use a new struct called `Mutex`. A mutex, short for *mutual exclusion*, serves as a synchronization primitive in Go, allowing multiple Goroutines to coordinate access to shared resources. When a Goroutine acquires a mutex, it locks it, ensuring exclusive access to the critical section of code. This prevents other Goroutines from accessing the same resource until the mutex is unlocked. Once the critical section execution is complete, the mutex is unlocked, allowing other Goroutines to acquire it and proceed with their execution concurrently. Let's see how we can use it. First, it needs the `sync` package to be imported. Then, we create a mutex like this:

```
mtx := sync.Mutex{}
```

But most of the time, we want to pass a mutex across several functions, so we'd better create a pointer to a mutex:

```
mtx := &sync.Mutex{}
```

This ensures we use the same mutex everywhere. It is important to use the same mutex, but the reason why the mutex must be only one will be clear after analyzing the methods in the `Mutex` struct. If all Goroutines have `mtx.Lock()` before modifying a value in a critical section of code such as in the following case, then only one Goroutine at a time can modify the variable due to the lock:

```
mtx.Lock()
s = s + 5
```

The preceding code snippet will lock the execution of all the routines, except the one that will change the variable. At this point, we will add 5 to the current value of s. After this, we release the lock using the following command so that any other Goroutine can modify the value of s:

```
mtx.Unlock()
```

From now on, any following code will run concurrently. We will see later some better ways to ensure safety when we modify a variable, but, for now, do not worry about adding much code between the lock/unlock part. The more code there is between these constructs, the less concurrent your code will be. So, you should lock the execution of the program, add only the logic required to ensure safety, unlock, and then carry on with the execution of the rest of the code, which does not touch the shared variables.

One important thing to notice is that the order of asynchronously performed code can change. This is because Goroutines run independently and you cannot know which one runs first. Furthermore, mutex-protected code can only be run by one Goroutine at a time, and you should then not rely on Goroutines to order things correctly; you might need to order your results afterward if you need a specific order.

Channels

We've seen how to create concurrent code via Goroutines, how to synchronize it with `WaitGroup`, how to perform atomic operations, and how to temporarily stop concurrency to synchronize access to shared variables. We will now introduce a different concept – the channel, which is typical of Go. A channel is what the name essentially suggests – it's something where messages can be piped, and any Goroutine can send or receive messages through a channel. Similar to that of a slice, a channel is created the following way:

```
var ch chan int
ch = make(chan int)
```

Of course, it is possible to instantiate the channel directly with the following:

```
ch := make(chan int)
```

Just like with slices, we can also do the following:

```
ch := make(chan int, 10)
```

Here, a channel is created with a buffer of 10 items.

A channel can be of any type, such as integer, Boolean, float, and any struct that can be defined, and even slices and pointers, though the last two are generally used less frequently.

Channels can be passed as parameters to functions, and that's how different Goroutines can share content. Let's see how to send a message to a channel:

```
ch <- 2
```

In this case, we send the value of 2 to the preceding ch channel, which is a channel of integers. Of course, trying to send something other than an integer to an integer channel will cause an error.

After sending a message, we need to be able to receive a message from a channel. To do that, we can just do the following:

```
<- ch
```

Doing this ensures that the message is received; however, the message is not stored. It might seem useless to lose the message, but we will see that it might make sense. Nevertheless, we might want to keep the value received from the channel, and we can do so by storing the value in a new variable:

```
i := <- ch
```

Let's see a simple program that shows us how to use what we've learned so far:

```
package main
import "log"
func main() {
  ch := make(chan int, 1)
  ch <- 1
  i := <- ch
  log.Println(i)
}
```

This program creates a new channel, pipes the integer 1 in, then reads it, and finally prints out the value of i, which should be 1. This code is not that useful in practice, but with a small change, we can see something interesting. Let's make the channel unbuffered by changing the channel definition to the following:

```
ch := make(chan int)
```

If you run the code, you will get the following output:

```
fatal error: all goroutines are asleep - deadlock!
goroutine 1 [chan send]:
main.main()
    /Users/ samcoyle/go/src/github.com/packt-book/Go-Programming---
From-Beginner-to-Professional-Second-Edition-/Chapter19/Exercise19.04/
main.go:8 +0x59Process finished with exit code 2
```

The message may be different depending on the version of Go you are using. Also, some errors such as these have been introduced in newer versions. In older versions, though, the compiler was more permissive. In this specific case, the problem is simple: if we do not know how big the channel is, the Goroutines wait indefinitely, and this is called a deadlock. You can think of an unbuffered channel as having a capacity of zero. If we try to put anything into it, it won't hold the item – instead, it will block until we can pass the item through the channel to a variable, for example. We will see later how to handle them, as they require more than one routine running. With only one Goroutine, after we send the message, we block the execution, and there is no other Goroutine able to receive the message; hence, we have a deadlock.

Before we go further, let's see one more characteristic of channels, which is that they can be closed. Channels need to be closed when the task they have been created for is finished. To close a channel, type in the following:

```
close(ch)
```

Alternatively, you can defer the closing, as shown in the following code snippet:

```
...
defer close(ch)
for i := 0; i < 100; i++ {
  ch <- i
}
return
```

In this case, after the `return` statement, the channel is closed as the closing is deferred to run after the `return` statement.

Exercise 18.04 – exchanging greeting messages via channels

In this exercise, we will use a Goroutine to send a greeting message, and then we will receive the greeting in the main process. The exercise is very simple and does not need concurrency, but it is a starting point to understand how message passing works:

1. Create a folder. In it, create a main.go file with the main package:

```
package main
import (
  "log"
)
```

2. Then, create a greeter() function:

```
func greet(ch chan string) {
  ch <- "Hello"
}
```

This function just sends a `Hello` message to a channel and ends.

3. Now, create a `main()` function where you instantiate a channel and pass it to the `greeter()` function:

```
func main() {
    ch := make(chan string)
    go greet(ch)
```

Here, only a channel of strings is created and passed as a parameter to the call to a new routine called `greet`.

4. Now, print the result and complete the function:

```
    log.Println(<-ch)
}
```

Here, we are printing whatever comes from the channel. The following part of the code returns a value, which is passed straight to the `Println` function:

```
<- ch
```

5. Run the program with the following:

```
go run main.go
```

You will see the following output:

```
2024/01/25 19:44:11 Hello
```

Now, we can see that the message has been delivered to the `main()` function through the channel.

In this exercise, you have seen how to use channels to make different Goroutines communicate with each other and synchronize their computations.

Exercise 18.05 – two-way message exchange with channels

What we want now is to send messages from the main Goroutine to the second Goroutine and then get a message back as a response. We will base our code on the previous one and expand it. The main Goroutine will send a `"Hello John"` message, while the second Goroutine will return `"Thanks"` for the message received, stating it in full, and will then add a `"Hello David"` message:

1. Create a folder. In it, create a `main.go` file with the `main` package:

```
package main
import (
    "fmt"
    "log"
)
```

With the necessary imports, we will use the `fmt` package to manipulate the strings.

2. Write a `greet()` function to return the expected messages:

```
func greet(ch chan string) {
    msg := <- ch
    ch <- fmt.Sprintf("Thanks for %s", msg)
    ch <- "Hello David"
}
```

The `greet()` function signature has not changed. However, now, before sending a message, it will first wait for a message and then reply. After receiving the message, this function sends a message back thanking for the greeting and then sends its own greeting.

3. Now, create a `main()` function and call the `greet()` function as a Goroutine:

```
func main() {
    ch := make(chan string)
    go greet(ch)
```

Here, the `main()` function is created, and a string channel is instantiated. Then, the second Goroutine is started. Next, we need to send the first message from the main Goroutine to the second, which is currently waiting.

4. Now, to send a `"Hello John"` message to the channel, write the following code:

```
ch <- "Hello John"
```

5. And finally, add the code that waits for the messages to come back before printing them:

```
log.Println(<-ch)
log.Println(<-ch)
}
```

You can see that you need to log twice as you expect two messages to come back. In many cases, you will use a loop to retrieve all the messages, which we will see in the next exercise. For now, try to run your code, and you will see something as follows:

```
2024/01/25 19:44:49 Thanks for Hello John
2024/01/25 19:44:49 Hello David
```

From the output, you can see that both messages have been received through the channel.

In this exercise, you have learned how a Goroutine can both send and receive messages through the same channel and that two Goroutines can exchange messages through the same channel in both directions.

Exercise 18.06 – summing numbers from everywhere

Imagine you want to add a few numbers, but the numbers come from several sources. They might come from a feed or from a database; we just do not know which numbers we are going to add and where they come from. However, we need to add them all in one place. In this exercise, we will have four Goroutines sending numbers in particular ranges, and the main Goroutine, which will calculate their sum:

1. Let's start by creating a new folder and the main file. After you've done that, write the package and imports:

```
package main
import (
  "log"
  "time"
)
```

Here, we also include the `time` package, which we will use to do a small trick that will help us to better visualize the effects of concurrency.

2. Now, write a `push()` function:

```
func push(from, to int, out chan int) {
  for i := from; i <= to; i++ {
    out <- i
    time.Sleep(time.Microsecond)
  }
}
```

This sends all the numbers in the `from, to` range to the channel. After each message is sent, the Goroutine sleeps for a microsecond so that another Goroutine will pick up the work.

3. Now, write a `main()` function:

```
func main() {
  s1 := 0
  ch := make(chan int, 100)
```

This code creates a variable for the final sum, `s1`, and one for the channel, `ch`, which has a buffer of 100.

4. Now, create four `go` routines:

```
go push(1, 25, ch)
go push(26, 50, ch)
go push(51, 75, ch)
go push(76, 100, ch)
```

5. At this point, we need to gather all the numbers to add, so we create a loop of 100 cycles:

    ```
    for c := 0; c < 100; c++ {
    ```

6. Then, read the number from the channel:

    ```
    i := <- ch
    ```

7. We also want to see which number came from which Goroutine:

    ```
    log.Println(i)
    ```

8. Finally, we calculate the sum and show the result:

    ```
    s1 += i
    }
    log.Println(s1)
    }
    ```

Here, we have the truncated output once you run the program:

```
2024/01/25 21:42:09 76
2024/01/25 21:42:09 26
2024/01/25 21:42:09 51
2024/01/25 21:42:09 77
2024/01/25 21:42:09 52

.........................................................
2024/01/25 21:42:09 48
2024/01/25 21:42:09 75
2024/01/25 21:42:09 100
2024/01/25 21:42:09 23
2024/01/25 21:42:09 49
2024/01/25 21:42:09 24
2024/01/25 21:42:09 50
2024/01/25 21:42:09 25
2024/01/25 21:42:09 5050
```

Based on the results, we can easily guess which number comes from which routine. The last line displays the sum of all numbers. If you run the program multiple times, you will see that the order of the numbers changes as well.

In this exercise, we saw how we can split some computational work across several concurrent Goroutines and then gather all the computation in a single Goroutine. Each Goroutine performs a task. In this case, one sends numbers, while another receives the numbers and performs a sum.

Exercise 18.07 – request to Goroutines

In this exercise, we will solve the same problem mentioned in *Exercise 19.06, Summing numbers from everywhere*, but in a different way. Instead of receiving numbers as the Goroutines send them, we will make the main Goroutine ask for numbers from the other Goroutines. We will play with channel operations and experiment with their blocking nature:

1. Create a folder and a `main.go` file with the `main` package. Then, add the following import:

```
package main
import (
  "log"
)
```

2. Then, write the signature of the `push()` function:

```
func push(from, to int, in chan bool, out chan int) {
```

Here, there are two channels – a Boolean one called `in`, which represents the incoming requests, and `out`, which will be used to send back messages.

3. Now, write a loop for sending numbers when a request comes in:

```
for i := from; i <= to; i++ {
  <- in
  out <- i
}
}
```

As you can see, the loop is still for a fixed number of items. Before sending anything, it waits for a request from the `in` channel. When it receives a request, it sends a number.

4. Now, create a `main()` function, where you call the `push()` function in four different Goroutines, each one sending a subset of the numbers 1 to 100:

```
func main() {
  s1 := 0
  out := make(chan int, 100)
  in := make(chan bool, 100)
  go push(1, 25, in, out)
  go push(26, 50, in, out)
  go push(51, 75, in, out)
  go push(76, 100, in, out)
```

This is pretty similar to the previous exercise, but it creates an extra channel, `in`.

5. Now, create a loop to request a number, print it, and add it to the total:

```
for c := 0; c < 100; c++ {
    in <- true
    i := <- out
    log.Println(i)
    s1 += i
}
log.Println(s1)
}
```

In this case, the loop first requests a number and then waits to receive another number. Here, we do not need to sleep for a microsecond because after we receive a number, the next request will go to any active Goroutine. If you run the program, you will again see something similar to what you saw in the previous exercise. Here, we have the truncated output:

```
2024/01/25 22:18:00 76
2024/01/25 22:18:00 1
2024/01/25 22:18:00 77
2024/01/25 22:18:00 26
2024/01/25 22:18:00 51
2024/01/25 22:18:00 2
2024/01/25 22:18:00 78

.........................................................
2024/01/25 22:18:00 74
2024/01/25 22:18:00 25
2024/01/25 22:18:00 50
2024/01/25 22:18:00 75
2024/01/25 22:18:00 5050
```

You can see that each number is printed in the order it is received. Then, the sum of all numbers is printed on the screen.

In this exercise, you've learned how you can use channels to request other Goroutines to perform some actions. A channel can be used to send some trigger messages and not only to exchange content and values.

The importance of concurrency

So far, we've seen how to use concurrency to split work over several Goroutines, but in all of these exercises, concurrency was not really needed. In fact, you do not save much time doing what we did, nor do you have any other advantage. Concurrency is important when you need to perform several tasks that are logically independent of each other, and the easiest case to understand is a web server. You saw in *Chapter 16, Web Servers*, that several clients will most likely connect to the same server and all these connections will result in the server performing some actions. Also, these actions are all independent; that's where concurrency is important, as you do not want one of your users to have to wait for all other HTTP requests to be completed before their request gets handled. Another case for concurrency is when you have different data sources to gather data and you can gather that data in different Goroutines and combine the result at the end. We will see now more complex applications for concurrency and learn how to use it for HTTP servers.

Exercise 18.08 – equally splitting work between Goroutines

In this exercise, we will see how we can perform our sum of numbers in a predefined number of Goroutines for them to gather the result at the end. Essentially, we want to create a function that adds numbers and receives the numbers from a channel. When no more numbers are received by the function, we will send the sum to the main() function through the channel.

One thing to note here is that the function performing the sum does not know in advance how many numbers it will receive, which means we cannot have a fixed from, to range. So, we have to find another solution. We need to be able to split the work in any number of Goroutines and not be bound by a from, to range. Also, we do not want to do the addition in the main() function. Instead, we want to create a function that will split the work over several Goroutines:

1. Create a folder and a main.go file with the main package and write the following:

    ```
    package main
    import (
      "log"
    )
    ```

2. Now, let's write a function to do a partial addition. We will call it worker() as we will have a fixed set of Goroutines running this same function, waiting for numbers to arrive:

    ```
    func worker(in chan int, out chan int) {
      sum := 0
      for i := range in {
        sum += i
      }
      out <- sum
    }
    ```

    As you can see, we have an in channel and an out channel of integers. Then, we instantiate the sum variable, which will store the sum of all numbers sent to this worker.

3. At this point, we have a loop that ranges over the channel. This is interesting because we do not use in directly, as follows:

    ```
    <- in
    ```

We, instead, rely only on the range to get the numbers in. In the loop, we just add `i` to the total and, at the end, we send the partial sum back. Even if we do not know how many items are going to be sent to the channel, we can still loop over the range without a problem. We rely on the fact that when no more items are sent, the `in` channel will be closed.

4. Create a `sum()` function:

```
func sum(workers, from, to int) int {
```

This is the actual `sum()` function that has the number of workers and the usual range for the numbers to add.

5. Now, write a loop to run the requested number of workers:

```
out := make(chan int, workers)
in := make(chan int, 4)
for i := 0; i <  workers; i++ {
    go worker(in, out)
}
```

This creates the two `in`/`out` channels and runs the number of workers set by the `workers` parameter.

6. Then, create a loop to send all numbers to the `in` channel:

```
for i := from; i <= to; i++ {
    in <- i
}
```

This sends all numbers to be summed to the channel, which will distribute the numbers across all Goroutines. If you were to print out the numbers received across with the index of the worker, you could see how the numbers are distributed uniformly across the Goroutines, which does not mean an exact split, but at least it's a fair one.

7. As we sent all the numbers, we now need to receive the partial sums back, but before that, we need to notify the function that the numbers to sum are finished, so add the following line of code. Closing a channel means nothing else can be sent, but data can still be received from the channel:

```
close(in)
```

8. And then, perform a sum of the partials:

```
sum := 0
for i := 0; i < workers; i++ {
    sum += <-out
}
```

9. Then, finally, close the `out` channel and return the result:

```
close(out)
return sum
}
```

10. At this point, we need to somehow execute this function. So, let's write a simple `main()` function to do that:

```
func main() {
    res := sum(100, 1, 100)
    log.Println(res)
}
```

This simply outputs a sum from a function that makes use of concurrency and then prints out the result.

If you run your program, you should see the log output of the sum of numbers split into different routines as follows:

```
2024/01/25 19:49:13 5050
```

As you can see, after splitting the computation across multiple Goroutines, the result is synchronized into one single result.

In this exercise, you've learned how to make use of concurrency to split your computation across several concurrent Goroutines and then combine all these computations into one single result.

Concurrency patterns

The way we organize our concurrent work is pretty much the same in every application. We will look at one common pattern that is called a *pipeline*, where we have a source, and then messages are sent from one Goroutine to another until the end of the line, until all Goroutines in the pipeline have been utilized. Another pattern is the *fan out/ fan in* pattern where, as in the previous exercise, work is sent to several Goroutines reading from the same channel. All these patterns, however, are generally made of a *source* stage, which is the first stage of the pipeline and the one that gathers, or sources, the data, then some internal steps, and at the end, a *sink*, which is the final stage where the results of the process from all the other routines get merged. It is known as a sink because all the data sinks into it.

Buffers

You've seen in the previous exercises that there are channels with a defined length and channels with an undetermined length:

```
ch1 := make(chan int)
ch2 := make(chan int, 10)
```

Let's see how we can make use of this.

A buffer is like a container that needs to be filled with some content, so you prepare it when you expect to receive that content. We said that operations on channels are blocking operations, which means the execution of the Goroutine will stop and wait whenever you try to read a message from the channel. Let's try to understand what this means in practice with an example. Let's say we have the following code in a Goroutine:

```
i := <- ch
```

We know that before we can carry on with the execution of the code, we need to receive a message. However, there is something more about this blocking behavior. If the channel does not have a buffer, the Goroutine is blocked as well. It is not possible to write to a channel or to receive a channel. We'll get a better idea of this with an example, and we will show how to use unbuffered channels to achieve the same result so that you will get a better understanding of what you've seen in the previous exercises.

Let's have a look at this code:

```
ch := make(chan int, 2)
ch <- 1
ch <- 2
fmt.Println(<-ch)
fmt.Println(<-ch)
```

If you put this code inside a function, you will see that it works perfectly and will display something as follows:

```
1
2
```

But what if you add an extra read? Let's take a look:

```
ch := make(chan int, 2)
ch <- 1
ch <- 2
ch <- 3
fmt.Println(<-ch)
fmt.Println(<-ch)
```

In this case, you will see an error:

```
fatal error: all goroutines are asleep - deadlock!
goroutine 1 [chan send]:
main.main()
    /tmp/sandbox223984687/prog.go:9 +0xa0
```

This happens because the routine running this code is blocked after the buffer of size 2 is filled with a data size of 2 coming from the read operations (commonly referred to as reads), which results in the buffer being filled with data, which, in this case, has 2 data, and the buffer has a size of 2. We can increase the buffer:

```
ch := make(chan int, 3)
```

And it will work again; we are just not displaying the third number.

Now, let's see what happens if we remove the buffer. Try, and again you will see the previous error. This happens because the buffer is always full and the routine is blocked. An unbuffered channel is equivalent to the following:

```
ch := make(chan int, 0)
```

We've used unbuffered channels without any issues. Let's see an example of how to use them:

```
package main
import "fmt"
func readThem(ch chan int) {
  for {
    fmt.Println(<- ch)
  }
}
func main() {
  ch := make(chan int)
  go readThem(ch)
  ch <- 1
  ch <- 2
  ch <- 3
}
```

If you run this program, you should see something as follows:

```
1
2
3
```

But there is a chance you could see fewer numbers. If you run this on the Go Playground, you should see this result, but if you run it on your machine, you might see fewer numbers. Try sending more numbers:

```
ch <- 4
ch <- 5
```

At each addition, run your program; you might not see all the numbers. Basically, there are two Goroutines: one is reading messages from an unbuffered channel, and the main Goroutine is sending these messages through the same channel. Due to this, there is no deadlock. This shows that we can make use of unbuffered channels for read and write operations flawlessly by using two Goroutines. We still have, however, an issue with not all numbers showing up, which we can fix in the following way:

```go
package main
import "fmt"
import "sync"
func readThem(ch chan int, wg *sync.WaitGroup) {
    for i := range ch {
        fmt.Println(i)
    }
    wg.Done()
}
func main() {
    wg := &sync.WaitGroup{}
    wg.Add(1)
    ch := make(chan int)
    go readThem(ch, wg)
    ch <- 1
    ch <- 2
    ch <- 3
    ch <- 4
    ch <- 5
    close(ch)
    wg.Wait()
}
```

Here, we iterate over the channel inside the Goroutine, and we stop as soon as the channel gets closed. This is because when the channel gets closed, the range stops iterating. The channel gets closed in the main Goroutine after everything is sent. We make use of a WaitGroup here to know that everything is completed. If we were not closing the channel in the main() function, we would be in the main Goroutine, which would terminate before the second Goroutine would print all the numbers. There is another way, however, to wait for the execution of the second Goroutine to be completed, and this is with explicit notification, which we will see in the next exercise. One thing to notice is that even though we close the channel, the messages all still arrive at the receiving routine. This is because you can receive messages from a closed channel; you just can't send more.

Exercise 18.09 – notifying when the computation has finished

In this exercise, we want to have one Goroutine to send messages and another one to print them. Moreover, we want to know when the sender has finished sending messages. The code will be like the previous example, with some modifications:

1. Create a new file and import the necessary packages:

    ```
    package main
    import "log"
    ```

2. Then, define a function that will first receive the strings and print them later:

    ```
    func readThem(in, out chan string) {
    ```

3. Then, create a loop over the channel until the channel is closed:

    ```
    for i := range in {
       log.Println(i)
    }
    ```

4. Finally, send a notification saying that the processing has finished:

    ```
    out <- "done"
    }
    ```

5. Now, let's build the main() function:

    ```
    func main() {
      log.SetFlags(0)
    ```

    Here, we've also set the log flags to 0 so that we do not see anything other than the strings we send.

6. Now, create the necessary channels and use them to spin up the Goroutine:

    ```
    in, out := make(chan string), make(chan string)
    go readThem(in, out)
    ```

7. Next, create a set of strings and loop over them, sending each string to the channel:

    ```
    strs := []string{"a","b", "c", "d", "e", "f"}
    for _, s := range strs {
      in <- s
    }
    ```

8.　After that, close the channel you used to send the messages and wait for the done signal:

```
close(in)
<-out
}
```

If you run your program, you will see the log output of code using a done channel:

```
a
b
c
d
e
f
```

We see that the `main()` function has received all the messages from the Goroutine and has printed them. The `main()` function terminates only when it has been notified that all incoming messages have been sent.

In this exercise, you've learned how you can make a Goroutine notify another Goroutine that the work has finished by passing a message through a channel without needing `WaitGroup`.

Some more common practices

In all these examples, we've created channels and passed them through, but functions can also return channels and spin up new Goroutines. Here is an example:

```
func doSomething() chan int {
  ch := make(chan int)
  go func() {
    for i := range ch {
      log.Println(i)
    }
  }()
  return ch
}
```

In this case, we can actually have the following in our `main()` function:

```
ch := doSomething()
ch <- 1
ch <- 4
```

We do not need to call the `doSomething` function as a Goroutine because it will spin up a new one by itself.

Some functions can also return or accept, such as this one:

```
<- chan int
```

Here's another example:

```
chan <- int
```

This makes clear what the function does with the channels. In fact, you could try to specify the direction in all the exercises we've done so far and see what happens if you specify an incorrect one.

HTTP servers

You've seen how to build HTTP servers in *Chapter 16, Web Servers*, but you might remember that there was something difficult to handle with HTTP servers, and this was the application's state. Essentially, an HTTP server runs as a single program and listens to requests in the main Goroutine. However, when a new HTTP request is made by one of the clients, a new Goroutine is created that handles that specific request. You have not done it manually, nor have you managed the server's channels, but this is how it works internally. You do not actually need to send anything across the different Goroutines because each Goroutine and each request is independent since they have been made by different people.

However, what you must think of is how to not create race conditions when you want to keep a state. Most HTTP servers are stateless, especially if you're building a microservice environment. However, you might want to keep track of things with a counter, or you might actually work with TCP servers, a gaming server, or a chat app where you need to keep the state and gather information from all the peers. The techniques you've learned in this chapter allow you to do so. You can use a mutex to make sure a counter is thread-safe or, better, routine-safe across all requests. I'd suggest you go back to your code for the HTTP server and ensure safety with mutexes.

Methods as Goroutines

So far, you've only seen functions used as Goroutines, but methods are simple functions with a receiver; hence, they can be used asynchronously too. This can be useful if you want to share some properties of your struct, such as for your counter in an HTTP server.

With this technique, you can encapsulate the channels you use across several Goroutines belonging to the same instance of a struct without having to pass these channels everywhere.

Here is a simple example of how to do that:

```
type MyStruct struct {}
func (m MyStruct) doIt()
. . . . . . .
ms := MyStruct{}
go ms.doIt()
```

But let's see how to apply this in an exercise.

Exercise 18.10 – a structured work

In this exercise, we will calculate a sum using several workers. A worker is essentially a function, and we will be organizing these workers into a single struct:

1. Create your folder and `main` file. In it, add the required imports and define a `Worker` struct with two channels – in and out. Ensure that you add a mutex as well:

    ```
    package main
    import (
      "fmt"
      "sync"
    )
    type Worker struct {
      in, out chan int
      sbw int // sbw: subworker
      mtx *sync.Mutex
    }
    ```

2. To create its methods, write the following:

    ```
    func (w *Worker) readThem() {
      w.sbw++
      go func() {
    ```

    Here, we create a method and increment the number of `subworker` instances. Sub-workers are basically identical Goroutines that split the work that needs to be done. Note that the function is meant to be used directly and not as a Goroutine, as it itself creates a new Goroutine.

3. Now, build the content of the spawned Goroutine:

    ```
    partial := 0
    for i := range w.in {
      partial += i
    }
    w.out <- partial
    ```

4. This is pretty similar to what you've done before; now comes the tricky part:

    ```
    w.mtx.Lock()
    w.sbw--
    if w.sbw == 0 {
      close(w.out)
    }
    w.mtx.Unlock()
    ```

```
    }()
  }
```

Here, we've locked the routine, reduced the counter on the sub-workers safely, and then, in case all the workers have terminated, we've closed the output channel. Then, we've unlocked the execution to allow the program to carry on.

5. At this point, we need to make a function that's able to return the sum:

```
func (w *Worker) gatherResult() int {
  total := 0
  wg := &sync.WaitGroup{}
  wg.Add(1)
  go func() {
```

6. Here, we create a total, then a `WaitGroup`, and we add 1 to it as we will spawn only one Goroutine whose content is as follows:

```
    for i:= range w.out{
      total += i
    }
    wg.Done()
  }()
```

As you can see, we have looped until the `out` channel is closed by one of the sub-workers.

7. At this point, we can wait for the Goroutine to finish and return the result:

```
  wg.Wait()
  return total
}
```

8. The main code just sets up variables for the worker and its sub-workers:

```
func main() {
  mtx := &sync.Mutex{}
  in := make(chan int, 100)
  wrNum := 10
  out := make(chan int)
  wrk := Worker{in: in, out: out, mtx: mtx}
```

9. Now, create a loop where you call the `readThem()` method wrNum times. This will create some sub-workers:

```
  for i := 1; i <= wrNum; i++ {
    wrk.readThem()
  }
```

10. Now, send the numbers to be summed to the channel:

```
for i := 1;i <= 100; i++ {
   in <- i
}
```

11. Close the channel to notify that all numbers have been sent:

```
close(in)
```

12. Then, wait for the result and print it out:

```
res := wrk.gatherResult()
fmt.Println(res)
}
```

13. If you run the program, you will see the log output of a sum made using structs to organize our work:

```
5050
```

In this exercise, you've learned how to use a method of a struct to create a new Goroutine. The method can be called like any function, but the result will be a new anonymous Goroutine being created.

Go context package

We've seen how to run concurrent code and run it until it has finished, waiting for the completion of some processing through `WaitGroup` or channel reads. You might have seen in some Go code, especially code related to HTTP calls, some parameters from the `context` package, and you might have wondered what it is and why it is used.

All the code we've written here is running on our machines and does not pass through the internet, so we hardly have any delay due to latency; however, in situations involving HTTP calls, we might encounter servers that do not respond and get stuck. In such cases, how do we stop our call if the server does not respond after a while? How do we stop the execution of a routine that runs independently when an event occurs? Well, we have several ways, but a standard one is to use contexts, and we will see now how they work. A context is a variable that is passed through a series of calls and might hold some values or may be empty. It is a container, but it is not used to send values across functions; you can use normal integers, strings, and so on for this purpose. A context is passed through to get back control of what is happening:

```
func doIt(ctx context.Context, a int, b string) {
   fmt.Println(b)
   doThat(ctx, a*2)
}
```

```
func doThat(ctx context.Context, a int) {
  fmt.Println(a)
  doMore(ctx)
}
```

As you can see, there are several calls, and `ctx` is passed through, but we do not do anything with it. However, it can contain data, and it contains functions that we can use to stop the execution of the current Goroutine. We will see how it works in the next exercise.

Exercise 18.11 – managing Goroutines with a context

In this exercise, we will start a Goroutine with an infinite loop counting from zero until we decide to stop it. We will make use of the context to notify the routine to stop and a sleeping function to make sure we know how many iterations we do:

1. Create your folder and a `main.go` file, then write the following:

    ```
    package main
    import (
      "context"
      "log"
      "time"
    )
    ```

    For the usual imports, we have `logs` and `time`, which we've already seen, plus the `context` package.

2. Let's write a function that counts every 100 milliseconds from 0:

    ```
    func countNumbers(ctx context.Context, r chan int) {
      v := 0
      for {
    ```

    Here, `v` is the value we count from zero. The `ctx` variable is the context, while the `r` variable is the channel returning the result. Then, we start defining a loop.

3. Now, we start an infinite loop, but inside it, we will have `select`:

    ```
        select {
          case <-ctx.Done():
          r <- v
          return
    ```

    In this `select` group, we have a case where we check whether the context is `done`, and if it is, we just break the loop and return the value we have counted so far.

4. If the context is not `done`, we need to keep counting:

```
        default:
        time.Sleep(time.Millisecond * 100)
        v++
    }
  }
}
```

Here, we sleep for 100 milliseconds, and then we increment the value by 1.

5. The next step is to write a `main()` function that makes use of this counter:

```
func main() {
  r := make(chan int)
  ctx := context.TODO()
```

We create an integer channel to pass to the counter and a context.

6. We need to be able to cancel the context, so we extend this simple context. For clarity, `cl` is the variable name for the cancelable context, and `stop` is the function name we have chosen to cancel it:

```
  cl, stop := context.WithCancel(ctx)
  go countNumbers(cl, r)
```

Here, we also finally call the counting Goroutine.

7. At this point, we need a way to break the loop, so we will use the `stop()` function returned by `context.WithCancel`, but we will do that inside another Goroutine. This will stop the context after 300 milliseconds:

```
  go func() {
    time.Sleep(time.Millisecond*100*3)
    stop()
  }()
```

8. Now, we just need to wait for the message with the count to be received and log it:

```
  v := <- r
  log.Println(v)
}
```

After 300 milliseconds have passed, the counter will return 3 since, due to context manipulation, the routine stopped at the third iteration:

```
2024/01/25 20:00:58 3
```

Here, we can see that even though the loop is infinite, the execution stops after three iterations.

In this exercise, you've learned how you can use a context to stop the execution of a Goroutine. This is useful in many cases, such as when performing long tasks that you want to stop after a maximum amount of time or after a certain event has occurred.

One thing to mention is that, in this exercise, we did something that in some situations could lead to problems. What we did was create a channel in one Goroutine, but close it in another one. This is not wrong; in some cases, it might be useful, but try to avoid it as it could lead to problems when somebody looks at the code or when you look at the code after several months because it is difficult to track where a channel is closed across several functions.

Concurrent work with sync.Cond

Efficient coordination between different Goroutines is crucial to ensure smooth execution and resource management. Another powerful synchronization primitive provided by the Go standard library is sync.Cond (condition). The Cond type is associated with sync.Mutex and provides a way for Goroutines to wait for or signal the occurrence of a particular condition or changes in shared data.

Let's explore how to use sync.Cond by creating a simple example of a **work-in-progress** (**WIP**) limited queue.

Exercise 18.12 – creating a WIP limited queue

Suppose you have a scenario where multiple Goroutines produce and consume items, but you want to limit the number of items in progress currently. sync.Cond can help achieve this synchronization. Here's how to use it:

1. Create your folder and a main.go file, then write the following:

```
package main
import (
  "fmt"
  "sync"
  "time"
)
```

We import fmt, sync, and time, which we've already seen.

2. Let's define a WorkInProgressQueue and function to create a new WorkInProgressQueue object:

```
type WorkQueue struct {
  cond *sync.Cond
  maxSize int
```

```
    workItems []string
}
func NewWorkQueue(maxSize int) *WorkQueue {
    return &WorkQueue{
        cond: sync.NewCond(&sync.Mutex{}),
        maxSize: maxSize,
        workItems: make([]string, 0),
    }
}
```

3. Now, we define an enqueue() function to add work items while respecting a maximum size constraint on the work queue:

```
func (wq *WorkQueue) enqueue(item string) {
    wq.cond.L.Lock()
    defer wq.cond.L.Unlock()
    for len(wq.workItems) == wq.maxSize {
        wq.cond.Wait()
    }
    wq.workItems = append(wq.workItems, item)
    wq.cond.Signal()
}
```

4. Then, define a dequeue() function where we consume work items:

```
func (wq *WorkQueue) dequeue() string {
    wq.cond.L.Lock()
    defer wq.cond.L.Unlock()
    for len(wq.workItems) == 0 {
        wq.cond.Wait()
    }
    item := wq.workItems[0]
    wq.workItems = wq.workItems[1:]
    wq.cond.Signal()
    return item
}
```

5. Now we define a main() function and a maximum capacity for our work queue at three items:

```
func main() {
    var wg sync.WaitGroup
    workQueue := NewWorkQueue(3)
```

6. Next, we define the first Goroutine. This one is responsible for producing work items:

```
wg.Add(1)
go func() {
  defer wg.Done()
  for i := 1; i <= 5; i++ {
    workItem := fmt.Sprintf("WorkItem %d", i)
    workQueue.enqueue(workItem)
    fmt.Printf("Enqueued: %s\n", workItem)
    time.Sleep(time.Second)
  }
}()
```

7. We then define the second Goroutine. This one is responsible for consuming work items:

```
wg.Add(1)
go func() {
  defer wg.Done()
  for i := 1; i <= 5; i++ {
    workItem := workQueue.dequeue()
    fmt.Printf("Dequeued: %s\n", workItem)
    time.Sleep(2 * time.Second)
  }
}()
```

8. Lastly, we wait for all Goroutines to complete and close our `main()` function:

```
  wg.Wait()
}
```

9. Run the program:

```
go run main.go
```

You will see the following output, where the items may be in different orders of being enqueued and then dequeued:

```
Enqueued: WorkItem 1
Dequeued: WorkItem 1
Enqueued: WorkItem 2
Dequeued: WorkItem 2
Enqueued: WorkItem 3
Enqueued: WorkItem 4
Enqueued: WorkItem 5
Dequeued: WorkItem 3
Dequeued: WorkItem 4
Dequeued: WorkItem 5
```

This exercise demonstrates a simple work queue where the Goroutine enqueues items up to the queue's maximum size. If the queue is full, then the Goroutine will wait until there is room for more items in the queue. Once an item is enqueued, then it signals other Goroutines that might be waiting on the condition variable. There is also the second Goroutine, or the consumer Goroutine dequeuing items. The consumer waits if the queue is empty up to the five items. After dequeuing an item, it signals to other Goroutines that might be waiting on the condition variable. As you can see, the sync.Cond variable is used for signaling and waiting for Goroutines.

The thread-safe map

In concurrent programming, safely managing access to shared data structures is crucial to avoid race conditions and ensure consistency. Go's standard library provides a powerful tool for concurrent map access – the sync.Map type. Unlike the regular Map type, sync.Map is specifically designed to be used concurrently without the need for external synchronization.

The sync.Map type is part of the sync package and provides fine-grained locking internally to allow multiple readers and a single writer to access a map concurrently without blocking operations. This makes it suitable for scenarios where you have multiple Goroutines that need to read or modify a map concurrently.

Let's look at an exercise showcasing the utility of sync.Map.

Exercise 18.13 – counting how many times random numbers are between 0 and 9 using sync.Map

Suppose we want to count how many times random numbers fall between the values of zero and nine in a concurrent setting. The sync.Map type will help us do this safely:

1. Create your folder and a main.go file, then write the following:

    ```
    package main
    import (
        "crypto/rand"
        "fmt"
        "math/big"
        "sync"
    )
    ```

2. Let's write a function to generate a random number in the range of [0, max):

    ```
    func generateRandomNumber(max int) (int, error) {
        n, err := rand.Int(rand.Reader, big.NewInt(int64(max)))
        if err != nil {
    ```

```
      return 0, err
   }
   return int(n.Int64()), nil
}
```

3. Let's write a helper function to update the count using load and store methods to safely access and update the count map:

```go
func updateCount(countMap *sync.Map, key int) {
  count, _ := countMap.LoadOrStore(key, 0)
  countMap.Store(key, count.(int)+1)
}
```

4. Now, write a function to print the counts from the sync.Map contents:

```go
func printCounts(countMap *sync.Map) {
  countMap.Range(func(key, value interface{}) bool {
    fmt.Printf("Number %d: Count %d\n", key, value)
    return true
  })
}
```

5. Lastly, we can define a main() function that will define our sync.Map type and a Goroutine to generate random numbers and update the counts in the sync.Map type:

```go
func main() {
  var countMap sync.Map
  numGoroutines := 5
  var wg sync.WaitGroup
  generateAndCount := func() {
    defer wg.Done()
    // Generate 1000 random numbers per Goroutine
    for i := 0; i < 1000; i++ {
      // Generate random number between 0 and 9
      randomNumber, err := generateRandomNumber(10)
      if err != nil {
        fmt.Println("Error generating random number:", err)
        return
      }
      updateCount(&countMap, randomNumber)
    }
  }
```

6. We will then end our `main()` function by spawning all our Goroutines and waiting for their completion before printing the counts from our concurrent safe map:

```go
for i := 0; i < numGoroutines; i++ {
    wg.Add(1)
    go generateAndCount()
}
wg.Wait()
printCounts(&countMap)
}
```

7. Run the program:

```
go run main.go
```

You will see the following output, where the items may be in different orders and with different counts:

```
Number 7: Count 480
Number 0: Count 488
Number 5: Count 506
Number 4: Count 489
Number 1: Count 472
Number 9: Count 499
Number 2: Count 499
Number 6: Count 515
Number 3: Count 481
Number 8: Count 533
```

In this exercise, we used the `sync.Map` type to safely maintain accurate counts for each random number generated by multiple Goroutines. We had the `updateCount` function responsible for updating the count in a thread-safe manner using the `LoadOrStore` and `Store` methods. We just saw how we can use this thread-safe map without additional synchronization mechanisms. Using `sync.Map` simplifies concurrent map access and eliminates the need for explicit locks, making the code cleaner and more efficient in scenarios where concurrent access to a map is required.

Summary

In this chapter, you've learned how to create production-ready concurrent code, how to handle race conditions, and how to make sure that your code is concurrent-safe. You've learned how to use channels to make your Goroutines communicate with each other and how to stop their executions using a context.

You've worked on several techniques to handle concurrent computation and learned about `sync.Cond` and `sync.Map` as powerful tools in your toolbelt for concurrent programming In many real-life scenarios, you might just use functions and methods that handle concurrency for you, especially if you're doing web programming, but there are cases where you must handle work coming from some different sources by yourself. You need to match requests with your response through different channels. You might need to gather different data into one single Goroutine from different ones. With what you've learned here, you'll be able to do all that. You'll be able to ensure you do not lose data by waiting for all Goroutines to finish. You'll be able to modify the same variable from different Goroutines, making sure you do not override a value if it is not what you want. You've also learned how to avoid deadlocks and how to use channels to share information. One of the Go mottos is *Share by communicating, do not communicate by sharing.* This means that the preferred way to share values is to send them via a channel and not rely on mutexes if not strictly necessary. You now know how to do all that.

In the next chapter, you will learn to make your code more professional. Essentially, you will learn what you are expected to do as a professional in a real working environment, which is testing and checking your code – making sure, essentially, that your code works and is valid.

19

Testing

Overview

Testing is a crucial aspect of software development that ensures the reliability and correctness of your code. In Go, a comprehensive testing approach covers various types of tests, each serving a unique purpose. This chapter explores different testing techniques and tools available in Go to empower developers in building robust and maintainable applications.

By the end of this chapter, you will understand the various types of tests Go developers implement. We will discuss the big three types of tests: unit, integration, and **end-to-end** (E2E) tests. We will then cover a few other types of tests, such as HTTP testing and fuzz testing. We will cover test suites, benchmarks, and code coverage, and even create a final test report for project stakeholders or just to share how well-tested your code truly is. You will also see the benefits of automated tests testing your code regularly while continuously iterating on your code base as it evolves. These skills are imperative to developing production-ready and industry-grade applications. Testing is also an important part of the **software development life cycle** (SDLC) that we, as developers, go through for our projects.

Technical requirements

For this chapter, you'll require Go version 1.21 or higher. The code for this chapter can be found at `https://github.com/PacktPublishing/Go-Programming-From-Beginner-to-Professional-Second-Edition-/tree/main/Chapter19`.

Introduction

Testing is a fundamental aspect of software development that ensures the reliability, correctness, and stability of applications. In Go, testing plays a crucial role in maintaining the robustness of software systems.

As I mentioned previously, testing is a crucial part of the SDLC that encompasses various phases, from requirements gathering to deployment. Quality assurance begins with the implementation of effective testing strategies. Robust testing not only identifies and rectifies bugs and errors in code but also promotes maintainability and scalability. Consider a scenario where a critical financial application lacks comprehensive testing. An innocuous code change might inadvertently introduce a bug that goes unnoticed until the application fails catastrophically. Testing, therefore, acts as a safety net, catching potential issues early in the development life cycle. If a team is impacted by a bug rolling out into their different environments, developers should proactively create tests that cover that scenario for the future – no matter what language they code in.

Go provides a built-in testing framework that is both simple and powerful. Leveraging the testing package, developers can create unit tests, benchmark tests, and even example-based documentation tests. The testing package is designed to be expressive, making it easy to write, read, and maintain tests. Through conventions such as test file suffixes (`_test.go`) and clear test function signatures prefixed with `Test`, Go encourages a standardized approach to testing that promotes consistency across all projects. It is also important to note that there is no `main()` function when it comes to testing in Go to control the program flow. Each test function is executed independently, and consecutively.

In this chapter, we will dive into the specifics of testing in Go, covering topics such as writing effective unit tests, benchmarking, table-driven tests, and more. Armed with a solid understanding of testing principles in Go, developers will be well-equipped to build reliable and maintainable software applications.

Unit tests

One of the fundamental aspects of testing your application starts with unit tests. Unit tests focus on individual components, verifying that each function or method works as intended. In Go, unit tests are written using the built-in testing package, making it easy to define test functions and assertions.

You will typically define positive and negative unit tests. For example, if you have a function to concatenate several strings together, then you would have some positive test cases, such as `"hi "` + `"sam"` = `"hi sam"`, and `"bye,"` + `" sam"` = `"bye, sam"`. You would also add a few negative test cases that verify that an error occurred for input, such as `"hi"` + `"there"` `expecting the result of "hi sam"`. This is not equivalent, nor what we would expect as output, so our negative test case would expect an error to arise.

You can also consider edge cases, such as concatenating strings that include punctuation marks and ensuring that they are included in the concatenation and that proper grammatical syntax and capitalization are enforced. This provides coverage on test cases you expect to work, test cases you expect will produce errors, and test coverage on edge or corner cases for your function or method.

Idiomatic and readable code should come first nature to Go programmers due to its idiomatic nature. Therefore, it should be of no surprise that Go adopts a table-driven test structure for all tests, including unit tests. Table-driven tests keep code readable, flexible, and adaptable to future changes. They include the definition of an anonymous `using` struct defined as *Tests* or *TestCases*, where you include the test case's name, inputs or arguments, and expected outputs. Let's see an example of this in action.

Exercise 19.01 – table-driven tests

Let's look at an example of creating idiomatic table-driven unit tests:

1. Create a new folder in your filesystem, and, inside it, create a `main_test.go` file and write the following code. We are including the `assert` package from the `gotest.tools` module as it provides utilities and enhancements for testing in Go. Specifically, the `assert` package offers assertions in an expressive and readable way, so it is a nice package to use:

    ```go
    package main
    import (
      "testing"
      "gotest.tools/assert"
    )
    ```

2. Create a function that sums two numbers:

    ```go
    func add(x, y int) int {
      return x + y
    }
    ```

3. Define the table-driven test function to check that the numeric addition is correct and add a few test cases to check. We will add a test case that expects an incorrect value to see what this looks like:

    ```go
    func TestAdd(t *testing.T) {
      tests := []struct {
        name string
        inputs []int
        want int
      }{
        {
          name: "Test Case 1",
          inputs: []int{5, 6},
          want: 11,
        },
        {
          name: "Test Case 2",
          inputs: []int{11, 7},
          want: 18,
        },
        {
          name: "Test Case 3",
          inputs: []int{1, 8},
          want: 9,
    ```

```
        },
        {
            name: "Test Case 4 (intentional failure)",
            inputs: []int{2, 3},
            want: 0, // This should be 5, intentionally incorrect to
    demonstrate failure
        },
    }
```

4. Loop over each test case, assert that the received value is what is expected, and close the function. We could just as easily use an `if` conditional instead of the `assert` package; however, it condenses and cleans up the code a bit, so you will typically see this package being used to assert that test values are correct:

```
    for _, test := range tests {
        got := add(test.inputs[0], test.inputs[1])
        assert.Equal(t, test.want, got)
    }
}
```

5. Run the program:

```
go test main_test.go
```

You will see the following output:

```
    main_test.go:45: assertion failed: 8 (test.want int) != 5
(got int)
FAIL
FAIL    command-line-arguments    0.168s
FAIL
```

As you can see, the `assert` package makes it easy to see what is failing in the test function. However, this output makes it somewhat difficult to know which test case in particular is failing.

6. Now, if we fix the intentionally incorrect test case, we will see the following output:

```
ok      command-line-arguments    0.153s
```

You've now seen what table-driven tests look like for unit testing in Go. However, there are improvements we can make to this code to make it even more readable – for example, we can adjust the code so that it utilizes subtests. Subtests in Go provide several benefits:

- Isolation of setup and teardown logic if applicable

- Clear test output

- Ability to add parallel execution

- Structured test organization

- Conditional test execution

- Improved test readability

Now that we've seen some of the benefits of subtests, let's see what this looks like when it's been added to our unit test function from before. For this, we can simply update the for loop logic:

```
for _, test := range tests {
    test := test
    t.Run(test.name, func(t *testing.T) {
        got := add(test.inputs[0], test.inputs[1])
        assert.Equal(t, test.want, got)
    })
}
```

7. Run the program again after the update:

```
go test main_test.go
```

You will see the following output:

```
--- FAIL: TestAdd (0.00s)
Running tool: /usr/local/go/bin/go test -timeout 30s -run ^TestAdd$
github.com/packt-book/Go-Programming---From-Beginner-to-Professional-
Second-Edition-/Chapter19/Exercise19.01
--- FAIL: TestAdd (0.00s)
--- FAIL: TestAdd/Test_Case_4_(intentional_failure) (0.00s)
/Users/samcoyle/go/src/github.com/packt-book/Go-Programming---From-
Beginner-to-Professional-Second-Edition-/Chapter19/Exercise19.01/main_
test.go:45: assertion failed: 0 (test.want int) != 5 (got int)
FAIL
FAIL github.com/packt-book/Go-Programming---From-Beginner-to-
Professional-Second-Edition-/Chapter19/Exercise19.01 0.164s
FAIL
```

From this, you can see how the failing test output helps determine which test case is failing thanks to the name field in our test cases. In addition, the test function's for loop now includes test := test. This is due to using the variable on the range scope in the function literal. If you do not include this line, then the linter will complain due to there being an issue with the usage of the test loop variable inside a function literal (closure) passed to t.Run or another function within the loop.

When you use a loop variable inside a function literal, it captures the loop variable by reference. This can lead to unexpected behavior because the loop variable is shared among all the iterations of the for loop. To correct this problem, you can create a local copy of the loop variable within the loop to avoid capturing it by reference using the line we have added.

> **Note**
>
> The full code for this exercise is available at `https://github.com/PacktPublishing/` `Go-Programming-From-Beginner-to-Professional-Second-Edition-/` `blob/main/Chapter19/Example01/main_test.go`.

We've now seen how to write unit tests to ensure the correctness of individual components and use table-driven tests in Go. You've also seen that all test functions in Go are prefixed with `Test` and involve passing the `testing.T` parameter. You now know the benefits of naming test cases, defining positive and negative test cases that cover corner cases, and being mindful of good practices and test coverage when it comes to unit tests. Unit tests are among the easiest of tests to add, so they should be plentiful and easy to adapt as your code grows.

Integration tests

Integration tests verify the interactions between different components or services in your application. This can include tests for one service interacting with another service, or one service interacting with many services. Overall, these tests ensure that the integrated system functions correctly as a whole. They also typically require more setup than your unit tests and take a bit more time to implement. These tests intend to validate the collaboration and communication between various parts of your application.

Integration tests play a crucial role in ensuring that the different components of your system work together seamlessly. They help uncover issues related to data flow, **application programming interface** (**API**) integrations, database interactions, and other collaborative aspects that may not be apparent during unit testing. These kinds of tests are important for detecting problems in real-world scenarios where components interact with each other.

When setting up integration tests, there are a few things you need to consider:

- **Test environment**: Integration tests often require a test environment that closely resembles a production environment or may require a dedicated test database and/or mocked services.

- **Data setup**: Preparing test data that simulates real-world scenarios can be common for integration tests. This may involve populating a database with specific data or configuring external services with test case data.

- **Service communication**: When testing interactions between services, you can consider mocking or stubbing to simulate the behavior of external services. Tools such as `gomock` and `testify/mock` can help in creating mocks for testing purposes.

Exercise 19.02 – integration test with a database

Using an in-memory database can be a good choice for integration tests as they do not affect a live database. Let's look at an exercise where we mock a database, expect certain events to occur on the database, and check our values using the `assert` package:

1. Create a new folder in your filesystem, and, inside it, create a `main_test.go` file and write the following:

```
package main
import (
  "context"
  "database/sql"
  "testing"
  "github.com/DATA-DOG/go-sqlmock"
  "github.com/stretchr/testify/assert"
  "github.com/stretchr/testify/require"
)
```

2. Define a `Record` data object that you can use to check the database operations:

```
type Record struct {
  ID int
  Name string
  Value string
}
```

3. Create the database structure and function for creating a new database:

```
type Database struct {
  conn *sql.DB
}
func NewDatabase(conn *sql.DB) *Database {
  return &Database{conn: conn}
}
```

4. Create the insertion function for the database:

```
func (d *Database) InsertRecord(ctx context.Context, record
Record) error {
  _, err := d.conn.ExecContext(ctx, "INSERT INTO records (id,
name, value) VALUES ($1, $2, $3)", record.ID, record.Name,
record.Value)
  return err
}
```

5. Create a function to retrieve inserted objects from the database:

```go
func (d *Database) GetRecordByID(ctx context.Context, id int)
(Record, error) {
  var record Record
  row := d.conn.QueryRowContext(ctx, "SELECT id, name, value
FROM records WHERE id = $1", id)
  err := row.Scan(&record.ID, &record.Name, &record.Value)
  return record, err
}
```

6. Create a test function to check integrations with an in-memory database and perform setup by creating the in-memory SQL mock, as well as a test record for interacting with the database:

```go
func TestDatabaseIntegration(t *testing.T) {
  db, mock, err := sqlmock.New()
  require.NoError(t, err)
  defer db.Close()
  testRecord := Record{
    ID: 1,
    Name: "TestRecord",
    Value: "TestValue",
  }
```

7. Set up the expectations for the SQL mock database:

```go
  mock.ExpectExec("INSERT INTO records").WithArgs(testRecord.
ID, testRecord.Name, testRecord.Value).WillReturnResult(sqlmock.
NewResult(1, 1))
  rows := sqlmock.NewRows([]string{"id", "name", "value"}).
AddRow(testRecord.ID, testRecord.Name, testRecord.Value)
  mock.ExpectQuery("SELECT id, name, value FROM records").
WillReturnRows(rows)
```
Create the database and insert a record into it:
```go
  dbInstance := NewDatabase(db)
  err = dbInstance.InsertRecord(context.Background(),
testRecord)
  assert.NoError(t, err, "Error inserting record into the
database")
```

8. Verify that you can retrieve the inserted record from the database, ensure all mocked expectations were met on the database, and close the test function:

```go
  retrievedRecord, err := dbInstance.GetRecordByID(context.
Background(), 1)
  assert.NoError(t, err, "Error retrieving record from the
database")
  assert.Equal(t, testRecord, retrievedRecord, "Retrieved record
```

```
    does not match the inserted record")
      assert.NoError(t, mock.ExpectationsWereMet())
  }
```

9. Run the program:

```
go test main_test.go
```

You will see the following output:

```
ok      command-line-arguments   0.252s
```

We've now seen what it looks like to use a mocked resource for our integration tests and performing database interactions. This test checked the insertion and retrieval of a record in the in-memory database. You can easily expand this code to check different databases that your project may interact with or use it for inspiration to check additional project interactions.

E2E tests

In Go, E2E tests are vital for assessing the system as a whole. Unlike unit tests, which focus on isolated units of code, or integration tests, which might check that certain components cooperate as expected, E2E tests exercise the entire system, simulating real user scenarios. These tests are good for catching issues that may arise from the integration of various components, ensuring the overall functionality of your application.

The purpose of E2E tests is to validate that the entire application, including its user interface, APIs, and underlying services, behaves as intended. These tests mimic the actions of a user interacting with the system, covering multiple layers and components. By testing the complete flow of an application, E2E tests help identify integration issues across the system, configuration problems, or unexpected behaviors that may arise in a real-world environment.

E2E tests have several distinctive characteristics:

-   **Realistic scenarios**: E2E tests simulate user flows or business processes, ensuring that the application behaves as expected from an end user's perspective. This realism helps catch issues that might not be apparent in more isolated testing.

-   **Multiple component interactions**: In a typical application, various components, such as databases, APIs, and user interfaces, work together to deliver functionality. E2E tests exercise these components simultaneously, verifying their interactions and compatibility.

-   **An environment that's similar to production**: E2E tests are usually run in an environment that closely resembles the production setup. This ensures that the tests accurately reflect how the application will behave in real-world conditions.

When implementing E2E tests in Go, tools such as **Selenium**, **Cypress**, or custom HTTP clients can be used to interact with the application. Go provides the `testing` and `testing/httptest` packages, which help structure and execute E2E tests effectively. These tests often involve setting up the application, interacting with it programmatically, and asserting that the expected outcomes match the actual results.

Here are some best practices for E2E testing:

- **Isolation**: E2E tests should run in an isolated environment to prevent interference with other tests or the production-level system. This ensures the reliability and consistency of the test results.

- **Automation**: Due to the complexity of these tests, automation is critical. Automated E2E tests can be integrated into the **continuous integration** (**CI**) pipeline, allowing for regular validation of the application's E2E functionality.

- **Clear test scenarios**: Define clear and representative test scenarios that cover critical user journeys. These scenarios should encompass the most common paths users take through the application.

- **Data management**: Set up and manage test data effectively. This includes creating data fixtures or using database migrations to ensure a consistent state for each test run where one test does not interfere with another.

E2E tests are some of the most involved tests to set up for a project and take the most time to complete. However, they help provide confidence in the overall functionality of the system and can catch integration issues early in the development process.

HTTP testing

In Go, HTTP testing helps validate the behavior and functionality of web services and applications. These tests ensure that the HTTP endpoints respond correctly to various requests, handle errors appropriately, and interact seamlessly with the underlying logic. Testing the HTTP layer is essential to building robust and reliable applications as it allows developers to verify the correctness of their API implementations and catch issues early in the development process.

The importance of HTTP testing can be summed up by the following aspects:

- **Functional validation**: HTTP tests validate the functional aspects of your API endpoints, ensuring that they produce the expected responses for different scenarios. This includes checking status codes, response bodies, and headers.

- **Integration verification**: HTTP tests facilitate the verification of integrations between different components of your application. They help confirm that various services communicate correctly over HTTP while respecting the defined contract.

- **Error handling**: Testing HTTP error scenarios is crucial to ensure that your API responds appropriately to erroneous requests. This includes testing for proper error codes, error messages, and error handling behavior.

- **Security assurance**: HTTP testing is an integral part of security testing. It allows developers to validate that the authentication and authorization mechanisms work as intended and that sensitive information is handled securely.

Go provides a powerful testing framework that makes it straightforward to write HTTP tests. The `net/http/httptest` package offers a testing server that enables the creation of isolated HTTP environments for testing. This is particularly useful for testing how your application interacts with external services or APIs.

Exercise 19.03 – authentication integration with a test server

Consider a scenario where we have an application that communicates via HTTP with an authentication service. We want a test server for the authentication service that simulates some authentication logic and then tests the main applications' user authentication function. Let's get started:

1. Create a new folder in your filesystem, and, inside it, create a `main_test.go` file and write the following:

```
package main
import (
  "net/http"
  "net/http/httptest"
  "testing"
  "github.com/stretchr/testify/assert"
)
```

2. Define a `User` struct and an `Application` struct, along with a new function for the application:

```
type User struct {
  UserID string
  Username string
}
type Application struct {
  AuthServiceURL string
}
func NewApplication(authServiceURL string) *Application {
  return &Application{
    AuthServiceURL: authServiceURL,
  }
}
```

3. Create a function to simulate the user authentication process:

```go
func (app *Application) AuthenticateUser(token string) (*User,
error) {
  return &User{
    UserID: "123",
    Username: "testuser",
  }, nil
}
```

4. Define the test function and set up a test server for the authentication service:

```go
func TestAuthenticationIntegration(t *testing.T) {
  authService := httptest.NewServer(http.HandlerFunc(func(w
http.ResponseWriter, r *http.Request) {
    if r.Header.Get("Authorization") == "Bearer valid_token" {
      w.WriteHeader(http.StatusOK)
      w.Write([]byte(`{"user_id": "123", "username":
"testuser"}`))
    } else {
      w.WriteHeader(http.StatusUnauthorized)
    }
  }))
  defer authService.Close()
```

5. Create the application, test the authentication process, and then close the test function:

```go
  app := NewApplication(authService.URL)
  token := "valid_token"
  gotUser, err := app.AuthenticateUser(token)
  assert.NoError(t, err)
  assert.Equal(t, "123", gotUser.UserID)
  assert.Equal(t, "testuser", gotUser.Username)
}
```

6. Run the program:

```
go test main_test.go
```

You will see the following output:

```
ok        command-line-arguments   0.298s
```

In this exercise, we used the `httptest.NewServer` function to create a test server for the authentication service, allowing us to control its behavior during the test. The test then set up the main application, triggered the authentication process, and asserted the expected outcomes. This helped highlight how to incorporate HTTP testing to build reliable web applications.

Fuzz testing

Fuzz testing, or fuzzing, involves providing random or malformed inputs to functions to discover vulnerabilities. In other words, it is a testing technique that involves providing invalid, unexpected, or random data as input to a program with the intent of discovering vulnerabilities and bugs. The testing package in Go's standard library includes support for fuzzing, enabling developers to uncover unexpected behaviors with their code.

Unlike traditional testing, which relies on predetermined test cases, fuzz testing explores the input space extensively. You can see this as fuzz testing often subjects programs to large amounts of random or malformed input data to see what happens. Because fuzz tests are so different from traditional test cases, they can help identify edge cases and unexpected input scenarios that might light up bugs or vulnerabilities. They can also provide ongoing security and stability verification if they're established in an automated fashion.

A simple example fuzz test for our add function from earlier looks as follows:

```go
func add(x, y int) int {
  return x + y
}
func FuzzAdd(f *testing.F) {
  f.Fuzz(func(t *testing.T, i int, j int) {
    got := add(i, j)
    assert.Equal(t, i + j, got)
  })
}
```

You can see a few differences in this function versus the previous test functions we've been seeing. For example, fuzz testing functions start with *Fuzz* and pass in f *testing.F instead of t *testing.T. You can also see that since we don't have to worry about generating our own inputs, the function is very simple and clean in comparison to all of our test cases from earlier in this chapter. In addition, instead of a t.Run execution, we have f.Fuzz, which takes a fuzz target function with our usual t *testing.T and the input types to fuzz.

Lastly, it is important to note that to see the fuzz testing results, you must run the following command:

```
go test -fuzz .
```

This will run the fuzz tests that are present in the test file. It is important to note that your fuzz tests can live alongside other tests in the test file. You will also see an output similar to the following:

```
fuzz: elapsed: 0s, gathering baseline coverage: 0/1 completed
fuzz: elapsed: 0s, gathering baseline coverage: 1/1 completed, now
fuzzing with 10 workers
fuzz: elapsed: 3s, execs: 331780 (110538/sec), new interesting: 0
(total: 1)
```

```
fuzz: elapsed: 6s, execs: 709743 (126040/sec), new interesting: 0
(total: 1)
fuzz: elapsed: 9s, execs: 1123414 (137875/sec), new interesting: 0
(total: 1)
fuzz: elapsed: 12s, execs: 1417293 (97927/sec), new interesting: 0
(total: 1)
fuzz: elapsed: 15s, execs: 1713062 (98627/sec), new interesting: 0
(total: 1)
fuzz: elapsed: 18s, execs: 2076324 (121080/sec), new interesting: 0
(total: 1)
^Cfuzz: elapsed: 20s, execs: 2237555 (107504/sec), new interesting: 0
(total: 1)
PASS
ok      github.com/packt-book/Go-Programming---From-Beginner-to-
Professional-Second-Edition-/Chapter19/Example    19.697s
```

The new interesting thing in the preceding output is the number of inputs that were added to the corpus that provide unique results. *Execs* is the number of individual tests that were run. As you can see, this is far larger than the amount we were manually testing in our unit test case from earlier. Fuzz testing can help provide lots of input. If you have a fuzz test that fails, then the failing seed corpus entry will be written to a file and placed in the package directory. You can then use that information to rectify the failure.

Benchmarks

Benchmarks assess the performance of your code by measuring the execution time of specific functions. The testing package provides support for benchmarks, allowing developers to identify performance bottlenecks, identify if developers are achieving their project's **service-level indicators** (**SLIs**) or **service-level objectives** (**SLOs**), and gain insights into their application.

Similar to how fuzz testing had a slightly different syntax, but followed our usual Go test setup expectations, benchmark tests also look different, but very similar to what we're used to. For example, benchmark tests start with the word *Benchmark* and accept b *testing.B. The testing runner executes each benchmark function several times, increasing the value of b.N on each run.

Here's a simple example benchmark function for our addition function:

```
func BenchmarkAdd(b *testing.B) {
  for i := 0; i < b.N; i++ {
    add(1, 2)
  }
}
```

To run the benchmark test, you must add the benchmark flag for the Go test framework:

```
go test -bench .
```

This will give you an output similar to the following:

```
goos: darwin
goarch: arm64
pkg: github.com/packt-book/Go-Programming---From-Beginner-to-
Professional-Second-Edition-/Chapter19/Example
BenchmarkAdd-10        1000000000        0.3444 ns/op
PASS
ok        github.com/packt-book/Go-Programming---From-Beginner-to-
Professional-Second-Edition-/Chapter19/Example    0.538s
```

The numerical value of 1000000000 indicates the number of iterations or operations the benchmark performed; in this case, it's 1 billion operations. 0.3444 ns/op is the average time taken per operation in nanoseconds. This indicates that, on average, each call to the add function took approximately 0.3444 nanoseconds.

You can write even more complex benchmark functions to derive more meaning out of your code's performance so that you can include heap allocations per operation and byte allocations per operation.

With benchmark tests, it is important to use real-world input to retrieve the most accurate performance metrics on your code. You should also break down benchmarks into multiple functions to attain better granularity as this will help you assess the performance of your code.

Test suites

Test suites organize multiple related tests into a cohesive unit. The testing package in Go supports test suites that use the TestMain function and the testing.M type. TestMain is a special function that can be used to perform setup and teardown logic for the entire test suite. This is particularly useful when you need to set up resources or configurations that are shared across multiple test suites.

Exercise 19.04 – using TestMain to execute several test functions

Consider a scenario where you have multiple test functions that you want to be grouped into a test suite. Let's see how that can be done using the native Go test framework:

1. Create a new folder in your filesystem, and, inside it, create a main_test.go file and write the following:

    ```
    package main
    import (
      "log"
      "testing"
    )
    ```

2. Define a setup and teardown function:

```
func setup() {
    log.Println("setup() running")
}
func teardown() {
    log.Println("teardown() running")
}
```

3. Create the `TestMain` function:

```
func TestMain(m *testing.M) {
    setup()
    defer teardown()
    m.Run()
}
```

4. Define a few test cases for `TestMain` to run:

```
func TestA(t *testing.T) {
    log.Println("TestA running")
}
func TestB(t *testing.T) {
    log.Println("TestB running")
}
func TestC(t *testing.T) {
    log.Println("TestC running")
}
```

5. Run the program in verbose mode to see `TestMain` executing our test functions:

```
go test -v main_test.go
```

You will see the following output:

```
2024/02/05 23:34:29 setup() running
=== RUN    TestA
2024/02/05 23:34:29 TestA running
--- PASS: TestA (0.00s)
=== RUN    TestB
2024/02/05 23:34:29 TestB running
--- PASS: TestB (0.00s)
=== RUN    TestC
2024/02/05 23:34:29 TestC running
--- PASS: TestC (0.00s)
PASS
```

```
2024/02/05 23:34:29 teardown() running
ok      github.com/packt-book/Go-Programming---From-Beginner-to-
Professional-Second-Edition-/Chapter19/Exercise20.04    0.395s
```

Here, you can see how `TestMain` executes the setup, then the test functions we've defined in the package, and then the teardown at the end thanks to the `defer` function. This allows you to write several test functions that might be related and group them into a suite to be run together. By using `TestMain`, you have more control over the global setup and teardown processes, allowing you to handle shared resources and configurations efficiently for your test suite.

Test report

Writing tests is crucial for maintaining the correctness of your application; however, knowing the results of your tests is equally as important. Generating a test report provides a clear overview of test results. This helps identify issues and track improvements to the code base over time. The Go `test` command supports various flags for customizing test output.

Go provides the `json` flag, which can be used to generate machine-readable JSON output. This output can then be processed or analyzed by various tools. To generate a test report in JSON format, run the following command:

```
go test . -v -json > test-report.json
```

This command runs the tests and redirects the JSON-formatted output to a file named `test-report.json` using the available test files denoted by the period, though you can specify certain test files instead of using a period. The resulting file contains information about each test, including its name, status, duration, and any failure messages.

You can then use this report with various tools to analyze and better visualize the test results. However, you have to be mindful that some packages might alter the output of your test results in unintended ways – or useful ways. For example, the `stretchr/testify` package can be used with the assertion functions that we've seen in a few of the exercises to provide more useful output in the test reports. Our simple assertion on the addition of values from previous exercises could be modified to provide clear output in the event of a failure.

So, let's say we have the following code:

```
assert.Equal(t, i+j, got)
```

This could be updated to the following:

```
assert.Equal(t, i+j, got, "the values i and j should be summed
together properly")
```

Additionally, you could update it further to provide even more insights into what values of `i` and `j` failed the test, and so forth.

Code coverage

Understanding the extent of code coverage ensures that your tests adequately exercise your code base. Go provides a built-in tool called `cover` that generates test coverage reports based on the test cases you have implemented and that it can identify. This is something you can easily add for unit tests and is a new feature that was added in Go 1.20 for integration test code coverage.

Industry standards for application development sit at an 80% code coverage average for projects to strive for. You will typically see the coverage tool used in CI tools that run pull requests against main/master branches to check that there are no large drops in code coverage that have been tested.

You can add the `cover` flag to calculate test coverage on your test functions. There is also a flag that you can include to specify an output file to generate from the code coverage tool running and gathering its results. This is a useful report to include when your project requires artifacts for stakeholders and leadership that want verification that proper test code coverage is included in the development of the project.

Let's look at an example of what that might look like for a package we've been using throughout this chapter in an `add.go` file. If you have an `add_test.go` file with the corresponding `TestAdd()` function, you can check the code coverage amount using the following command:

```
go test . -cover
```

You can also update the period so that it points to a specific package or directory that you want code coverage on. You should see the typical test output, followed by the coverage amount:

```
ok      github.com/packt-book/Go-Programming---From-
Beginner-to-Professional-Second-Edition-/Chapter19/
Example02      0.357s  coverage: 100.0% of statements
```

As you can see, since there is a test function for our add function, we have 100% coverage. If, by chance, we add an addition function for a different type of input, such as float64 values, then our coverage amount would drop to 50% until we add the test function that corresponds to our new function.

> **Note**
>
> The full code for this exercise is available at https://github.com/PacktPublishing/
> Go-Programming-From-Beginner-to-Professional-Second-Edition-/
> tree/main/Chapter19/Example02.

A development team can use the results from the code coverage tool to determine if they need to increase the amount of test cases for their projects, or in certain areas of the project, as the output file can demonstrate the areas lacking in code coverage. This is one of the many powerful ways Go enables developers to write properly tested code.

Summary

In this chapter, we explored the diverse landscape of testing in Go, from unit tests to integration and E2E tests, and a few other types of tests, including HTTP tests and fuzz tests. We also learned about test suites and industry best practices when it comes to code coverage for our projects. We wrapped this chapter up with what we can do with our tests, which includes creating a test report to share for our test coverage, as well as benchmarks that highlight the performance of our code base.

Armed with these tools and techniques, developers can ensure the reliability and stability of the Go code that they write. We covered a lot of ground when it comes to testing with Go, and barely scratched the surface of the capabilities that the Go toolchain offers us developers. In the next chapter, we'll take a closer look at the Go tools and the capabilities they offer us.

20

Using Go Tools

> **Overview**
>
> This chapter will teach you how to make use of the Go toolkit so that you can improve and build your code. It will also help you build and improve your code using Go tools and create binaries using `go build`. Furthermore, you'll learn how to clean up library imports using `goimports`, detect suspicious constructs with `go vet`, and identify race conditions in your code using the Go race detector.
>
> By the end of this chapter, you will be able to run code with `go run`, format code with `gofmt`, automatically generate documentation using `go doc`, and download third-party packages using `go get`.

Technical requirements

For this chapter, you'll require Go version 1.21 or higher. The code for this chapter can be found at `https://github.com/PacktPublishing/Go-Programming-From-Beginner-to-Professional-Second-Edition-/tree/main/Chapter20`.

Introduction

In the previous chapters, you learned how to produce concurrent and well-tested code. Although Go makes the task of creating concurrent and tested code much easier compared to other languages, these tasks can be intrinsically complex. This is when learning to use tools to write better code that will simplify the complexity comes in handy.

In this chapter, you will learn about Go tools. Go comes with several tools to help you write better code. For example, in the previous chapters, you came across `go build`, which you used to build your code into an executable. You also came across `go test`, which you used to test your code. There are also a few more tools that help in different ways. For example, the `goimports` tool will check if you have all the import statements required for your code to work and if not, it will add them. It can also check if any of your import statements are no longer needed and remove them. While this seems like a very simple thing, it means you no longer need to worry about the imports and can instead focus on the code you are writing. Alternatively, you can use the Go race detector to find race conditions hidden in your code. This is an extremely valuable tool when you start writing concurrent code.

The tools provided with the Go language are one of the reasons for its popularity. They provide a standard way to check code for formatting issues, mistakes, and race conditions, which is very useful when you are developing software in a professional setting. The exercises in this chapter provide practical examples of how to use these tools to improve your code.

The go build tool

The go build tool takes Go source code and compiles it so that it can be executed. When creating software, you write code in a human-readable programming language. Then, the code needs to be translated into a machine-readable format so that it can be executed. This is done by a compiler that compiles the machine instructions from the source code. To do this with Go code, you can use go build.

Exercise 20.01 – using the go build tool

In this exercise, you will learn about the go build tool. This will take your Go source code and compile it into a binary. To use it, run the go build tool on the command line while using the -o flag to specify the output file or executable name:

```
go build -o name_of_the_binary_to_create source_file.go
```

If the -o flag is omitted, the output file will be named by the package or folder that contains the source file.

Let's get started:

1. Create a new directory called Exercise20.01. Within that directory, create a new file called main.go.

2. Run the following two commands to create the Go module for the exercise:

    ```
    go mod init
    go mod tidy
    ```

3. Add the following code to the file to create a simple Hello World program:

    ```
    package main
    import "fmt"
    func main() {
       fmt.Println("Hello World")
    }
    ```

4. To run the program, you need to open your Terminal and navigate to the directory that you created the `main.go` file in. Then, run the `go build` tool by writing the following:

```
go build -o hello_world main.go
```

5. This will create an executable called `hello_world` that you can execute the binary in by running it on the command line:

```
./hello_world
```

The output will look as follows:

```
Hello World
```

In this exercise, you used the `go build` tool to compile your code into a binary and execute it.

The go run tool

The `go run` tool is similar to `go build` in that it compiles your Go code. However, the subtle difference is that `go build` will output a binary file that you can execute, whereas the `go run` tool doesn't create a binary file that you need to execute. It compiles the code and runs it in a single step, with no binary file output in the end. This can be useful if you want to quickly check that your code does what you expect it to do, without the need to create and run a binary file. This would be commonly used when you're testing your code so that you can run it quickly without needing to create a binary to execute.

Exercise 20.02 – using the go run tool

In this exercise, you will learn about the `go run` tool. This is used as a shortcut to compile and run your code in a single step, which is useful if you want to quickly check that your code works. To use it, run the `go run` tool on the command line in the following format:

```
go run source_file.go
```

Perform the following steps:

1. Create a new directory called `Exercise20.02`. Within that directory, create a new file called `main.go`.

2. Run the following two commands to create the Go module for this exercise:

```
go mod init
go mod tidy
```

3. Add the following code to the file to create a simple `Hello Packt` program:

```
package main
import "fmt"
func main() {
    fmt.Println("Hello Packt")
}
```

4. Now, you can run the program using the `go run` tool:

```
go run main.go
```

This will execute the code and run it all in one step, giving you the following output:

```
Hello Packt
```

In this exercise, you used the `go run` tool to compile and run a simple Go program in a single step. This is useful to quickly check whether your code does what you expect.

The gofmt tool

The `gofmt` tool is used to keep your code neat and consistently styled. When working on a large software project, an important but often overlooked factor is code style. Having a consistent code style throughout your project is important for readability. When you must read someone else's code, or even your own code months after writing it, having it in a consistent style makes you focus on the logic without much effort. Having to parse differing styles when reading code is just one more thing to worry about and leads to mistakes. To overcome this issue, Go comes with a tool to automatically format your code in a consistent way called `gofmt`. This means that, across your project, and even across other Go projects that use the `gofmt` tool, the code will be consistent. So, it will fix the formatting of the code by correcting the spacing and indentation, as well as trying to align the sections of your code.

Exercise 20.03 – using the gofmt tool

In this exercise, you'll learn how to use the `gofmt` tool to format your code. When you run the `gofmt` tool, it will display how it thinks the file should look with the correct formatting, but it won't change the file. If you would like `gofmt` to automatically change the file to the correct format, you can run `gofmt` with the `-w` option, which will update the file and save the changes. Let's get started:

1. Create a new directory called `Exercise20.03`. Within that directory, create a new Go file called `main.go`.

2. Run the following two commands to create the Go module for this exercise:

```
go mod init
go mod tidy
```

3. Add the following code to the file to create a badly formatted `Hello Packt` program:

```
package main
import "fmt"
func main(){
   firstVar := 1
   secondVar := 2
   fmt.Println(firstVar)
   fmt.Println(secondVar)
   fmt. Println("Hello Packt")
}
```

4. Then, in your Terminal, run `gofmt` to see what the file will look like:

```
gofmt main.go
```

This will display how the file should be formatted to make it correct. Here is the expected output:

```
> gofmt main.go
package main

import "fmt"

func main() {
        firstVar := 1
        secondVar := 2

        fmt.Println(firstVar)
        fmt.Println(secondVar)
        fmt.Println("Hello Packt")
}
```

Figure 20.1: Expected output from gofmt

However, this only shows the changes it would make; it doesn't change the file. This is so that you can confirm you are happy with the changes it will make.

5. To change the file and save those changes, you need to add the `-w` option:

```
gofmt -w main.go
```

This will update the file and save the changes. Then, when you look at the file, it should look like this:

```
package main
import "fmt"
func main() {
   firstVar := 1
   secondVar := 2
   fmt.Println(firstVar)
```

```
      fmt.Println(secondVar)
      fmt.Println("Hello Packt")
  }
```

You may observe that the badly formatted code has been realigned after using the gofmt tool. The spacing and indentation have been fixed, and the new line between func and main() has been removed.

> **Note**
>
> Many **integrated development environments (IDEs)** come with a built-in way for you to use gofmt on your code when you save. It is worth researching how to do this with your chosen IDE so that the gofmt tool will run automatically and fix any spacing or indentation mistakes in your code.

In this exercise, you used the gofmt tool to reformat a badly formatted file into a neat state. This can seem pointless and annoying when you first start coding. However, as your skills improve and you start working on larger projects, you will start to appreciate the importance of a neat and consistent code style.

The goimports tool

Another useful tool that comes with Go is goimports, which automatically adds the imports that are needed in your file. A key part of software engineering is not reinventing the wheel and reusing other people's code. In Go, you do this by importing the libraries at the start of your file, in the import section. It can, however, be tedious to add these imports each time you need to use them. You can also accidentally leave in unused imports, which can pose a security risk. A better way to do this is to use goimports to automatically add the imports for you. It will also remove unused imports and reorder the remaining imports into alphabetical order for better readability.

Exercise 20.04 – using the goimports tool

In this exercise, you will learn how to use goimports to manage the imports in a simple Go program. When you run the goimports tool, it will output how it thinks the file should look with the imports fixed. Alternatively, you can run goimports with the -w option, which automatically updates the imports in the file and saves the changes. Let's get started:

1. Create a new directory called Exercise20.04. Within that directory, create a new file called main.go.

2. Run the following two commands to create the Go module for this exercise:

    ```
    go mod init
    go mod tidy
    ```

3. Add the following code to the file to create a simple Hello Packt program with incorrect imports:

```
package main
import (
    "net/http"
    "fmt"
)
func main() {
    fmt.Println("Hello")
    log.Println("Packt")
}
```

You will notice that the log library has not been imported and that the net/http import is unused.

4. In your Terminal, run the goimports tool against your file to see how the imports change:

```
goimports main.go
```

This will display the changes it would make to the file to correct it. Here is the expected output:

```
> goimports main.go
package main

import (
        "fmt"
        "log"
)

func main() {
        fmt.Println("Hello")
        log.Println("Packt")
}
```

Figure 20.2: Expected output for goimports

This won't have changed the file but shows what the file will be changed to. As you can see, the net/http import has been removed and the log import has been added.

5. To write these changes to the file, add the -w option:

```
goimports -w main.go
```

6. This will update the file and make it look as follows:

```
package main
import (
    "fmt"
    "log"
)
```

```
func main() {
    fmt.Println("Hello")
    log.Println("Packt")
}
```

In this exercise, you learned how to use the `goimports` tool. You can use this tool to detect incorrect and unused import statements and automatically correct them. Many IDEs come with a built-in way to turn on `goimports` so that when you save your file, it will automatically correct the imports for you.

The go vet tool

The `go vet` tool is used for static analysis of your Go code. While the Go compiler can find and inform you of mistakes you may have made, there are certain things it will miss. For this reason, the `go vet` tool was created. This might sound trivial, but some of these issues could go unnoticed for a long time after the code has been deployed, the most common of which is passing the wrong number of arguments when using the `Printf` function. It will also check for useless assignments, for example, if you set a variable and then never use that variable. Another particularly useful thing it detects is when a non-pointer interface is passed to an `unmarshal` function. The compiler won't notice this as it is valid; however, the `unmarshal` function will be unable to write the data to the interface. This can be troublesome to debug but using the `go vet` tool allows you to catch it early and remediate the issue before it becomes a problem.

Exercise 20.05 – using the go vet tool

In this exercise, you will use the `go vet` tool to find a common mistake that's made when using the `Printf` function. You will use it to detect when the wrong number of arguments are being passed to a `Printf` function. Let's get started:

1. Create a new directory called `Exercise20.05`. Within that directory, create a new go file called `main.go`:

2. Run the following two commands to create the Go module for this exercise:

    ```
    go mod init
    go mod tidy
    ```

3. Add the following code to the file to create a simple `Hello Packt` program:

    ```
    package main
    import "fmt"
    func main() {
        helloString := "Hello"
        packtString := "Packt"
        jointString := fmt.Sprintf("%s", helloString, packtString)
    ```

```
        fmt.Println(jointString)
    }
```

As you can see, the `jointString` variable makes use of `fmt.Sprintf` to join two strings into one. However, the `%s` format string is incorrect and only formats one of the input strings. When you build this code, it will compile into a binary without any errors. However, when you run the program, the output will not be as expected. Luckily, the `go vet` tool was created for this exact reason.

4. Run the `go vet` tool against the file you created:

```
    go vet main.go
```

5. This will display any issues it finds in the code:

```
        > go vet main.go
        # command-line-arguments
        ./main.go:9:17: Sprintf call needs 1 arg but has 2 args
```

Figure 20.3: Expected output from go vet

As you can see, `go vet` has identified an issue on line 9 of the file. The `Sprintf` call needs 1 argument, but we have given it 2.

6. Update the `Sprintf` call so that it can handle both arguments we want to send:

```
    package main
    import "fmt"
    func main() {
        helloString := "Hello"
        packtString := "Packt"
        jointString := fmt.Sprintf("%s %s", helloString, packtString)
        fmt.Println(jointString)
    }
```

7. Now, you can run `go vet` again and check that there are no more issues:

```
    go vet main.go
```

It should return nothing, letting you know the file has no more issues.

8. Now, run the program:

```
    go run main.go
```

Here's the output after making the corrections in the string:

```
Hello Packt
```

In this exercise, you learned how to use the `go vet` tool to detect issues that the compiler might miss. While this is a very basic example, `go vet` can detect mistakes such as passing a non-pointer to `unmarshal` functions or detecting unreachable code. You are encouraged to run `go vet` as part of your build process so that you can catch these issues before they make it into your program.

The Go race detector

The Go race detector was added to Go so that developers can detect race conditions. As we mentioned in *Chapter 18, Concurrent Work*, you can use goroutines to run parts of your code concurrently. However, even experienced programmers might make a mistake that allows different goroutines to access the same resource at the same time. This is called a race condition. A race condition is problematic because one goroutine can edit the resource in the middle of another reading it, meaning the resource could be corrupted. While Go has made concurrency a first-class citizen in the language, the mechanisms for concurrent code do not prevent race conditions. Also, due to the inherent nature of concurrency, a race condition might stay hidden until long after your code has been deployed. This also means they tend to be transient, making them devilishly difficult to debug and fix. This is why the Go race detector was created.

This tool works by using an algorithm that detects asynchronous memory access, but a drawback of this is that it can only do so when the code executes. So, you need to run the code to be able to detect race conditions. Luckily, it has been integrated into the Go toolchain, so we can use it to do this for us.

Exercise 20.06 – using the Go race detector

In this exercise, you will create a basic program that contains a race condition. You will use the Go race detector on the program to find the race condition. You will learn how to identify where the problem lies and then learn ways to mitigate the race condition. Let's get started:

1. Create a new directory called `Exercise20.06`. Within that directory, create a new file called `main.go`.

2. Run the following two commands to create the Go module for this exercise:

    ```
    go mod init
    go mod tidy
    ```

3. Add the following code to the file to create a simple program with race conditions:

    ```
    package main
    import "fmt"
    func main() {
        finished := make(chan bool)
        names := []string{"Packt"}
        go func() {
    ```

```
        names = append(names, "Electric")
        names = append(names, "Boogaloo")
        finished <- true
    }()
    for _, name := range names {
      fmt.Println(name)
    }
    <-finished
  }
```

As you can see, there is an array called `names` with one item in it. A goroutine then starts appending more names to it. At the same time, the main goroutine is attempting to print out all the items in the array. So, both goroutines are accessing the same resource at the same time, which is a race condition.

4. Run the preceding code with the `race` flag activated:

```
go run --race main.go
```

Running this command will give us the following output:

```
Packt
==================
WARNING: DATA RACE
Write at 0x00c0000aa000 by goroutine 6:
  main.main.func1()
      /Users/samcoyle/go/src/github.com/packt-book/Go-Programming---
From-Beginner-to-Professional-Second-Edition-/Chapter20/Exercise20.06/
main.go:10 +0xe0
Previous read at 0x00c0000aa000 by main goroutine:
  main.main()
      /Users/samcoyle/go/src/github.com/packt-book/Go-Programming---
From-Beginner-to-Professional-Second-Edition-/Chapter20/Exercise20.06/
main.go:14 +0x170
Goroutine 6 (running) created at:
  main.main()
      /Users/samcoyle/go/src/github.com/packt-book/Go-Programming---
From-Beginner-to-Professional-Second-Edition-/Chapter20/Exercise20.06/
main.go:9 +0x168
==================
Found 1 data race(s)
exit status 66
```

In the output, you can see a warning, informing you about the race condition. It tells you that the same resource was read and written in the code on lines `main.go:10` and `main.go:15`, which look as follows:

```
names = append(names, "Electric")
for _, name := range names {
```

As you can see, in both cases, it is the `names` array that is being accessed, so that is where the problem lies. The reason this happens is that the program starts to print `names` before it waits for the `finished` channel.

1. A solution could be to wait for the `finished` channel before printing the items:

   ```
   <-finished
   for _, name := range names {
       fmt.Println(name)
   }
   ```

2. This means that the items will have all been added to the array before you start to print them out. You can confirm this solution by running the program again with the `--race` flag activated:

   ```
   go run --race main.go
   ```

3. This should run the program as normal and show no race condition warnings. The expected output after the corrections have been made is as follows:

   ```
   Packt
   Electric
   Boogaloo
   ```

The final program with the race condition now fixed would look as follows:

```
package main
import "fmt"
func main() {
    finished := make(chan bool)
    names := []string{"Packt"}
    go func() {
        names = append(names, "Electric")
        names = append(names, "Boogaloo")
        finished <- true
    }()
    <-finished
    for _, name := range names {
        fmt.Println(name)
    }
}
```

While the program in this exercise was quite simple, as was the solution, you are encouraged to return to *Chapter 18, Concurrent Work*, and use the `--race` flag in the activities there. This will provide a better working example of how the Go race detector can help you.

> **Note**
> The Go race detector is often used by professional software developers to confirm that their solution doesn't contain any hidden race conditions.

The go doc tool

The `go doc` tool is used to generate documentation for packages and functions in Go. An often neglected part of many software projects is their documentation. This is because it can be tedious to write and even more tedious to keep up to date. So, Go comes with a tool to automatically generate documentation for package declarations and functions in your code. You simply need to add comments to the start of functions and packages. Then, these will be picked up and combined with the function header.

This can then be shared with others to help them understand how to use your code. To generate the documentation for a package and its function, you can use the `go doc` tool. Documentation like this helps when you are working on a large project and other people need to make use of your code. Often, in a professional setting, different teams will be working on different parts of a program; each team will need to communicate to the other teams about what functions are available in a package and how to call them. To do this, they could use `go doc` to generate the documentation for the code they've written and share it with other teams.

Exercise 20.07 – implementing the go doc tool

In this exercise, you will learn about the `go doc` tool and how it can be used to generate documentation for your code. Let's get started:

1. Create a new directory called `Exercise20.07`. Within that directory, create a new file called `main.go`.

2. Run the following two commands to create the Go module for this exercise:

    ```
    go mod init
    go mod tidy
    ```

3. Add the following code to the `main.go` file you created:

    ```
    package main
    import "fmt"
    // Add returns the total of two integers added together
    func Add(a, b int) int {
    ```

```
    return a + b
}
// Multiply returns the total of one integer multiplied by the
other
func Multiply(a, b int) int {
    return a * b
}
func main() {
    fmt.Println(Add(1, 1))
    fmt.Println(Multiply(2, 2))
}
```

This creates a simple program that contains two functions: one called Add, which adds two numbers, and one called Multiply, which multiplies two numbers.

4. Run the following command to compile and execute the file:

    ```
    go run main.go
    ```

5. The output will look as follows:

    ```
    2
    4
    ```

6. You will notice that both functions have comments above them that begin with the name of the function. This is a Go convention to let you know that these comments can be used as documentation. What this means is that you can use the go doc tool to create documentation for the code. In the same directory as your main.go file, run the following:

    ```
    go doc -all
    ```

This will generate documentation for the code and output it, as follows:

```
> go doc -all


FUNCTIONS

func Add(a, b int) int
    Add returns the total of two integers added together

func Multiply(a, b int) int
    Multiply returns the total of one integers multipled the other
```

Figure 20.4: Expected output from go doc

In this exercise, you learned how to use the go doc tool to generate documentation on the Go package you created, as well as its functions. You can use this for other packages you have created and share the documentation with others if they would like to make use of your code. If you would like to capture this documentation, you can use godoc package/path > output.txt.

The go get tool

The go get tool allows you to download and use different libraries. While Go comes with a wide range of packages by default, it is dwarfed by the number of third-party packages that are available. These provide extra functionality that you can use in your code to enhance it. However, for your code to make use of these packages, you need to have them on your computer so that the compiler can include them when compiling your code. To download these packages, you can use the go get tool.

Exercise 20.08 – implementing the go get tool

In this exercise, you will learn how to download a third-party package using go get. Let's get started:

1. Create a new directory called Exercise20.08. Within that directory, create a new file called main.go.

2. Run the following two commands to create the go module for this exercise:

    ```
    go mod init
    go mod tidy
    ```

3. Add the following code to the main.go file you created:

    ```
    package main
    import (
      "fmt"
      "log"
      "net/http"
      "github.com/gorilla/mux"
    )
    func exampleHandler(w http.ResponseWriter, r *http.Request) {
      w.WriteHeader(http.StatusOK)
      fmt.Fprintf(w, "Hello Packt")
    }
    func main() {
      r := mux.NewRouter()
      r.HandleFunc("/", exampleHandler)
      log.Fatal(http.ListenAndServe(":8888", r))
    }
    ```

4. This is a simple web server that you can start by running the following command:

    ```
    go run main.go
    ```

5. However, the web server uses a third-party package called mux. In the import section, you will see that it has been imported from github.com/gorilla/mux. However, since we don't have this package stored locally, an error will occur when we try to run the program:

```
main.go:8:2: no required module provides package github.com/
gorilla/mux; to add it:
    go get github.com/gorilla/mux
```

6. To get the third-party package, you can use go get. This will download it locally so that our Go code can make use of it:

```
go get github.com/gorilla/mux
```

7. Now that you have downloaded the package, you can run the web server again:

```
go run main.go
```

This time, it should run without any errors:

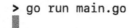

Figure 20.5: Expected output when running the web server

8. While the web server is running, you can open http://localhost:8888 in your web browser and check that it works:

Hello Packt

Figure 20.6: Web server output when viewed in Firefox

In this exercise, you learned how to download third-party packages using the go get tool. This allows the use of tools and packages beyond what comes as a standard package in Go.

Activity 20.01 – using gofmt, goimport, go vet, and go get to correct a file

Imagine that you are working on a project with poorly written code. The file contains a badly formatted file, missing imports, and a log message in the wrong place. You want to use the Go tools you've learned about in this chapter to correct the file and find any issues with it. In this activity, you will use gofmt, goimport, go vet, and go get to fix the file and find any issues within it. The steps for this activity are as follows:

1. Create a directory called Activity20.01.

2. Create a file called main.go.

3. Add the Go module for your activity code.

4. Add the code from the Activity20.01/example directory to main.go so that you can correct and properly format it and install its dependencies.

5. Fix any formatting issues.

6. Fix any missing imports from main.go.

7. Check for any issues the compiler may miss by using go vet.

8. Ensure the third-party gorilla/mux package has been downloaded to your local computer.

   Here is the expected output:

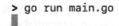

```
> go run main.go
```

Figure 20.7: Expected output when running the code

You can check that this worked by going to http://localhost:8888 in your web browser:

Hello Packt

Figure 20.8: Expected output when accessing the web server through Firefox

> **Note**
>
> The solution for this activity can be found in this book's GitHub repository at https://github.com/PacktPublishing/Go-Programming-From-Beginner-to-Professional-Second-Edition-/tree/main/Chapter20/Activity20.01.

Here is the example code to correct:

```go
package main
import (
  "log"
  "fmt"
  "github.com/gorilla/mux"
)
// ExampleHandler handles the http requests sent to this webserver
Func ExampleHandler(w http.ResponseWriter, r *http.Request) {
  w.WriteHeader(http.StatusOK)
  fmt.Fprintf(w, "Hello Packt")
  return
  log.Println("completed")
```

```
}
func main() {
    r := mux.NewRouter()
    r.HandleFunc("/", ExampleHandler)
    log.Fatal(http.ListenAndServe(":8888", r))
}
```

You've now seen several of the Go tools in action in one coding exercise.

Summary

Go tools are invaluable to a programmers when they're writing code. In this chapter, you learned about go build and how to compile your code into executables. Then, you learned how consistent neat code is important when working on a project and how you can use gofmt to automatically neaten the code for you. This can be further improved with goimports, which can remove unnecessary imports for better security and automatically add imports you may have forgotten to add yourself.

After, you looked at go vet and how it can be used to help you find any mistakes that the compiler may have missed. You also learnt how to use the Go race detector to find race conditions hidden in your code. Then, you learned how to generate documentation for your code, which makes for easier collaboration when working on larger projects. Finally, you looked at downloading third-party packages using the go get tool, which allows you to make use of numerous Go packages that are available online to enhance your code.

In the next chapter, you will learn about running your Go code in the cloud, and considerations developers make when this occurs.

21

Go in the Cloud

Overview

This chapter will show you how to take your Go application to the next level of readiness for deployment. It will cover the considerations you have to make your Go application run reliably once deployed to your server or cloud infrastructure by demonstrating how to add monitoring capabilities to the system through an open source monitoring and alerting toolkit known as **Prometheus**. The chapter will also discuss how to run your application using an orchestrator and all of the benefits you get out of the box. Lastly, the chapter will cover insights that **OpenTelemetry** allows, as well as best practices for containerizing your Go application code.

By the end of this chapter, you will be empowered to deploy your Go application reliably, and with valuable insights into the system to ensure its success.

Technical requirements

For this chapter, you'll require Go version 1.21 or higher. The code for this chapter can be found at `https://github.com/PacktPublishing/Go-Programming-From-Beginner-to-Professional-Second-Edition-/tree/main/Chapter21`.

Introduction

In the previous chapter, you learned about the various Go tools that enable developers to write better code and be more productive. We covered the Go tools to compile and run your Go code using the `go build` and `go run` commands. We then looked at how to format Go code using `gofmt`. We also saw the power of working with the Go ecosystem through its dependencies with the `goimports` and `go get` command-line tools. After having functional dependencies in our code, we can see issues that might be present using the `Go vet` tool and the `Go race` detector. Lastly, with any good code comes a well-rounded project through proper documentation using the `Go doc` tool. The previous chapter empowered you with the tools right at your fingertips in the Go ecosystem.

In this chapter, we focus on the fact that at some point in a project, your application development journey will lead you to the final frontier: deploying the application. But, before you hit the deploy button or run the final command, there are essential considerations to ensure your application runs reliably and efficiently in its destination environment.

Where your Go application will be deployed depends on numerous factors. This can be a stakeholder and leadership-led decision, based on existing infrastructure, or even based on the specifications of your project or customer base. No matter the destination, your Go code will be able to be packaged up and shipped to it. However, it is on you to ensure your project is ready for deployment.

This chapter will teach you about running your application in the cloud successfully and some of the considerations you might make before deploying it into the cloud, or wherever you choose to deploy it to really. We will cover topics such as monitoring, orchestration, tracing, and containerization, equipping you with the knowledge and tools to navigate the complexities of cloud infrastructure effectively.

First and foremost, we'll discuss the importance of monitoring your application's performance and health in a cloud-native environment. We'll explore how to integrate monitoring systems such as Prometheus into your Go application, enabling you to gather vital metrics and gain insights into its ongoing behavior.

Next, we'll delve into the realm of distributed tracing and logs with OpenTracing. By implementing tracing and logging into your Go application, you'll gain visibility into the flow of requests and responses across microservices. This will provide you with additional insights to make debugging issues a breeze – hopefully – and provide you with insights to potentially make performance optimizations in the future.

Finally, we'll cover essential containerization practices for Go applications, including image optimization, dependency management, and security considerations. You'll learn how to build robust container images for your Go application, ready for deployment in any environment. That will allow for a seamless transition to where we'll tackle the challenge of orchestrating your application using platforms such as Kubernetes. Orchestrators allow for scalability, resiliency, and ease of management for your application at a greater scale.

By the end of the chapter, you will be well equipped to deploy your Go application confidently to the cloud, armed with the knowledge and tools to ensure its reliability, scalability, performance, and visibility into production environments. Let's dive in!

Making your app monitorable by systems such as Prometheus

Monitoring is a critical aspect of maintaining the health and performance of any application, no matter the language. Monitoring is especially important in a cloud-native environment where resources are dynamic and distributed. There are certain nuances as to the differences between monitoring and observability in software engineering.

The monitoring aspects abide more by collecting data through predefined metrics and thresholds to detect and alert upon issues to define the overall health of the system, whereas observability is much more investigative and goes into a more comprehensive understanding of system behavior and performance to enable effective debugging and troubleshooting in complex environments. To focus on enabling monitoring capabilities and insights into the health of our application, we will focus on monitoring instead of observability in this book chapter.

Prometheus is a powerful tool when it comes to enabling monitoring capabilities on an application. It operates on a pull-based model, where it scrapes metrics from instrumented applications at regular intervals. These metrics are then stored in a time-series database, allowing developers to query, visualize, and alert them in real time. As a Go developer, integrating Prometheus into an application enables you to gain valuable insights into its performance and behavior.

To make your Go application monitorable with Prometheus, you need to instrument it with metrics that capture relevant information about its internal state and performance. This involves adding instrumentation code to your application's code base to expose metrics endpoints that Prometheus can then scrape.

The Prometheus Go client library provides a convenient way to instrument your Go application with metrics. It offers a range of metric types that allow you to capture different aspects of your application's behavior:

- **Counters**: Monotonically increasing values used to track the number of occurrences of an event over time. They reset to zero when the application restarts and are useful for measuring event frequencies, such as the number of requests or errors.

- **Gauges**: Instantaneous measurements of a particular value at a specific point in time. They can increase or decrease and represent the current state of a system, such as CPU usage, memory consumption, or the number of active connections.

- **Histograms**: A means to track the distribution of values over time, allowing you to understand the variability and spread of data. They collect observations into configurable buckets and provide metrics such as percentiles, median, and average, which are useful for understanding response times, latencies, and request durations.

- **Summaries**: Similar to histograms, summaries provide a more accurate representation of the data distribution, especially for high-cardinality datasets. They calculate quantiles and percentiles dynamically, allowing you to analyze data distribution with precision and granularity, making them suitable for measuring latency, duration, and response-time distributions.

Once you've instrumented your application using the aforementioned metric types that are appropriate to the metrics you desire and use case, you then need to expose metrics endpoints for Prometheus to scrape. These endpoints typically serve metrics in a format compatible with the Prometheus exposition format, such as `/metrics`.

Prometheus uses configuration files called scrape configs to define targets it should scrape for metrics. You'll need to configure Prometheus to scrape your application's metrics endpoint(s) and specify the scrape interval to collect data at regular intervals.

With Prometheus collecting metrics from your Go application, you can now visualize them using tools such as Grafana and set up alerts based on predefined thresholds or conditions. This allows you to proactively monitor your application's health and performance and take corrective action when necessary.

Exercise 21.01 – Creating an app with a /healthz endpoint

We've just walked through an overview of how monitoring works, a powerful tool you can utilize to capture metrics, and how you can then visualize those metrics and use them for the betterment of your project. We will now take a look at what this looks like in code:

1. Create a new directory called `Exercise21.01`. Within that directory, create a new file called `main.go`.

2. Run the following two commands to create a go module for the exercise:

    ```
    go mod init
    go mod tidy
    ```

3. Add the following code to the file to create a simple application we can monitor:

    ```
    package main
    import (
      "fmt"
      "net/http"
      "time"
      "github.com/prometheus/client_golang/prometheus"
      "github.com/prometheus/client_golang/prometheus/promhttp"
    )
    ```

4. Add a counter metric we will use to monitor the count of calls to the endpoint:

    ```
    var (
      healthzCounter = prometheus.NewCounter(prometheus.CounterOpts{
        Name: "healthz_calls_total",
        Help: "Total number of calls to the healthz endpoint.",
      })
    )
    ```

5. Register the metric with Prometheus:

```
func init() {
    prometheus.MustRegister(healthzCounter)
}
```

6. Define a handler for the `/healthz` endpoint:

```
func main() {
    http.HandleFunc("/healthz", func(w http.ResponseWriter, r
*http.Request) {
        healthzCounter.Inc()
        w.WriteHeader(http.StatusOK)
        fmt.Println("Monitoring endpoint invoked! Counter was
incremented!")
    })
```

7. Define a handler for viewing the metrics:

```
    http.Handle("/metrics", promhttp.Handler())
```

8. Define and start the server, and then close the function:

```
    server := &http.Server{
        Addr: ":8080",
        ReadTimeout: 10 * time.Second,
        WriteTimeout: 10 * time.Second,
    }

    fmt.Println("Server listening on port 8080...")
    if err := server.ListenAndServe(); err != nil {
        fmt.Printf("Error starting server: %s\n", err)
    }
}
```

9. To run the program, you need to open your terminal and navigate to the directory that you created the `main.go` file in. Then, run the `go build` tool by writing the following:

```
go build -o monitored_app main.go
```

10. This will create an executable called `monitored_app` that you can execute the binary in by running it on the command line:

```
./monitored_app
```

The output will look as follows:

```
Server listening on port 8080...
```

The server is now listening for requests. You can now navigate to the /healthz endpoint in your web browser, or through a curl command to perform the HTTP request. Navigate to the web browser at the endpoint, and reload the page a few times: http://localhost:8080/healthz.

If you return to your terminal, you will see that the counter was incremented with each request or, in other words, each time you refreshed the web page:

```
Monitoring endpoint invoked! Counter was incremented!
Monitoring endpoint invoked! Counter was incremented!
Monitoring endpoint invoked! Counter was incremented!
```

You will see the same number of lines of that output as the number of times you made a request to the web server for that endpoint. Now that we've made a few requests to the server, we've generated some data on our monitored application. We can view the available Prometheus metrics at http://localhost:8080/metrics.

If you go to the web browser at the /metrics endpoint, you will see the metric we created, among a bunch of other metrics that have been abbreviated with three dots, as there are too many to list nicely on a page:

```
...
# HELP healthz_calls_total Total number of calls to the healthz
endpoint.
# TYPE healthz_calls_total counter
healthz_calls_total 3
# HELP promhttp_metric_handler_requests_in_flight Current number of
scrapes being served.
# TYPE promhttp_metric_handler_requests_in_flight gauge
promhttp_metric_handler_requests_in_flight 1
# HELP promhttp_metric_handler_requests_total Total number of scrapes
by HTTP status code.
# TYPE promhttp_metric_handler_requests_total counter
promhttp_metric_handler_requests_total{code="200"} 0
promhttp_metric_handler_requests_total{code="500"} 0
promhttp_metric_handler_requests_total{code="503"} 0
```

You can see our custom metric:

```
healthz_calls_total 3
```

We invoked our endpoint three times; therefore, we see a counter value of 3.

The additional metrics you are seeing are provided by the Prometheus client library itself and are related to Go runtime metrics, including memory allocation, garbage collection, goroutines, and other runtime statistics. These metrics are automatically exposed by the Prometheus client library when you import and use it in your Go application.

In this exercise, you defined a counter metric for an endpoint on an HTTP server using Prometheus. By instrumenting your Go application with Prometheus and following best practices for monitoring, you can gain valuable insights into its behavior and performance in a cloud-native environment. With Prometheus, we saw how you can use it to be well equipped to define the monitoring capabilities of an application.

Expanding the example by adding additional custom metrics allows teams to detect issues early on, effectively troubleshoot their applications, and ensure the reliability and scalability of Go applications in production-level environments. Prometheus also enables alerting upon metrics upon certain criteria, proving it to be quite a powerful tool when gaining insights into your application.

Enabling deep insights through OpenTelemetry

In today's complex distributed systems landscape, understanding how our applications behave and perform is crucial for maintaining reliability and performance. We will now take a look at another useful monitoring tool readily available. **OpenTelemetry** is a pivotal tool for gaining profound insights into the functionality and performance of distributed systems. OpenTelemetry, often referred to as OTel, provides a standardized approach to collect and correlate data across various components of the system.

By incorporating OpenTelemetry into your Go applications, you can seamlessly capture telemetry data, including traces, metrics, and logs, to gain a holistic understanding of your system's operation. Let's take a look at the three main pillars OpenTelemetry encompasses:

- **Tracing** allows us to track the flow of requests as they travel through different services and components, providing invaluable insights into latency, dependencies, and error propagation. For tracing, we create and propagate trace contexts across service boundaries in order to achieve end-to-end visibility into request flows. This enables us to visualize requests as they flow through the system, identify performance bottlenecks, diagnose errors, and optimize resource utilization.

- **Metrics** offer a quantitative view of our system's health and performance, enabling us to monitor key indicators and identify potential bottlenecks or anomalies. OpenTelemetry provides a means of collecting metrics similar to providing insights into the health and performance of our applications.

- **Logs** provide a narrative of events and actions within our applications, aiding in troubleshooting and debugging efforts. This also allows us to trace the flow of information across our distributed systems and capture logs as events occur internal to the application.

To harness the power of OpenTelemetry in your application, you must first instrument the application with the necessary instrumentation libraries and **software development kits**, or **SDKs**. This is similar to how we saw you must instrument the application for Prometheus in the previous section of this chapter. For OpenTelemetry, it is a similar process of integrating the OpenTelemetry SDKs into the code base and configuring instrumentation for tracing, metrics, and logging.

Let's see what some of this looks like in practice.

Exercise 21.02 – Using OpenTelemetry for queryable logs and tracing

We now understand the monitoring capabilities that OpenTelemetry allows developers. We will now see how it helps to make structured logs that enable developers to more easily query their logs later on, as well as see what tracing is like with OpenTelemetry.

Create a new directory called `Exercise21.02`. Within that directory, create a new Go file called `main.go`, then do the following:

1. Run the following two commands to create a go module for the exercise:

    ```
    go mod init
    go mod tidy
    ```

2. Add the following code to the file, including all of the imports necessary for our OpenTelemetry monitoring:

    ```
    package main
    import (
        "context"
        "fmt"
        "log"
        "net/http"
        "time"
        "go.opentelemetry.io/contrib/instrumentation/net/http/
    otelhttp"
        "go.opentelemetry.io/otel"
        "go.opentelemetry.io/otel/exporters/otlp/otlptrace"
        "go.opentelemetry.io/otel/exporters/otlp/otlptrace/
    otlptracegrpc"
        "go.opentelemetry.io/otel/exporters/otlp/otlptrace/
    otlptracehttp"
        "go.opentelemetry.io/otel/exporters/stdout/stdouttrace"
        sdktrace "go.opentelemetry.io/otel/sdk/trace"
        "go.opentelemetry.io/otel/trace"
        "go.uber.org/zap"
    )
    ```

3. Create a function to initialize a trace exporter:

```go
func initTraceExporter(ctx context.Context) *otlptrace.Exporter
{
  traceExporter, err := otlptracegrpc.New(
    ctx,
    otlptracegrpc.WithEndpoint("http://localhost:4317"),
  )
  if err != nil {
    log.Fatalf("failed to create trace exporter: %v", err)
  }
  return traceExporter
}
```

4. Create a function to initialize a log exporter:

```go
func initLogExporter(ctx context.Context) *otlptrace.Exporter {
  logExporter, err := otlptracehttp.New(
    ctx,otlptracehttp.WithEndpoint("http://localhost:4318/v1/
logs"),
  )
  if err != nil {
    log.Fatalf("failed to create log exporter: %v", err)
  }
  return logExporter
}
```

5. Create a function to initialize a structured logger:

```go
func initLogger() *zap.Logger {
  logger, err := zap.NewProduction()
  if err != nil {
    log.Fatalf("failed to create logger: %v", err)
  }
  return logger
}
```

6. Create a function to initialize the tracing provider:

```go
func initTracerProvider(traceExporter *otlptrace.Exporter)
*sdktrace.TracerProvider {
  exp, err := stdouttrace.New(stdouttrace.WithPrettyPrint())
  if err != nil {
    log.Println("failed to initialize stdouttrace exporter:",
err)
  }
  bsp := sdktrace.NewBatchSpanProcessor(exp)
```

```
    tp := sdktrace.NewTracerProvider(
      sdktrace.WithBatcher(traceExporter),
      sdktrace.WithSpanProcessor(bsp),
    )
    return tp
}
```

Then, define an HTTP handler that will handle the incoming monitored request and capture log information, as well as start the span for the incoming request:

```
func handler(w http.ResponseWriter, r *http.Request){
    ctx := r.Context()
    span := trace.SpanFromContext(ctx)
    defer span.End()
    logger := zap.NewExample().Sugar()
    logger.Infow("Received request",
      "service", "exercise22.02",
      "httpMethod", r.Method,
      "httpURL", r.URL.String(),
      "remoteAddr", r.RemoteAddr,
    )
    w.WriteHeader(http.StatusOK)
    fmt.Fprintf(w, "Monitoring endpoint invoked!")
}
```

7. Last, define a `main()` function where you will call all of the initialization helper functions we just defined:

```
func main() {
    ctx := context.Background()
    traceExporter := initTraceExporter(ctx)
    defer traceExporter.Shutdown(context.Background())
    logExporter := initLogExporter(ctx)
    defer logExporter.Shutdown(context.Background())
    tp := initTracerProvider(traceExporter)
    otel.SetTracerProvider(tp)
    logger := initLogger()
    defer logger.Sync()
```

8. Wrap the HTTP handler with OpenTelemetry instrumentation, start the HTTP server, and close the `main()` function:

```
    httpHandler := otelhttp.NewHandler(http.HandlerFunc(handler),
    "HTTPServer")
```

```go
    http.Handle("/", httpHandler)
    server := &http.Server{
      Addr: ":8080",
      ReadTimeout: 10 * time.Second,
      WriteTimeout: 10 * time.Second,
    }
    fmt.Println("Server listening on port 8080...")
    if err := server.ListenAndServe(); err != nil {
      fmt.Printf("Error starting server: %s\n", err)
    }
  }
}
```

9. To run the program, you need to open your terminal and navigate to the directory that you created the `main.go` file in. Then, run the `go build` tool by writing the following:

```
go build -o monitored_app main.go
```

10. This will create an executable called `monitored_app` that you can execute the binary in by running it on the command line:

```
./monitored_app
```

The output will look as follows:

```
Server listening on port 8080...
```

The server is now listening for requests. You can now navigate to the `/healthz` endpoint in your web browser, or through a `curl` command to perform the HTTP request. Navigate to the web browser at the endpoint, and reload the page a few times: `http://localhost:8080/healthz`.

The web page will now show the following:

```
Monitoring endpoint invoked!
```

If you return to your terminal, you will see the structured log we defined:

```
{"level":"info","msg":"Received
request","service":"exercise22.02","httpMethod":"GET","httpURL":"/
healthz","remoteAddr":"[::1]:51082"}
```

You will also see the results of the tracing information exported to standard output, so we can see the trace in the terminal. Here, you can see part of the output, shortened to allow ease of visibility:

```
{
        "Name": "HTTPServer",
        "SpanContext": {
                "TraceID": "0008b00a820c440f298f1b025af72723",
                "SpanID": "79335a8c461c36d6",
                "TraceFlags": "01",
                "TraceState": "",
                "Remote": false
        },
        "Parent": {
                "TraceID": "00000000000000000000000000000000",
                "SpanID": "0000000000000000",
                "TraceFlags": "00",
                "TraceState": "",
                "Remote": false
        },
        "SpanKind": 2,
        "StartTime": "2024-02-25T10:02:46.771872-06:00",
        "EndTime": "2024-02-25T10:02:46.772208-06:00",
        "Attributes": [
                {
                        "Key": "http.method",
                        "Value": {
                                "Type": "STRING",
                                "Value": "GET"
                        }
                },
                {
                        "Key": "http.scheme",
                        "Value": {
                                "Type": "STRING",
                                "Value": "http"
                        }
                },
                {
                        "Key": "net.host.name",
                        "Value": {
                                "Type": "STRING",
                                "Value": "localhost"
                        }
                },
                {
                        "Key": "net.host.port",
                        "Value": {
                                "Type": "INT64",
                                "Value": 8080
                        }
                },
                {
                        "Key": "net.sock.peer.addr",
                        "Value": {
                                "Type": "STRING",
                                "Value": "::1"
                        }
                },
                {
                        "Key": "net.sock.peer.port",
                        "Value": {
                                "Type": "INT64",
                                "Value": 51475
                        }
                },
                {
                        "Key": "user_agent.original",
                        "Value": {
                                "Type": "STRING",
```

Figure 21.1: OpenTelemetry tracing output – this image is meant to show the output and text; readability is not essential

In this exercise, you worked with OpenTelemetry to gain valuable monitoring insights into the application, including structured logging and tracing information on requests. The logs help to provide information on what occurred, and we saw how you can structure the logs to include information relevant to your use case and project. From there, you can use different aspects of the logs to query. For example, our logs included the service name, HTTP method used, and endpoint invoked. We could easily create queries based on all service requests or all requests to a specific endpoint. This could provide valuable insights to enable teams to practice on their projects. We also saw tracing information using OpenTelemetry. This information is useful for timing insights and execution flow if there are sub-requests made. We can also visualize these results with different exporters or UI tools to more easily see what is going on in our request flows in more complex use cases.

Best practices for putting your Go application in a container

In recent years, containerization has revolutionized the way software engineers deploy and manage software applications. By encapsulating an application along with its dependencies into a lightweight, portable container, containerization provides numerous benefits, including consistency, scalability, and portability for our applications. This approach has gained widespread adoption across industries and is considered a standard practice for modern software development and deployment workflows.

Containerization is essential to software nowadays as it ensures consistency by packaging the application and its dependencies into a single unit, eliminating the infamous and dreaded "it works on my machine" problem This consistency extends to different environments, including production, reducing the risk of configuration drift. It also allows scalability on demand, as it is efficient to add or remove instances of the application when it is lightweight and fast to spin up in a container. Lastly, containers can be run on-premises, in **cloud service providers** (CSPs), or even in hybrid environments. Therefore, it is essential to understand how to package up your Go application dependencies into a container to run your Go code to be consistent, scalable, and portable.

Docker is a big player in the containerization ecosystem, serving as one of the most widely used containerization platforms. Docker provides a containerization engine, image management, container orchestration, and a widely integrated ecosystem. It provides tools, workflows, and infrastructure for creating, deploying, and managing containers effectively.

There are a few best practices to keep in mind when containerizing your Go application:

- **Leverage Go modules for dependency management**: Go modules provide a convenient way to manage dependencies for your Go applications. When containerizing your Go application, ensure that you are using Go modules to manage dependencies effectively. Go modules were covered early on in the book in *Chapter 9, Using Go Modules to Define a Project*.

- **Keep containers lightweight**: One of the fundamental principles of containerization is to keep containers lightweight. This means minimizing the size of your container images to reduce deployment times and resource usage. When building container images for Go applications, use multi-stage builds to compile your application binary and copy only the necessary files into the final image. Additionally, leverage Alpine-based or scratch images as base images to further reduce image size.

- **Optimize Dockerfile instructions**: When writing Dockerfiles for your Go applications, optimize Dockerfile instructions to improve build performance and reduce image size. Use multi-stage builds to separate the build environment from the final production image, minimizing the size of the final image. Additionally, leverage Docker's layer-caching mechanism by ordering your Dockerfile instructions from least frequently changing to most frequently changing, ensuring that only necessary steps are executed when rebuilding the image.

- **Secure your container environment**: Security should be a top priority when containerizing your Go applications. Follow security best practices such as using minimal and trusted base images, scanning container images for vulnerabilities using tools such as **Trivy**, and applying least privilege principles by running containers with non-root users whenever possible. Additionally, ensure that sensitive information such as credentials or API keys are not hardcoded into your container images but instead provided as environment variables or mounted as secrets at runtime. Lastly, consider leveraging Chainguard images for your Dockerfiles to enhance the security of container images by relying upon their enhanced security measures.

- **Implement health checks and logging**: Implement health checks and logging in your Go applications to improve observability and reliability in a containerized environment. Define health check endpoints to allow container orchestration platforms such as Kubernetes to monitor the health of your application and automatically restart unhealthy containers. Additionally, use structured logging to provide valuable insights into the behavior of your application, making it easier to troubleshoot issues and debug problems in production.

- **Use container orchestration platforms**: We will discuss why this is important in the next section of this chapter.

Now that we understand why it is crucial to know how to containerize our Go applications, let's see what this looks like in practice.

Exercise 21.03 – Creating a Dockerfile for a Go application

To containerize your Go application, you'll need to create a Dockerfile, which is a text document that contains instructions for Docker on how to build your application's image. Let's walk through the process of creating a Dockerfile for a simple Go application and then see how to build and run the container. We will use the code from earlier on in the chapter, in the Exercise21.01 directory:

1. Create a new directory called Exercise21.03. Within that directory, create a new file called main.go.

2. Copy the contents of `Exercise21.03/main.go`, `Exercise21.03/go.mod`, and `Exercise21.03/go.sum` into the new directory.

3. Create a new file called `Dockerfile` that contains instructions.

4. Start with the official Go image as the base image:

    ```
    FROM golang:latest AS builder
    ```

5. Ensure the Go compiler builds a statically linked binary, including all necessary libraries within the binary:

    ```
    ENV CGO_ENABLED=0
    ```

6. Set the working directory inside of the container:

    ```
    WORKDIR /app
    ```

7. Copy over the Go modules files and our code for the monitored application:

    ```
    COPY go.mod go.sum ./
    COPY main.go ./
    RUN go mod download
    ```

8. Build our Go binary:

    ```
    RUN go build -o monitored_app .
    ```

9. Start a new stage to create a minimal final image:

    ```
    FROM scratch
    ```

10. Copy over the binary to our final stage:

    ```
    COPY --from=builder /app/monitored_app /.
    ```

11. Expose the port we will use to interact with our application:

    ```
    EXPOSE 8080
    ```

12. Run our monitored application:

    ```
    CMD ["./monitored_app"]
    ```

13. Now that we have filled the contents of our `Dockerfile` file, we can build our Docker image by running the following command in the terminal:

    ```
    docker build -t monitored-app .
    ```

14. We can then run our Docker container using the following command, which will start a container based on our monitored application image and map port 8080 on our host machine to port 8080 of the container:

```
docker run -p 8080:8080 monitored-app
```

15. We can now access our application at the same URL we've been hitting: `http://localhost:8080/healthz`.

We still see the same output as we did before with the application:

```
Monitoring endpoint invoked! Counter was incremented!
```

We've now seen how to take our Go application into a lightweight, ephemeral container and run it using Docker commands. Docker is a platform that enables us to build, ship, and run our application in a Docker container by packaging up our Go application dependencies into a portable container that can be deployed across different environments.

Let's now expand on this idea of portability and container orchestration.

Making your app ready to work with orchestrators such as Kubernetes

Kubernetes, often abbreviated as **K8s**, has emerged as the de facto standard for container orchestration and management. It provides the capabilities to automate the deployment, scaling, and management of containerized applications. At its core, Kubernetes abstracts away the complexities of managing individual containers and offers a unified API and control plane for orchestrating containerized workloads across a cluster of machines. Orchestrators such as Kubernetes are what you turn to when you want to streamline the deployment and management of modern, cloud-native applications.

In today's dynamic and rapidly evolving software landscape, where microservices architectures and containerization have become mainstream, Kubernetes offers a scalable and resilient platform for deploying and operating these distributed applications. However, it is not without its complexities and learning curve.

There are a few things to do in order for your application to work with orchestrators such as Kubernetes:

- **Containerize your application**: Package your Go application and its dependencies into a Docker container, as we saw in the previous section.

- **Deploy your containerized application**: Once you've built your container image, you need to deploy it into your Kubernetes cluster. This typically involves pushing your container image to a container registry (such as Docker Hub, **Google Container Registry** (**GCR**), or **Amazon Elastic Container Registry** (**Amazon ECR**), and then deploying it into your Kubernetes cluster using Kubernetes deployment manifests.

- **Define Kubernetes resources**: In Kubernetes, you define the desired state of your application using Kubernetes resources such as Deployments, Services, ConfigMaps, and Secrets. You will need to create Kubernetes manifests (YAML files) that describe these resources and specify how Kubernetes should manage your Go application.

- **Handle application life cycle**: Kubernetes manages the life cycle of your application, including scaling, rolling updates, and monitoring. Ensure that your application is designed to work well with Kubernetes by implementing features such as health checks, readiness probes, graceful shutdowns, and logging/metrics instrumentation.

- **Service discovery and load balancing**: Use Kubernetes services to expose your application internally within the cluster and to external clients. This allows other parts of your application to discover and communicate with your Go application and enables Kubernetes to load-balance traffic to multiple instances of your application.

- **Monitoring and logging**: Instrument your Go application for monitoring and logging using tools such as Prometheus, Grafana, Fluentd, OpenTelemetry, and so on. Emit metrics, logs, and trace information in a structured format so that Kubernetes can collect and analyze them. This allows you to gain visibility into the health and performance of your application running in Kubernetes.

By following these steps, you can successfully deploy and run your Go application using an orchestrator, such as a Kubernetes environment. It's important to familiarize yourself with Kubernetes concepts and best practices to ensure that your application runs smoothly and efficiently in production. You should also acknowledge a much more complex environment and learning curve to bring yourself up to speed on working with Kubernetes.

Summary

This chapter was an exciting one that expanded our understanding of where we are running the Go applications that we write. We learned how to run our Go code in the cloud, all packaged up nicely and providing us with the monitoring insights that we need to ensure success for our services.

We started with understanding why and how to make our Go application code instrumented with monitoring using Prometheus. That was a nice segue into gaining even richer insights into our application using OpenTelemetry. We then demonstrated how to containerize our application using Docker, and then looked at how to run that containerized application in an orchestrated environment, such as in Kubernetes. We've covered a lot of ground in this chapter and in this book in its entirety.

Over the course of the book, we have covered the basics of Go with variables and various type declarations. We moved into control flow and data rules with Go, to include some of the newest features of working with complex types such as using generics and interfaces. We covered good software engineering practices as they apply to Go through code reuse, error handling, and how to work with large-scale projects through Go modules and packages. We even touched on time and files and systems.

The book transformed our skills to a professional level demonstrating debugging best practices with Go, crafting state-of-the-art CLI applications, and how to perform application development by connecting to databases, and working with web servers and clients. We tied everything up with a nice bow ending with covering the concurrency Go primitives, strong testing practices, and even highlighting the best of the Go ecosystem with the tools it offers. Lastly, we saw how to run our Go code in the cloud and gain insights into how our application is performing. This book should provide you with the tools and knowledge to transform your Go knowledge into a professional Go developer!

Index

packtpub.com

Subscribe to our online digital library for full access to over 7,000 books and videos, as well as industry leading tools to help you plan your personal development and advance your career. For more information, please visit our website.

Why subscribe?

- Spend less time learning and more time coding with practical eBooks and Videos from over 4,000 industry professionals

- Improve your learning with Skill Plans built especially for you

- Get a free eBook or video every month

- Fully searchable for easy access to vital information

- Copy and paste, print, and bookmark content

Did you know that Packt offers eBook versions of every book published, with PDF and ePub files available? You can upgrade to the eBook version at packtpub.com and as a print book customer, you are entitled to a discount on the eBook copy. Get in touch with us at customercare@packtpub.com for more details.

At www.packtpub.com, you can also read a collection of free technical articles, sign up for a range of free newsletters, and receive exclusive discounts and offers on Packt books and eBooks.

Other Books You May Enjoy

If you enjoyed this book, you may be interested in these other books by Packt:

gRPC Go for Professionals

Clément Jean

ISBN: 978-1-83763-884-0

- Understand the different API endpoints that gRPC lets you write
- Discover the essential considerations when writing your Protobuf files
- Compile Protobuf code with protoc and Bazel for efficient development
- Gain insights into how advanced gRPC concepts work
- Grasp techniques for unit testing and load testing your API
- Get to grips with deploying your microservices with Docker and Kubernetes
- Discover tools for writing secure and efficient gRPC code

Building Modern CLI Applications in Go

Marian Montagnino

ISBN: 978-1-80461-165-4

- Master the Go code structure, testing, and other essentials

- Add a colorful dashboard to your CLI using engaging ASCII banners

- Use Cobra, Viper, and other frameworks to give your CLI an edge

- Handle inputs, API commands, errors, and timeouts like a pro

- Target builds for specific platforms the right way using build tags

- Build with empathy, using easy bug submission and traceback

- Containerize, distribute, and publish your CLIs quickly and easily

Packt is searching for authors like you

If you're interested in becoming an author for Packt, please visit authors.packtpub.com and apply today. We have worked with thousands of developers and tech professionals, just like you, to help them share their insight with the global tech community. You can make a general application, apply for a specific hot topic that we are recruiting an author for, or submit your own idea.

Share Your Thoughts

Now you've finished *Go Programming - From Beginner to Professional,* we'd love to hear your thoughts! Scan the QR code below to go straight to the Amazon review page for this book and share your feedback or leave a review on the site that you purchased it from.

https://packt.link/r/1803243058

Your review is important to us and the tech community and will help us make sure we're delivering excellent quality content.

Download a free PDF copy of this book

Thanks for purchasing this book!

Do you like to read on the go but are unable to carry your print books everywhere?

Is your eBook purchase not compatible with the device of your choice?

Don't worry, now with every Packt book you get a DRM-free PDF version of that book at no cost.

Read anywhere, any place, on any device. Search, copy, and paste code from your favorite technical books directly into your application.

The perks don't stop there, you can get exclusive access to discounts, newsletters, and great free content in your inbox daily

Follow these simple steps to get the benefits:

1.   Scan the QR code or visit the link below

https://packt.link/free-ebook/9781803243054

2.   Submit your proof of purchase
3.   That's it! We'll send your free PDF and other benefits to your email directly

Made in the USA
Coppell, TX
22 November 2024

40802523R00374